Gestures of Music Theater

GESTURES OF MUSIC THEATER

THEATER

The Performativity of Song and Dance

Edited by Dominic Symonds

and

Millie Taylor

Oxford University Press is a department of the University of Oxford.
It furthers the University's objective of excellence in research, scholarship,
and education by publishing worldwide.

Oxford   New York
Auckland   Cape Town   Dar es Salaam   Hong Kong   Karachi
Kuala Lumpur   Madrid   Melbourne   Mexico City   Nairobi
New Delhi   Shanghai   Taipei   Toronto

With offices in
Argentina   Austria   Brazil   Chile   Czech Republic   France   Greece
Guatemala   Hungary   Italy   Japan   Poland   Portugal   Singapore
South Korea   Switzerland   Thailand   Turkey   Ukraine   Vietnam

Oxford is a registered trademark of Oxford University Press
in the UK and certain other countries.

Published in the United States of America by
Oxford University Press
198 Madison Avenue, New York, NY 10016

© Oxford University Press 2014

Library of Congress Cataloging-in-Publication Data
Gestures of music theater : the performativity of song and dance / edited by
Dominic Symonds and Millie Taylor.
     pages cm
Includes bibliographical references and index.
ISBN 978–0–19–999715–2 (alk. paper)—ISBN 978–0–19–999716–9 (alk. paper) 1. Music and
dance. 2. Music—Performance. 3. Musical theater. 4. Singing. I. Symonds, Dominic, editor of
compilation. II. Taylor, Millie, editor of compilation.
ML3858.G38 2013
782.1'4–dc23   2013016327

9 8 7 6 5 4 3 2 1
Printed in the United States of America
on acid-free paper

CONTENTS

LIST OF ILLUSTRATIONS

ACKNOWLEDGMENTS

This volume of essays has arisen from discussions by the Music Theatre Working Group of the International Federation for Theatre Research. Our thanks go to all members of the group, particularly those who shared their thoughts during initial discussions at the IFTR world congress, Ludwig-Maximilians-Universität, Munich (2010). Contributors to this volume have also shared their work through the "Song, Stage and Screen" conference series, notably in gatherings at the University of Winchester, UK (2010), University of Missouri–Kansas City, United States (2011), and University of Groningen, Netherlands (2012). We are very grateful to the host institutions and organizers of all these events for facilitating ongoing international scholarship in this area. We would also like to express our thanks to the staff of Oxford University Press and in particular to our acquisitions editor, Norm Hirschy, whose unshakeable support for the development and publication of high-quality scholarship in this area is matched only by his generosity, guidance, and goodwill.

ABOUT THE CONTRIBUTORS

Zeynep Bulut is a Lecturer in Music at King's College London. She was previously a postdoctoral research fellow at the ICI Berlin Institute for Cultural Inquiry. She received her Ph.D. in critical studies/experimental practices in music from the University of California at San Diego. Analyzing contemporary classical and experimental music, her work theorizes the physical and phenomenal emergence of the human voice and its role in the constitution of the self.

Ainhoa Kaiero Claver holds a Ph.D. in musicology from the University Autonomous of Barcelona and held a postdoctoral fellowship at the École des Hautes Études en Sciences Sociales (EHESS) in Paris. Her research interests are centered on the modern and postmodern aesthetic, focusing on issues related to the construction of the self in contemporary high-tech societies.

Kathryn Edney is an Assistant Professor in the History and Heritage Department at Regis College. She earned her Ph.D. in American studies from Michigan State University and has published articles on musical theater in *The Journal of Popular Culture*, *Studies in Musical Theatre*, and several book anthologies. She served as the managing editor for the *Journal of Popular Culture* for two years and now serves on its editorial board.

Bethany Hughes is currently a doctoral student at Northwestern University. Her educational background includes degrees in music theater (performance) and drama (musical theater history and dramaturgy). Her professional experiences encompass performing, directing, choreographing, teaching, and working in development for the not-for-profit company Music Theatre of Wichita. Current research interests include musical theater, ethics, and Native American performance.

Matthew Lockitt is currently completing his Ph.D. at Monash University, Australia, where he also teaches musical theater within the Centre for Theatre and Performance. His research and work have led to the writing of three original performance-as-research musicals, and he is published in *Australasian Drama Studies* and *Studies in Musical Theatre*.

Mary Jo Lodge is an Associate Professor of English and Theater at Lafayette College in Easton, PA, United States, and has directed and choreographed numerous productions in professional, summer stock, and college theaters. She holds a Ph.D. from Bowling Green and has published several articles and book chapters as a scholar of the musical. She received a Fulbright Scholar award in 2013–2014 to teach at the University of Roehampton in London and to conduct research for her book on liminality and other challenges of the musical.

Ben Macpherson is a Lecturer in Musical Theatre at the University of Portsmouth. His research interests include musical theater; corporeality and reception studies; spaces and sites of music theater performance; and actor-musicianship. Publications include articles on voice and the body in *Studies in Musical Theatre* and the corporeal response to multimedia performance in the *International Journal of Performance Arts and Digital Media*. He is currently reviews editor for *Studies in Musical Theatre*, and co-convenor of the Centre for Interdisciplinary Voice Studies.

George Rodosthenous is Lecturer in Music Theatre at the School of Performance and Cultural Industries of the University of Leeds. His research interests are the body in performance; refining improvisational techniques and compositional practices for performance; devising pieces with live musical soundscapes as interdisciplinary process; the director as coach; updating Greek tragedy; and the British musical.

Judith Sebesta serves as Director of Distance Learning for the Texas Higher Education Coordinating Board. She is the coeditor, with Bud Coleman, of *Women in American Musical Theatre*. Her essays on musicals have appeared in such journals as *Studies in Musical Theatre* and *Studies in American Culture*, as well as the anthologies *Theatre Historiography* and the *Cambridge Companion to the Musical*.

Marianne Sharp currently teaches at the University of Winchester, specializing in contemporary theater practice. She previously worked for several years as an actress in touring theater in the UK and continental Europe, and as a director and workshop facilitator in theater schools, Universities, youth theater and applied contexts, including theater in prisons. Her research and practice is focused broadly around questions of acting, identity, ethics and the body.

Jessica Sternfeld focuses on the role of musicals in popular culture. Her book *The Megamusical* (2006) examines hit Broadway shows of the 1980s; her current work explores the proliferation and impact of musicals on television. She teaches music history, musical theater, and popular music at Chapman University in California.

Dominic Symonds is Reader in Drama at the University of Lincoln. He is joint editor of *Studies in Musical Theatre*, and coedited *Contemporary Theatre Review* issue 19.1, "The Broadway Musical: New Approaches"; he is also a convenor of the Music Theatre Working Group of the International Federation for Theatre Research. He is currently preparing the monographs *We'll Have Manhattan: The Early Work of Rodgers and Hart* for Oxford University Press, and *Broadway Rhythm: Imaging the City in Song* for University of Michigan Press.

Millie Taylor is Professor of Musical Theatre at the University of Winchester. She worked as a freelance musical director for many years on shows such as *West Side Story*, *Rocky Horror Show*, *Little Shop of Horrors*, and *Sweeney Todd* before becoming an academic. Recent publications include *British Pantomime Performance* (Intellect,

2007), *Singing for Musicals: A Practical Guide* (Crowood Press, 2008), and *Musical Theatre, Realism and Entertainment* (Ashgate Press, 2012). With Dominic Symonds she is currently preparing a textbook for musical theater students, *Studying Musical Theatre* (Palgrave Macmillan).

Konstantinos Thomaidis recently completed his Ph.D. on the materiality of the voice in Gardzienice training, Korean *pansori*, and vocal dance at Royal Holloway, University of London. He is Lecturer in Drama and Performance at the University of Portsmouth, co-founder of the Centre for Interdisciplinary Voice Studies, and Head of Movement of Opera in Space. His recent publications include contributions to *Theatre, Dance and Performance Training* (Routledge) and *Body and Performance* (Triarchy Press).

Sabine Wilden is a multidisciplinary artist from Germany. She holds master's degrees in piano performance and music theory and composition from the University of New Mexico (United States). There, she also studied dance. After her graduation in 2012, Sabine accepted a teaching position at the Robert Schumann University of Music in Germany, where she taught a wide range of music theory classes. Currently, Sabine works as independent pianist, music theorist, and music teacher.

Caroline Wilkins comes from a background of new music performance, composition, and theater, and has worked extensively on collaborative productions involving a combination of these disciplines. She studied piano and composition at the Royal College of Music, and new music theater composition with Mauricio Kagel in Cologne. Since 1989 her music has received performances and broadcasts worldwide. In 2000 she was awarded the Karl-Sczuka Prize from South West German Radio for her radio composition *Mecanica Natura*. She completed a practice-based Ph.D. in sound-theater composition at Brunel University in 2012. Her works are published by G. Ricordi & Co., Berlin.

Carlo Zuccarini holds a Ph.D. in psychology and an M.A. in psychoanalysis and contemporary society, both from Brunel University. His published research interests include psychoanalysis, neuroscience, and neuropsychoanalysis applied to music reception, in particular the operatic voice. He is also a longtime practicing linguist and translator.

PART ONE

Singing the Dance, Dancing the Song

Friday, July 27, 2012. Former Beatle Sir Paul McCartney leads 80,000 people singing the familiar refrain from "Hey Jude"; it is a—well, let us say a very *British* finale to what has been a spectacular opening ceremony to the 30th Olympiad in London: "Come on chaps, sing along," he yells (more or less). First the men, then the women, then everybody altogether—80,000 voices sing in unison, and the sheer power of that cumulative vocal energy is felt bodily in the stadium. This is a power that will continue to be felt in the stadium over the ensuing weeks, as the crowd performs its part in the celebration of sporting excellence and participation that is the Olympics. Bodies on the grass and on the track will be stretched to the limits of physical agility, while the constant surge and roar of thousands of other bodies and voices will act not as an accompaniment to the main event, but as an integral part of it—the song and dance of the stadium, you might say.

This collection of essays is an exploration of song and dance as performative gestures, though in introducing our discussion with this example it is clear that we intend to broaden the assumption of what song and dance is. When we use the phrase "song and dance" we undoubtedly conjure up something in our minds, a point of reference that we culturally share: perhaps song and dance is what Fred Astaire does with Ginger Rogers in *Swing Time* (1936); perhaps *Song and Dance* refers to the 1982 show by Andrew Lloyd Webber; perhaps song and dance is what kids do in creative learning classes to help them bond, build confidence, and explore expressiveness. Already we have several quite distinct points of reference, and other examples show an even broader diversity of forms and practices that could be labeled "song and dance": the family ritual of "Auld Lang Syne" on New Year's Eve; the spirited bouncing of clubbers at the Ministry of Sound; the healing ceremonies of Navajo Indians in Arizona; the call to prayer of the muezzin or whirl of the dervish in Turkey. In this confusion, we could turn to the aphorisms of experts to help us find a frame of reference through their definitions, though when Bob Dylan labels song as "anything that can walk by itself,"[1] and Baudelaire considers dance to be "poetry with arms and legs," it is clear that song and dance are more evocative than simple definitions would suggest.[2]

What these diverse examples have in common is that, whether primarily song or dance, they are all corporeal gestures of vocality and physicality that engage bodies in acts of expressive commitment. That—the idea that song and dance are corporeal gestures—is our first assertion. The second is that these practices "say" something in the very act of their performance about the bodies that are their source and raw material, about the contexts in which they are uttered, and about the idioms they use. In all of these respects they reflect our second assertion, the fact that these are acts that resonate with performativity. "Gestures of music theater," we have therefore called this collection, "the performativity of song and dance."

This summation determines the focus of our exploration, establishing some boundaries and offering a way of seeing its conceptual terrain, but we still need to understand the complexity of that terrain and to recognize its different features. Here, rather than turning to *points* of reference to explore what those features might be, it is perhaps more helpful to think about *axes* of reference within that terrain, along each of which a continuum of practices, affordances, or encounters takes place. One axis might deal with an awareness of composition, recognizing a continuum between fluid or ephemeral gestures of song and dance (idle humming, for example) and rigidly defined constructs (a choreographed routine); another might trace the role of identity within song and dance, ranging from acts that are consciously articulating self to acts that adopt the persona of character; a third axis might consider song and dance in terms of their musicality, recognizing varying degrees of proficiency, cultural idiom, and resonances of rhythm, timbre, and tone. There are, of course, many such axes, and their interplay creates within this terrain further complexity. In this the web becomes a better representation than the axis of the intricate mutations and flows between composition, performance, interpretation, musicality, identity, affect, efficacy, excess, transformation, and…well, that is why we are evoking the concept of a web, not a list.

ENGAGING THE BODY: PERFORMANCE AND PERFORMATIVITY

If the power of 80,000 massed voices in the Olympics opening ceremony generates a physical and corporeal weight, this was a deliberate intention from the moment deaf percussionist Evelyn Glennie led a team of 1,000 drummers as the soundtrack to the Industrial Revolution sequence, "Pandemonium": "She feels the music and it vibrates through her feet," remarks BBC commentator Hazel Irvine: "Here in the stadium 80,000 people can hear the pounding energy pulsating through the stadium right now from these 1000 drummers." Such a corporeal experience is clearly a part of the euphoria-building momentum that this high-profile spectacle demands, and confirms performance to be far more than something we hear with our ears or watch with our eyes. This kind of experience—feeling the vibrations impacting on your whole body—is familiar from rock concerts, nights at the opera, and community sing-alongs led by Paul McCartney, even if it is more muted for the estimated

900 million viewers watching the ceremony on television. For the audience at home (though *audience* is an interesting word), the performativity of the event is compromised: we *see Live Aid, The Last Night of the Proms,* and *The X Factor* but don't really *witness* them; we *listen* to them but don't really *hear* them. Removed from the liveness and presence of the experience, our bodies cannot partake.

We draw attention to this to recognize what Marvin Carlson picks up on as "the return of the body" in recent critical thinking about performance.[3] This is significant for our study not only because both song and dance clearly use the body as raw material, as tool and canvas, as it were, but also because there is an assumption of an experiencing (or perhaps an *engaging*) body in most song and dance contexts. It is in this matrix of presence, liveness, and corporeality that the performativity of song and dance can most sharply be felt, and it is, to call on contemporary terminology about performance, in the tacit "knowledge" of the body (*through* the body rather than *about* the body) that song and dance—indeed, what song and dance is—become understood.[4]

On the other hand, this is just one particular way of understanding the term "performativity," in which it is used in association with expressly theatrical events, acts of performance. The idea that performativity is a quality of liveness and presence that stimulates above (i.e., more so) and beyond (i.e., irrespective of) the material of performance reminds us that "performativity" is not *just* "performance"; indeed, it is something inherently different, and it need not even be associated with events that are theatrical. McCartney and the crowd *performed* "Hey Jude," though it could just as easily have been "Let it Be"; the performativity was something distinct from that.

The idea of the performative has had currency at least since J. L. Austin's publication of *How To Do Things with Words*, in which he formulated the tenets of speech act theory.[5] For him, the performative statement is one whose very utterance does (or *performs*) something, rather than one that simply describes something.[6] It was not really until the 1990s that the distinctions between "performance" and the "performative" were properly explored. Around this time, and following important discussions of performativity by scholars such as Jean-François Lyotard and Jacques Derrida,[7] in which the term was put to specific uses, a number of theater and performance scholars including Richard Schechner, Judith Butler, Eve Kosofsky Sedgwick, Jon McKenzie, Peggy Phelan, and Dwight Conquergood embarked on a careful consideration of what "the performative" means in performance studies.[8] Beyond theatrical concerns such as "pretending" or "entertaining," their understanding of performativity exceeds the discrete encounter of the performed and moves into a space in which performance is a cultural discourse:

> This is very far now from any sense of performing as illusion, the pale imitation of a real life lived elsewhere. If performance matters, it is because it is in a crucial sense infrastructural: it is fundamental to the constitution of our social and cultural world.[9]

In terms of McCartney's sing-along, we can understand this to magnify the meaning of "performativity" in several ways: rather than simply being a performance, this activity performed beyond itself to make important statements about community, nostalgia, and national identity; in other ways it commented on the status and cultural significance of Paul McCartney, and the Britishness of this billionaire pop icon engaging in cheeky-chappy sing-along antics as if he was once again a working-class teenage mop-top. In a similar way we can expand the way in which we understand the Olympics themselves to be performative. Markedly and ostensibly the performativity of the Olympics is in its commitment to sporting excellence, achievement, and participation: these are the values it carries on its sleeve, so to speak, emblemized in the five interlocking rings of the Olympic flag, the constant burning of the Olympic flame, and the rewarding of victory with medals of culturally determined value. The performativity of these ideals in an intensive period of mass engagement both magnifies them and seals into them a further dimension of value: these ideals become ethical or even ideological in their potency, and our cumulative complicity in supporting them escalates this ideology to the level of a universal credo. Nevertheless, in projecting this forceful ethics, the Olympics also makes other significant performative statements: in emphasizing the universal, for example, it diminishes difference; in favoring the body it spurns the mind; and (in the context of song and dance) in glorifying physicality it marginalizes vocality, vividly and literally to the displays of the opening and closing ceremonies, to the commentary, to the crowd responses, or to disruptions by errant voices, perhaps even—thinking of the responses to "grunts" made by female tennis players at Wimbledon—considered vulgar affronts to sport's implicit ethics of the body beautiful. As performativity moves beyond performance we begin to see its extremely complex and textured web of affordances—resonant dynamics that reach out and signify through interrelation with, among many other things, contexts and identities; affordances that continue to galvanize discourse through different media, in informal conversations, and in the zeitgeist of a moment.

MUSIC THEATER, SONG, AND DANCE

But why focus on song and dance—and by extension music theater—in exploring the dynamics of performativity? Of course there are other strategies we could use to engage with this discussion. However, the idea of song and dance seems a particularly appropriate prism through which to engage with performativity because of two key qualities that make it powerful as a rhetorical metaphor. First, as we have noted, song and dance are both corporeal gestures that demand commitment in performance and cause affect in reception: song and dance are performative in their very nature. Second, song and dance also defy structural boundaries, their effects seeping fluidly through conventional modalities of understanding and affecting us therefore in tangential and peripheral ways. Defined by these two qualities, the term "song and dance" can embrace a broad and diverse range of artistic and cultural practices that engage with voice and/or music with physical commitment, and whose resonances move fluidly through the porous membranes of conventional systems.

This interpretation of song and dance is more conceptual than might at first be imagined, though we certainly don't intend to claim that there is song and dance in everything. It does shift our study of song and dance away from actual forms or artifacts that we call "songs" and "dances," though, and adjusts it to focus on the physical and vocal expression of the human body and voice, particularly when it is used in excess and above all when it resonates in performative ways.[10]

In understanding such gestures to operate not only in forms that we know as "song" and "dance" but also in a wide range of cultural behaviors and practices, our study broadens the field of enquiry normally constituted as music theater, and enables a dialogue to emerge between different embodied expressions of the voiced and the moved, and thus to challenge a disciplinary approach to music theater. Music theater is often positioned somewhere between opera and the musical, though this classification projects upon it a number of problematic resonances, causing it to sit uncomfortably between ideological assumptions (high versus low, the classical versus the popular, Europe versus America, for example). Squeezed between opera and the musical, it is also limited in scope: neither one thing nor the other and restricted to a very localized cultural identity. For us, music theater is not a canonic literature of the musical stage, a repertoire of texts whose merits represent some pinnacle of achievement—though this collection does include discussion of some canonical texts. Rather, the field is expanded by a focus on the expressive gestures through which music theater is articulated; and our approach to this field is expanded to consider it from a wider perspective rather than one bound by the disciplinary assumptions of, for example, musicology or theater studies.

Our exploration is therefore fundamentally interdisciplinary, and in this sense it is difficult to categorize—we seek in many ways to resist and explode discrete discipline-based enquiry, so although we share methodologies and performance repertoires with discipline-based scholarship from theater studies, musicology, and cultural studies, there are many other approaches and case studies that we also embrace. Together, we view these as neighboring voices whose dialogue enriches the landscape of contemporary music theater, and although this book's chapters will explore discrete forms such as the Broadway musical, opera, sound installation, and devised theater, we move away from constructed cultural forms and phenomena such as opera or the musical to see the performative gestures of song and dance operating fluidly through the whole performance landscape. Therefore the range of performances considered as music theater is deliberately wide, encompassing the devised musicality of theater performers in Gardzienice, the corporeality of the trained voice in opera performance, the choreographic expression of the Broadway musical, and the mediatized performativity of sound installation. What brings a dialogue to this range of practices is our focus on the expressive potency of the voice in the body or the body in the voice as it performs: the song and dance that is music theater. Through this open approach to music theater, some striking themes emerge, allowing us to explore the mediatization of voice and body; the construction of gender and identity; the recontextualization of discrete practices; the expression of individuals within a community; and the consequences for reception, pleasure, and intoxication produced through watching, listening, and performing. Our book—while by no means exhaustive in its consideration of different senses of the performative—will consider performativity in terms of its affordances of dramaturgy, transition, identity, context, practice, and community.

As we have implied, raising the idea of performativity reminds us that to speak of performance is not simply to infer a display of skill, an act of entertainment, the interpretation of a text, or the telling of a story. Instead, performativity invokes complex dynamics meted out between performer and audience, transgressing established sites of discourse and bleeding across/through embodied identities: if the audience is affected physically by the encounter, they are not simply objective observers. If this disrupts conventional sites of engagement such as the identities of "performer" and "audience," it also points to conventional structures of engagement being disrupted: dialogue, narrative, drama, character, diegesis, and mimesis.

This blurring of boundaries between sites of definition has been widely discussed in terms of theatrical performance and performance art, and Carlson's seminal book *Performance*, referred to above, suggests that such "flux, with the porous or contested borders replacing centers as the focus of interest," is a condition of our experience of the contemporary world "with its new patterns of global communication [...] and the continual movement and displacement of peoples."[11] This is not to say that the porosity itself is a new phenomenon, but it is to say that our critical eyes are only recently becoming attuned to such flux,[12] which, in common with other emerging trends in critical thinking, is a symptom of the poststructural turn.

Over a similar time frame, the field of music theater has been exploring the effects of performativity in discrete music theater scenarios in studies as diverse as Slavoj Žižek and Mladen Dolar's *Opera's Second Death*[13] and Simon Frith's *Performing Rites: Evaluating Popular Music*.[14] Still, there is more to be said, especially in areas not yet so well explored as opera and pop music—or rather, in performance practices whose dimensions and boundaries are less well defined than in traditional opera or commercial pop.

Part of the reason for the slow take-up of this development outside such areas is perhaps the fact that music theater engages with this porosity—with this bleeding between and across boundaries; with the scrapping of boundaries, even—*in excess*. Put another way, the self-conscious expressive gestures of music theater, in particular vocality and physicality (song and dance), are not easily contained within the (apparently) hermetically sealed boundaries of established structures. Indeed, as we have seen from the challenge of defining "song and dance," music theater struggles even with terminology to define those boxes in respect of its practices. So although terms like "diegesis" and "dialogue" may make sense, they are confounded by music theater as its musical and physical energies flood uncontrollably over the structural defenses: Are those choral voices in the story or not? Is that expressive dance move a part of the conversation or not? What about other traditional "givens" like characters, voices, or even songs?

If this seems to claim for music theater some sort of higher state of performativity than other practices, we should acknowledge a different though equally pervasive rhetoric in writings about song and dance: Philip Auslander critiques it in the work of Susan Leigh Foster, for whom postmodern dance seems to be "beyond," "outside," "superior" to (in this case) other types of dance;[15] Roland Barthes's famous article "The Grain of the Voice" invokes a sort of mystical power in the experiencing of singing: "something is there, manifest and stubborn [...] beyond (or before) the meaning of the words";[16] meanwhile the hyperbole surrounding operagoers' fascination with the voice is captured vividly in discussions of jouissance such as Michel Poizat's *The Angel's Cry*.[17] If we are to be honest, we should concede that we don't fully understand these dynamics, at least not to the same extent that we understand the dynamics of, say, language. We can talk about *that* because our mode of critical articulation also uses language, and thus there is at least a metonymical relationship between the object of study and the way we think about it. But in trying to fold other performative dynamics into the same mode of critical articulation (or even the same patterns of thought), we attempt an act of illusion or subterfuge the type of which Wittgenstein discusses in his famous adage "If lions could speak..."

These concerns notwithstanding, a perspective on music theater's performativity is one that suffuses the writing of all of our contributors, and will be expanded on as the book progresses in editorial commentaries positioned at appropriate points between chapters. The chapters are organized to allow their thematic links to emerge, and their sequence reflects one path constructed by the editors that traces a trajectory from an exploration of the function of song and dance, through an exploration of identities forged in the discourse of music theater's song and dance, to a series of works that explore different media, different modalities of song and dance, and more communal understandings of identity. It is not the intention to separate these discussions, however, and the reader will find that by dipping into the book a different journey will be created through these discussions in which other themes and possibilities can spring into sight. We hope that our curation of the chapters will allow these ideas—like song and dance—to flow throughout the collection, allowing discrete chapters to find dialogue with one another and infusing the whole book with a coherent and contemporary view of music theater. Indeed, what we hope for with this book is that it will work for the reader in a similar way to a music theater performance, whose gestures intertwine to create a dense intertextural fabric.

So "Let's start at the very beginning," as someone once sang, with a pair of essays that explore the material of song and our engagement with it.

The first two chapters focus on song: Dominic Symonds's chapter considers the way that our conceptualization of song changed as recording technology replaced oral performance traditions; he argues that the ephemeral "sung" became sedimented into "song" and therefore became perceived as an object ripe for commoditization. Carlo Zuccarini, in the next chapter, continues with the discussion of the object, articulating the Lacanian idea that song, or what Symonds introduces as "the sung," is seen as fractured from the body that produces it. He explores neuroscience and the psychology of reception to discover the performative affect of operatic song on the listener. Focusing on the particular sound of operatic song, he discovers in the experience of its aesthetic of vocal beauty an exhilaration that transcends other dynamics of reception.

NOTES

1. Bob Dylan, *Bringing It All Back Home*, sleeve notes, CBS 62515, 1965.
2. Charles Baudelaire, *Paris Spleen and La Fanfarlo*, trans. Raymond N. Mackenzie (Indianapolis: Hackett, 2008), 128.
3. Marvin Carlson, *Performance: A Critical Introduction* (London: Routledge, 1996), 191.
4. See John Freeman, *Blood, Sweat and Theory* (Faringdon: Libri, 2010), 179.
5. J. L. Austin, *How to Do Things with Words* 2nd ed. (Oxford: Clarendon Press, 1975).
6. Austin uses the examples of a bet being made, a marriage vow being taken, and a ship being launched.
7. In Jean-François Lyotard, *The Postmodern Condition: A Report on Knowledge*, trans. Geoff Bennington and Brian Massumi (Minneapolis: University of Minnesota Press, 1979); Jacques Derrida, *Margins of Philosophy*, trans. Alan Bass (Chicago: University of Chicago Press, 1982).
8. Richard Schechner, *Performance Theory*, rev. ed. (New York: Routledge, 1988); Judith Butler, "Performative Acts and Gender Constitution: An Essay in Phenomenology and Feminist Theory," in *Performing Feminisms: Feminist Critical Theory and Theatre*, ed. Sue-Ellen Case (Baltimore: John Hopkins University Press, 1990) and most of her subsequent writing; Andrew Parker and Eve Kosofsky Sedgwick, eds., *Performativity and Performance* (New York: Routledge, 1995); Jon McKenzie, *Perform or Else: From Discipline to Performance* (New York: Routledge, 2001); Peggy Phelan, *Unmarked: The Politics of Performance* (London: Routledge, 1993); Dwight Conquergood, "Performance Studies: Interventions and Radical Research," *Drama Review* 46 (2002): 145–56.
9. James Loxley, *Performativity* (London: Routledge, 2007), 154.
10. It is no coincidence that the International Federation for Theatre Research's Music Theatre Working Group, which has initiated this collection of essays, positions "performance, experience and emergence" at the heart of its discussions.
11. Carlson, *Performance*, 188.
12. Carlson was writing in 1996, alongside a number of other scholars on performance—Phelan, *Unmarked*; Jill Dolan, *Presence and Desire: Essays on Gender, Sexuality and Performance* (Ann Arbor: University of Michigan Press, 1993); Philip Auslander, *Liveness: Performance in a Mediatized Culture* (New York: Routledge, 1999).
13. Slavoj Žižek and Mladen Dolar, *Opera's Second Death* (London: Routledge, 2002).
14. Simon Frith, *Performing Rites: On the Value of Popular Music* (Cambridge, MA: Harvard University Press, 1996).
15. Auslander, *Liveness*, 75.
16. Roland Barthes, "The Grain of the Voice," in *Image, Music, Text*, trans. Stephen Heath (London: Fontana Press, 1975), 181.
17. Michel Poizat, *The Angel's Cry: Beyond the Pleasure Principle in Opera*, trans. Arthur Denner (Ithaca, NY: Cornell University Press, 1992).

CHAPTER 1

The Song's the Thing

Capturing the "Sung" to Make It "Song"

DOMINIC SYMONDS

Perhaps the most significant dramatic moment in Disney's *The Little Mermaid* (1989) is the Faustian pact in which she sells her metaphorical soul to the sea witch, Ursula. Ursula has positioned herself as troubleshooter for the "poor unfortunate souls" in the undersea kingdom, and in a diabolic exchange (fee: one voice) she arranges for Ariel to grow legs so that she can walk on land.[1] There she can meet and marry her sweetheart Eric and live, she hopes, happily ever after in domestic and human bliss. In the Broadway show, this dramatic highpoint is also a theatrical coup de grâce, in which, with appropriate aerial trickery, Ariel the mermaid metamorphoses into Ariel the girl, tumbling upward toward the flies, shedding her fishy tail and then emerging from the stage-level surf like a different Ursula—Andress—from the waves. This transitional moment is significant on lots of levels, but in a broadly mythical way it signals the rite of passage from one state to another (sea to land; child to adult; mermaid to human), a transition that has often been marked on the musical stage by a significant use of song: think of *Orfeo* (1607) and *The Magic Flute* (1791), for example. In all of these cases song is a potent symbol, not just because it accompanies the dramatic transition, but also because it holds some symbolic or magical potency: it is the *possente spirto*, the powerful spirit, as Monteverdi has it, a performative act. It both represents the transition from one state to another and performs the symbolic act that enables the individual to reterritorialize in a new state on the other side, as it were. For Ariel, this process of reidentifying is particularly significant: in becoming girl she loses identity as mermaid; she also loses identity in the sense that one of her other defining features—her voice—is wrapped up both in the bargain she has made with the sea witch and with the magical potency of that song.

This transition serves as an interesting metonym of other larger yet perhaps less visible paradigm shifts, and the fact that voice and the performativity of song are central to this dramatizing of the transition is very important. In the Broadway show, the transaction is simple: Ariel sings into a gramophone-like shell, willingly giving herself to the exchange and committing her voice to some sort of subaqua recording device. Thus Ariel's offering is, in one sense, simply to sing, and Ursula's gain from the transaction is a pressing of this incantation on whatever wax cylinder she is using, thereby creating, or at least capturing the song. This restages the primitive processes of recording and promises to preserve the voice of the little mermaid, just as we have preserved for posterity the voices of Thomas Edison, Queen Victoria, or Alessandro Moreschi. And it sites technology at the threshold of this mythical rite of passage. There is one difference, though, because when Edison, Victoria, and Moreschi gave their voices to the gods of technology in literal enactments of a different song's narrative ("My gift is my song, and this one's for you"),[2] they were able to swim off with larynxes intact. In the fantasy of *The Little Mermaid*, the offering is far more sacrificial: in singing, Ariel actually gives her voice (not only gives but *gives away*); this offering is not *to sing*, but is instead *the voice*. Here, then, technology is not only placed at the point of transition but also becomes culpable as the tool of reification that turns practice into product. Ursula's technological device is not only a capturing system but also a sort of gateway from the primitive undersea community, in which song is a performed practice, to the cynical world on dry land, in which song becomes a commodity. In allegorical terms, this becomes the shift from an oral tradition with prelapsarian, pre-Oedipal, pastoral overtones, to a modernist, twentieth-century, capitalizing (American) "civilization." It is a paradigm shift that marks the moment at which the sung becomes the song.

It is interesting to consider how a perception of "thingness" has dogged the song, how we have come to think of the song-object and identify it as such in the language we use and the contexts in which we situate it, though if we perceive song as a thing (the song), this idea is very much a posttechnological, twentieth-century phenomenon, occurring since the turn away from the oral tradition. This is a discussion that clearly invites consideration of that tradition and the fundamental quality of song that can't (or can?) be objectified: its sound, intrinsically linked to the voice, the body, and therefore the practice of the sung. In evoking that oral tradition, an almost poetic nostalgia for the pretechnological remains: a memory of song as an oral practice that seeps into our romantic imagination and exposes the paradoxically silent song. Through strategies of interpellation and as part of the sedimentation of oral practices into objects in the literizing of culture, we have rhetoricized song as a commodity, affirming the product rather than the process, yet creating a tension between the song as thing and the song as practice. These are contradictions worth exploring; this tension is the psychological determinant that makes so bewitching, bothering, and bewildering the thing we call "song."

THE SONG AS OBJECT

Unlike Ursula the sea witch I don't enter into dodgy bargains with pretty mermaids, but like millions of others, I do like to get my hands on songs. For me the most exciting way of collecting songs is as songsheets; opening the package I have won on eBay, there is a thrill as I hold the music in my hands: I can own the song! Not that this is an original copy, or even a limited edition; but the songsheet has a definite materiality, an authenticity, perhaps helped by its age and by the quirky illustrations that decorate the front cover. The song can be held in my hand, whether as a song-sheet or a seven-inch single: the song is tangible, the song is a thing.

This is a thingness that is pervasive. In long-running UK radio show *Desert Island Discs*, celebrities choose eight precious songs to take with them to a desert island, along with the complete works of Shakespeare, the Bible, a book of choice, and a luxury item. The celebrities surround themselves with thingness, the luxury of commodity, with no consideration that food or shelter may be more practical. At the end of the program, current presenter Kirsty Young asks the castaway to select one of these songs, usually presenting this choice as a salvage operation: "If you could save just one song from the waves," she often phrases it, confirming the fact that these are tangible objects that can be broken, lost, or washed away by the sea. Are we intended to picture the castaway rescuing a seven-inch? Or a songsheet? Or maybe nowadays a WAV file downloaded onto a memory stick?

The way in which these songs have become tangible objects is comparable to the way in which tales became inscribed as texts in a parallel fixing of the oral tradition into literature; indeed, it is worth noting how often scholarship has treated songs as texts. Alec Wilder's prodigious but selective *American Popular Song* (1972) is one example that, through reproducing notated sections of sheet music, makes song manifest both visibly—as visibly, say, as *écriture*—and as an object of study whose "certain native characteristics" ("verbal, melodic, harmonic, and rhythmic")[3] can be used to classify in rather scientific terms the genus and species of song. This sort of analysis acquiesces to the rhetoric of materiality, consolidating the impression with structural vocabulary that establishes concepts like song form. Thus in the evolutionary narrative of song development, various subspecies of song eventually mature into a thirty-two-bar standardized model, typically coded in DNA-like formats: AABA, ABAC, and so on. In some cases, song even becomes anthropomorphized ("A pretty girl is like a melody"),[4] and implicitly seen as the offspring of its composer; David Margolick's account of Billie Holliday's "Strange Fruit" is not the only recent publication labeled "The Biography of a Song"; nor is the 1948 Danny Kaye film the only example of the phrase *A Song is Born* conceptualizing it as an infant just starting life; meanwhile, in his book *They're Playing Our Song*, Max Wilk evokes "the meeting of a good song with a great composer,"[5] as if over coffee they collaborate on a plan. Even when songs do not bear explicitly human names ("Mandy," "Maria," "Jeanie with the Light Brown Hair"), they are given titles—names—with capitalized letters, suggesting a certain humanist encoding that we also bring to our novels, films, and artworks. And this has been the case ever since early broadsides were given descriptive titles, such as "The Wandering Jew's Chronicle" that Schwegler discusses from the early seventeenth century.[6] Although this "song" embraces in its title the performative voicing of its singer (the wandering Jew) and the archiving principle behind its documentation (a chronicle), the sedimentation of the sung into the song is an endemic procedure that over time has increasingly entrenched the thingness of song. In a macabre twist on this anthropomorphizing, historian Nicholas Tawa writes about songs being "dissected"[7] by scholars, as if they are bodies—corpses—that can be sliced apart and scientifically explored.

Perhaps surprisingly, Theodor Adorno's take on this thingness gives it the most hefty substance of all, though it is not surprising that his perspective is linked to the burgeoning recording industry, which offers "the first means of musical presentation that can be possessed as a thing."[8] Among his many essays published on popular music is one, "The Curves of the Needle," in which he compares the matter of song to a physical lump of clay: "The turntable of the talking machines is comparable to the potter's wheel," he begins; "a tone-mass [*Ton-Masse*] is formed upon them both, and for each the material is preexisting."[9] Here, as translator Thomas Levin reminds us, "the untranslatable polyvalence of *Ton* [...] in German means both 'sound' or 'tone' and also 'clay,'" giving Adorno the opportunity to perceive song as if it is made up of that solid, physical matter, and evoking the idea that song is somehow born out of the very resources of the earth, a sort of variation of Wagner's summoning of life in music from the waters of the Rhine. In this analogy, song matter has consistency and apparently, in its unformed state, a claggy wetness, waiting to be shaped. It's an insistent Germanic motif, and if nothing else, this alerts us to the fact that language can create strong associations: *Ton* in German means both "sound" and "clay" and therefore links the two in conceptual ways that seem to transcend or prefigure the mechanical pertinence of vocabulary.[10] On the other hand, he says, "the material is preexisting," giving the impression of capture rather than sedimentation, just like Ursula captures the object that is Ariel's voice.

THE VOICE AS OBJECT

The voice has been seen as an object of Lacanian desire by many theorists, and the *Little Mermaid* scene stages a fetishization of the voice as object. In Lacanian psychoanalysis the infant's recognition of self-identity occurs at what he calls the "mirror stage," when the child realizes he or she is a separate being from the mother. It is in part this psychological trauma that enables the newly articulated subject to embrace the symbolic and therefore emerge into language. The voice becomes a tool by which the infant can articulate self and communicate with Other, but a residual desire to restore a condition of wholeness as the mother-child leads the individual's adult psyche to fetishize the voice. In Michel Poizat's terms, "it is insofar as the voice is indeed an object, an autonomous object detached from the body that produces it, that it can become the object of the fan's jouissance."[11]

Ursula's desire for Ariel's voice is palpable and explicit, and in coveting the beauty of the sound she hears, Ursula the monster of adulthood also covets the innocence of Ariel's childlike beauty. Having made the exchange, Ariel is left bereft, though this literal reification of the voice (in this transaction and in Poizat's Lacanian reading) raises some questions about the objectivity of this treasure that is exchanged. Carried by the breath to be held hostage, her voice is trapped inside the shell and, presumably, stoppered to prevent it from escaping. But what is it exactly that is inside that shell?

In the 1989 Disney film the transaction is far more violent. A spectral hand reaches into Ariel's throat and plucks out her larynx, physically pulling the voice from the mermaid, leaving Ariel not just voiceless but without the means of even producing voice; the object-voice is literally taken. This metaphorical rape fits in the context of a powerfully mythologized relationship between woman and voice: it provides a mirror image to the narrative of the Garden of Eden, in which the larynx is formed by Eve choking on the apple with which the serpent tempts her. In that narrative, Eve is banished from the earthly paradise; in *The Little Mermaid*, Ariel is allowed back into the metaphorical garden, and is able to journey onto dry land and become constituted as a human. Ariel's passage is nothing if not a symbolic gesture of birth, and the brutal amputation involved in this transaction is another Lacanian separation that articulates the subject as an individual.

Nevertheless, whether given away or brutally torn out, the way that this separation is voiced (the magical potency of song that accompanies the dramatic moment) is no literal voicing of this surgery: we do not hear in the music this amputation as the removal of a voice; there is no scream, no violence, no wrenching. Instead, we hear Ariel's beautiful, pure leitmotif first heard as "Part of Your World." It is this sound, this song that Ursula covets, a double articulation of both the metatheatrical *possente spirto* and the mythical aesthetic of the mermaid's song. As she seizes it we hear the song become audibly muffled, trapped within the stolen larynx—or at least within the sea witch's jewelry box—as object.

In this transaction, it is clear that the relationship between voice and song is complex: Ariel sells her voice, her vocal apparatus is taken, but the transaction is mimetically performed through singing. The only thing that can seemingly evidence the fact that the voice has been taken is not the material musculature and ligaments of the ripped-out organ (it is not that gory object that Ursula covets), nor the immateriality of the voice itself (what precisely would that be: textured breath?), but the performative token of *song*: the machinations of the larynx given the aesthetic form of voice and captured for posterity in a discernible form. Ethereality is reified in a series of maneuvers that give song its shape and substance.

THE PRACTICE OF THE SUNG

In this dramatization of the vocal object it becomes clear that what we understand as song is inextricably tied to the voice and the body that produces it. It is worth exploring the complex metaphysical dynamics that this involves: the corporeality of the body that creates it, the personality of the apparatus that shapes it, the movement of its residue once it has been performed, and the reception of its vibrations when it is heard. It is worth also noting over the next few paragraphs the way that this discussion of the voice calls regularly on the notion of the song, as if these are synonymous. This slippage in our perceptual handling of voice and song, and in the language we use to discuss them, is an important complexity to unravel.

Roland Barthes's essay "The Grain of the Voice" has perhaps done most to invoke the significance of "the body in the voice as it sings" "from deep down in the cavities, the muscles, the membranes, the cartilages."[12] If nothing else, this reminds us that the voice is created by muscular effort. It is not ambient, as Ariel's ethereal leitmotif might suggest, but instead it starts as a very defined entity and at a very defined point, with the impetus of the diaphragm reversing the flow of inbreath to outbreath and forcing it between the vocal folds, vibrating and expanding into the cavity of the mouth from which it spews into the world. Perceptually, the sound of song ends when that breath comes to an end and that energy expires. In this articulation song is given body and the fluidity of sound is given shape (a beginning and end). Thus the shape of voice takes the materiality of breath, and the narrative of a single breath serves as a metonym for the whole articulation of what is sung.

If breath creates that material terrain, its shape is molded by our mouth—the tongue and the teeth and the lips that in parallel articulate language. The sharp attacks and closures of consonants encage the liquidity of vowels; meanings fix specifics, and textures create form. Sometimes the sound is literally starting-gunned or cut off with the crack of "K," the bite of "T," or the mumming of "M." At other times the sound seems to seek release, escape through small fissures in the leisurely fricatives like "SH," "V," "TH," or "J." Physically our mouths both create and perform an entrapment, our lips squeezing the roundness of vowels into the bottleneck of "W," tripping the sound's flow with the obstacle of "P" or clamping shut "M" to stifle the hostage within. Many writers discuss this sound-shaping,[13] and Poizat reminds us that another feature of its play is "the cutting apart of vocal sound by the scalpel of silence."[14] These are individual phonemes, though the effect can be magnified throughout a song in the articulation of its units: the line, the phrase, the verse, and even the rhetoricizing of its unity within a title. Thus "Crazy" metaphorically starts with the hard "K" as something breaks inside Patsy Cline; she pours out her endless sob, whose sound is left to go on indefinitely with only a partial closure in "E" ("I'm crazy...") In the song itself the pattern extends, the sound and breath extend, and that open ending becomes "OO" ("I'm crazy for trying and crazy for crying and I'm crazy for loving you").[15] We indulge in its bittersweet continuation, brought to an end only by the human limitations of that corporeal breath.

Yet even in performance the song is a funny thing, for though it is literally breathed into life and molded into shape within the body and by the body, it is quickly—immediately—ejected; indeed, like movement, its ejection from the body is an integral condition of song, and paradoxically, this is the point at which the shape, breath, and texture of song all disappear. In fact, it is not even always true to say that the song is created in one body: its component voices often emerge from the many, where outside the bodies that have given life and shape to each sound, the individual voices become layered, creating a new texture. Consider Rodolfo's first encounter with Mimi in act 1 of *La Bohème*:[16] "Ma per fortuna é una notte di luna e qui la luna l'abbiamo vicina" ("By luck there is a moon tonight and the moon will keep us company"), he sings, answering the gentle droplets of "moonlight" from the harp, and duetting with the rising scale of the flute motif. This song is made by several bodies—by the singer's breath and voice issuing the melody and lyrics; by the flautist's breath and fingers piping counterpoint out of the flute; by the harpist manipulating pedals and strings to generate their vibrations; and by a team of cellos and violins that resonate to create a bed of warm texture. Two dozen individuals create this music and eject it. Outside their bodies in that moment of release it hangs in the air. Only there can it coalesce to become the sound of song.

In this respect, song is "music in the air," whose sound waves disperse to resonate within the soundbox of the opera house, and to reach our ears, where the song can finally be heard. Sound moves in waves after all, and dynamics of movement are fundamental to its production, its reception and its resonance. Though we can't see or feel it, sound travels, using other invisible and intangible matter as its conduit, resonating in "empty" cavities that aren't really as empty as they appear to be. And it is only now that we, the listeners, can become aware of the sound of the voice or song, after this long journey it has taken, following its creation, its shaping, its movement, and its resonance. Now we sense it in another phenomenological encounter of body and voice—this time the vicarious enactment of the listener with the corporeality of the voice that is heard, as Millie Taylor writes: "the voice in that moment draws together the listening and singing bodies," she suggests; "And when I remember that moment I feel the thrill of a voice reverberating in my body, I feel the physical action through which that sound is created."[17] If the song itself does not have any tangible matter, it at least seems to affect the matter from which we are formed. It causes us to vibrate, it impacts on our equilibrium, and even if we can't say definitively that it has matter, the solidity of clay, we can pick up on the words of Tim Rice and suggest that we have found "what's the buzz":[18] the vibration of affect on our corporeal and psychological matter that the song elicits. In this sense, no matter how objectified (distinct from us) it is, the song as an ecology (sound in our presence) needs and becomes, subjectively, a part of us.

If song is of necessity carried by the traffic of the voice, this complex sequence of processes shows it to be something far more dynamic than a tangible lump (of clay?) that we see and touch with our hands. Instead, as Steven Connor describes it, voice is something more fluid that "tends to occupy space, spreading into and blending with it indivisibly."[19] And it is presumably through this indivisible blending of substances that the Phantom (of the Opera) talks of "floating, falling" (now liquid, now gas) in "The Music of the Night." Indeed, for him, what is sung blends even with the porosity of the body: you succumb to its "sweet intoxication" (within); you let it "secretly caress you" (without), as if its substance and our own were intermingling.[20] Yet paradoxically, the very dispersal and intermingling that enables sound is also the dissipation that makes it fade in time and memory. So the dispersal is both a reaching out and a fading out; voice dies even as it lives. Indeed, as David Burrows reminds us, the "deflating irony" is that it is not the oxygen of existence that breathes life into the voice in the first place, but the expiration of carbon monoxide: "all our spoken eloquence, all our arias, and all our prayers are qualifications of the waste-removal phase of breathing."[21]

As these examples reinforce, what is sung is more than just sounds, the complex coalescence of its many different textures and resonances; voice has a visceral presence, the mark of a singer whose corporeality creates the sound of song. In this sense, song is the shaping of the voice, and any conceptualization of the song, one might think, must necessarily also conceptualize the singer and that act of singing.

THE SONG IS YOU

Given the close connection of song, voice, and body, it is not surprising that many writers have sought to conflate them, or at least to locate the song *within*: "If I sing, you are the music," write Richard Maltby Jr. and David Shire in *Closer Than Ever* (1989); "You are the music in me," Zac Efron tells us more recently—"You're harmony to the melody that's echoing inside my head" (2007). In an extreme of this anthropomorphism, Max Wilk evokes the final scene from Ray Bradbury's *Fahrenheit 451* (1953), in which bohemian fugitives from the state that has banned all books gather in the forest to live out their days as the books that are being lost. In Bradbury's novel the exiles learn by heart their narratives and spend their days endlessly replaying the tales so that the stories will not be lost. On their deathbeds, the elderly "books" pass on their embodied narratives to the young generation, the dissemination of literature returning to an oral tradition in an evocative vision: "We'll pass the books on to our children, by word of mouth, and let our children wait, in turn, on the other people."[22] Wilk imagines the same thing happening to song, describing a world in which "gallant individuals would tomorrow stroll from person to person, humming, singing, and chanting songs [...] in an effort to keep our treasures alive for generations to come."[23] The songs, then, become embodied and humanized, given tangible form and the identity of subject. Perhaps the most defining example of this working its way into the dynamics of a musical is in the 1952 radio adaptation of Jerome Kern and Oscar Hammerstein II's *Music in the Air* (1932). In this narrative, "The Song is You" is one of those songs that seem to ooze from the very matter of the world they inhabit. Young romantic lead Karl Reder is put on the spot to come up with lyrics for a melody by his father-in-law-to-be, music teacher Dr. Lessing. Ultimately, Karl and his fiancée Sieglinde will travel to Vienna to make the song a successful hit and make Dr. Lessing a published songwriter; but this is the first iteration of what both inside and outside the show becomes a popular success.

In the scene in which "The Song is You" first appears, Dr. Lessing demands from Karl the promised lyrics, but Karl has been so preoccupied with his feelings for Sieglinde that he has clean forgotten. "I'll write them right now, Sieglinde," he offers, and turning to his overblown passion for inspiration, he conjures up the lyrics in an instant: "Look at me. Can't you read the words in my eyes?" he says. "What are your eyes saying, Karl?" Sieglinde replies, and then Karl sings, both explaining why the lyrics are so readily accessible to him and simultaneously using this explanation as the material from which the song is made: "I hear music when I look at you [...] Down deep in my heart I hear it play [...] The song is you."[24]

It is a moment of romantic hyperbole, of course, but Karl's apparently mystical summoning forth of song is a part of the creative process that many composers experience. Granted, many popular tunesmiths have worked with pianos to bash out (and therefore hear) prototype cadences and melodies, and many songwriters have turned to professional orchestrators to adapt the sparse bones of their ditty into the full flesh of a song. However, this is not the case for all (or for those orchestrators), and certainly anecdotal accounts attest to the fact that composers somehow hear the song internally: "What impresses me most about Irving Berlin is that his inner ear is tremendous," wrote Robert Russell Bennett, "*inside*, he hears it."[25] The magic of creative inspiration is even more impressive than it seems; for Karl not only spontaneously creates lyrics for the song, but also seems uncannily to know the music to which he is creating the lyrics—that sound which is fundamental to song, yet paradoxically silent inside him. It is as if the song surges out of his body, already fully formed, a creative conceit in which "the character appears to be the actual site of the music's production."[26] What is more, Sieglinde joins Karl in his iteration, affirming their compatibility for sure, but showing a similarly uncanny prior knowledge of the song, as if it—the object-song replete with form, music, lyrics, and orchestration—has also incubated inside her, just waiting for this moment to be emphatically born. So does song exist *before*?

This idea that we can hear song bodily—without its materiality (sound) being ordinarily audible—is curiously persistent, however metaphorical. Yesterday for the entire day my thoughts kept returning to "Some People" from *Gypsy* (1959), like a hangover from a student seminar I had delivered the day before: "that's living for some people, For some humdrum people I suppose."[27] In fact, to say that my thoughts kept returning is not quite right; this was clearly a subconscious memory of the song that was looping repetitively in my head and of which my consciousness became relentlessly aware. Yet I seemed to hear the song almost palpably inside my head: this was Ethel Merman's distinctive foghorn of a voice, with her mannered New York–Jewish vowel sounds and her iconic Broadway nasality: a memory of the Original Broadway Cast recording, to be sure. It's a common experience for us all to hear songs in our head, though these songs are clearly not "heard" "sound" in the conventional senses of either word. "I hear singing and there's no one there," writes Berlin,[28] and this observation calls into question the earlier assertion that sound—human sound, the voice—is an integral part of song.

In romanticizing the internalized song, both Kern/Hammerstein and Wilk invoke a nostalgia for what seems to have been lost, or in Wilk's terms, what threatens to be lost. He writes of Bernard Herrmann predicting a gloomy future for the Tin Pan Alley song: "the future of American popular music would probably relegate the works of Messrs. Gershwin, Berlin, Kern, Rodgers & Hart, Porter, et al., to the status of *leider*."[29] I suspect Wilk intended to write "*Lieder*," referring to the German canon of songs now only heard as formalized concert pieces. "*Leider*," his misprint, is the German word for "unfortunately," which is an ironic misspelling if ever there was one, though it reminds me once again of "Those Poor Unfortunate Souls" of whom the sea witch Ursula sings.

Of course, Wilk's fanciful solution to the loss of our songs—whereby "gallant individuals" hand them down through singing—is a historical flashback rather than a futuristic vision. The practice of "humming, singing and chanting songs" he imagines is the practice of strolling players and wandering minstrels, a practice now so fantastical and alien to us simply because the vicissitudes of technology have enabled us to substitute the oral practice with the archiving of thingness. In order to consider this it is useful to turn attention to that oral practice, and in particular to its "song," which is difficult to write about, much less analyze, because, of course, "it" ("the song") has not been preserved, and no "text" that could be studied defines its identity (until, as we have seen, broadsides like "The Wandering Jew's Chronicle" start to appear).

However, such a practice is articulated in one of those songs about songs that crop up throughout the musical theater repertoire, Nanki-Poo's "A Wandering Minstrel I" from Gilbert and Sullivan's *The Mikado*. Here, Gilbert and Sullivan stage a conceptualization of song in the oral tradition—song being something that is offered in performance by a singer whose identity is embodied in the act of singing.

Nanki-Poo's act is to suit mood to occasion: "Are you in sentimental mood? I'll sigh with you."[30] Here, couched in active terms as a verb, the practice of singing (rather than the object of the song) characterizes the minstrel; with these words, Sullivan's music sighs ("Oh, sorrow"), also actively, recalling the observation of Theo van Leeuwen that "melodies do not only 'express tenderness,' they also and at the same time caress, they do not only 'express scorn,' they also and at the same time mock, they do not only 'express longing,' they also and at the same time plead."[31] And though Gilbert also invokes the idea of "song" as a noun ("To your humours changing I tune my supple song"), there is a sense that in this impression of the oral enterprise, the term "song" reaches beyond the discrete fixity of a particular song-object to signify the complex ecology of a cultural practice (as in the expression "song and dance"). This is a subtle distinction, though it points to the complex nuances that are at play in the way that language encodes certain assumptions in its use. In another example, Gilbert and Sullivan exploit the same distinction to slide beguilingly from the particular to the mythic: "I have a song to sing, O!" sings Jack Point in *The Yeomen of the Guard*, as if referring to one specific song:

> It is sung to the moon
> By a love-lorn loon,
> Who fled from the mocking throng, O!
> It's a song of a merryman, moping mum,
> Whose soul was sad, and whose glance was glum
> Who sipped no sup, and who craved no crumb,
> As he sighed for the love of a ladye.[32]

But this is not a song that can be simplistically identified; instead Gilbert uses the suggestion of the singular song (it even has lyrics: "Heighdy! Heighdy! Misery me, lackadaydee!") as a metonym to stand for a greater mythical potential: song here is the human expression of sighing (active) "for the love of a ladye" (elsewhere of loving "with a love life-long, O!"). Again, Sullivan's music enacts the melancholy of this sighing in a shimmering ostinato that seems to articulate the mesmeric ephemerality of the unquantifiable. The fact that there is in these stagings of the tradition a double articulation of the performative act (Nanki-Poo singing to Titipu; Julian Jensen singing to D'Oyly Carte audiences)[33] is significant, for it means that even in this updated (posttechnological) revisiting of the pastoral past, the engagement and experience of song is a performative and live phenomenon.

In this, two important dynamics emerge that are useful to this discussion, and which are poetically rehearsed in the concept of "The Song is You." The first of these is that the song of the oral tradition is carried silently and voicelessly within the individual; the second is that the passing on of this song happens as a performative act in which the voice makes the song textured and audible. Thus what is sung is either internalized (a state of being), or voiced (an act of performing). In either case, the word "song" seems too physical—it has not yet taken its place in the symbolic order; rather than "the song," the material that will be performed is *the sung*. As wispy as a dream, the sung has an ephemeral identity as an utterance in a moment whose resonance may linger, but whose form cannot be perceived: a nebulous, unformed practice.[34]

I'm deliberately making a distinction here in my use of language (between *the sung* and *the song*), because it seems to me that one of the reasons we perceive song as *thing* is because of a pervasive cultural rhetoric that has positioned it as such, one tool of which is language. The "literizing" of the sung, capturing the intangible and sedimenting it onto the paraphernalia of literacy (the songsheet, the wax cylinder) perhaps marks a significant point at which the conceptualization of song as a material entity is born. That this effect was exponentially accelerated as the mass technologies of mechanical reproduction heralded the real onslaught of popular music in America is significant. So while the long tradition of musical literacy and associated language in Europe had clearly already had interpellative effect in constructing the authority of the musical work and the attendant ideology surrounding the great composers, it is reasonable to suggest that the parcelling and commodification of short-form song structures onto songsheet and recording both magnified and popularized that interpellation. Thus it was in America and in the twentieth century, as both a byproduct and marketing tool of what for the purposes of simplicity we can call Tin Pan Alley, that the thingness of song became a pronounced conceptual rhetoric.

Along with the technological paradigm shift comes an ideological maneuver to rhetoricize this literizing in the language that attends upon the shift. Thus language is clearly tremendously significant in the way we perceive song, and, much as Lacanian theory has the original lack replaced by the constitution of identity through the symbolic substitution of language, there is a similar, complex relationship between the sung and its symbolic substitution by "song." Karl and Sieglinde's song, symbolic of their parental love, is metaphorically born, as the song enacts a Lacanian separation from its host and emerges into the symbolic order; here it is articulated as music and lyrics and also as a discrete entity, the object that is separate from its "mother," *that song*. And this birth enacts the broader separation of subjectivity that occurred historically in the transition from the oral to the literary traditions, when the immediacy of the sung as practice gained a second articulation in the sedimentation of the song as text.

FIXING THE SONG AS THING

The oral tradition, though, is a transient practice, confounding discussion that seeks to tie down examples and enactments in linguistic fixity. Scholarly sources to which we now turn in order to learn about the oral tradition (for example, Hamm's

Music in the New World) objectify both practices and utterances, giving names to styles of singing ("ballads, songs and snatches, and dreamy lullaby") and labeling discrete examples based on the subject matter of the what-is-sung. In this way the literary tradition fixes the mythical song into the mundane; and it is in forging terms for a practice (naming it) that language conceives the thingness of the what-is-sung: the "what" of the object and the "is" of existence. Texture becomes text and the sung becomes the song; just as myth becomes reified into a literary economy, the song becomes a commodity and practice fades into product. In this way, language interpellates the metaphysical into the material world. By the twentieth century the ideologies of this literizing culture are unequivocally absorbed into the exchanges of song, and with the printing, sale, and ownership of the notated songsheet (and later the vinyl disc), the perception that songs are things is performed into certainty.

NOTES

1. Howard Ashman and Alan Menken, "Poor Unfortunate Souls," from *The Little Mermaid*, 1989 by Walt Disney Records, Walt Disney Records 60841-2, CD-018, D190113, compact disc.
2. Elton John, "Your Song," from *Elton John*, 2004, 1970 by DJM Records, Island Records B0003607-36, compact disc.
3. Alec Wilder, *American Popular Song: The Great Innovators* (New York: Oxford University Press, 1972), xxiv.
4. Irving Berlin, "A Pretty Girl Is Like a Melody," from *The Ziegfeld Follies of 1919* (1919).
5. Max Wilk, *They're Playing Our Song: Conversations with America's Classic Songwriters* (New York: Da Capo Press, 1997), 221.
6. Robert A. Schwegler, "Oral Tradition and Print: Domestic Performance in Renaissance England," *Journal of American Folklore* 93: 370 (1980): 435–441.
7. Nicholas Tawa, *The Way to Tin Pan Alley: American Popular Song, 1866–1910* (New York: Schirmer Books, 1990), xi.
8. Theodor W. Adorno, "The Form of the Phonograph Record," *October* 55 (1990): 58.
9. Theodor W. Adorno, "The Curves of the Needle," *October* 55 (1990): 55.
10. Although other cultures with different linguistic influences might not share the same connotations evoked in German, it's interesting to consider how, on a much broader level and across cultures, song (and dance) maintain a close association with what we see as natural and born of the earth: song is used ritually as an accompaniment to the natural cycle (dawn and dusk, spring and harvest); pastoral tropes depict nymphs and shepherds of the land always singing and dancing; and song to the Australian aborigines becomes fundamental to the way they understand their homeland and their nomadic life within it.
11. Michel Poizat, *The Angel's Cry: Beyond the Pleasure Principle in Opera*, trans. Arthur Denner (Ithaca, NY: Cornell University Press, 1986), 35.
12. Roland Barthes, *Image-Music-Text*, trans. Steven Heath (London: Fontana, 1977), 188, 181.
13. See, for example, R. Murray Schafer, *When Words Sing* (Scarborough, ON: Berandol Music, 1970); Jean-Jacques Nattiez, *Music and Discourse: Toward a Semiology of Music* (Princeton, NJ: Princeton University Press, 1990); Roman Jakobson, *The Sound Shape of Language* (The Hague: Mouton de Gruyter, 2002); David Burrows, *Sound, Speech, and Music* (Amherst: University of Massachusetts Press, 1990); Steven Connor, "Chiasmus," *Studies in Musical Theatre* 6: 1 (2012): 9–27.
14. Poizat, *Angel's Cry*, 43.

15. Patsy Cline, "Crazy," *Patsy Cline*, 1962 by Decca, Decca ED 2707, LP.
16. Giacomo Puccini, Luigi Illica, and Giuseppe Giacosa, "Che gelida manina," from *La Bohème* (1896).
17. Millie Taylor, " 'If I Sing': Voice, Singing and Song," *Studies in Musical Theatre* 6: 1 (2012): 4.
18. Tim Rice and Andrew Lloyd Webber, "What's the Buzz?" from *Jesus Christ Superstar*, 1972 by Fanfare, Fanfare SIT 60006, LP.
19. Connor, "Chiasmus," 21.
20. Andrew Lloyd Webber and Charles Hart, "The Music of the Night," from *The Phantom of the Opera*, 1987 by Polydor, Polydor 831 273-2 Y-2, compact disc.
21. Burrows, *Sound, Speech, and Music*, 16.
22. Raymond Bradbury, *Fahrenheit 451* (London: HarperCollins, 2008), 196.
23. Wilk, *They're Playing Our Song*, 291.
24. Jerome Kern and Oscar Hammerstein II, "The Song is You," from *Music in the Air* (original cast recording: radio broadcast), 1952 by AEI, AEI CD024, compact disc. The radio adaptation (1952) offers a narrative markedly different from the original stage play (1932), in which the characters are based in Munich (rather than Vienna) and launch the hit song "I've Told Every Little Star" (rather than "The Song is You"). In the original libretto, "The Song is You" is sung by the Macchiavellian Bruno Mahler in an apparently spontaneous expression of adoration for Sieglinde. Bruno is later exposed as a Casanova, notorious for deceiving young ladies with this tried-and-tested romantic gesture.
25. Cited in Wilk, *They're Playing Our Song*, 266.
26. Heather Laing, "Emotion by Numbers: Music, Song and the Musical," in *Musicals: Hollywood and Beyond*, ed. Bill Marshall and Robynn Stilwell (Exeter: Intellect Books, 2000), 7.
27. Jule Styne and Stephen Sondheim, "Some People," from *Gypsy*, 1959, in *Ten Great Musicals of the American Theatre*, ed. Stanley Green (Radnor, PA: Chilton Book Company, 1973), 422.
28. Irving Berlin, "You're Just in Love," from *Call Me Madam*, 1950.
29. Wilk, *They're Playing Our Song*, 291.
30. William Schwenk Gilbert and Arthur Sullivan, "A Wand'ring Minstrel, I," from *The Mikado* (1885), in *The Complete Annotated Gilbert and Sullivan*, ed. Ian Bradley (New York: Oxford University Press, 1996), 561.
31. Theo Van Leeuwen, *Speech, Music, Sound* (Basingstoke: Macmillan, 1999), 97.
32. William Schwenk Gilbert and Arthur Sullivan, "I Have a Song to Sing, O!" from *The Yeomen of the Guard* (1888), in Bradley, *Gilbert and Sullivan*, 779.
33. Julian Jensen is just one performer who has taken this role, in the 1990 Buxton Opera House production, captured in a BBC video recording: *The Mikado*, VHS, directed by John Michael Phillips and Andrew Wickes (London: BBC, 1992). Online. Available: https://www.youtube.com/watch?v=ZRCbKHegzZk, December 2, 2012.
34. In this, of course, song shares qualities with other performative forms/practices such as "play"—and it is useful to consider the more performative meaning of this word in a line like "The play's the thing wherein I'll catch the conscience of the King." Instantly, Hamlet's chicanery becomes the symptom of a dynamic encounter rather than the result of a staged exposé.

CHAPTER 2

The (Un)Pleasure of Song

On the Enjoyment of Listening to Opera

CARLO ZUCCARINI

You are ensconced in your seat, immersed in the plot of your favorite opera, or perhaps an opera that is unfamiliar to you, and you are enveloped by a mantle of aurally seductive orchestral and vocal music. You may be enjoying a recording in the comfort of your armchair, or sitting in the charged atmosphere of an opera house auditorium. As the action unfolds, you become increasingly oblivious to your surroundings and the reality that lies beyond the fictional operatic space you have willingly chosen to enter. Your surroundings and the agency of your selected listening or viewing media no longer have any significance. Without realizing it, you have been transported to another time and place. The space of illusion in which you now find yourself has managed to suspend reality. Even though you know that this newfound reality that you inhabit temporarily is fictional, you nonetheless allow this suspension of disbelief to continue. Your interaction with the story being enacted on the stage operates within an intermediate area that provides a bridge between your inner and outer worlds. The fusion of the constituent elements of the opera—the dramatic action, the music, and the singing—that is occurring out there is somehow able to draw upon what is inside you, evoking real feelings and emotions despite the illusion that is mediating them. You go along with this secondary belief until, suddenly, something resonates within you. In one of the musical numbers, a voice reaches its peak of expressiveness, soaring to its highest register, and you are inexplicably overcome by a transcendent state—an intense mixture of sadness and bliss. Yet what you are feeling may not have any correspondence with the affective color or content of the musical number, or the dramatic action. You are enjoying the intensity of the emotion that has been evoked within you, realizing that you have been moved by the singing itself, yet you do not know why. You feel uneasy. You feel a lump in your throat, choked up. You try to suppress the utterly enjoyable feeling, which for some unexplained reason is becoming increasingly uncomfortable. You are overwhelmed by a sense of loss. You try to catch your breath, as your eyes well up despite your best efforts to prevent them from doing so.

This "sonorous envelope" fantasy[1] is a familiar scenario for many operaphiles, even though the emotive charge is unlikely to be as powerful each and every time. The intensity of the emotion that can be evoked in the reception of an opera, a specific musical number or a "song" within it and, most often, one particular voice, is perhaps directly proportional to its being perceived as "a great performance." On the other hand, a performance that leaves the operaphile emotionally cold and unmoved rarely achieves any measure of greatness, even though it may be very good in many other respects. This raises several questions. Why do operaphiles seek out this bittersweet emotional experience that has the power to make them cry? Why do they enjoy it? And what is it about operatic singing that can evoke such intense emotion? This is not to say that other genres of music, songs, or types of singing are unable to evoke equally intense emotion. However, based on the material discussed here, it may be plausible to claim that, although the neural underpinnings are essentially the same in the reception of all music, an operaphile's affective response to operatic singing involves specific unconscious dynamics. These questions can be fruitfully explored using a two-pronged neuropsychoanalytic approach. In order to do so, the findings of neuroscientific research on music perception will be combined with psychoanalytic theory applied to the reception of operatic singing, drawing mainly from the theories of Freud, Lacan, and Winnicott.

NEUROSCIENCE AND MUSIC

A good place to start the discussion might be to dip a toe into the substantial pool of neuroscientific findings related to music reception. However, there is little empirical research on the reception of vocal music, and even less in the case of opera. The main reason for this is the need to limit confounding factors, so that neuropsychophysiological responses to music itself can be studied independently of the language and meaning of lyrics. Among the studies that have investigated vocal music,[2] a few have focused on opera. They have provided convincing evidence in support of the two opposing views as to whether music and lyrics are processed separately or jointly in the brain. The reason for this apparent contradiction has been clarified by the research of Sammler and colleagues,[3] which showed that music and lyrics are actually processed both jointly *and* separately to varying degrees. The study used functional magnetic resonance imaging (fMRI) to observe blood flow in the brains of the non-musician participants while they listened to unfamiliar nineteenth-century French folk songs performed by trained singers. The researchers found that passive listening to unfamiliar songs involves various degrees of integration and separation during the processing stages, from the back to the front of the brain. Music and lyrics at a phonemic level are processed together at first, followed by increasingly abstract and independent processing of the lyrics in terms of structure and semantics. The research highlighted a couple of interesting points. First, while the processing of music and lyrics is closely bound, lyrics are processed in a more independent manner.

Second, there is a similarity with the findings of speech perception studies, which also show increasingly complex and abstract hierarchical stages of processing.

A significant overlap between the processing of music and language in the brain has been identified by a number of researchers.[4] Investigation in this area has been increasing consistently over the years, in line with the growing realization that both music and language recruit a wide range of neural processing systems relating to memory, attention, classification, and identification of specific elements.[5] However, music processing involves an even greater number of areas in the brain than language.[6] Beyond the fact that music and language processing each involve complex neural structures, both also share many cognitive features, such as the way in which structured sound is encoded, and how words in language and tones in music may function in relation to a governing syntax.[7]

Another area of neuroscientific research that is of relevance to the psychoanalytic themes that will be discussed here concerns the innate capacity of human beings to acquire both language and music abilities. There is considerable evidence that this ability to process features of music and syntactic rules (of music and language) is innate, present from birth, and similar to that of adults.[8] This evidence indicates that the natural ability of infants to process music is closely related to their natural ability to acquire language.[9] Listening to vocal music, such as lullabies, is generally among the earliest activities of most newborns.[10] Babies display a preference for singing and speech at higher pitches,[11] and vocal music compared to instrumental music.[12] They also prefer their mother's voice rather than the voices of strangers.[13] Given that sound perception begins at approximately thirty weeks of gestation, newborns have a fair amount of exposure to the sounds in their environment even before birth, including a good knowledge of the mother's voice.[14] After birth, the affective state or mood of preverbal infants is regulated by mothers/caregivers through voice modulation and singing.[15] It seems plausible, then, that interest in and affective response to music in adults is the result of their exposure to the melodious nonverbal vocal communication of their mothers and caregivers, which is aimed at regulating mood, affect, and engagement.[16] This early exposure to the affective content of music and musicality, in addition to the comfort of the mother/infant dyad, promotes learning and social bonds throughout life, so that a listener's response to music in adulthood retains social features of affective regulation and relatedness to others.[17] Therefore, music may be considered to involve a communication process originating in vocal affect aimed at obtaining a specific response in the listener, either emotional or behavioral, and this dynamic has in turn shaped the whole process in evolutionary terms.[18] Experiences during early development allow infants to learn the features of the music in their culture, and it is against this knowledge that all future listening is based.[19] The brain learns the rules of the musical tradition in which we are raised, and our neural networks are shaped accordingly, in the same way that we innately learn the rules of the language of the culture into which we are born.[20] We tend to enjoy, understand, and listen most often to music that is part of the musical tradition in which we have been raised, or to which we have been habituated through consistent exposure. As such, acculturation and memory also have a significant role in the neural processing and enjoyment of music.

Numerous areas of the brain are involved in the reception of music, including those associated with reward, motivation, emotion, and arousal.[21] The neural process of listening to music may be described in basic terms as involving a deconstruction or parsing of incoming auditory information. The separate strands of information are then reconstructed or reassembled, drawing on memory, to produce an abstract and seemingly unitary neural representation of the music. An appropriate emotional response is then formed based on this mental "sound image." The auditory system has a hierarchical organization, both anatomically and functionally, in which there is a bidirectional flow of information from lower to higher levels.[22] As the information moves toward higher levels, the degree of abstraction and complexity increases. This allows representations to be constructed of specific instruments or melodies, based on information that is stored in memory and other cognitive areas.[23] When this process has been completed, an emotional response is then prepared.[24] The lyrics of vocal music activate the brain's language networks in the temporal and frontal lobes.[25] The structure of music is also processed in the frontal regions of the brain that are associated with language.[26] The involvement of language networks may explain why we tend to focus a great deal on the higher notes when listening to music, given that most of the energy released by consonants in speech is within the same range as most melodies.[27] Emotion evoked by music activates the frontal lobes, cerebellum, amygdala, and nucleus accumbens, which are components of a neural system that processes any pleasurable and rewarding activity, such as eating or having sex.[28]

PSYCHOANALYSIS AND OPERA

The heterogeneous mix of artistic "languages" in opera poses significant challenges when we attempt to analyze their simultaneous reception without dissecting opera.[29] Words and empirical methods are imperfect tools in their ability to account for the otherworldly nature of the performativity of the reception experience. Any analysis of opera must inevitably consider the constituent performance elements side by side, rather than together, exploring the way in which they combine to shape the reception experience as a whole. This situation is reflected in the parallel approach used here to try to account for the related axes of mind and body, brain and psyche.

In philosophy and aesthetics since the eighteenth century, music has been located beyond linguistic signification, as a discourse of the unsayable.[30] From a deconstructive viewpoint, meaning may be found in that which cannot be integrated and is therefore not present in the discourse itself, or has been eliminated from the discourse, or is in excess of the discourse.[31] Indeed, as many musicologists would agree, some of the most powerful emotions experienced by operaphiles occur precisely when the words become unintelligible, namely when the voice becomes music and loses its connection with language, thereby destroying language itself.[32] This phonic materiality of the voice, which lies beyond the meaning of the words that are being sung, is what Michel Poizat[33] is referring to when he claims that the voice follows a trajectory both because of the dramatic action and despite it. The singing ultimately transcends the storyline, the visual elements, and the music, and follows its own trajectory to its final destination of the cry at the higher registers of the voice—the soprano being the most likely to achieve this, although by no means to the exclusion of other upper vocal ranges. Poizat's examples of this dynamic highlight an operaphile's baffling phenomenological encounter with the performative, such as Lulu's death cry in *Lulu* (1937); Kundry's score in act 2 of *Parsifal* (1878); Brünnhilde's cry when the ring is taken from her in act 1, scene 3 of *Götterdämmerung* (1876); Brünnhilde's cry of joy in act 2, scene 2 of *Die Walküre* (1862); the love duet in act 2 and also Isolde's Transfiguration in *Tristan und Isolde* (1865); the Queen of the Night's arias "O zittre nicht, mein lieber Sohn" and "Der Hölle Rache" in *The Magic Flute* (1791); the "Mad Scene" (the F major version) in *Lucia di Lammermoor* (1839); and the "Bell Song" in *Lakmé* (1883).

It is of significance that these examples relate to entire sections or musical numbers, rather than specific passages or "high points." There may be more to this than mere convention, or a convenient method of signposting, or considerations of musical order and structure. The structure of opera (and similar forms of musical theater), with its separate yet concatenated "songs" or musical numbers in the form of arias, duets, trios, and so on, provides a framework within and across which the trajectory of the voice develops. Each musical number or "song" functions like a sort of pressure vessel that serves to contain, focus, and intensify the power of the operatic voice, pumping it up to achieve the "excess of songness" that characterizes opera, yet keeping it (mostly) at a safe distance to prevent the listener from being completely overwhelmed. This "song framework" can be identified throughout the history of opera, starting from a more distinct alternation between singing and recitative, right down to and including Wagnerian continuous melody with its leitmotifs.

When the operatic voice completes its trajectory, transcending and undoing the language of the lyrics, and its excess is such that it manages to erupt from its safe containment, the operaphile experiences jouissance, a Lacanian term referring to an "excess of enjoyment" that is so intense as to be painful. However, it is not the voice's asemic phonic materiality per se that produces this vocal jouissance, but rather the fact that the language and meaning of the lyrics have been undone by the singing in the performativity of the encounter. This may be more likely to happen in opera because of the particular vocal techniques and dynamics that are involved, among other contributory elements. The operaphile is seeking what is in excess of language—the characteristically operatic "excess of songness," in the form of embellishments and ornamentation. This involves an encounter with the voice as *objet a*, to introduce Lacan's term, a partial lost object cause of desire.

Lacan added the voice and the gaze as two partial objects of desire to Freud's list of lost objects: breast, feces, and phallus.[34] As Lacan affirms, the voice and the gaze are partial objects of a drive, where the object is the cause of desire, or *objet a*.[35] He describes these objects as being partial not because they are part of the body as a whole, but rather because they "only partially represent the function that produces them."[36]

The singing voice in opera functions as a partial object, a lost object, the operaphile's object of desire, that is, *objet a*. As the path of desire is circuitous, the operaphile is driven in an attempt to obtain the voice as *objet a*, but being a partial lost object, it is characterized by lack and is ultimately unattainable. The singing voice as *objet a* is the cause of desire in the operaphile and, as it is lacking, causes desire to circle endlessly around it. The sole aim is to ensure the continuation of desire itself and not the obtaining of *objet a*, as this would result in desire being annihilated. Consequently, *objet a* remains just beyond the operaphile's reach. It is close enough to be tantalizing, yet far enough away to be unattainable, ensuring the function of desire in its perpetual circuit. The song framework of opera contributes to and heightens this circularity, providing a dynamic of alternation that repeatedly reveals and conceals the vocal object. It functions all at once like a resonating chamber, a hall of mirrors, a smoke screen and a maze, ensuring that the desired object remains so by virtue of its utter unattainability. However, the operaphile's quest for wholeness in trying to obtain the vocal object involves more than just the phonic materiality of the singing voice. That is to say, the vocal high points of opera are sought because the vocal object is no longer under the sway of linguistic meaning.[37] All of the other elements of opera, such as the orchestral music, drama, stage sets, and so forth, serve the auxiliary purpose of supporting and contributing to the undoing of language by the singing voice as it gradually becomes a meaning-less vocal object, the "pure" cry with its attendant jouissance.

The song framework of opera sets up the additional illusion that the vocal object can be attained in the neat package of a musical number, which accounts for operatic concert programs consisting entirely of isolated bravura pieces. Yet the vocal object remains ever elusive, whether it is sought in the showcase of a particular musical number, or in the original context of the full work where it functions to best effect, gaining power and impetus gradually through a sort of affective fractional distillation process.

The operaphile's constant quest for the vocal object should be understood in the context of Lacan's description of the pleasure principle that "makes man always search for what he has to find again, but which he will never attain,"[38] which is similar to Freud's description of the repetition compulsion and link to the death drive.[39] Lacan subsequently restates this repetition as jouissance continually transgressing the pleasure principle to seek death.[40] This is Freud's "death instinct" or drive.[41] Lacan referred to the death drive as "nostalgia for wholeness," a "return to the mother's womb," which "dominates the whole of the life of man," and the weaning complex "leaves in the human psyche the permanent trace of the biological relationship it interrupts."[42] This notion is echoed below in the context of Winnicott's theories. For Lacan, then, "every drive is virtually a death drive,"[43] given that drives are taken to their limits, through repetition, toward the painful enjoyment of jouissance beyond the pleasure principle.

Opera creates and operates within an intermediate area that allows the listener to relate inner and outer worlds through illusion and fantasy. Illusion has a central role in Winnicott's theories about the transitional object and transitional phenomena, which will be discussed later. Illusion and its opposite, disillusionment, provide the basis not only for infant individuation and separation from the mother (weaning), but also for creativity itself. According to Winnicott, illusion is "that which is allowed to the infant, and which in adult life is inherent in art and religion."[44] Both the creation and reception of cultural products, such as music and art, involve sharing illusory experiences in a common intermediate area. As Winnicott explains, this is an unchallenged area, where cultural products are conceived and enjoyed, and he likens it to "the play area of the small child who is 'lost' in play."[45] Through the fiction of the story being enacted, opera creates what Winnicott calls a "holding environment"[46] that allows the listener to "practice" experiencing intense emotions without having to endure the associated real-life trauma situations. In this way, like other cultural products, opera functions as a derivative transitional experience, providing a source of comfort and solace.[47] It is capable of relieving the strain of negotiating reality by maintaining a symbolic link with the (M)Other.

Winnicott used the term "transitional object" to describe the infant behavior involving attachment to a special object, such as the corner of a sheet or blanket.[48] The cherished object has a transitional function, between the two stages of oral erotism and subsequent play with dolls and teddy bears, before true object-relationships are formed, and "between the subjective and that which is objectively perceived";[49] it is viewed by the infant as his/her "first not-me possession."[50] Transitional phenomena (i.e., nonmaterial objects), may include, for example, babbling in the younger infant, or singing songs and humming tunes before sleep in older children. According to Winnicott, this "intermediate area" creates a space of illusion.[51] In this transitional experience, the child's inner and outer worlds merge and overlap, and the boundaries between the two become indistinct. The intermediate area develops as a result of the gradual separation from the breast and the mother—from illusion to disillusionment—leading to the child's individuation and the formation of other object-relationships in the external world. Although the transitional object may symbolize a part object, for example the mother's breast, its significance lies in the overlapping position that it occupies, representing the mother's breast while not actually being the mother's breast. Because of the symbolism involved in this intermediate position, the transitional object marks the beginning of an infant's ability to distinguish between inner and outer worlds, fantasy and reality, subjectivity and objectivity. In this way the transitional object is at the same time neither entirely an external object, nor an internal one. It represents the external reality of the mother's breast, but only through the infant's internal symbolization of it.

In Winnicott's view, the successful establishment of object-relationships in the external world is dependent upon a "good enough mother" who facilitates the infant's individuation through the process of illusion and disillusionment. In other words, the mother initially creates the illusion that her breast is part of the infant. Subsequently, the mother's decreasing adaptation to the infant's needs produces gradual disillusionment and allows the infant's separation and individuation to be achieved. The infant's increasing ability to tolerate frustration through this process has the result of juxtaposing love and hate, making external objects real and distinguishable. The illusion-disillusionment process is therefore related to the weaning of the infant, yet its effects continue long after weaning has been completed.

The transitional object is one of many transitional phenomena, which include sounds such as babbling, lullabies, songs and tunes, movements such as rocking, patting, and rubbing by the mother, and the mother herself.[52] Although they are transitory, different forms of these transitional phenomena persist into adulthood and continue throughout life.[53] Thus, the transitional experience can be identified in the uses of sounds and language that have a comforting quality, an element of maternal presence and the combination of these features with actual or perceived external reality, allowing anxiety to be relieved.[54] Vocalizations, for example, can range from preverbal sounds "to the most complex cultural productions (e.g. an operatic love duet)."[55] According to Horton, an infant's transitional relatedness may be observed before or at the same time as early language competence.[56] This point is of interest when considered alongside the Lacanian theory discussed earlier.

Coppolillo explains that the enjoyment of a cultural product may occur at two different levels.[57] For example, a song can be enjoyed both in terms of its aesthetic qualities (i.e., as it exists in a listener's external reality) and the experience that it provides for the listener in an intermediate area. This intermediate area of experience is capable of mediating fantasy, allowing the listener to draw upon elements from his or her inner world and relate them to the external reality of the song. In other words, the listener continues to enjoy the song for its aesthetic qualities too.

The continuing need for solace in adulthood, to allay pain, anxiety, and stress through the transitional experience of adaptation to changing circumstances results in an attachment, for example to art, poetry, and music. In its broadest sense, the transitional experience involves relatedness to animate or inanimate, tangible or intangible objects, activities or sounds that provide solace through their symbolic and associative links "with an abiding maternal primary process presence."[58] The ability of the transitional experience to provide solace by relieving anxiety stems from "the first and most meaningful, psychologically internalized relationship with a loving presence."[59]

NEUROPSYCHOANALYSIS AND THE ENJOYMENT OF OPERA

Weaving together the neuroscientific and psychoanalytic themes that have been discussed up to now, we can develop a tentative neuropsychoanalytic understanding about the nature of an operaphile's enjoyment. This interdisciplinary approach has the advantage of combining the objectivity of neuroscience with the subjective insight of psychoanalysis.

In a neuropsychoanalytic interpretation of the material that was discussed earlier, three key stages can be identified in the reception of opera. The first stage relates to initial reception, when patterns are extracted from the musical sound and processed by neural networks that deal with meaning, memory, sensation, and movement. In this stage, an operaphile's subjective impressions and associations come into play. At first, the meaning of the words that are being sung may be interpreted, as well as the meaning of the musical piece or "song" as a whole. If the piece is known to the listener, specific memories and associations may be automatically elicited. In the case of a first hearing, memories and associations may be conjured up by particular elements of the music, singing, or lyrics. These personal memories and associations are unconsciously recruited in relation to the piece overall, as well as to specific constituent elements, such as certain qualities of the singing. Features of the music and the singing, both in combination and separately, such as rhythm and timbre, among others, may also contribute to the evocation of memories and associations. These may or may not be directly related to the features themselves. For example, it can be readily understood how the lilting rhythm in 6/8 time of the singing and music in the "Barcarole" ("Belle nuit, ô nuit d'amour") from act 2 of *Les Contes d'Hoffmann* (1881) by Jacques Offenbach may immediately conjure up a gondola ride, or fond memories of a trip to Venice. These associations and memories can be said to relate directly to a feature of the music. By contrast, the piece may evoke negative associations that are specific to a listener, whereby the otherwise appealing musical qualities are lost. In this case, the listener is relating to a personal meaning that has come to be associated for whatever reason with the piece as a whole, rather than to specific features of the singing and music. Although a listener may be intensely moved in both cases—though for completely different reasons—neither scenario illustrates how vocal jouissance functions as proposed here. The associations in these examples are direct and relate to memory rather than to drives and unconscious processes. Yet both of the examples do have some of the ingredients that are constitutive of vocal jouissance.

In the second stage, the brain produces increasingly complex representations by recruiting various specialized networks for this purpose, dealing with music, language, meaning, and the interpretation of the words that are being sung. As mentioned earlier, research has found that lyrics and music are processed jointly at first, followed by an increasing degree of separation as the brain interprets the meaning of the words, until the lyrics are finally processed independently of the music.[60] While there is greater independence in the processing of the lyrics alone, possibly in terms of their meaning rather than their melodic aspect, the music is closely bound to the lyrics. Leaving aside possible influencing factors, as mentioned by these researchers, relating to memory, familiarity of the musical pieces, and musical expertise of listeners, these findings are nonetheless thought-provoking and would appear to tie in with the psychoanalytic theory relating to the dynamics of vocal jouissance. In the trajectory toward vocal jouissance, language and meaning are gradually undone by the singing, whereby the words become harder to understand, leaving the phonic materiality of the vocal embellishments to be enjoyed for their own sake in excess of meaning. There may be a parallel here with the fact that in neural processing terms, music is closely bound to the lyrics, yet the lyrics are also processed independently of the music. Whereas the music and the melodic element of the lyrics are processed together, the semantic component of the lyrics is processed separately. As this particular research did not investigate emotional response or make use of operatic excerpts as stimuli, a connection cannot be made between peak affective response and vocal jouissance. However, the neuropsychoanalytic overlap does apply in theory to the listening dynamics in opera prior to peak affective response/vocal jouissance. A previous study investigating this relationship between the processing of lyrics and music in operatic songs also found this separation in processing, although not the initial integration of music and lyrics.[61] The findings of this research confirmed that the semantic element of the lyrics and the melodic element of music are processed independently of each other. Importantly, this study found that the semantic and melodic elements of language are also processed separately, both by musicians and by nonmusicians.

The third stage follows on from the previous one in several ways. Language continues to play a role here. It is involved in the interplay between words and music, in the progress toward vocal jouissance/peak affective response during which language is gradually undone by the singing. This trajectory of the singing voice within the song framework of opera, which, as suggested earlier, functions independently of other considerations and even despite the voice itself, corresponds to the anticipation that causes dopamine to be released in the brain just before peak affective response. As research has found, dopamine activity in the brain's reward system determines the anticipatory pleasure in response to music, or "wanting" the musical stimulus.[62] The connection proposed by these researchers between this dopamine activity and the reinforcement of rewarding stimuli would perhaps account for an operaphile "wanting" to repeat the listening experience—even despite the resulting bittersweet enjoyment of vocal jouissance. Conversely, when the operatic voice reaches its final destination, after language has been undone and all that remains is asemic phonic materiality, the resulting peak affective response in the form of vocal jouissance can be said to correspond to the release of dopamine in the nucleus accumbens, which is linked to areas in the limbic system that are responsible for processing emotion. The limbic system and the nucleus accumbens are involved in the processing of emotion related to music. They are activated by music much as by the consumption of other pleasurable biological functions, as mentioned earlier.[63]

A little more needs to be mentioned here about hormone release in the brain, as this is relevant to understanding an operaphile's enjoyment of the bittersweet experience of vocal jouissance. A neurochemical explanation has been advanced by David Huron for the apparently paradoxical enjoyment of sad emotions evoked by music.[64] According to Huron, when we cry in response to music, our tears contain prolactin, a hormone that is associated with bonding experiences, such as breastfeeding, the mother/infant bond, or sexual intercourse. Prolactin has a tranquilizing effect and is released when an individual feels sad, as well as following childbirth and orgasm. Significantly, prolactin is only present in tears of sorrow, such as those that can be evoked by music. The release of other hormones in the brain, including dopamine and oxytocin, also replicate the feelings that we experience during an intimate connection with others.

FINALE

In terms of an operaphile's reception, the performative features of opera are embodied psychically as the subjectively experienced "pleasure in suffering" of vocal jouissance, and physically as measurable neurophysiological processes with their attendant bodily manifestations, such as goosebumps, piloerection, frissons, sweating, feeling choked up, crying, and so on. The power and particular characteristics of operatic singing penetrate the body, resonating within it to elicit a visceral, sensually erotic response that recruits unconscious dynamics. The singing is felt as well as heard—physically and emotionally. Despite the inherent (un)pleasure of vocal jouissance, it functions as an enjoyable reward in the brain by virtue of the unconscious meaning that it has for the listener. The neurobiological connection between pain and pleasure can be adduced in support of this claim, where meaning determines "the subjective interpretation of a sensory stimulus," so that "even suffering can be rewarding if it has meaning to the sufferer."[65] For an operaphile, this meaning derives from the subjectivity of the resonance between vocal jouissance and the unconscious, that is, the preverbal bond with the mother, separation and individuation from this first Other, and the acquisition of language and meaning. The loss of the preverbal "pure" cry, and the consequent entry into the order of language and meaning, sets up the circuitous dynamics of desire in the impossible pursuit of the unattainable *objet a*. The abiding link with the (M)Other underpins the operaphile's repetition compulsion.

While the reception of opera may not involve distinct neurophyisological processes, which are common to the reception of all music, it can nonetheless recruit specific subjective dynamics in the operaphile. This is most likely to occur in the operaphile, rather than the casual listener, because of an intimate knowledge of the structure of opera (which need not be technical, but is always visceral). These subjective dynamics function as an unconscious subtext to what is being played out on the stage, irrespective of the characters and plot. In the end, it is the singing, in combination with the auxiliary elements that are idiosyncratic to opera, that mediates the fundamental narrative of an operaphile's anxiety and desire. The resulting space of illusion (re)creates a preverbal, preoedipal holding environment with an enduring maternal link. The fleeting encounter with the operatic object-voice affords the operaphile an opportunity for unbounded enjoyment outside the order of language, in the preverbal at-oneness with the (M)Other. Yet this can only be achieved for a brief and painfully ecstatic moment.

NOTES

1. David Schwarz, *Listening Subjects: Music, Psychoanalysis, Culture* (Durham, NC: Duke University Press, 1997), 7.
2. For example see Mireille Besson et al., "Singing in the Brain: Independence of Lyrics and Tunes," *Psychological Science* 9: 6 (1998): 494–98; Emmanuel Bigand et al., "The Effect of Harmonic Context on Phoneme Monitoring in Vocal Music," *Cognition* 81: 1 (2001): B11–B20; Anne-Marie Bonnel et al., "Divided Attention between Lyrics and Tunes of Operatic Songs: Evidence for Independent Processing," *Perception and Psychophysics* 63: 7 (2001): 1201–13; Robert G. Crowder et al., "Physical Interaction and Association by Contiguity in Memory for the Words and Melodies of Songs," *Memory and Cognition* 18: 5 (1990): 469–76; Pascale Lidji et al., "Integrated Pre-attentive Processing of Vowel and Pitch: A Mismatch Negativity Study," *Annals of the New York Academy of Sciences* 1169: 1 (2009): 481–84; Bénédicte Poulin-Charronnat et al., "Musical Structure Modulates Semantic Priming in Vocal Music," *Cognition* 94: 3 (2005): 67–78; Daniela Sammler et al., "The Relationship of Lyrics and Tunes in the Processing of Unfamiliar Songs: A Functional Magnetic Resonance Adaptation

Study," *Journal of Neuroscience* 30: 10 (2010): 3572–78; Daniele Schön et al., "Musical and Linguistic Processing in Song Perception," *Annals of the New York Academy of Sciences* 1060 (2005): 71–81; Mary Louise Serafine et al., "Integration of Melody and Text in Memory for Songs," *Cognition* 16: 3 (1984): 285–303; Mary Louise Serafine et al., "On the Nature of Melody-Text Integration in Memory for Songs," *Journal of Memory and Language* 25: 2 (1986): 123–35.

3. Sammler, "Relationship of Lyrics and Tunes."

4. For example, see Evelina Fedorenko et al., "Structural Integration in Language and Music: Evidence for a Shared System," *Memory and Cognition* 37: 1 (2009): 1–9; Stefan Koelsch et al., "Neural Substrates of Processing Syntax and Semantics in Music," *Current Opinion in Neurobiology* 15: 2 (2005): 1–6; Stefan Koelsch et al., "Musical Syntax Is Processed in the Area of Broca: An MEG Study," *NeuroImage* 11: 5 (2000): 56; Stefan Koelsch et al., "Bach Speaks: A Cortical 'Language-Network' serves the Processing of Music," *NeuroImage* 17: 2 (2002): 956–66; Stefan Koelsch et al., "Interaction between Syntax Processing in Language and in Music: An ERP Study," *Journal of Cognitive Neuroscience* 17: 10 (2005): 1565–79; Daniel J. Levitin and Vinod Menon, "Musical Structure Is Processed in 'Language' Areas of the Brain: A Possible Role for Brodmann Area 47 in Temporal Coherence," *NeuroImage* 20: 4 (2003): 2142–52; Burkhard Maess et al., "Musical Syntax Is Processed in Broca's Area: An MEG study," *Nature Neuroscience* 4: 5 (2001): 540–45; Aniruddh D. Patel, *Music, Language and the Brain* (New York: Oxford University Press, 2008); Nikolaus Steinbeis and Stefan Koelsch, "Comparing the Processing of Music and Language Meaning Using EEG and fMRI Provides Evidence for Similar and Distinct Neural Representations," *PloS ONE* 3: 5 (2008): 1–7.

5. Daniel J. Levitin and Anna K. Tirovolas, "Current Advances in the Cognitive Neuroscience of Music," *The Year in Cognitive Neuroscience 2009: Annals of the New York Academy of Sciences* 1156 (2009): 211–31.

6. Oliver Sacks, *Musicophilia: Tales of Music and the Brain* (New York: Picador, 2007).

7. Luciano Fadiga et al., "Broca's Area in Language, Action, and Music," *The Neurosciences and Music III—Disorders and Plasticity: Annals of the New York Academy of Science* 1169 (2009): 448–58.

8. Judit Gervain et al., "The Neonate Brain Detects Speech Structure," *Proceedings of the National Academy of Sciences of the USA* 105 (2008): 14222–27; Birgit Mampe et al., "Newborns' Cry Melody Is Shaped by Their Native Language," *Current Biology* 19: 23 (2009): 1994–97; Christine Moon et al., "Two-Day-Olds Prefer Their Native Language," *Infant Behavior and Development* 16: 4 (1993): 495–500; Thierry Nazzi and Franck Ramus, "Perception and Acquisition of Linguistic Rhythm by Infants," *Speech Communication* 41: 1 (2003): 233–43; Patel, *Music, Language and the Brain*; Daniela Perani et al., "Music in the First Days of Life," *Nature Precedings*, July 2008; Gábor Stefanics et al., "Newborn Infants Process Pitch Intervals," *Clinical Neurophysiology* 120: 2 (2009): 304–8.

9. Patel, *Music, Language and the Brain*, 361.

10. Vinod Menon and Daniel J. Levitin, "The Rewards of Music Listening: Response and Physiological Connectivity of the Mesolimbic System," *NeuroImage* 28: 1 (2005): 175–84; Sandra E. Trehub, "The Developmental Origins of Musicality," *Nature Neuroscience* 6: 7 (2003): 669–73.

11. Laurel J. Trainor, "The Neural Roots of Music," *Nature* 453: 7195 (2008): 598–29; Laurel J. Trainor and Christine A. Zacharias, "Infants Prefer Higher-Pitched Singing," *Infant Behavior & Development* 21: 4 (1998): 799–805.

12. Sandra E. Trehub et al., "Perspectives on Music and Affect in the Early Years," in *Handbook of Music and Emotion: Theory, Research, Applications*, ed. Patrick N. Juslin and John A. Sloboda (Oxford: Oxford University Press, 2010), 645–68.

13. Patel, *Music, Language and the Brain*, 382.

14. Anthony J. DeCasper and Melanie J. Spence, "Prenatal Maternal Speech Influences Newborns' Perception of Speech Sounds," *Infant Behavior and Development* 9: 2 (1986): 133–50.

15. Trainor, "Neural Roots of Music," 598.
16. Trehub et al., "Perspectives on Music," 660.
17. Ibid., 661.
18. Ibid., 646.
19. Trainor, "Neural Roots of Music," 599.
20. Daniel J. Levitin, *This Is Your Brain on Music: The Science of a Human Obsession* (New York: Plume, 2007), 26, 108.
21. Auditory cortex, frontal regions, mesolimbic dopamine system, cerebellum, and basal ganglia. Anne J. Blood and Robert J. Zatorre, "Intensely Pleasurable Responses to Music Correlate with Activity in Brain Regions Implicated in Reward and Emotion," *Proceedings of the National Academy of Sciences of the United States of America* 98: 20 (2001): 11818–23; Anne J. Blood et al., "Emotional Responses to Pleasant and Unpleasant Music Correlate with Activity in Paralimbic Brain Regions," *Nature Neuroscience* 2: 4 (1999): 382–87; Levitin, *This Is Your Brain on Music*; Menon and Levitin, "Rewards of Music Listening."
22. Jason D. Warren, "How Does the Brain Process Music?" *Clinical Medicine—Medicine, Music and the Mind* 8: 1 (2008): 32–36.
23. Ibid., 33.
24. Ibid.
25. Levitin, *This Is Your Brain on Music*, 86.
26. Ibid., 191.
27. Robert Jourdain, *Music, the Brain and Ecstasy: How Music Captures Our Imagination* (New York: HarperCollins, 2002), 250.
28. Levitin, *This Is Your Brain on Music*, 91.
29. Carolyn Abbate, "Analysis," in *The New Grove Dictionary of Opera*, ed. Stanley Sadie (London: Macmillan, 1992), 118.
30. Martin Scherzinger, "When the Music of Psychoanalysis Becomes the Psychoanalysis of Music," review essay on *Listening Subjects: Music, Psychoanalysis, Culture* by David Schwartz, *Current Musicology* 66 (1999): 95–114.
31. Ibid., 96.
32. Michel Poizat, *The Angel's Cry: Beyond the Pleasure Principle in Opera* (Ithaca, NY: Cornell University Press, 1992), 37.
33. Ibid., 145.
34. Renata Salecl and Slavoj Žižek, *Gaze and Voice as Love Objects* (Durham, NC: Duke University Press, 1996).
35. Jacques Lacan, *The Seminar of Jacques Lacan. Book XI: The Four Fundamental Concepts of Psychoanalysis*, trans. Alan Sheridan, ed. Jacques-Alain Miller (New York: Norton, 1998), 103–4.
36. Lacan, "The Subversion of the Subject and the Dialectic of Desire in the Freudian Unconscious," in *Écrits: The First Complete Edition in English*, trans. Bruce Fink (New York: Norton, 2007), 693.
37. Poizat, *The Angel's Cry*, 103.
38. Lacan, *The Seminar of Jacques Lacan. Book VII: The Ethics of Psychoanalysis,* trans. Dennis Porter, ed. Jacques-Alain Miller (New York: Norton, 1997), 68.
39. Sigmund Freud, "Beyond the Pleasure Principle," in *The Standard Edition of the Complete Psychological Works of Sigmund Freud*, ed. James Strachey (London: Vintage, 1920).
40. Lacan, *The Seminar of Jacques Lacan. Book XVII: Psychoanalysis Upside-Down / The Reverse of Psychoanalysis* (unpublished).
41. Freud, "Beyond the Pleasure Principle," 44–61.
42. Lacan, *Family Complexes in the Formation of the Individual* (unpublished), 4–13.
43. Lacan, "Position of the Unconscious," in *Écrits*, 719–20.
44. Donald W. Winnicott, "Transitional Objects and Transitional Phenomena: A Study of the First Not-Me Possession," *International Journal of Psychoanalysis* 34 (1953): 90.
45. Ibid., 96.

46. Donald W. Winnicott, *Playing and Reality* (London: Routledge Classics, 2005), 150.
47. Paul C. Horton, *Solace: The Missing Dimension in Psychiatry* (Chicago: University of Chicago Press, 1981).
48. Winnicott, "Transitional Objects."
49. Ibid., 90.
50. Ibid., 89.
51. Ibid., 90.
52. Michael K. Hong, "The Transitional Phenomena: A Theoretical Integration," *Psychoanalytic Study of the Child* 33 (1978): 47–79.
53. Ibid., 64.
54. Horton, "Language, Solace," 172.
55. Ibid.
56. Ibid., 173.
57. Henry P. Coppolillo, "Maturational Aspects of the Transitional Phenomenon," *International Journal of Psychoanalysis* 48 (1967): 237–46.
58. Horton, "Language, Solace," 168.
59. Ibid., 169.
60. Sammler et al., "Relationship of Lyrics and Tunes."
61. Bonnel et al., "Divided Attention."
62. Valorie N. Salimpoor et al., "Anatomically Distinct Dopamine Release during Anticipation and Experience of Peak Emotion to Music." *Nature Neuroscience* 14: 2 (2011): 257–62.
63. Levitin, *This Is Your Brain on Music*; Warren, "How Does the Brain Process Music?"
64. Described in Conrad McCallumo, "Why They Call it the Blues," *The Star*, November 13, 2007. Online. Available: http://www.thestar.com/living/article/275759. March 28, 2012.
65. Siri Leknes and Irene Tracey, "A Common Neurobiology for Pain and Pleasure," *Nature Reviews Neuroscience* 9: 4 (2008), 318.

PART TWO

Performativity as Dramaturgy

The performativity of song and dance has been linked in the previous chapters to the pleasure of the audience experiencing song; excessive vocal gestures and vocal body, sung performance and song text recreate for the listener pleasure, jouissance, and the loss of self. But song and dance don't exist bereft of context, and that context often constructs a dramaturgical frame through which their reception is refracted.

Dramaturgy, like performativity, is a slippery term. It can refer to the composition of a work as a text and as a performance (its structure and its meaning making), but it can also apply to the discussion of the composition of a work or a performance, and in this sense of creating a discourse about composition the chapters that follow are dramaturgical. However, we can go further, noting explicitly performative dynamics in what Eugenio Barba identifies as three dramaturgies of the performance: a narrative dramaturgy (of events and characters), an organic or dynamic dramaturgy (the rhythms and dynamisms that affect spectators sensually), and a dramaturgy of changing states (when the whole evokes more than the parts).[1] These are all present in understanding the compositional, the interpretative, and the sensorial in what follows. Even more than this, though, as Cathy Turner and Synne Behrndt note, dramaturgy implies observation of the performance, the context of the event, the structure of the work in all its elements, and awareness of the live process of performance, and thus "there is a dynamic, contextual and, indeed, political dimension to dramaturgical practice":[2] dramaturgy itself is performative, adding a further dimension to the performativity of performance.

An example of how performativity can be read dramaturgically derives from *The Voice UK* (2012), a singing competition with the same format as NBC's *The Voice* in which vocalists perform well-known popular songs mentored by star judges. The context for each sung performance—as with many other TV talent show formats—is structured around a narrative of competition, including filmed background information about the competitors, and a "live" performance of well-known songs in front of a studio audience and a television audience at home.[3] An understanding of the structural framework and context, what Andrew Parker and Eve Kosofsky Sedgwick describe as "the quality and structuration of the bonds that unite auditors or link them to speakers" contributes to making meaning and causing affect, and it is implicit in the audience's following of the show.[4] As we follow the rags-to-riches trajectory of the amateur performers, both within single episodes and across the whole series, we map their narrative of competition on to aspirations of success in our own lives, relating to the mundanity of their home and family life (the rags), and vicariously delighting in the achievement of their spectacular performance (the riches) on the show. It's a classic dramaturgy that here becomes the pragmatic motor for the TV show.

In the final episode of *The Voice UK*,[5] competitor Leanne Mitchell sang "Mama Told Me Not to Come" in a duet with the celebrated singing star Tom Jones.[6] First Jones sang the A section, repeated and adapted by the pupil, Mitchell. Then the refrain, in harmony, blended their voices. Even aside from the entertaining effect of the sung performance, its framing within a dramaturgical structure articulated meaning in association with context. It embodied the mentoring process as the contestant learned from her coach until she arrived at this performance as his equal, able to take her place beside him in the world of vocalists and performers. This compositional structure mirrored the narrative of the journey the contestants undertake from naive amateur to the consummate and comfortable professional able to hold her own with an experienced star. Mitchell's obvious pleasure, her enjoyment of the experience, and her empowerment through it performed the arrival point of the journey—a dramaturgy of changing states.

To root this in a discussion of performativity, it's worth reminding ourselves of J. L. Austin's original ideas in *How to Do Things with Words*. For him, part of the performativity of an utterance—the locutionary element—involves the relationship it has with certain sense and reference, its "meaning" within a context; another part involves the perlocutionary affect that causes some change in the receiver. Siting the narrative trajectory of this TV show within a corelational web of recognition and desire gives it both a locutionary context and perlocutionary affect and relates to Barba's dramaturgies of narrative and dynamism.[7]

The contextual dramaturgy of the show's narrative arc is not its only point of reference. In the semifinal of *The Voice UK* Mitchell sang "It's a Man's Man's Man's World" and set the audience on fire. [8] [9] Every repetition was different, every ornament considered. The voice was excessive and playful, at times liquid and at other times harsh and punched, and Mitchell drew the cheering audience to its feet in rapturous applause. This is a song I know, a song I've heard sung many times. But Mitchell's performance—her musical elaborations, her vocal dexterity, her gendered voice—was new. It made the song appear fresh, and it added to the sum of my understanding of this song and to my sensual pleasure. The "present experience," as Marvin Carlson suggests, "is always ghosted by previous experiences and associations."[10] This experience opened up a conceptual space that linked my memories and this rearticulation. Thus the performance of the song was performative as its meaning was recreated through my associations and memories in a particular time and place, and this discourse links Barba's dramaturgy of changing states to the efficacy or perlocutionary effect of performativity. This event, unique to my experience and memory, demonstrates the instability and insecurity of reception and meaning: even as I'm able to share with you a sense of the experience through these words and the

URL address of the YouTube clip, your understanding of this phenomenon can only be gauged by your own set of references, your own cultural memory, and both the performance and this writing therefore become further acts of performative ghosting. "Ghosts are simultaneously shifted and modified by the processes of recycling and recollection"[11] so that all future listenings and rememberings will contain these experiences blending memories—mine or yours—into a momentary thrill of complex pleasure and extreme attachment.[12]

This is the dramaturgy that George Rodosthenous explores in the next chapter as Lennon and McCartney songs are relocated and regendered in Julie Taymor's *Across the Universe* (2007). He explores the performative effect of a dramaturgical composition that resituates and recontextualizes songs, thereby inviting political dimensions to emerge between the immediacy of the song-event in its local context and our remembrance of the (performative) original. This naturally has many similarities with the performances of well-known songs in a reality show, and the contexts of narrative, character, and sometimes celebrity performer all play into that performative dynamic.

Mitchell's final solo before she was voted the winner of the series was "Run to You."[13] This ballad was controlled and quiet, as she breathed a husky intimacy through the words. Gradually the vocal and dynamic range of the song grew as she extended her voice through louder and bolder sounds, up to its brightest, highest, dripping, tripping notes before returning to the quiet question "Will you stay or will you run away?" The dynamic shape gave an emotional arc to the performance as the dramatic middle section expanded on and revealed the underpinning depths of emotion behind the quiet, vulnerable start and finish of the song. As the pitch range, the volume, and the emotional display increased, so too did the audience excitement and energy, so that the effect of the performance on the listener—me—was as much driven by its dynamic dramaturgy and the audience's role in building that energy as it was on the voice or the song.

In the chapters that follow, Rodosthenous's consideration of *Across the Universe* incorporates a reading of plot and lyrics, song structures, and the gendered and geographical relocation of Beatles' songs within plot, to argue that the work's alienation is political and performative. Ben Macpherson, meanwhile, develops the idea of dynamic shape beyond thinking of it in relation to musical pitch, range, and volume, instead relating it to Barba's organic or dynamic dramaturgy: he develops an analysis of the energy and affect produced by the singing and dancing bodies within the stage space in the West End musical *Cats* (1981). He reads the dramaturgy of *Cats* as a series of contrasting moments of generic song and dance styles, and of arcs of expansion and restriction, some complex and dense, others simple and direct. Both these chapters explore the consequences for reception, pleasure, and intoxication of watching, listening, and re-embodying song and dance. The analysis in them draws attention to the performative dramaturgies of changing states that results from the composition of the performances, and the sensual, the interpretative, and the transformational effects they trigger.

1. Eugenio Barba, "The Deep order Called Turbulence," in *The Performance Studies Reader*, ed. Henry Bial (London: Routledge, 2004), 255–56.
2. Cathy Turner and Synne Behrndt, *Dramaturgy and Performance* (London: Palgrave, 2008), 4.
3. *The Voice* is a franchised reality television competition that began in the Netherlands. It has so far appeared in versions as far afield as the United States, Ukraine, Korea, Australia, Thailand, and Argentina with many more countries developing programs. In it experienced stars pick vocalists from blind auditions and mentor them through a series of singing battles, live shows and public votes. For more information see online. Available: http://en.wikipedia.org/wiki/The_Voice_(TV_series). September 20, 2012.
4. Andrew Parker and Eve Kosofsky Sedgwick, "Sexual Politics, Performativity and Performance," in *The Routledge Reader in Politics and Performance*, ed. Lizbeth Goodman and Jane de Gay (London: Routledge, 2000), 176.
5. June 2, 2012.
6. "Mama Told Me (Not to Come)" was written by Randy Newman for Eric Burdon in 1966 but was later recorded by Newman himself, among others. Online. Available: http://en.wikipedia.org/wiki/Mama_Told_Me_Not_To_Come. October 7, 2012. The performance discussed here is available online. Available: http://www.youtube.com/watch?v=g9iGRoH82zQ. October 7, 2012.
7. Marvin Carlson, *Performance: A Critical Introduction* (London: Routledge, 1996), 60.
8. As Jon McKenzie argues in *Perform or Else* (London: Routledge, 2001), "Performative desire is not molded by distinct disciplinary mechanisms. It is not a repressive desire; it is instead 'excessive,' intermittently modulated and pushed across the thresholds of various limits by overlapping and sometimes competing systems" (19). Some of the language in this part draws attention to this by deliberately exploring the boundaries between academic writing and a more descriptive or playful expression.
9. "It's a Man's Man's Man's World" is a song by James Brown and Betty Jean Newsome recorded by Brown in 1966. The song's chauvinistic lyrics were written by Newsome based on her perception of gender relations. Online. Available: http://en.wikipedia.org/wiki/It's_a_Man's_Man's_Man's_World. October 7, 2012. The performance discussed here is available online. Available: http://www.youtube.com/watch?v=gClh69oPmUE. October 7, 2012.
10. Marvin Carlson, *The Haunted Stage* (Ann Arbor: University of Michigan Press, 2001), 2.
11. Ibid.
12. This refers to the idea of meaning being the result of combinations of materials overlaid and blended into complex articulations individually interpreted in Amy Cook, "Interplay: The Method and Potential of a Cognitive Scientific Approach to Theatre," *Theatre Journal* 59 (2007): 579–94.
13. Run to You" is a song written by Jud Friedman and Allan Rich for the film *The Bodyguard*, sung by Whitney Houston. Online. Available: http://en.wikipedia.org/wiki/Run_to_You_(Whitney_Houston_song). October 7, 2012. The performance discussed here is available at http://www.youtube.com/watch?v=q2_0XDwfEoE. October 7, 2012.

CHAPTER 3

Relocating the Song

Julie Taymor's Jukebox Film Musical

Across the Universe *(2007)*

GEORGE RODOSTHENOUS

Six years after Baz Luhrmann's groundbreaking *Moulin Rouge!* (2001), which suc-
ceeded in redefining the film "jukebox" musical and reintroducing the genre to
younger generations, Julie Taymor's *Across the Universe* (2007) used the music of
the Beatles to tell the story of Jude, a young Liverpudlian who works in a shipyard,
and his journey to the United States in search of his father. Like a modern Odysseus, he makes new friends including Lucy, Max, and Daniel and encounters a series
of adventures of love (the Vietnam) war, and betrayal. In bringing the idiom of the
jukebox musical to the screen, yet incorporating her characteristic theatrical style,
Taymor explores the presumption of a linear narrative in film musicals, using the
distancing effect of diegetic and nondiegetic singing as part of a complex dramaturgy. The transitions to the song-and-dance sequences appear in unexpected, inventive, and surprising moments in the film and reflect her rich experience as stage
director—most notably of Disney's *The Lion King* (1997). Her use of metatheatrical
devices, also present in her films *Titus* (1999), *Frida* (2002), and *The Tempest* (2010),
transform the concept of linear narrative in film musicals to a three-dimensional
experience with colorful, poetic, and quasi-drug-induced moments.

Through the use of diegetic and nondiegetic music, Taymor and her creative team
constructed a new jukebox musical, a "kaleidoscopic odyssey in human warmth and
passion,"[1] which was heavily attacked by film critics. It was released only a year after
Cirque du Soleil created its own theatrical homage to the music of the Beatles in
the "circus-based, artistic and athletic" production *Love* (2006).[2] The fact that these
two large-scale artistic productions using the same musical material were released in
close proximity with each other removed some of the media spotlight from the film
musical.

Taymor's "reputation for profligacy"[3] is demonstrated in *Across the Universe* in moments of reckless extravagance and a great abundance of visual and aural episodes. In addition, even though she took a financial risk in casting young, unknown actors for the lead roles (Jim Sturgess, Evan Rachel Wood, Joe Anderson), she also employed a range of celebrities for small cameo appearances (Bono, Joe Cocker, Eddie Izzard, and Salma Hayek). Her non-celebrity casting approach may have had a negative impact on box office sales but contributed to the new dramaturgy of the work. Since the characters played by unknown actors do not carry the "ghosting" of other roles into this performance, they can be perceived as "people like us" and identified with on their journey. The celebrities are "ghosted" by the memory of their previous roles, which feeds into the reading of those roles, and to the perception of the characters as different: separate and exotic.

The director's approach to relocating the songs and giving them a new context within the narrative of the piece will be examined with a focus on the gender reversals that Taymor introduced in the performance of the Beatles' songs. In this way, the performativity of songs that are remediated, regendered, and relocated into a new dramaturgical context will be explored in depth. The analysis will be completed by considering the more spectacular scenes of the film, and suggesting how reading them in new metatheatrical contexts creates a hyperreality that contributes to the complex and textured dramaturgy of the work. Selected songs/scenes from the musical will be discussed in detail to exemplify the challenge to integration of technologized dance, puppetry, liveness, and constructedness. As Dolan writes in *Presence and Desire* "musicals' complicity in gender arrangements is insidious, but it's also very easy to turn familiar songs against their own meanings through parodic juxtaposition."[4] Extracts from the critical and academic reception of the work will help to demonstrate how this work contributes to the development of dramaturgy within twenty-first-century film musicals.

GHOSTING THE ORIGINAL VOICE

There has been a huge increase in the numbers of jukebox stage musicals since the beginning of the decade, and the trend has also moved to the film medium with works such as *Moulin Rouge!* (2001), the Cole Porter biopic *De-lovely* (2004), *Mamma Mia!* (2008) (which uses ABBA songs), and the film adaptation of *Rock of Ages* (2012). Since 2009, two major television musical series have been extremely successful and have generated new audiences for the genre: *Glee* (2009), a television jukebox musical comedy series (discussed later in this volume), and *Smash* (2012), a television musical series that includes a mixture of existing and original songs.

Stacy Wolf believes that "when the songs are heard outside the musical itself, they are always ghosted by the original voice."[5] The audience experience of the songs in jukebox formats seems curiously situated between the presence of the now (watching the current musical) and the absence of something that previously existed (remembering the Beatles' originals). Thus the reading of the musical contains the ghosts of those past incarnations, the original renditions of the songs that exist in our memories. The dramaturgy of this work assumes that the audience will not hear and see the new versions with fresh ears and eyes, but instead will have an active role in interpreting them as they are reused and reexamined in a new narrative. This works as a palimpsest in which there are reverberations between what we hear and our "historical" involvement with the original song. Since most people will be familiar with the original renditions of these songs, audiences discover in the relocation of the songs a double-reading, an intertextual "ghosting" of the original songs that brings out a dialogue between one incarnation and the next.

Comparing the songs with the Beatles' recorded versions, and all the other cover versions that have since appeared, and establishing what is different can be a distracting process, but a blend is created from the combination of memory and this new experience. Expectations of how the songs were previously sung may blind audiences, and stop them from accepting the dramaturgical interpolation of the songs into the new context, and the treatment of the material as a "new" piece of work. Such expectations may to some extent account for the negative reactions to the work. All these thoughts, the ghosts of the past, can affect an audience's appreciation of the new work.

The jukebox musical and the interpolation of familiar songs into new contexts is not a new phenomenon. Since the 1920s familiar songs have been reintroduced into other narratives to express love, anger, frustration, desire, and so on through the sung words. For Marvin Carlson, in *The Haunted Stage,* this recycling of narrative material and characters develops into semiotic building blocks that "carry much of their reception burden in their combinations."[6] Barrie Gelles suggests further that "ghosting is the beginning of a recontextualisation that includes the process of 'de-integration' and 're-integration.'"[7] In *Across the Universe,* it is during that process of reintegration that the meanings of the Beatles' songs as performed by the Beatles are subverted and new signifiers emerge. The Beatles' songs with their inherent countercultural associations and highly commercial history are transformed, and new narratives appear and reperform the identity of the singer.

Kelly Kessler in *Destabilizing the Hollywood Musical: Music, Masculinity and Mayhem* discusses the genre's "narrative reflexivity" using examples from *Mamma Mia!* and *Moulin Rouge!* She feels that the songs in such jukebox musicals as *Moulin Rouge!* provide "a similar sense of nostalgic reminiscence and intertextuality while embracing a stronger sense of gratification and irony."[8] She writes that their characteristic is an "ever increasing sense of generic reflexivity, parody and pastiche," and comments that the "disconnect between the sincere projection of musical reality (Look, if we can do it, you can do it) and the ironic sense of the millennial musical (This musical thing is just too silly) emerge partially through the repeated use of pre-existing musical numbers in new contexts."[9] On the other hand, Kessler's reading of *Across the Universe* is directly opposed to mine: I viewed the film and its ability to relocate the songs as innovative and dramaturgically complex. Kessler, rather categorically, dismisses the jukebox musicals' treatment of the songs and claims that the music now

comes equipped with its own ironic baggage. These films reposition music initially intended for other purposes. Lyrics no longer evoke the unique thoughts of the narrative's character as popularized by the book musicals. They recall their previous context and announce their own insincerity and displacement [...] As *Across the Universe* transplants iconic Beatles tunes into the story of romance and revolution, the film begs for a pat on the head for its witty combination of classic lyrics and narrative and musical integration. As each character takes his or her name from a lyric, the film reinforces its own artifice.[10]

Kessler's discussion of the jukebox musical fails to acknowledge that "song migration" has been a regular practice since the early twentieth century. The difference, though, is that Taymor's consistently imaginative dramaturgy has reworked those songs into the narrative in a clear, sensitive, and, at times, startling way. She is exploiting the musical's unique power to invoke the sort of cultural patterns that have been habituated by postmodern culture's intertextual weaving of material.

This is important when it comes to considering the performativity of the work: the consequences for reception of the political statements made by the Beatles' songs, but in their new refashioned versions. Because changing the gender associated with a well-known song allows a new semiotic layer to emerge, the audience's reception of the song needs to take into account all the intertextual presentations of the material that have existed in their cultural memory and allow them to place the song in a new context. These processes might be seen as an exercise for the intellect rather than a deep engagement with the energies of the performance—the voice and its display of virtuosity and skill—but they reflect the craft of the dramaturgical approach. Singing these relocated songs, the new characters can state their intentions and express their identities through song.

Writing about the film musical genre, Brett Farmer explains that genres are

exceedingly complex signifying formations, made of literally thousands of texts and intertexts, including most obviously the films themselves and their myriad structural interrelations as well as the wide range of interreferential discourses that circulate around and help constitute genre films—advertisements, studio publicity, critical reviews, popular and academic studies, fan discourses, and so on. This (over)abundant intertextuality means that the genres are sites of a radical semiotic polysemy, a plurality of meanings, replete with all the complexities, discrepancies, contradictions, and possibilities of variable interpretation that this entails.[11]

The jukebox film musical adds to the levels of intertextual reference available to directors through the addition of song.

Moulin Rouge! was certainly an important contributor to recognition of this in the film musical. A significant part of the enjoyment of this text is hearing songs relocated into a narrative in ways that seem "even better than the real thing," to use a very postmodern phrase: gestures from *The Sound of Music* (1960) relocated to turn-of-the-century bohemian Paris seem simultaneously out of place and perfectly appropriate; hearing Jim Broadbent sing "Like a Virgin" not only offers a ridiculous scenario, entertaining in its playfulness, but also overcodes the performance with significant nods back to Madonna's original performance of gender and sexuality, and the cultural power of her authorial performance. *Across the Universe* presents a similar layering of prior and current performance texts. Grant states that it "views popular music—specifically, the music of The Beatles—as accurately expressing, reflecting, and influencing personal and social history."[12] And the process of engaging as a spectator with these layers of signification is far more than an act of understanding (with our minds). While spectating a piece of musical theater (on stage or screen), we allow our senses to be seduced by the overwhelming sounds and visual images, and we are thus engaged in what Wolf defines as "performative spectatorship," which is

> the visceral experience of watching and listening to a musical play. In this way, the spectatorship of musicals is literally active. The musical offers not only the sensory experience of music and dance, voice and body, but also often a physicalized memory of the performance [. . .] What we take from musicals is embodied.[13]

Perhaps, by watching *Across the Universe*, we are experiencing a double embodiment of a doubly layered multitextured spectacle which mixes the ghosts of the past with an assault of images, in the present.

Taymor uses three relocation techniques to incorporate the thirty-two Beatles songs: *geographical* relocations (moving from the UK to the United States and vice versa); *gender* relocations (where songs originally sung by the male members of the Beatles are now given to female vocalists/characters); and *surreal* relocations (where the songs are treated either as [day-]dream sequences or moments of musical theater spectacle in an abundance of show-stopping numbers and a barrage of visual imagery and colorful invention). In order to analyze these three features, the focus of the discussion will be largely on the four songs "I Want to Hold Your Hand," "I Want You," "Let it Be," and "Happiness Is a Warm Gun."

ENGAGING WITH A DIFFERENTLY GENDERED PERFORMATIVITY THROUGH SONG

> Suburban Massachusetts, all golden light and green grass. Liverpool, England, cramped alleyways and dark muted tones. The lower East side of Manhattan, early 60s, with colored grafitti [sic] and crowded sidewalks. A drug trip in a psychedelic school bus. A dreamy gorgeous underwater sequence. Strawberries pinned to the wall of a bohemian apartment. The Detroit riots, with cars burning, and handheld cameras. Each world created with total confidence in the story being told, and also the genre itself. There is maybe half an hour of straight dialogue in the film. The rest is told through song.[14]

From the very beginning of the film, Taymor destroys the fourth wall by having her lead protagonist Jude (Jim Sturgess) address the audience (camera) directly through the character-driven opening "Girl." His performative invitation is his desire to communicate with us, his audience, and he encourages us to associate with his story. It is explicitly clear in the words "is there anybody going to listen to my story."

This approach of singing thoughts directly to the audience demonstrates a negotiation of distance and a breaking down of the fourth wall—or the screen. Its effect is to draw the audience into the performance, implicating them in its address, and increasing the sensation of liveness and responsiveness to the experience.

Jude is commenting on the action, setting the tone for the film: it is a film in which its protagonists sing and its characters are intimately connected with their audiences. Because of this intimacy, which is created by the close-up shots and the direct address to the audience, I propose that we can apply Millie Taylor's observations on the power of "live" musical theater onto the mediated recording of *Across the Universe*. Taylor explains that

> voice and song in musical theatre have the capacity to move audiences through pre-motor responses and mirror neurons that create a mimetic response to the portrayal of emotion in the voice and body of the performer. This is amplified by the musical stimulation and a physically embodied witnessing of the performance events. In other words the presence of music and the response to song has the capacity to elicit a greater emotional release than performance without those elements.[15]

This feature of direct address contributes to the physically embodied witnessing that Taylor describes in relation to the live event, but applied to film. She further explains that the mirror neuron system through which mirroring occurs is a response to all sorts of events (action, emotion, melodic line, vocal timbre but also response to other audience members, etc.). Music also stimulates physical/biological/chemical responses. As we watch a film musical in a cinema full of like-minded viewers the response of the mirror neuron system and the effects of liveness are sustained, and thus, with the added effects of direct address in this film musical, a similar kind of response from audiences could be anticipated as is apparent in a live performance.[16] It is a different experience, though, when watching it on a DVD at home without the possibility of witnessing other audience member's responses, but still the urge to empathize with the material and its dynamic energies is stimulated by direct address.

Song and dance in musicals can (and do) have a stronger emotional release for audiences than spoken theater. And because of the emotional, cultural, social, and historical baggage that these songs might have for some of the members of the audience, there is a multilayering of emotions: a complex reception of the work in its "altered" version that includes joy, reversal, and cohesion. A "conceptual blending"[17] of genres and materials can work in different ways for the audience as "categories can slip, expand, constrict and change."[18] And different meanings emerge "through a negotiation or a 'struggle over meaning' among text, context, and spectator."[19]

In the character-driven "I Want to Hold Your Hand" sequence, there is a fascinating treatment of the material in a slowed down version of the original song. The character Prudence appears in a daydream sequence that mixes reality and illusion. Her inner world is projected as a fantasy world that is shared with the audience. This is where the gender relocation plays into rereadings of lyrics that cast them in a new light. It is where conceptual blending comes into play and our brains perceive the current and the remembered simultaneously and can be linked to Freud's *unheimlich* or uncanny.

According to Grant, "film musicals typically present their song-and/or-dance numbers in an imaginary space, even if this space is ostensibly a real location, and contained within a narrative framework."[20] Prudence in her performative daydream sequence is speaking her thoughts out . . . to another girl. She hopes the other girl will understand her desire to hold her hand, and in a further development she asks her to "Let me be your man, Please say to me, You'll let me hold your hand."[21]

In this sequence Taymor uses an important device of gender reversal to approach her material. This might come as a surprise to audiences who know the songs intimately, but this conjunction of genders provides new opportunities for complex gender and role reversals and power shifts. By giving this song to a female character, the director challenges the heterosexual context of the original songs. This song is now sung by the female character Prudence to another female character Lucy in a moment of "coming out": Prudence sings out her sexual identity. She does not perform her sexual identity for the community within the film, but she performs it in song for the audience. She states her intention for physical contact: "And when I touch you, I feel happy inside." It is like a tantric performative expression of sexual energy that appears from a different voice (and regendered timbres, pitches, and associations). It forces the audience to renegotiate the sexual chemistry of the number, and its familiarity facilitates our understanding and acceptance of the song and the singer. "The voice is an apparently transparent reflection of feeling: it is the sound of the voice, not the words sung, which suggests what a singer really means."[22] This implies that we, as audiences, register the song through the emotion triggered by the sound of the voice, even though it is blended with a cultural memory that takes audiences back to their own childhood (perhaps first love) and makes them rethink the content and the relationship they have with it.

Prudence is also shaping the present to what-she-would-want-it-to-be, singing in her well-created "bubble" and planning the future. But in the film's present it is not a flashback or a flash-forward. The song is simply shaping the present in a dense conglomeration of signifiers. In a remarkable sequence female-to-female romantic love is juxtaposed with an aggressive game of American football (in slow motion). The violence the game entails is presented in a balletic way and underlines the "realistic" and emotionally affecting sensitivity of the girl singing. The slow motion walk among the players, in an untouchable bubble, is theatrical in its essence, and the relocation is a direct confession statement (singing to the audience) that creates dramatic irony through a rich and textured blend of hetero- and homosexual signification.

The sequence "I want you" portrays another performative moment: the poster of Uncle Sam is reaching out both vocally and physically to the character of Max and sings the lines "I want you" in a declamatory manner. This statement is now denuded of its sexual implications and functions as a military call recruiting young men for the Vietnam War. The whole sequence is a rite of passage for Max. From the surreal moment where the poster of "Uncle Sam" actually talks to Max at the army induction center to the sequence involving Max's journey, the scene exudes a muscular acuteness. The bodies of the sergeants dancing with masks (like Action Man dolls), versus the bodies of recruits, creates a visceral masculine clash of identities: an explicit demonstration of power and loss of power. It raises the question of power shifts and makes the audience wonder who ultimately has power: the robotic masked sergeants or the physically free but institutionally powerless new recruits. And during this MTV-like animation the song is relocated both geographically and surreally to a new location where the recruits on the front line carry the Statue of Liberty on their shoulders, creating the visual image of carrying all of America on their shoulders. This surreal moment represents the prize of freedom as a combination of national identity and personal freedom that the recruits bear on their march through the forests of Vietnam. This combination of images might be perceived as taking an American idea of freedom and forcing it on others through war.

According to Taymor "the sergeants [...] were stripping Max now and getting him in his underwear for this physical where he is slightly dehumanised because his identity is being pulled away as he is becoming part of a martial machine."[23] All the sergeants have identical masks and the whole mise en scène seems like a computer game. Grant describes its movement as "a peculiar choreography, as much military drill as dance, with crisply angular, somewhat threatening movements of their arms and legs."[24] The scene, one of the most powerful of the film, has a malicious, passive-aggressive violence influenced by the discipline and inhumanity of computer games and computer animations. This combination performatively juxtaposes the discipline of military life, the inhuman automata of computer games with the entertainment of games, song, and dance.

Just before the song ends, there is a third gender relocation, during which Prudence, who is part of an emotional love triangle, sings to Lucy while watching her from outside a kitchen window. Prudence sings "I want you" in a strained voice, full of desire.[25] The words of the song now sound different and provide new sexual contexts and relationships that were not apparent in the Beatles' performance of the original song. Through the song Prudence's voyeuristic tendencies are highlighted and the three words "I want you" move seamlessly from the "Uncle Sam" reference to a more personal context. In this scene Taymor uses inventive, eloquent physical language, puppetry, and a remarkable technologized dance sequence to produce a powerfully memorable scene.

I would agree with Grant's observations that "for many viewers, *Across the Universe* ends on a sentimental, if not saccharine, endorsement of 'love,' whether in personal or public politics [...] it brings us back once again to the romantic and utopian thrust at the heart of the genre."[26] Even if the work challenges heteronormative traditions and values, it remains closely focused on the subject of love and understanding that comes after the transformation brought by a revolution (whether personal or social).

METATHEATRICAL CONTEXTS: THE PERFORMATIVITY OF DRUG-INDUCED OUTBURSTS AND HYPERREALITIES

In *The Play within the Play* Ken Woodgate comments on the dream sequences in another major film musical of the twenty-first century, *Dancer in the Dark* (2000), which was directed by the enfant terrible of contemporary cinema, Lars von Trier:

what we see may be conceived of as a transformation or idealisation of the world, but it is nevertheless an extension of that world. In fact, the world of the musical is a world that is always on the brink of bursting into song and dance, on the brink of transfiguration into something larger than life...The transfigured world is suddenly interrupted by the world of mundane reality. Rather than being contiguous, the two realms are antagonistic. The numbers cannot be read as part of the film's diegesis, but as figments of [...] imagination. They are daydreams that impose on real time and have real consequences [and] escape mechanisms.[27]

Dream sequences are inherent parts of the film musical and have often been the opportunity for the spectacle in films. They are refreshing, breathtaking, and, for some, unnecessary. Woodgate's claim that "the ease with which the musical mirrors itself might well be seen, from a rationalistic point of view, as a form of theatrical narcissism, or even syllogism"[28] is applied by Taymor to the musical's filmic counterpart. These moments of extreme visual beauty and hyperreality are features of Taymor's directorial excess, but are also reflexive of musical theater and musical film. Here directorial excess becomes a performative action confirming her past as a theater director but also increasing the dramaturgical complexity of the film. Altman notes, in relation to the film musical, that

the use of art forms and dream sequences within the musical contributes strongly to the genre's tendency to blend the real and the ideal or imaginary, yet we will be able to say little about the style of any given film as a whole if we must treat it simply as an alternation between set pieces each employing a radically different set of conventions, techniques, and concerns.[29]

In this work, everything is rich in color, size, and scope. It is theatrical, in essence, with several intertextual references to the genre of the film musical.

The naked bodies in "Because" singing a cappella in close harmonies provide yet another performative statement about their political stance: an earthly denotation of love and peace and a reflexive reference to an earlier antiwar musical, *Hair*. The inviting bodies evoke a statement of freedom and sexual tolerance. The crane shots are metatheatrical in the sense that they are referencing and reflecting on Busby Berkeley's spectacular film musicals of the 1930s with their sweeping camera angles, overhead shots, and rows of dehumanized bodies. The action then moves to an underwater scene. When Jude, like a new Odysseus escaping from the Sirens, reemerges from the water, the music stops and is replaced with the sound of helicopters: Bohemia versus real life (war). Taymor wanted "to create a musical that feels as if these songs emerge from the characters" and that "the songs are forwarding the action and [...] the emotions and they are not laid on top."[30] She introduces theatrical artifice to confront cinematic realism and creates a complex and textured dramaturgy. Her approach has come under attack because it created moments "which threaten to turn the film into merely a game of spotting the reference, the reliance on the Beatles' music as a lens through which to view the history of their times."[31] She raises the question of whether audiences can still be moved by political theater in the contemporary world or whether we are so completely inundated with real images of war and atrocities that audiences can only be satisfied with real, documentary-style imagery.

In the location-driven "Let it Be" song sequence the scene begins, underscored by the song, as the bad news of a soldier's death is announced to his family. The scene then cuts to a young boy singing the song amid a revolution—it is a raw war zone. The continuity of the music links these two sequences and challenges the linear construction and the diegetic continuity of the scene. The song also contributes to the religious context of the scene as the boy sings a prayer that is both performative and political in its essence: "When I find myself in times of trouble, Mother Mary comes to me, speaking words of wisdom, let it be."

A female gospel voice takes over as the film cuts to the boy's funeral. The gospel chorus resembles a Greek chorus commenting on the action. The dead boy's voice is heard again (like a ghost figure),[32] while the soloist and chorus ornament the song, which is accompanied by organ and piano. This is a complex treatment of the song and makes full use of the theatricality of the church setting and the religious associations that go with it. The music has a huge emotional impact and elevates the song from a pop song to an antiwar hymn about personal freedom.

There is further transformation during the song "Happiness Is a Warm Gun," which resembles a morphine-induced dream sequence: hospital beds as platforms of spectacle. Song and dance heal Max's pain in a sequence that references a number of theatrical and filmic devices. A revolving stage is a standard theatrical device, while the use of digital technology multiplies the nurse Salma Hayek to a kaleidoscope of singing/dancing nurses who each hold syringes containing dancing girls in shiny electric blue liquid. This is a reference to the filmic excess of classic Hollywood musicals and the dehumanization of Busby Berkeley film musicals as well as to the drug-induced spectacles of pop and rock music films such as *Yellow Submarine* (1968), *Tommy* (1975), and *Hair* (1967). Max sings "I need a fix because I am going down" as his internal worries are externalized through his drug-induced fantasies involving the nurses who provide safety and "happiness."

He is allowed to touch the nurses simply by singing "When I hold you in my hand, When I feel my finger on your trigger." In the same way as Prudence has physical contact with her object of desire through song, Max allows his sexual fantasies to become alive simply by projecting them: with specific pitch, rhythm, and "imaginary" accompaniment. After the injection, Max flies (to ecstatic heights) and returns to his hospital bed at the end of the sequence. Still, this physicalization of his internal turmoil turned out to be too much for Kessler; she felt that Taymor's

> trippy hyper-stylized montage sequences and riots repeatedly deny music's primary power of narrative unification. Although [. . .] integrated music stands as the center of the narrative, it often appears to be swirling around an induced soldier, frightened child, or riotous mob, as a flood of bold and quick images truly keep the characters outside of a seamlessly flowing diegesis. Individuals do not sing the music to each other or for each other. It emerges amid a rush of visual and aural chaos.[33]

What Taymor achieves is something different than narrative integration. She challenges the normativity of narrative integration and linear narrative through the dramaturgy of the work, even as the complex content of the work challenges political and gender norms. Taymor's theatrical direction has infiltrated her directorial style throughout this film, but it is most obvious in the frequent "show within a show" sequences. These include bands performing live in proms dances, concerts on buildings' terraces, gigs in seedy clubs and singing at art gallery openings, singing on buses, choral singing in fields, and solo singing in the streets. The celebrity comedian Eddie Izzard[34] is featured in his own outdoor circus-like scene peopled by huge puppets,[35] which then transforms into an indoor hallucinatory animated sequence. This pays homage to the *Yellow Submarine* film of the Beatles[36] but also to such popular comic phenomena as *Monty Python's Flying Circus* in its use of surreal animation. Eddie Izzard, an entertainer in his professional life, encourages us "not to be late" for this spectacular show, reminding us that this is a show-within-a-film. In it, he reaffirms his theatrical past, so that the sequence performatively identifies both celebrity and character.[37]

NEW RELOCATIONS

The chapter's aim is to analyze the gendered and geographical relocations of the Beatles' songs and show how Taymor's dramaturgy transformed them into complex emotional and performative signifiers for a contemporary audience. It demonstrated how these recontextualizations contribute to a reconsideration of personal and national identity constructions, much of which was achieved through spectacular moments of hyperreality. The creative team of *Across the Universe* worked consistently to find a new visual language for every song. The musical director Elliot Goldenthall stated that "every song is a small solar system"[38] and production designer Mark Friedberg added that it was an "explosion of emotion, explosion of colour." And all those moments of visual excess work within the dramaturgy of the piece as drug-induced moments of bliss and as political commentary. In reviewing the film musical, Peter Travers has acknowledged that "to call [*Across the Universe*] trippy would be an understatement. Your head might explode. Just don't accuse Taymor of playing it safe."[39]

Taymor's style has been criticized for separating the vocal lines from the characters and not succeeding in integrating the elements together. Kessler wrote that "Julie Taymor uses her trademark hyper-stylization to create a visual/aural estrangement between character, action, music, and voice."[40] While Alan Jacobson talks about it as a "love letter to an era" and relates his experience in watching the work, "the viewer learns to trust and understand that Julie Taymor has done the impossible: crafted a jaw-hander of a clever musical that teeters on the electric precipice but never collapses into selfconsciousness."[41]

The influence of Taymor's *Across the Universe* is now beginning to be apparent as new ghosts of the work appear in new works such as the television series *Glee*. In the fifth episode of the fourth series of *Glee* (November 8, 2012), the song "Hopelessly

Devoted to You" gets a near-identical treatment to "I Want to Hold Your Hand" in this film.[42] However, in *Glee* a young homosexual man, Blaine, is singing the song walking through American football players. The comparison is playful here and the reference is unashamed in the double-ghosting of the scene and song. Taymor seems also to have inspired the director and choreographer of the American stage punk rock musical *American Idiot* (2009). There are traces from the songs "I Want You" and "Happiness Is a Warm Gun" in the stage adaptation including flying, moments of out-of-body experiences, and hallucinatory visions. Taymor's visual style has already been embedded in our popular culture, but in this work she has managed to preserve the freshness and cutting edge of the original songs, creating a performative context of reflexivity and irony, and a complex political commentary. In doing this, she has elevated the jukebox film musical into a panorama of filmic abundance, a barrage of visual surprises and inventions that characterize her own recklessly extravagant directorial style, and inspired the makers of the stage and television musicals of the future. Musicals are often, wrongly, regarded as a globalized art form of effortless innocence that is designed to bring simple pleasures to its audiences. What musicals truly offer their audiences are complex interdisciplinary creations that allow their creators to articulate the audience's deepest fantasies, fears, and anxieties through a subversive presentation of song and dance.[43]

NOTES

1. Nick Prescott, "Across the Universe," online. Available: https://dspace.flinders.edu.au/xmlui/handle/2328/7496. April 10, 2012.
2. This is performed at a specially built theater at the Mirage hotel and casino resort in Las Vegas.
3. Elizabeth Wollman and Jessica Sternfeld, "Musical Theatre and the Almighty Dollar: What a Tangled Web They Weave," *Studies in Musical Theater* 5: 1 (2011): 4.
4. Jill Dolan, *Presence and Desire: Essays on Gender, Sexuality, Performance* (Ann Arbor: University of Michigan Press, 1993), 118.
5. Stacy Wolf, *A Problem Like Maria: Gender and Sexuality in the American Musical* (Ann Arbor: University of Michigan Press, 2002), 42.
6. Marvin Carlson, *The Haunted Stage: The Theater as Memory Machine* (Ann Arbor: University of Michigan Press, 2001), 7.
7. Barrie Gelles, "*Glee* and the 'Ghosting' of the Musical Theatre Canon," *Popular Entertainment Studies* 2: 2 (2011): 73.
8. Kelly Kessler, *Destabilizing the Hollywood Musical: Music, Masculinity and Mayhem* (Basingstoke: Palgrave Macmillan, 2010), 198.
9. Ibid., 197–98.
10. Ibid., 198.
11. Brett Farmer, *Spectacular Passions: Cinema, Fantasy, Gay Male Spectatorships* (Durham, NC: Duke University Press, 2000), 70.
12. Barry Keith Grant, *The Hollywood Film Musical*, (Oxford: Wiley Blackwell, 2012), 153.
13. Wolf, *A Problem Like Maria*, 33.
14. Sheila O'Malley, online. Available: http://www.sheilaomalley.com/?p=9942. April 10, 2012.
15. Millie Taylor, "Experiencing Live Musical Theatre Performance: *La Cage Aux Folles and Priscilla, Queen of the Desert*," *Popular Entertainment Studies* 1:1 (2010), 53.

16. A further example is the urge of the audience to clap after the end of screening of a filmed lived performance during the NT Live series, online, http://microsites.nation-altheatre.org.uk/ntlive or the Met Live, online,http://www.metoperafamily.org/metopera/liveinhd/LiveinHD.aspx?sn=watch.
17. See Amy Cook, *Shakespearean Neuroplay: Reinvigorating the Study of Dramatic Texts and Performance through Cognitive Science* (Basingstoke: Palgrave Macmillan), 2010.
18. Ibid., 2.
19. Wolf, *A Problem Like Maria*, 4.
20. Grant, *The Hollywood Film Musical*, 1.
21. Lennon and McCartney, Northern Songs Ltd., 1963.
22. Simon Frith, "Why Do Songs Have Words?" in *Lost in Music: Culture, Style and the Musical Event*, ed. Avron Levine White (New York: Routledge, 1987), 98.
23. Taymor in "Creating the Universe," featurette, *Across the Universe*,Sony C8283549, DVD. This scene resembles the iconic recruitment scene in the film musical *Hair*.
24. Grant, *The Hollywood Film Musical*, 59.
25. For more on desire and the singing voice see Wayne Koestenbaum, *The Queen's Throat: Opera, Homosexuality and the Mystery of Desire* (London: Penguin, 1993).
26. Grant, *The Hollywood Film Musical*, 163.
27. Gerhard Fischer and Bernhard Greiner, eds., *The Play within the Play: The Performance of Meta-theater and Self-Reflection* (Amsterdam: Rodopi, 2007), 396.
28. Ibid.
29. Rick Altman, *The American Film Musical* (Bloomington: Indiana University Press, 1987), 62.
30. Taymor in "Creating the Universe."
31. Grant, *The Hollywood Film Musical*, 154.
32. There is an interesting use of double-ghosting effects here by Taymor.
33. Kessler, *Destabilizing the Hollywood Musical*, 188.
34. The extra layer of the celebrity cameos adds to the dream sequence elements of the film. Bono is leading the spectacle-driven "I Am the Walrus" song sequence during which he performs live at an art gallery before moving onto a bus. This has definite connotations of *Priscilla, Queen of the Desert: The Musical* (2006), but it can also be associated with Jack Kerouac, Neal Cassady, and the infamous road trips of the Beat Generation with Warholesque (and other) pop art references.
35. In the song "Dear Prudence," the audience appears to be transferred from an interior space to an antiwar demonstration with walking masked peaceful demonstrators surrounded by larger-than-life puppets of skeletons. The use of puppets is a feature of much of Taymor's work.
36. Online. Available: http://www.youtube.com/watch?v=vefJAtG-ZKI. December 6, 2012.
37. Other striking scenes include "Strawberry Fields Forever," during which an image of Max is projected onto the face of Jude. The strawberries become the hearts of soldiers dying, blood, and hand grenades. Toward the end of the film Max sings his thoughts in a daydream sequence of "Hey Jude" during which he telepathically encourages Jude to return to the United States. This sequence contains references to *American in Paris* and other films and musicals.
38. "All about the Music," *Across the Universe*.
39. Peter Travers, online. Available: http://www.rollingstone.com/movies/reviews/across-the-universe-20071018. April 10, 2012.
40. Kessler, *Destabilizing the Hollywood Musical*, 199.
41. See Jacobson, online. Available: http://www.brightlightsfilm.com/61/61universe.php. December 6, 2012.
42. See further comment at http://deconstructingglee.wordpress.com/2012/11/11/hopelessly-devoted-to-you-staging/. December 6, 2012.
43. Many thanks to Tony Gardner, Alison Andrews, and Jordan Taylor for their input, and Kristina Wells for introducing me to this work.

CHAPTER 4

Dynamic Shape

The Dramaturgy of Song and Dance in Lloyd Webber's Cats

BEN MACPHERSON

When Valerie Eliot, the widow of poet T. S. Eliot, presented Andrew Lloyd Webber with old drafts and discarded fragments from the writing of her husband's volume *Old Possum's Book of Practical Cats* at a production workshop in 1980, one abandoned poem prompted the composer to declare, "What you've just given me is the difference between a song cycle that could be done by children in school and a musical."[1] The rejected draft in question was in fact originally intended to conclude Eliot's collection of feline poetry, and contained ideas that centered on aspects of the physical, and the dance of the cats. This idea of physicality and movement so galvanized Lloyd Webber that it formed the basis upon which he shifted his attention from the song cycle he was creating based on Eliot's poetry, to the idea of a staged project; ultimately, that discarded draft shaped the work's form into what is often credited as the progenitor of the "megamusical": *Cats*. The reason for this may now appear obvious, for as choreographer Gillian Lynne notes, "there is no limit to what cats can do with their bodies, if you watch."[2]

In light of this volume's thematic concerns with the performative gestures of music and physicality as agents of meaning and transformation, it is provocative to explore the use of song and dance in *Cats* with reference to the idea of dramaturgical shape, from which a sense of narrative might be derived. Just as the discarded draft gave form to what became *Cats*, and just as cats can make multiple physical "shapes" with their bodies, it is interesting to explore how the performative shape of this musical—with reference to its intense physicality, vocality, and insistence on ensemble—might create a sense of performative shape and narrative through its dramaturgy, a position that many reviewers have thus far dismissed.[3] To do this, Kathryn Lowerre's article "Fallen Woman Redeemed: Eliot, Victorianism, and Opera in Andrew Lloyd Webber's *Cats*" (2004) provides a useful springboard. Lowerre argues that *Cats* has a definable dramaturgical shape, operating "through the juxtaposition of characters, rather than through their development [...] characters come and go [arbitrarily] without disturbing the pleasures of high-energy presentation."[4] The performative experience of these juxtapositions within the dramaturgy can be explored by examining the physical and aural shapes created by song and dance. To do this, four visual schematics (what I am calling *dynamic shape* schemas) will illustrate graphically the shapes of these juxtapositions in performance, after which neurobiological research will be applied to an understanding of them, articulating the corporeal and cognitive experience of song and dance. This analysis is further examined to explore how the dynamic shape of *Cats* in performance may directly relate to, subvert, challenge, or confirm Lowerre's suggestion of arbitrary juxtapositions. In short, it might be suggested that the corporeal and cognitive experience of *Cats* in performance has a direct bearing on our understanding of its content and complexity, producing meaning through the dramaturgical interrelationships of physicality, voice, and music.

THE DRAMATURGY OF DYNAMIC SHAPE SCHEMAS

In exploring the dramaturgy of song and dance through the performative shape(s) of *Cats,* the work of neurobiologist Antonio Damasio is particularly helpful. Borrowing specific aspects of corporeal experience from his book *The Feeling of What Happens: Body, Emotion and the Making of Consciousness* (2000), we find that three areas prove particularly useful in isolating the different shapes created through *Cats*. In his definition of consciousness as it relates to experience, Damasio writes that "consciousness begins as the feeling of what happens when we see or hear or touch [...] that accompanies the making of any kind of image."[5] Damasio's trio of bodily sensations that contribute to cognitive and corporeal experience is useful here because it allows an exploration of the shapes created through "sight," "hearing," and "touch." Through this simple but easily identifiable framework, the idea of "sight" will be examined first—in reference to the intense focus on ensemble performance evident in *Cats*. This is important, as it establishes the performative aesthetic within which the shapes of song and dance may be assessed, using "hearing" and "touch" as sensorial labels respectively.

In considering the ensemble nature of *Cats*, the schematic in figure 1 provides evidence of a sense of shape in the performative dynamic. Yet, on closer inspection, it is interesting to extrapolate some statistics from the information it provides.

As demonstrated, of the thirty-four separate vignettes that make up *Cats*, twenty-nine of them see the majority of the actors onstage throughout.[6] In fact, only five sequences (less than 15 percent of the whole work) have fewer than three performers onstage: Victoria's solo ballet, "Invitation to the Jellicle Ball," "Mungojerrie and Rumpleteaser," Grizabella's dance at the end of act 1, and Bombalurina and Demeter's ode to Macavity.[7] Of these, only Victoria's dance sees the space inhabited by a solo performer for an extended period of time.[8]

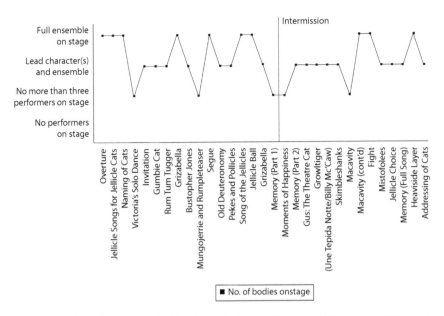

Figure 1 Number of performing bodies (dynamic shape of the ensemble) on stage. © Benjamin Macpherson.

Given such an intensive focus on ensemble, Richard Schechner's theory of performance and reception becomes provocative here. In *Performance Theory* (2003), Schechner argues that one of the defining characteristics of experiencing live performance is the unique sense of "cocreation" between the actors and the audience.[9] Elsewhere, Erika Fischer-Lichte has conceptualized this cocreativity as a "feedback loop" between performers and spectators.[10] To this end, the intensity of ensemble in *Cats* theoretically includes the audience in its dynamic. In fact, in the original production this sense of community was intensified by the spatial arrangement of a thrust stage that destabilized conventional modes of reception between performers and audience.

Interestingly, neuroscience underpins this theoretical suggestion of cocreation, providing two very specific ways of conceptualizing the sense or shape of shared bodily experience in the immediacy and intensity of performance. For over fifteen years, Vittorio Gallese and Giacomo Rizzolati have been engaged in the—sometimes contentious—study of the existence and function of mirror neurons in the pre-motor cortex of the brain.[11] Gallese, Rizzolati, and their colleagues have presented evidence that suggests motor simulation on the part of subject A (audience member) when he or she witnesses subject B's action or movement (the dancer on stage). It would appear that the pre-motor cortex vicariously mirrors subject B's action, sending signals to the relevant muscles in subject A. This may explain why, when watching a trapeze artist cross from one wire to another, we gasp uncontrollably, our stomachs reeling at the sight. It also suggests that the physical stylization and movement, and the shape of the ensemble in *Cats*, are experienced by the audience vicariously; chemical signals flooding the spectator's body in a space where kinetic immediacy heightens physical awareness of the actors in performance.[12] In this case, the intensive feeling of ensemble seen in figure 1 must also include—to an extent—the audience, who cognitively and corporeally respond to the performing ensemble.

Discussing this copresence of multiple bodies onstage—and by extension the ongoing negotiation and vicarious experience of the differing levels of intensity between them—Marvin Carlson suggests that in responding to the ensemble as cocreators, the audience is forced to negotiate "multiple individual psyches" during performance.[13] The amount of body energies existing together forcibly narrows both the conceptual and the physical distance between the actors and the audience, multiplying the number of "psyches" the audience is required to negotiate. Echoing this, but from a more explicitly somatic perspective, Fischer-Lichte analyzes the copresence of actors and audience as a meeting place for biological "body rhythms."[14] She suggests that each subject has his or her own unique (circadian) body rhythm, which can be used to negotiate and interact with other human beings. Performance thus constitutes a "body rhythm struggle" that perpetuates and sustains the intense sense of presence and energy.[15] Such a struggle is seen in the intense concentration of ensemble in *Cats*, further intensified through its reliance on dance and movement (discussed below). To this end, some suggestions can be made.

While the dynamic shape of ensemble (figure 1) does not suggest a constant intensity of bodies, and does evidence a sense of shape, there is an obvious concentration of ensemble for upward of 85 percent of the performance. This intensity is not simply a specular or spatial one, emanating from the physical placement of bodies. Via motor simulation and vicarious corporeal experience, the audience may also physically experience a sense of intensity as cocreators in the performance. The plurality of body rhythms enhances the sense of physical presence on the part of both actors and audience, and increases the sense of corporeal awareness that enables the struggle and negotiation of body rhythms to take place. It is within this dynamic shape of ensemble that the dramaturgy of song and dance is experienced, with the two elements often juxtaposed against each other as performative gestures.

With specific reference to voice as a contributing gesture to the musical properties of the dramaturgy, there are varied uses of choral voices, group voices, and solo voices that contribute to the dynamic shape here. From a neurobiological perspective, Fischer-Lichte has suggested that "vocality [...] brings forth corporeality," further contributing to a sense of bodily presence in performance that may contribute to the ebb and flow of ensemble through the textural shifts of song (see figure 2).[16]

Likewise, Paul Robertson's findings on the power of music suggest that we react bodily to what we hear.[17] At a colloquium on this subject,[18] Robertson explored the release of chemicals into performer's and audience member's bodies during live musical performance. Referring to mirror neuron theory, Robertson identified an almost like-for-like experience between performers and audience. Specifically, he emphasized that the release of chemicals including dopamine and serotonin enhanced the subject's sense of physical presence and corporeal experience, prompted by shifts in texture and structure (or shape). On this basis, the shifting dynamics of voice in *Cats* not only enhances the juxtaposition of characters, but contributes to the interplay

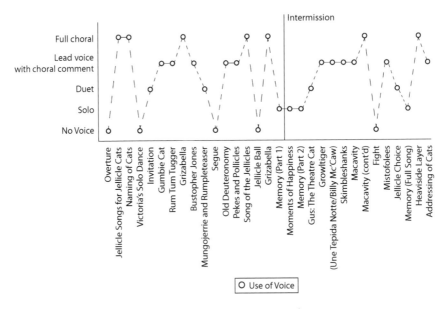

Figure 2 The dynamic shape of voice in *Cats*. © Benjamin Macpherson.

of immediacy and distance within the aural shape of the work, increasing or decreasing volume and density, set against the backdrop of bodily intensity—adding to it.

Less than half the musical settings are written to include the entire ensemble even though, as figure 1 demonstrates, the ensemble are physically present for just over 90 percent of the time. Songs including "The Old Gumbie Cat," "Bustopher Jones: The Cat About Town," and "Magical Mister Mistofolees" all include solo lines, usually with a lead narrator and comment from the chorus. "Jellicle Songs for Jellicle Cats" and "Heaviside Layer" are both choral, while "Memory" (parts 1 and 2) and "Moments of Happiness" are the only uses of solo voice. In *Cats*, the use of voice may be grouped into five categories: full choral community voice (which may also include anonymous or arbitrary use of solo or group lines), lead voice and choral commentary (where the lead voice is character based), duet, solo voice, and no voice. Figure 2 shows the varied use of voice that gives shape to the characters and performers.

As noted above, the opening and finale of the performance contain elements of choral voice, and there are only three moments of extended solo voice in between, in which the lead vocal with choral comment is the aesthetic that dominates. However, before exploring the use of song in more detail, the final element of dynamic shape needs to be considered.

The juxtaposition of dance, movement, and stasis within the work, aligned to the dynamic shapes of voice and ensemble and Lowerre's dramaturgical exploration of juxtapositions, adds another layer to the way an audience might understand the drama through bodily engagement in performance. *Cats* has often been lauded as a dance musical, with Lloyd Webber—at the time of its production in 1980—suggesting: "We are creating a world of dance not seen before, to this degree, in a British

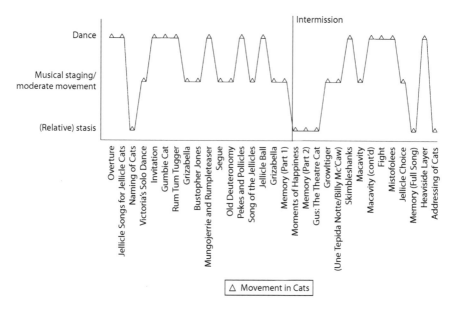

Figure 3 The dynamic shape of movement in *Cats*. © Benjamin Macpherson.

musical."[19] Dividing this element of the dynamic shape into discrete categories, the sense of movement and dance directly relates to the shape of the ensemble outlined in figure 1, with corresponding (and at times divergent) moments of choreographed dance, musical staging, and something that may be called "relative stasis." This last category includes movement by characters as part of the stage direction, but which does not constitute musical staging, such as the show's finale.

As with voice, figure 3 demonstrates a permanently changing physical dynamic in performance, with defined oscillation between musical staging and choreographed dance. The moments of relative stasis therefore provide either respite or an interruption to the proceedings. As explored in more detail below, the constant dynamic shifts between these three forms of physical gesture promote a sense of rhythm in performance, experienced by both performers and audience, a rhythm that might be seen also to contribute to the dramaturgy of the piece as well.

Along with theories on ensemble and voice, the effect dance has on its receiver draws specific corporeal attention to the performing body. Scholars including Corrine Jola (2010), Christian Keysers (2010), Bruce McConachie (2008), and Maaike Bleeker (2002) have also used scientific notions of inner mimicry, vicarious enactment, or corporeal entrainment to articulate the physical effect dance has on spectators from the comfort of their theater seats.[20] Discussing this in more detail, and analyzing the foregoing figures in depth, we see what happens when the dynamic shapes of ensemble, dance and movement, and voice are combined together.

To visualize this, figure 4 demonstrates that while there is an intense concentration on the performing ensemble throughout, the dynamics of voice and movement are fluid and divergent. These textural changes add a feeling of shape, pace, and shift

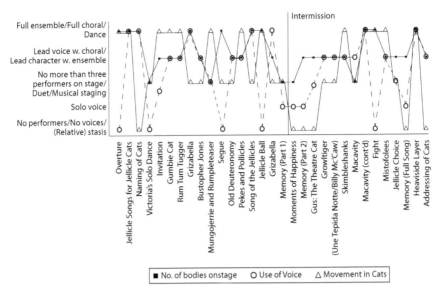

Figure 4 Composite "dynamic shape" schema of *Cats*. © Benjamin Macpherson.

to the performance. In the experience of these interactions, the corporeal energies of the performance are perpetuated between the actors and audience. Additionally, such shifting dynamics constantly reconfigure the sight, sound, and sense of physical contact that might feed the audience's conceptual engagement with the juxtapositions Lowerre has explored.

Figure 4 highlights, for example, that there are only three moments of extended solo voice in the entire performance: at the end of act 1, during the opening scene of act 2, and when Grizabella sings "Memory." Aurally, these are the only moments when attention is focused on one individual character, perpetuating a sense of shared community voice throughout the majority of the performance. This sense of community is evident in four specific sections of the schema, at points when the ensemble comes together in full choral voice and unison movement. These moments are represented by the numbers 1–4 in figure 5. In essence, they serve to bookend the performance at the opening and finale, and lift the energy at approximately the midpoint.

Dramaturgically, the content of these four moments is the question of Jellicle identity, confirming Jessica Sternfeld's assertion that the overarching concern in *Cats* is the quest to define what exactly a Jellicle cat might be.[21] Structurally then— as far as one could ever describe *Cats* as having a dramatic arc—these moments of intense ensemble, when this recurring question comes to the fore, create a sense of order, unity, and coherence. Corporeally, the way these moments frame the character vignettes between them is fascinating. If we explore this with reference to the dynamic shapes at play, it is interesting to analyze the first section from figure 5, from the Overture through to Victoria's solo dance.

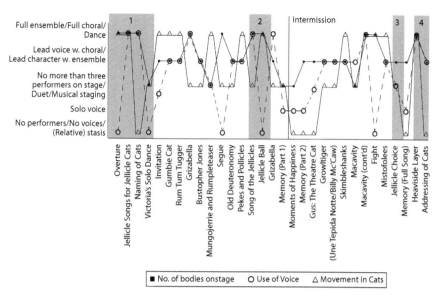

Figure 5 Moments of the "ensemble effect." © Benjamin Macpherson.

DYNAMIC SHAPES OF ENSEMBLE, VOICE, AND MOVEMENT

At the opening of the performance (No. 1, fig. 5), the sense of ensemble and movement is quickly established through the bodily immediacy of actors and audience members in the auditorium. During the Overture, for example, the cats run riot through the aisles, clambering on audience members and causing mischief. Literally—physically—closing down the distinctions between spectating and performing, this intense physical gesture destabilizes conventional boundaries, leading to an instant "body rhythm struggle" and sense of shared corporeal energy. This opening therefore establishes the sense of ensemble that the audience have become a part of. Following this, "Jellicle Songs for Jellicle Cats" begins with a series of rhetorical questions. The song climaxes with a full choral refrain set to choreographed movement. The build is gradual both vocally and corporeally, with individual voices slowly multiplying until all thirty-three cats are onstage, singing and dancing. The progression to simultaneity acclimatizes the audience to the corporeal immediacy of the performance.

Once at its peak, the celebratory opening song creates what Scott McMillin has termed "the ensemble effect."[22] Defining this as a mechanism of musical theater performance, he suggests that it achieves two things simultaneously. Dramatically, it allows for "characters to express themselves simultaneously."[23] Such a moment transcends the limits of the individual characters embodied in the drama, becoming a universalized mechanism: "the voice of the musical making itself heard."[24] In this sense, when all thirty-three cats sing the refrain of "Jellicle Songs for Jellicle Cats" (No. 1, fig. 5) they assume a sense of anonymity, become a community voice. Likewise, when words give way to dance in "The Jellicle Ball," the effect is the same; the voice of the musical becomes embodied in thirty-three physically energized, intensely present dancers.

Such an effect is corporeally provocative in terms of the dynamic shape of the performance as a whole. The intensity of bodies in space has already been established, but with respect to the ensemble effect, neuroscience provides further explanation for cognitive engagement independent of the rhetoric of the lyrics. Studies of kinesthetic empathy suggest that responses to dance and movement through the mirror neuron system are inherent: "even without physical training, spectators can simulate the movements they are visually familiar with, and that empathy increases resonance."[25] So an audience member may see movements associated with felines—Skimbleshanks twitching his whiskers prior to the opening of "Jellicle Songs for Jellicle Cats," or Alonzo slinking along the back of the junkyard set—and vicariously relate to those visual cues, by fictional character-based association with a pet, or perhaps through a process of anthropomorphism.

Further, in these ensemble numbers—which largely focus on the build to synchronized movement and dense vocal presentation—such a vicarious reaction on the part of the audience becomes amplified.[26] Literally, corporeal motor simulation occurs through a focus on the dancing body, and the audience members' body rhythms attune to those of the dancers, intensified in these moments by a factor of up to thirty-three if we account for every "individual psyche" the audience witnesses onstage.[27] This consistently enlarged set of movements by the actors, which builds from the Overture and which is sustained through the opening song, creates a real sense of intensity and immediacy, one that corporeally induces the audience at large to engage and react as a community. This is particularly the case in the middle chorus of "Jellicle Songs for Jellicle Cats," when all performers dance in unison, recalling McMillin's "ensemble effect," achieved through a discrete dynamic shape within this song's structure.[28] Such a sensory experience of ensemble can be suggested here in light of specific neurobiological research into music and movement, which finds that when these two elements occur together there is greater synchronicity in the sensory appreciation of experience between audience members; a synchronicity that enhances feelings of community, unifies body rhythms in space, and intensifies the sense of shared bodily copresence.[29] The fact that this occurs to a factor of at least thirty-three for each audience member (not including recognition of other audience members), suggests an intense experience of the performance, which both begins with and results in sensory appreciation within the body.

This "ensemble effect"—a performative gesture of dance in this case—bookends the entire performance and introduces the audience to these characters, creating a heightened sense of presence, engagement, and community, through which the audience might continue to engage with the performance. According to Damasio, such corporeal stimulation is what enables the production of "images" in the consciousness, the mechanism that increases and sustains the suspension of disbelief enough to try to find an answer to the question: what's a Jellicle?[30] Having established this sense of ensemble dramatically and physically, the dynamic shape of the performance shifts from a focus on ensemble intensity at the opening (No. 1, fig. 5) to the juxtapositions Lowerre explores, through which the answer to that question may be found.

After the intense ensemble effect of "Jellicle Songs for Jellicle Cats," the poem "The Naming of Cats" and Victoria's balletic solo slows the pace; physiologically the audience's heart rates and body rhythms attune to a slower tempo. There is no longer the multiplicity of performing energies and bodies in confrontation or collusion; there is simply one character—Victoria—dancing center stage. This relatively sudden shift distances the audience conceptually and physically. The ensemble effect that built upon the physical and conceptual claustrophobia of the performance space gives way to a different dynamic shape. As Fischer-Lichte argues, the resultant spectatorial distance encourages dramatic engagement over and above the performative engagement felt through the enlarged gestures of ensemble.[31] This change in dynamic shape to Victoria's dance therefore shifts the experience from a focus on performative spectacle, to an enhanced focus on the drama, allowing the audience to engage more fully in the character studies that follow.[32] This focus on the individual continues through the four vignettes following Victoria's dance, and which (as Lowerre suggests) juxtapose characters one against another. The characters portrayed in these four vignettes are the Old Gumbie Cat (named Jennyanydots), the Rum Tum Tugger, Grizabella, and Bustopher Jones.

THE DRAMATURGY OF MUSICAL THEATER SIGNIFICATION

The way corporeal engagement is achieved and sustained through the dynamic shape of *Cats* having been schematized, it is appropriate to explore the way in which the dynamic shape of the performance gives rise to a sense of narrative in the dramaturgical juxtapositions of these characters. As noted by Sternfeld, the score for *Cats* achieves momentum and interest through its textural or rhythmical shifts, and—crucially—through its use of pastiche and parody in musicalizing each feline character.[33] For example, Eliot's poem characterizes the Old Gumbie Cat in ways reminiscent of an Edwardian schoolmistress. She teaches the mice music, crocheting, and tatting, and she makes the beetles "well disciplined."[34] The setting of this text by Lloyd Webber evokes a specific character type, redolent of prewartime Edwardian domesticity and patriotism. It is upbeat, sung in a high register, and complete with a borrowing from "Rule Britannia."[35] In addition to the prewar nostalgia of the Old Gumbie Cat, *Cats* indeed borrows from a broad range of musical idioms including jazz ("Macavity: The Mystery Cat"), rock ("The Jellicle Ball"), romantic ("Memory"), music hall ("The Ballad of Billy McCaw"), and liturgical ("Journey to the Heaviside Layer"). Such references pulse through the score and have far-reaching effects, going "beyond the [simple] recycling of references, tropes, even structural elements."[36] Providing a musical representation of character types, these choices enhance the nature of the juxtapositions while highlighting another important element in the performance experience: cultural associations.

Echoing Raymond Williams, Bruce Kirle has suggested that an audience member's experience and understanding of live musical theater can only be complete when considering the influence cultural factors have on his or her reading of a work at a given moment in time.[37] Capitalizing on extrinsic cultural references, Lloyd Webber assists the audience in engaging with what they hear through musical gestures that prompt prior knowledge, memory, or cultural associations. Such intertextual signification, including all aspects of the production, extends beyond the fiction, once again drawing attention to the theatricality and artifice of the performance, enhancing the dynamic shape of song and dance in the show. In tandem with the bodily immediacy of the performance itself, this intertextuality excites both present senses of the live experience, and conjures mental associations of cultural icons from the past. Therefore, the audience may engage with the performance through the heightened sensory inputs of the dynamic shape, but may also respond to the character *types* presented in song and dance (discussed below). In effect, the characters become ciphers of recognized human beings.

As we reflect on these textual, musical, and cultural signifiers, it is interesting to consider how the dynamic shape of the performance complements the juxtaposition of the characters. Returning to Jennyanydots, many of the ensemble reenter the space after "Invitation to the Jellicle Ball," reestablishing the sense of copresence and community introduced in the opening number. In addition to the corporeal presence of the ensemble, there are two aspects worthy of comment here. Firstly, the dynamic shape of the voice changes. The opening ensemble section relied on shared solo lines and full choral groups. Here—in the first of many vignettes to use this pattern—the vocal style is presentational and in the third person: Munkustrap and three female cats describe and comment on Jennyanydots, with only occasional interjections from her. The full embodied voices of the ensemble give way to attention on solo voices. A form of corporeal distance is created through this use of voice, for it is Munkustrap and his companions who vocally provide most energy, through their commenting on Jennyanydots in the third person. Second, while the intertextual references here (Jennyanydots's costume, musical borrowings, and stylistic features), highlight Jennyanydots's domesticated, orderly personality (and in many ways paint her as a musical version of 1950s British children's entertainer Joyce Grenfell), the dynamic shape of the performance embodies this when she marshals the ensemble into a dance troupe. The tap dance that develops creates a sense of excitement and nostalgic recall to musicals of a bygone era, prompting a different set of cultural associations, and providing a physiological lift to the performance in much the same way that the opening sequence did.

The "ensemble effect" once again celebrates the creation of community, in the immediacy of the performance space, and heightens bodily presence and energy exchange as the dancers perform in perfect unison. Once again, a sense of entrainment and synchronization identified on the receivers' part also comes into play.[38] The lyrical description of this cat—distanced through its aural shape and use of the third person—gives way to a return of performative immediacy and energy. The dynamic shape has shifted even within this one vignette, creating a sense of interplay between the immediacy of the ensemble and the intertextual elements of the drama.

In contrast, "The Rum Tum Tugger" is written as a contrary and mischievous cat, who when offered pheasant would rather have grouse, and once indoors wants to exit immediately.[39] Within the dramatic space, the character type that follows the bustling Jennanydots is disjunctive, juxtaposed against what preceded it. This cat is characterized musically by soft rock, with physicality and vocal inflections reminiscent of Elvis or Mick Jagger. He flirts with all the female kittens and gyrates his pelvis to the upbeat electric guitars of his musical setting. The corporeal experience of the Rum Tum Tugger's song is chaotic and boisterous. The ordered ensemble, with their synchronized body rhythms, literally collapses into chaos after Jennyanydots's tap dance, with small groups all doing different things. The element that unites this now disparate ensemble in the performance space is the dynamic shape of the voice. In unison, the chorus repeatedly exclaim, "The Rum Tum Tugger is a curious cat!"[40] This direct address creates an immediacy and intensity in the aurality of performance, while the previously synchronous corporeal exchanges between the actors and audience once more engage in a "body rhythm struggle."[41] The immediacy of presence and chaotic energy in the experience of performance therefore aptly embodies the character of the Rum Tum Tugger.

The subsequent shift in dynamic shape and dramatic atmosphere to introduce Grizabella is marked. The original poem, which told of Grizabella whom other character's almost wish dead, was not included in Eliot's *Old Possum's Book of Practical Cats* because he felt it too depressing for children.[42] Such a depressing characterization by Eliot is matched in Lloyd Webber's music, through its slow tempo, somber tonality, and bluesy harmonic progressions in sharp contrast to both of the preceding songs.

Unlike either of the previous vignettes, the dynamic shape of Grizabella's song is relatively static and the ensemble concludes by physically grouping together in a mob; their body rhythms concentrated, ushering Grizabella offstage. From the multiple body rhythms in "The Rum Tum Tugger," or the heightened sense of unison in "The Old Gumbie Cat," here, the bodies are together—but in stasis. This shift in corporeal energy prompts an audience member's motor simulation pattern to change, physically stopping him in his tracks as the dynamic shape shifts. The written text paints Grizabella as an embittered outcast, while the dynamic shape of performance literally embodies this isolation through the ensemble's physicality. Vocally, after a short solo Grizabella is silent as the other cats tell of her exploits. Once again, an aural distance is created between her, the ensemble onstage, and the audience. The fact that Grizabella's presence is muted when the other cats sing literally seems to embody their dominance over her.

Finally, the juxtaposition that sets Grizabella's character in relief is that of "Bustopher Jones: The Cat About Town." Set to a moderately paced wistful hymnal, this cat is fond of gentleman's clubs and venison.[43] The ensemble returns to small groups in the playing space for Bustopher's entrance. Larger than life, he is dressed in a morning suit, with a monocle and a walking cane. Importantly, the anthropomorphism of the actor/character is here subverted by the human attire. The audience's physical and visual orientation from the intense physical gesture of the mob that ushered Grizabella offstage, and gradual crescendo in the music of "Grizabella" now focuses on this imposing figure in a fat suit. Being placed center stage, his presence is different again from that of Old Gumbie Cat, Rum Tum Tugger, or Grizabella. His corporeality is more intense than Grizabella's, for example. For part of the song he is seated on a large top hat center stage, with all of the younger male cats sat at his feet, listening intently to his exploits. Visually, this concentrates the audience's focus on the character, and is a sign of respect and status. Here too, the dynamic shape of the performance supports the content of the drama.

THE DYNAMIC SHAPES OF DRAMATURGY: SOME FINAL THOUGHTS

In the opening scenes, and in all four vignettes considered above, the sense of presence and interplay within the dynamic shape of the performance provides a strong corporeal experience for the audience, with a sense of shifting body rhythms, levels, and layers throughout. However, as this chapter has demonstrated, the physical gestures of dramaturgy here go further. These dynamics form a physical embodiment, or activation, of the juxtapositions and connotations of the drama. As defined earlier in this volume, song and dance work as performative gestures with an active sense of agency in constructing meaning, identity, and transformation. Thus, the performance in *Cats* embodies and gives a sense of corporeal movement to the dramaturgical juxtapositions Lowerre has explored, using the physical staging to construct what might be termed micronarratives within *Cats*. For the brief section explored above, this micronarrative might be represented as in figure 6.

Thus, the dramaturgy of the dynamic shapes of song and dance—order and unison, chaos, stasis and status—directly enhance the corporeal and cognitive agency for the juxtapositions of character. A cause-and-effect narrative is then created through the dynamic shapes of *Cats*: from order (Jennyanydots), through rebellion (Rum Tum Tugger), the consequences of the rebellion (Grizabella), and then a return to the status quo (Bustopher Jones). What might such a reading demonstrate?

With specific reference to *Cats,* it may belie the suggestion that this musical is more "experience" than "meaning,"[44] allowing the dynamic shape schemas to suggest

	Eliot's character type	Musical reference (cultural)	Micro-narrative (Juxtaposition)
The Old Gumbie Cat	Fun, order, domesticity, 'Nanny'	Glen Miller, pre-war, jazz	Social Order
The Rum Tum Tugger	Mischievous character,disruptive, playful, flirtatious, anti-establishment	Elvis, Mick Jagger, rebellion,youth, fun, freedom, sexuality	Rebellion against the social order
Grizabella: The Glamour Cat	Bedraggled, solo, outcast	Blues, dirge, minor key	Exclusion from social acceptance
Bustopher Jones:The Cat About Town	The 'cat about town', social order,class, carica- ture, Beau Brummel	Hymn-like, wistful	Celebration of social status

Figure 6 Diagram of the dynamic shape of act 1 micronarrative. © Benjamin Macpherson.

an implicit sense of narrative within the agency of the physical dramaturgy. Second, it also presents the possibility for a broader application in dialogue with other contributions in this volume, and speaks to the plurality of forms that contribute to musical theater performance, including song, dance, language, costume, and the material shape of the performance. We might identify an intrinsic link between the physical experience of the gestures of song and dance as dramaturgical substance within the performance of musical theater, and a subsequent sense of narrative or meaning that such gestures may imply in the received content of a performance. This connection between the physical activation and dramatic substance is demonstrated through the dynamic shape schemas above, and importantly draws on elements of neuroscientific research, including vicarious enactment, conceptual blending, the mirror neuron system, and body rhythm clashes, in application to the way audience members may engage with the narrative suggested in the corporeal experience of performance. To this end, exploring the corporeal intensity of song and dance, the physical dramaturgy implicit in such intensity, and the presence of a sense of narrative within the dynamic shape of this piece, the gestures of musical theater are evident both for the actors in performance and for the audience as cocreators, who in this case work together to answer the question: what's a Jellicle cat?[45] Perhaps the answer, in Old Deuteronomy's words, is that, in the end, they are "very much like you."[46] Likewise, in a more general sense, perhaps through exploring the dynamic shape of dramaturgical gestures, including the physical embodiment of ensemble, the textural shifts in vocal and musical content, and the sense of motion created by dance, we are able to understand and articulate the effects of musical theater performance as an active, bodily experience that provides both performers and audiences alike with corporeal, ephemeral, and incredible "moments of happiness."

NOTES

1. Keith Richmond, *The Musicals of Andrew Lloyd Webber* (London: Virgin Publishing, 1995), 73.
2. In Richmond, *Andrew Lloyd Webber,* 75.
3. Reviewing the Broadway production of *Cats* in 1982, T. E. Kalem reported in *Time* magazine that "We had the experience but missed the meaning." Cited in Michael Walsh, *Andrew Lloyd Webber: His Life and Works* (New York: Harry N. Abrams, 1997), 127.
4. Kathryn Lowerre, "Fallen Woman Redeemed: Eliot, Victorianism, and Opera in Andrew Lloyd Webber's *Cats," Journal of Musicological Research* 23: 3 (2004): 303.
5. Antonio Damasio, *The Feeling of What Happens: Body, Emotion and the Making of Consciousness* (London: Vintage, 2000), 26.
6. This is several more than listed in the original musical score or even souvenir program. In the original production, Victoria's solo dance early in act 1 was part of "Invitation to the Jellicle Ball." Here, it becomes a separate vignette due to its dynamic shift in staging, as do the individual occurrences of "Memory."
7. The thirty-four sequences include song numbers with more than one presentational style, including "Invitation to the Jellicle Ball," Victoria's solo, "The Old Gumbie Cat," "Grizabella: The Glamour Cat," "Magical Mister Mistofolees," and "The Addressing of Cats." For the purposes of exploring this with regards to the number of bodies on

stage, a distinction has been made between Bombalurina and Demeter's expository passage and the choral refrain in "Macavity: The Mystery Cat."

8. Although Grizabella's dance at the end of act 1 is a solo, the presence of Old Deuteronomy upstage evidently alters the dynamic of the space.

9. Richard Schechner, *Performance Theory* (London: Routledge, 2003), 230.

10. Erika Fischer-Lichte, *The Transformative Power of Performance: A New Aesthetics*, trans. Saskya Iris Jain (London: Routledge, 2008), 39.

11. Vittorio Gallese et al., "Action Recognition in the Premotor Cortex," *Brain Research* 119 (1996): 593–609; Giacomo Rizzolatti and Corrado Sinigaglia, *Mirrors in the Brain: How We Share Our Actions and Emotions* (New York: Oxford University Press, 2008).

12. Gregory Hickok has identified eight problems with the use of mirror neuron theory, notably regarding the lack of action recognition, or an understanding of context in the actions mirrored. However, in the context of theatrical performance, that understanding seems to be supported through reference to the dramatic space. See Gregory Hickok, "Eight Problems for the Mirror Neuron Theory of Action Understanding in Monkeys and Humans," *Journal of Cognitive Neuroscience* 21: 7 (2008): 1229–43.

13. I am using Carlson's discussion of "psyches" here to refer to the subject's sense of self as a whole, and not merely to a mental constitution of presence. See Marvin Carlson, "Theatre and Dialogism," in *Critical Theory and Performance*, ed. Janelle G. Reinelt and Joseph R. Roach (Ann Arbor: University of Michigan Press, 1992), 313–24.

14. Fischer-Lichte, *Transformative Power*, 58.

15. Ibid., 59.

16. Ibid., 125.

17. Paul Robertson, "Music, Mind and Brain," conference paper, Music Colloquium Series, King's College, London, December 5, 2007.

18. Ibid.

19. Lloyd Webber cited in Richmond, *Andrew Lloyd Webber*, 75.

20. Corrine Jola, "Merging Dance and Cognitive Neuroscience," in *The Neurocognition of Dance: Mind, Movement and Motor Skills*, ed. Bettina Blasing, Martin Puttke-Voss, and Thomas Schack (Hove: Psychology Press, 2010), 203–34; Christian Keysers and V. Gazzola, "Social Neuroscience: Mirror Neurons Recorded in Humans," *Current Biology* 20: 8 (2010): 353–54; Bruce McConachie, *Engaging Audiences: A Cognitive Approach to Spectating at the Theatre* (New York: Palgrave MacMillan, 2008); Maaike Bleeker, "Disorders That Consciousness Can Produce: Bodies Seeing Bodies Onstage," in "Bodycheck—Relocating the Body in Performing Art," special issue of *Critical Studies* (2002), 131–60.

21. For a specific discussion of the music of the "Jellicle theme" that Lloyd Webber develops through these sections, and in *contrafactum* throughout the work, see Jessica Sternfeld, *The Megamusical* (Bloomington: Indiana University Press, 2006), 133–44.

22. Scott McMillin, *The Musical as Drama* (Princeton, NJ: Princeton University Press, 2006), 78.

23. Ibid., 79.

24. Ibid., 79–80.

25. M.-H. Grosbras et al., "Enhanced Cortical Excitability Induced by Watching Dance in Empathetic and Visually Experienced Dance Spectators," conference paper for "Kinaesthetic Empathy: Concepts and Contexts," Manchester University, April 22–23, 2010.

26. The unison of choreography may well create simultaneity of motion, a huge energetic visual stimulus of one single set of movements that become enlarged. However, the moments of separate movement by individuals or groups of performers during these points creates its own visual energy and spatial variety that forms a bustling and bristling sense of motion. The spectators will also corporeally respond to this as part of the dramatic event, a heightened sense of body energy, within the performance space.

27. Carlson, "Theatre and Dialogism," 320.
28. McMillin, *Musical as Drama*, 79.
29. See McConachie, *Engaging Audiences,* 39–74, 92–114; Katie Overy and Istvan Molnar-Szakacs, "Being Together in Time: Musical Experience and the Mirror Neuron System," *Music Perception* 26: 5 (2009), 489–504; Jola, "Merging Dance."
30. See Damasio, *What Happens*. Importantly, this effect is achieved at two other key points of the work: just before Grizabella's second entrance in act 1, and immediately after Grizabella's redemption in act 2, concluding the performance with a celebration of community. The ensemble effect is therefore used as a dramatic device to propel the quest along, and also to highlight Grizabella's importance in the work, setting her entrance and redemption in relief.
31. Fischer-Lichte, *Transformative Power*, 60–61.
32. Even here, the mirror neuron system and vicarious enactment may occur, maintaining corporeal engagement throughout this slower and less immediate moment. Likewise, the fact that inputs from the performance space may prompt engagement with the dramatic space is not undermined by this shift in focus.
33. Sternfeld, *Megamusical*, 112–75.
34. T. S. Eliot, *The Complete Poems and Plays of T. S. Eliot* (London: Book Club Associates, 1969), 210.
35. The borrowing from "Rule Britannia" did not occur in the original production, and was expanded in later productions of the show.
36. Marvin Carlson, *The Haunted Stage: The Theatre as Memory Machine* (Ann Arbor: University of Michigan Press, 2001), 17.
37. Bruce Kirle, *Unfinished Show Business: Broadway Musicals as Works-in-Process* (Carbondale: Southern Illinois University Press, 2005).
38. See Jola, "Merging Dance"; McConachie, *Engaging Audiences*.
39. Eliot, *Complete Poems and Plays*, 214.
40. Ibid.
41. Fischer-Lichte, *Transformative Power*, 58.
42. Sternfeld, *Megamusical*, 115.
43. Eliot, *Complete Plays and Poems*, 230–31.
44. Kalem in Walsh, *Andrew Lloyd Webber*, 127.
45. Schechner, *Performance Theory*, 230.
46. Eliot, *Complete Poems and Plays*, 234.

PART THREE
Performativity as Transition

If our instinctive responses to the dynamics of a show's shape or the density of vocality or corporeality become filtered into "narrative" or "motivic" tropes, as Macpherson suggests, this emphasizes how dominant the pull of structuring forces can be, even though the dynamics of song and dance move more fluidly beyond these forces. Even in texts that confront dominant expectations like (in the case of *Cats*) the need for dialogue, we seem to be committed to certain other structuring forces (such as narrative) and assumptions (for example, that naturalism is both desirable and natural). If this identifies a tension between the active performativity of certain practices and the passive complacency of others, we are reminded that performance can be and has been used both to galvanize and pacify disruptive forces. The potentially libidinal play of performativity is often countered by the controlling mechanisms of institutions, structures, and commodification: one only has to turn to Bertolt Brecht's writings to find his lament that opera has indoctrinated the public into a passive complicity with the status quo; and one only has to turn to another common lament to hear members of that public criticize music theater because it disrupts this passive complacency. "They are uncomfortable," writes Jill Gold Wright, "with the 'unrealistic' convention of characters 'suddenly bursting' into song and dance."[1]

In the following two chapters Mary Jo Lodge's discussion of dance and Matthew Lockitt's discussion of song in the Broadway musical explore the use of the liminal and liminoid in constructing coherent narratives that nevertheless embrace the excesses of song and dance. The liminal spaces in these otherwise naturalistic narratives—dream spaces or dance breaks, as Lodge observes—are ways of excusing the play of song and dance within an otherwise conservative form, though to explain their function in such simplistic terms rather misses the point. Smuggled in under the cover of that excuse, song and dance in music theater can, as elsewhere, engage performers and audiences—in part through vicarious association, in part through direct play and affect—in a number of crucial performative transactions.

The terminology of the liminal comes from anthropological and ethnographic scholarship relating to the enactment of ritual during rite-of-passage encounters. In these liminal rituals the magnified experience energizes transition, and the heightened expression of the enacted statement—often in song and dance—both gives body to and serves as metaphor for the shift. One such rite-of-passage, almost universally practiced, is the coming together of partners in the ritual of a wedding ceremony. In the Christian ceremony, music, song, and dance play key functions both in the service, in which processual choreography and choral song serve to formalize the solemnity of the oath, and in the reception, which usually culminates in a participatory celebration of song and dance.

That the notion of the liminal recognizes both a transition between one mode and another and a free-play of excess often expressed in performative modes means that the term has become appropriated very extensively by performance scholars, as Jon McKenzie notes.[2] First, it is invoked in respect of the audience encounter with performance and with performativity, an encounter that is between the real world of their lives and the representational world of the performance; second, it is referred to in relation to performance studies as a genre (or gender) being established "between" other stable genres; and third, it is used to recognize the way that performance transcends discipline boundaries to engage in interdisciplinary ("between") modes of expression and affect—as we have noted.[3] In all of these spaces, between boundaries that structural thinking inevitably but unhelpfully conceptualizes, performance allows the free-play of the liminal, and without the strict conventions of other bounded spaces, the efficacy of the liminal can become performative, flowing between spaces through porous boundaries, and enabling transition (affect) rather than stasis (complacency). These understandings of the liminal support the project of this whole book and recognize in its song and dance—as we will discuss later—a performative energy that seeks to identify, explore, and articulate music theater as a critical tool. In more focussed ways, though, understanding the performativity of the liminal in relation to music theater can be helped by exploring two balancing mechanisms: the way that song and dance is used as a liminal device in music theater texts, which the following chapters explore, and the way that song and dance is used as a liminal device in life's ritual encounters.

In YouTube's "Dirty Dancing UK—Julia and James first dance,"[4] we can see the first dance of a British couple marrying in 2005. The video shows the couple dancing to the hit song "(I've Had) The Time of My Life" from the film *Dirty Dancing* (1987), with which Jennifer Grey and Patrick Swayze memorably ended this cult teen movie (figure 7). Julia and James's version of the dance is a close copy of Kenny Ortega and Miranda Garrison's original choreography. First she (Julia) enters, to the cheers of the invited guests; then he (James) enters down the stairs, reversing the expected framing of genders to give him higher status; he has changed from his formal groom's attire into a casual all-black shirt and trousers modelled on Patrick Swayze's costume in the film.

The dance begins, mimicking the gestures of the original to the crowd's obvious appreciation. Around three minutes into the video, the couple move to the stairway, and once again James takes center stage, making a stylized leap from the bottom step into the room and then—as Swayze does in the original film—strutting across the dance floor. The camera returns to pick up Julia, now observing the dance, and when it pans back to James we find he has been joined by four friends, choreographed into the sequence with a simple routine, again emulating the choreography from the film. Finally, two of the friends take Julia and launch her up above James's head to hold her in the classic flying lift from the movie. It's cheating—Swayze had

Figure 7 Patrick Swayze and Jennifer Grey perform the iconic lift in *Dirty Dancing* (1987). Photo courtesy of Vestron Pictures Ltd/Photofest.

no assistance—but they have fulfilled the expectations of this routine and to the crowd's delight, the lift offers a climax to this dance routine.

As it appears in the film, the dance to "(I've Had) The Time of My Life" offers obvious performative punctuation to a narrative love story. The role of the dance in Julia and James's routine is somewhat different: there is undoubtedly a narrative arc for which the lift is an obvious ending; but this narrative, rather than being part of a longer storyline per se (or even being contained within the five minute duration of the first dance), is housed within the ritual framework of the wedding ceremony, itself one of the crackles that illuminates the difference between the before and after of Julia and James's marital status.

In this capacity, the first dance is a liminal and performative act in many ways, representing the moment of recognition by the community that two people are united, symbolizing sexual union in a public simulation of reproduction, and framing the moment at which the heightened celebration of the wedding ceremony returns, through communal release, to the mundane. This particular example is liminal in other ways: it takes place in a stately hallway into which a sweeping stairway descends—a threshold between the interior and exterior of the house, and between the private upstairs and the public downstairs. The participants are also sited in interesting roles whose performative responsibility is blurred: the audience/guests are invited into the dance, both in their aural responses and in later taking to the dance floor; and even the bride and groom (especially she) from time to time slip in and out of being the performance focus of the crowd to observe the action from a distance.

There is an enormous amount of complexity in the first dance, even when it is a far more casual affair than this example. When we take to the dance floor (with varying degrees of discomfort or ability), we are stepping beyond our normative behaviour into a self-conscious use of our bodies that approaches performance but which does not necessarily complete the performative transaction (it does not necessarily climax with a lift, engage an audience or solicit applause, for example). These acts are caught between the publicness of performance and the privacy of the personal; we slip in and out of them, and though they may have a structure forced upon them, they do not necessarily operate in narrative or linear terms. In this, some interesting critical concerns spring to light, which our next two chapters explore.

These chapters discuss the liminal encounters of music theater, looking particularly at how the typical structuring of dialogue with song and dance works in the Broadway tradition. Mary Jo Lodge focuses on dance, noting the way in which Broadway choreographers have consolidated dominant tendencies towards narrative and integration, creating heightened moments of suspension within which the stylized expression of dance can flourish. In doing this, practitioners like Agnes de Mille and Jerome Robbins have both amplified the idea of narrative trajectory and created dream-like spaces in which the self-contained logic of spatial and corporeal expression can echo the narrative frameworks of wider practices. Matthew Lockitt focuses his discussion on songs, and asks whether these work as moments of suspension or moments of animation. One of the key considerations here is whether song and dance simply exists for its aesthetic enjoyment, whether it serves the two masters of narrative and integration, or whether it offers some other more elusive dynamic function that transcends or even baffles our entrenched assumptions: what might be the relationship between the liminal, the performance and the performative?

NOTES

1. Jill Gold Wright, *Creating America on Stage: How Jewish Composers and Lyricists Pioneered American Musical Theater* (Saarbrucken: VDM Verlag, 2009).
2. Jon McKenzie, "Genre Trouble: (The) Butler Did It," in *The Ends of Performance*, ed. Peggy Phelan and Jill Lane (New York: New York University Press, 1998), 219.
3. Ibid., 218–19.
4. Online. Available: http://www.youtube.com/watch?v=ZYhlm9GTAQ0. December 13, 2012. This video "seems to have taken the world by storm," write the couple in their own commentary, and with almost 10 million hits and subsequent appearances on BBC TV news, daytime UK talk show *Richard and Judy*, and US hit *The Oprah Winfrey Show*, their assertion seems to be accurate.

CHAPTER 5

Dance Breaks and Dream Ballets

Transitional Moments in Musical Theater

MARY JO LODGE

Here I sit, on my farm's front porch, in my beloved Oklahoma, and I know that Ado Annie and the other girls think I'm a silly for takin' up with my farmhand Jud for the Box Social today. It's just that that stuck up cowboy Curly is always teasin' me and lyin' about havin' a fancy surrey with a fringe on it, and I don't want anyone sayin' Laurey Williams is a fool! Still, that awful Curly is mighty handsome in his hat, and while Jud has always been a great help here on the farm, he's just so serious and gloomy—he even scares me a bit. I know this Elixir of Egypt from Ado Annie's Peddler Man will help me figure out what to do. I've sniffed it, like the bottle says to, and I've gotten a might sleepy, and now the strangest thing has happened. It's like I've walked right out of my dreams and I'm standing right in front of me. And I can see the real me—not that tomboy that Annie and Gertie and even Curly and Jud think I am. The *me* that I see is a woman, not a girl, and moves with the grace and elegance I can't quite find on the farm. And I find that *that* me is drawn to Curly. I want to fly into his arms, and the *me* I see can do that—she can say with her body what I can't seem to with my words.

The original Broadway production of the musical *Oklahoma!* (1943) famously featured a dream ballet, wherein Laurey, the heroine, falls asleep and the audience sees her dream life made real (see figure 8). Dream Laurey, the real Laurey's ballet dancing double in "The Dream Ballet," not only embodies Laurey's anxiety at accepting the invitation of the villainous Judd for the Box Social, instead of the hero cowboy Curly's, but also gives tomboyish Laurey a chance to explore her femininity and indeed, her sensuality, through dance. In doing so, she uses her body in ways previously unseen from the character in the context of the show. Through dance, she can accept Curly's courtship, and even "marry" him, though in her real life, and in speech and song, she cannot yet do so in the musical. Laurey is transformed in the moment of transition to her dream ballet, both physically (she is so transformed that

Figure 8 Laurey (Shirley Jones) meets her double, Dream Laurey (Bambi Lynn), at the start of "The Dream Ballet" in the 1955 film version of Rodgers and Hammerstein's *Oklahoma!* Photo: © Photofest.

an entirely different actress must play her) and psychologically, as she reveals her true feelings both to herself and to the audience. This physicalization and revelation of Laurey's inner life is important not only for the character, but also for the musical's audience because it allows them to see how differently Laurey views herself and her situation from the external image she projects, and to see how her performance of resistance to Curly's charms shapes the show. Also, the moment when the audience moves from viewing one actress as Laurey to another, and when Laurey's story begins to be told only through dance, rather than through singing or speaking, as had previously been done, is critically important for *Oklahoma!* both because of the plot development it offers, and because it represents one of the musical's most significant liminal or transitional moments.

Musicals' liminal moments, like the one described above in *Oklahoma!*, are challenges because they exist at moments of change in the show when, for instance, a song is introduced or a dance concludes. These moments are among the most frequently critiqued in Broadway musicals because they are the moments when characters suddenly begin to or stop singing and/or dancing. Graham Wood, in his essay "Examining the Film Musical," asks, in regard to one type of liminal moment in the musical: "What is it about that moment where song takes over from speech that when treated with skill and finesse can seem like the most natural thing in the world, yet when carelessly done is jarring and comic in the extreme?"[1]

Yet it is not only the transition from speech to song that is challenging for the musical—the shift from speech to dance, or from song to dance can be equally problematic. Dance in the musical, as a visual rather than aural element, presents a particular challenge for musicals, as it is an entirely different mode of communication from the more common aurality of speech or song. Indeed, there are many famous musicals that feature very little or even no dance—most of Stephen Sondheim's shows fall into this category, with their focus on the aural (intricate music and complex lyrical rhyming)—perhaps because of the hurdles of using this alternative way of communicating and because of the particular challenges that the transition into these visual, movement based moments can present. Certainly, many musicals do include dance, and it is these shows, and their requisite treatment of moments of transition—ones that move from one mode of communication to another, particularly ones involving dance—that, while fraught with challenges for their creators, define dance in the musical. Exploring how dance is used successfully in musicals can offer insight into how the creative teams of musicals can address the inherent challenges of the form. In particular, examining how liminal moments involving dance function, especially when characters in musicals stop singing and begin dancing, typically midsong (the dance break), or sometimes midshow (often a dream ballet) can help both choreographers and director/choreographers determine how to introduce and integrate dance successfully into a song or show in innovative ways.

DIEGESIS, SPECTACLE, LIMINALITY

The term "liminality" was originally coined by theorist Victor Turner to describe the transitional space of rituals, wherein the participants move from one state of being to another. His work on liminality is rooted in the study of tribal culture, in which, for instance, an initiation ritual moves the participant through a transition ceremony of some sort into a new position in the tribe and thus, the world. Turner is especially interested in what happens in those moments of transition, during the ritual, and how those moments impact the individual and the community, noting that during these transitional times, "what is mundanely bound in sociostructural form may be unbound and rebound."[2] Erika Fischer-Lichte, in *The Transformative Power of Performance*, applies Turner's ideas on liminality to theater and expands them, drawing a distinct contrast, when she says: "While the liminal experience in ritual may transform the participants' social status and alter their publicly recognized identity, no comparable effect seems to exist for the aesthetic experience of artistic performance."[3]

In spite of the differences in their work, both Turner and Fischer-Lichte focus on liminality as a means of transformation for an individual, with Turner exploring how the liminal moment transforms the participant, while Fischer-Lichte explores how the transformation affects the spectator of a performance. Certainly, though, both argue for the importance of these moments, with Fischer-Lichte noting that "the transitional moment is accompanied by a profound sense of destabilization."[4] It is this description of destabilization that aptly describes the moment in a musical when dance is first introduced. It profoundly changes the moment that came before, when the participants were communicating in some way other than dance. But if these moments of transition in a musical, as liminal moments, are transformative, as both Fischer-Lichte and Turner argue, who or what is transformed? Certainly, in the musical, the means of storytelling changes—in this case to a movement-based means that causes the musical itself to change. Yet the transformation can be even more profound than that—indeed both the participant in the transformation (the character, in this case, as distinguished from the actor) *and* the spectator are also transformed as part of the communal nature of the theater. The performance needs a spectator in order to exist as performance, and the presence of the spectator inherently shapes that which is performed for him or her. Certainly, the character who suddenly begins to dance experiences what Fischer-Lichte calls "a physical transformation, in other words a change to the physiological, energetic, effective and motoric state," though she notes that "the transformations caused by liminality are predominantly temporary," which might describe what happens when characters stop dancing and return to other modes of communication.[5] The spectator of the musical, too, is transformed, either by being pulled out of the experience when characters burst into song or dance—the negative audience experience noted above, which Fischer-Lichte describes as audience members dismissing "their transitory destabilization as silly and unfounded"—or by embracing this new mode of communication and participating more fully in the entertainment experience.[6] The musical itself is also transformed as new modes of communication are introduced; it experiences a ritual of sorts, when, for instance, characters first engage in dance in a show, and disrupt the stability of the form that had previously been established (and did not include dance). For instance, in *Oklahoma!* it isn't immediately established that the story will be told through dance, since it doesn't appear until several minutes into the first act when it is introduced in rodeo cowboy Will Parker's number "Kansas City." When that song and its accompanying dance end, the form of *Oklahoma!* is stabilized into a new normal that can include eruptions of dance.

Certainly, the musical is transformed by the moments of liminality described above, which Fischer-Lichte says exist in the "betwixt and between," yet it is somewhat surprising that these transitional moments exist at all in musicals, and have such a profound effect on both the characters within them and the spectators watching them, given that many musicals, particularly since *Oklahoma!* in 1943, have struggled to achieve integration of their various components—song, speech, and movement—and effectively erase, or at least control, the transitional spaces between those elements.[7] Jane Feuer calls this phenomenon, at least in relationship to dance in film musicals, an attempt to "naturalize all effort," which can be expanded to describe movement in the many musicals that strive for integration—in normalizing and naturalizing the movement, dance becomes more integrated with the nonchoreographed, natural movements in the nonmusical scenes that precede and follow it and thus the border space between dance and *not dance* is minimized, or even erased.[8] It is important to note, however, that many other musicals, particularly those that do not aim for naturalism, are less concerned with integration, and they often do just the opposite in including dance, and in fact call attention to it by its dissimilarity to movement in real life. More recent shows like *Spring Awakening* (2006) and *Matilda* (2010) deliberately use dance nonnaturalistically, yet even these shows must acknowledge that moments within them that include dance are different from those moments that do not include dance. Both naturalistic and nonnaturalistic musicals deal with the same challenges raised by the uneasy marriage of the various forms of communication found in the musical—songs, dances, and nonmusical scenes. In all cases, the interplay between these modes of communication is complex, and not as easily "naturalized" as Feuer might suggest. For instance, the modes of communication in a musical may not happen in isolation; indeed, musicals rarely provide neat and orderly internal borders between those modes. Shows as disparate as *Carousel* (1945) and *Rent* (1996) include lengthy musical scenes ("If I Loved You" in *Carousel* and "Light My Candle" in *Rent*) that navigate the delicate line between recitative and song, and utilize a scene that is simultaneously a song to further the dramatic action of the musical. Thus, the "integrated" musical, long touted in histories of the musical as an ideal example of the form, is something of a myth, since musicals tend to remain the sum of their disparate parts and their related liminal spaces; musicals rarely coalesce into an orderly, unified whole. Also, there is no single ratio of song to dance that can predict the success of a musical, since shows with both a great deal of dance and with none have joined the musical theater canon.

Acknowledging that liminality is, therefore, an inherent part of the form of the musical, regardless of its integrated status, raises the question of how musicals might best deal with their liminal spaces, particularly as related to dance. While there is no single solution to the problems (and possibilities) of these moments of liminality, ones that Turner calls "both more creative and more destructive than the structural norm," it does seem that handling the delicate shifts between the various components of a musical more seamlessly (or perhaps more thoughtfully) can improve a musical's reception.[9] Indeed, the moments when the internal boundaries of a production become apparent—for example, when a group stops singing in the middle of a production number and instead begins dancing—are when much of the craft involved in shaping the musical is revealed. These transitional moments are also critical for audiences since, when successful, they can transform spectators, as Fischer-Lichte would argue, by pulling them more deeply into the story told. Also, transitional moments as related to dance, when used nonnaturalistically, can serve to highlight the skill of the performers and the virtuosity of the choreography, both of which also serve to heighten the spectators' involvement in, or at least appreciation of, the performance. Alternatively, unsuccessful transitions into dance, which can occur both when dance is integrated into the story and when it stands apart to highlight its performance *as* dance, can create jarring transitions for spectators that negatively disrupt the viewing experience.

A useful first step in effectively approaching the liminal spaces in a musical is determining the musical's dominant mode of communication—song, dance, or speech—since it helps to determine how the show's structure supports its ideas and their execution. Usually, though not always, the mode of communication introduced first in a musical denotes the primary mode of communication for a production, something consistent with Fischer-Lichte's view that the "beginning and end of a performance represent[s] a special type of transition."[10] It follows, then, that when shows embrace their dominant mode, they are often most successful and cohesive. For example, shows that begin with a focus on dance (*West Side Story* (1957) is the obvious example here) often struggle less with embracing their later dance moments, since the musical immediately establishes a convention that dance is the primary way in which the people within the musical communicate. In musicals where dance is not introduced first (and is therefore not the dominant mode), and/or is only employed sporadically, the moments of liminality involved in the shift away from the dominant mode into dance are more challenging. *Rent*, for example, uses little dance in the show, so the sudden introduction in the original Broadway production of several ensemble members doing abstract movement in the background as they sing backup for the number "Santa Fe" is, at best, jarring, and at worst, very distracting from the rest of the number. While it might be argued that the dancers' movements in "Santa Fe" are intended to be expressive rather than naturalistic, because movement on stage nearly always draws the spectator's eye, it risks distracting them from the important lyrics Collins is singing, and might instead cause them to wonder about the identities of these dancers, whose characters are unclear. While dance can be used effectively in a musical to force spectators into Fischer-Lichte's moments that exist "betwixt and between," in the case of *Rent*'s "Sante Fe," dance fragments the number, and in doing so, stunts the character development of a critical player in the musical's action.[11]

THE HIERARCHY OF MODES OF COMMUNICATION

Dance typically fills one of three distinct roles in a musical—it either accompanies singing, or is featured during a song when singing stops (the dance break), or is showcased in a number entirely dedicated to dance (the dream ballet). The first of these roles, dance as movement that accompanies singing, is the one that dance most frequently fills. Many choreographers and directors refer to these dance steps that accompany singing as staged movement, rather than dance, a distinction employed because the movements are usually simpler and on a smaller scale than featured dance moments, and are generally more realistic and more closely resembling real-life movement than those that appear at moments when dance is the only action happening. Jane Feuer says of this sort of dance that "by cancelling choreography as a calculated dance strategy, non-choreography implies that dancing is utterly natural and that dancing is easy."[12] Also, because the performers are usually singing while doing the movements, the steps must, by necessity, not cause the dancers to be winded and unable to deliver their song. The staged movement is not the primary focus of the song (singing is), and it therefore plays a supporting role in the number. Still, staged movement can be a powerful component of a musical, even though it often requires less technical mastery from those performing it. It might give a group an identity, as they move in unison, or it might match the energy of the lyrics and rhythm of the high-energy piece being sung. This type of dance can serve both diegetic and nondiegetic functions—that is, it may advance the musical's story, but this is not strictly necessary. It may instead simply serve as a stimulating visual echo or even counterpoint for the lyrics of the song.

The next two roles dance plays in the musical have in common that they occur at moments when dance is used as the sole means of communication in a musical, without singing or speaking happening simultaneously with it. As a result, the steps used in both are typically more sophisticated. Both dance breaks and extended dance sequences (often dream ballets) in musicals usually rely on a more formal dance vocabulary and, particularly in the case of the extended dance-only number, require trained dancers who can execute complex movements that are typically unlike those used at any other time (except in other dance sequences) in the show. These dance moments are generally among the least realistic in a show, and while they may tell the musical's story, because they are movement and not language-based (as both song and spoken scenes are), they do so in a different and more abstract way.

In spite of all of these commonalities, dance breaks and dream ballets are also uniquely different from each other and need to be examined separately. To that end, the second role dance plays in a musical is as part of the dance break. Technically speaking, dance breaks occur when the singing stops but a musical number continues, and thus dance becomes the primary mode of communication for the number at that moment. Dance breaks can range from a few measures (or seconds) to several minutes in length, and they typically showcase only one specific dance language or style. Curiously, dance breaks in the musical tend to overwhelmingly feature Broadway style jazz dance or tap dance, though those are not the only kinds of movement featured in the musical theater. For instance, one rarely sees a dance break (a short sequence *within* a song) featuring ballet, and even more rarely, featuring a ballet performed en pointe. Modern shows might feature hip-hop dance breaks, and classic pieces might showcase ballroom or Latin moves in their dance breaks, but, like the more dominant tap and jazz sequences that most frequently appear in musical theater dance breaks, the movements in the break, regardless of their style (or perhaps, *because* of their style) tend to serve as spectacle in the show, wowing the audience with the virtuosity of the performers (the lengthy tap break in the title number of the 2011 Broadway revival of *Anything Goes* is an excellent example of this). In fact, dance breaks are usually intentionally performative and highlight dance *as* dance—while they might advance the story, they more typically do not. As Scott McMillin notes in *The Musical as Drama*, "most songs and dances do not advance plots. Usually the book sets forth the turn of plot and the number elaborates it, in the spirit of repetition and the pleasure of difference."[13]

The third role dance plays in a musical is typically as part of an extended showcase piece that features only dance and functions similarly to the way that concert dance, and especially classical ballet, works. Often called the dream ballet, after Agnes de Mille's famed example in *Oklahoma!*, these numbers need not actually feature only ballet (though they typically do), and the circumstances that call for them need not be based in a fantasy or dream sequence within the show. The modern dream ballet came into prominence in the 1930s and 1940s, when important ballet choreographers, starting with George Balanchine, and then continuing with Agnes de Mille, began choreographing Broadway musicals and included short, usually story-driven ballets (performed by a dancing chorus who needed only be expert in dancing) into their projects. The most famous of these is de Mille's *Oklahoma!* and the moniker came from the fact that this ballet actually occurred in the context of *Oklahoma!*'s plot as a dream (heroine Laurey falls asleep to the strains of her song "Out of My Dreams," before her dream double appears to dance her role in the lengthy feature). After de Mille's string of successes with similarly styled dance pieces in the subsequent musicals she choreographed, the name stuck for many dance sequences of this kind. Like many of its successors, de Mille's original dream ballet advanced both plot and character, serving a diegetic function, while also offering up an elegant and unique dance vocabulary—not traditional ballet, but rather ballet adapted for the

Broadway stage (and "westernized," given *Oklahoma!*'s cowboy content) and enacted by skilled dancers. While these extended sequences are most commonly ballet (as in all of de Mille's work), they sometimes feature jazz dance that is infused with ballet (as in the opening of *West Side Story*) but almost never, for instance, showcase flashy, rhythmically driven styles like tap or hip-hop (which are nearly always confined to dance breaks). Since the aim of the dream ballet in the musical is usually to tell a story, virtuosic tap movements, like those in the aforementioned *Anything Goes* sequence, draw attention away from the plot, even though they are engaging and entertaining.

Dream ballets were most commonly featured in musicals during the golden age of the American musical, but the rise of the director/choreographer during the end of that period brought about a shift in how musicals were constructed (which will be examined in a greater detail below) and as a result, dream ballets and other extended numbers featuring only dance became far less common, except in revivals drawn from the period (though these, too, often evolve greatly in their "revisal" form).

The three roles that dance plays—as staged movement, as featured break (dance break) or as extended feature (dream ballet)—are also affected by the particular function that dance assumes in a given musical. This function is dictated both by *who* dances in the show, and by whether or not those characters understand that they are dancing at a given moment in a musical. First, the conversation regarding who dances in a musical is deeply tied to the larger development of the musical, and in particular, as noted above, to the rise of the director/choreographer in the musical, an era usually considered to have reached its maturity with Jerome Robbins's work on *West Side Story* in 1957. With the exception of just a few prominent practitioners like George M. Cohan and, later, George Balanchine and Agnes de Mille, who served as both director and choreographer on at least one show, musicals prior to *West Side Story* typically had a director, responsible for the concept, scenes, and songs (to varying degrees), and a dance director (later called the choreographer), who handled the specialty dance moments and those moments involving the dancing chorus. In this pre-director/choreographer era, musicals typically featured a dancing chorus who rehearsed separately from the principal actors. The most demanding dance was not typically enacted by the principal performers, but was instead delegated to these featured performers. Thus, the actress playing Laurey in the original Broadway production of *Oklahoma!*, Joan Roberts, only ever watched her famous dream ballet unfold—she played no role in it, as she was the "dreamer," and the dancer playing Dream Laurey, Katharine Sergava, instead danced it, and performed the role of Laurey for the time of the ballet.

The rise of the director/choreographer brought fundamental changes to the personnel of musicals, however, leading to the development of the "triple threat" performer—one who excels in singing, acting, and dancing. With one person controlling the concept and staging the libretto-driven scenes, the staged movement that accompanied singing and the more sophisticated dance movements, the director/choreographer could demand unity both in the larger production, and within the individual performers (so, for instance, Laurey would have to be part of her dream ballet in this new paradigm, a change the 2002 revival of *Oklahoma!* included—even though the show was actually staged with separate creative artists—Trevor Nunn and Susan Stroman, in the roles of director and choreographer, respectively). Since only one person (the director/choreographer) would be the driving creative force, and that person could not stage multiple rehearsals at once (so that the dancing chorus could not, for instance, learn the dream ballet while the principals worked other scenes), the dancing chorus gradually fell out of favor. Thus, in *West Side Story*, which ushered in the first of the true triple-threat casts (and was created by a director/choreographer—Jerome Robbins) and which, based on the analysis offered above, featured dance in the dominant role in the musical because the characters are first seen dancing, the show couldn't work unless the principals could communicate in that dominant mode—they had to dance. The era of the triple-threat performer not only led to changes in who danced, but in fact, since dance could be interspersed throughout the production, in how dance could be used in a given musical. Dream ballets were often no longer needed as the musical became more integrated, not simply in form and content, but much more significantly, in the bodies of the performers, as the principal actors could tell their story through multiple modes of communication, and in multiple modes at once, leading to less necessity for the isolated, dance-only dream ballet.

THE FUNCTION OF DANCE AS DIEGESIS OR AESTHETIC

The function of dance in a given show extends beyond who dances to include the level of knowledge the characters have about the dance they are doing. That is, while it is certain that the actors know that they are dancing in a musical, not all characters in musicals are knowledgeable of that fact. (This of course, also applies to characters' knowledge about their own singing, which often goes hand in hand with their knowledge of their own dancing, but the focus here is limited to a discussion of dance). Thus, dance function breaks down into two distinct choices—characters either know they are dancing or they don't. In the first choice, characters know and acknowledge, often openly (with lyrics or text) or gesturally (with reactions or movements), that they are dancing. Typically, the circumstances of the dance are part of the diegesis, most often as a show-within-a-show or backstage musical. In this case, the dancers often perform in a metatheatrical context, with the plot of the show often following the rehearsal or performance of a show. Thus, one of the great hurdles of believability for the musical, or at least for the integrated musical, is overcome through the context—the characters all know the same dance steps and when and how to execute them—because they (as characters) rehearsed them. In the second choice, the characters do not know that they are dancing, and while they do dance, they don't, for instance, acknowledge that they are doing anything unusual by dancing. Dance, like singing in these contexts, is simply another way the characters "speak" to one another. Thus, the convention of musicals using dance in this way (aesthetically or nondiegetically) relies on the fact that the characters do not acknowledge anything has changed when the mode of communication changes, moving, for instance, from song to dance. In this context, then, the audience must suspend disbelief and accept that the characters know all of the steps because they simply *do*. Alternatively, characters may not acknowledge they are dancing because the normal rules of logic are suspended because the action is happening *between* diegetic and nondiegetic spaces: in a dream world (i.e., the *Oklahoma!* "Dream Ballet") or in some sort of fantasy sequence (a device often used for musicals that happen in the more inherently realistic media of television and film). While there is a long list of musicals that rely on the backstage conceit, with characters in shows ranging from *Show Boat* (1927) to *Kiss Me, Kate* (1948) and the more recent *The Producers* (2001) being knowledgeable about the fact they are dancing, the iconic dance-centered show *West Side Story* actually falls into the second category of dance function, as the characters, except in the specifically performative numbers "Dance at the Gym" and "America," do not seem to know they are dancing. However, because dance is the dominant mode in *West Side Story*, it is easier for the audience to accept the convention that the entire group knows the steps and can perform them in unison, since these characters have a history with each other, and dance is the way they "speak" to one another; they perform their coherent group identity through a shared physicality. Other dance-oriented shows, like the more recent *Contact* (1999), use this same approach.

A greater understanding of dance as a mode of communication in musicals, and of the circumstances that cause it to be the dominant one, and of the role and function of dance in musicals in general, provides a basis for a more in-depth analysis of liminality as it is related to dance in musicals. While liminal challenges related to dance abound in musicals, they may be less obvious in their original Broadway productions because of the skill of the performers, but they become immediately apparent when danced in amateur productions by performers who lack the virtuosity of professionals. Thus, while the extended dance breaks in *Damn Yankees* (1955) performed by the athletic baseball players dazzled on Broadway, they can become awkward and disjointed when danced by inexperienced schoolboys. Still, the performers' skills alone cannot fully address the questions raised in musicals wherein characters that have just communicated solely by speaking or singing suddenly abandon those modes and begin dancing. Indeed, although a smooth transition from one presentational form (singing) to another (dancing) might have become normalized during the rise of the integrated musical, and therefore expected in musical theater, some musicals simply sidestep the liminal challenges of introducing dance, and instead allow their characters to "burst out dancing." In musicals that deliberately reject the earlier integrated model, like *Spring Awakening*, the sudden eruption of dance makes sense, for the show's structure from the start establishes that movement is divorced from the more realistic scenes and nonphysicalized songs. In *Spring Awakening*, dance serves a clear dramatic function—it comments upon the turmoil of the inner lives of the tormented teens at its heart (a similar function to its use in *Oklahoma!*'s "Dream Ballet," but with a critical change—the audience is not asked to view the dancing in *Spring Awakening* as occurring in some separate dream state). The challenge arises when considering dance in musicals that live in the space between integrated and nonintegrated musical, a liminal arena of its own that creates challenges for audiences. For example, in many of the recent live-action musicals that Disney has produced for television and film, characters "burst out dancing," often with large groups doing synchronized choreography. While this mirrors the approach noted above that *Spring Awakening* uses, there is a critical change—in *Spring Awakening*, the characters never seem cognizant of the fact they are dancing (an approach that supports the idea that their dancing embodies their inner lives), whereas in the Disney pieces, like *High School Musical* (2006), at times the characters know they are dancing, and at other times they don't. The distinctions are not particularly clear and can lead to a convention that is confusing. Thus, when the elaborate dance breaks out in the middle of "Get'cha Head in the Game" in Disney's film version of *High School Musical*, not only is there no explanation given for why the young basketball players suddenly begin dancing in unison (which would suggest a world in which the characters don't know they are singing and dancing), but the number also defies all logic, since the high school pupils are singing and then dancing about keeping leading man Troy from singing and dancing (thus acknowledging that singing and dancing happen in this world, or at least in the backstage musical world the film sometimes embraces, while *also* embracing the convention that they don't know they are dancing). Simply put, if the characters, like those in *High School Musical*, do not understand that they are participating in this ritual of dance and therefore experiencing, by dancing, the transformation that Turner describes, the liminal moment has actually been avoided, not addressed. While technically, the introduction of dancing does still force a transition, and does indeed cause Fischer-Lichte's sense of "destabilization," muddying the circumstances of the transition as in the example described above causes not only destabilization but also confusion, which impedes the spectators' engagement with the performance, either as diegesis or performative feature.[14]

When dance in a musical is used in such a way that it is not "jarring or comic in the extreme" (particularly when that is not the musical's desired effect) and instead engages the spectators more fully in the performance, either by seeming "like the most natural thing in the world" or alternatively, like a deliberately nonnaturalistic performance (as in the aforementioned *Spring Awakening*), a variety of factors come into play.[15] All are indicative of a creative process in the original structuring of the musical that includes input from the choreographer in its early stages. While it is difficult to tell in a collaborative art form like the musical who specifically is responsible for each decision, certainly the major Broadway choreographers (and director/choreographers in a more significant way) have played a critical role in shaping their successes in the area of dance. For those musicals that feature dance as their dominant mode of communication, the challenge is more easily overcome, as dance is introduced first and is frequently returned to throughout, since it is the primary language of the piece. However, for shows that do not feature dance as their dominant mode of communication, but still feature at least some dance, which are certainly the norm for Broadway, their creators have generally used three ways to successfully navigate the liminal spaces. First, they might incorporate dance in a diegetic fashion—often the choice of so-called integrated musicals (usually as part of an in-show performance, where the characters know that they are dancing); second, they might use dance in an overtly nonrealistic context (where the characters typically don't know that they are dancing, though they might), as in many modern, postintegration musicals; or third, they embrace an aesthetic that was more common in the preintegration era, in which plot is less dominant and shows can function, for the most part, as revues.

ANALYZING MUSIC THEATER PRACTICES

The choice to use dance in a diegetic manner is a common technique by which choreographers deal with the liminality that exists when introducing dance. Most often in musicals, the liminal moments are addressed by placing the show in a metatheatrical context. While not all backstage musicals feature diegetic numbers, wherein the characters know they are dancing, most do, and they are common staples of the genre, both on Broadway and on film. These diegetic dance numbers function in a performative context in the show; the dancers *know* they are dancing, and they dance to entertain. The transitional moment is minimized, and indeed naturalized, since the circumstances of the musical's book call for dance to begin then. In addition, in the context of the show, rehearsal for the number is often shown or implied (*A Chorus Line* [1975] is an excellent example of this). Thus, as noted above, the characters can do complex steps in unison because they have all learned them, either at some earlier time, or in the context of the show. Most Fosse shows embrace this performative aesthetic: *Chicago* (1975) functions as a series of vaudeville acts (the audience is even directly addressed), while *Pippin* (1972) embraces the performative convention of a narrator, and commedia-style performance as its unifying concept. Jerome Robbins makes use of diegetic dance numbers in the performance-centered *Gypsy* (1959), in "The Small House of Uncle Thomas" ballet in *The King and I* (1951), danced in the context of the show as a performance, and even in the less overtly dance-oriented *Fiddler on the Roof* (1964), where the famed bottle dance is danced by men attending a wedding who are performing a traditional wedding feat. This performance context eliminates the need for elaborate justifications in the integrated musical since the dance is a performance within the show, the characters recognize that, and the plot calls for it. Indeed, this mostly diegetic approach is what American television musical series *Glee* (2009) and *Smash* (2012) do differently from their failed predecessors, most notably *Cop Rock* (1990) and *Viva Laughlin* (2007), and may have contributed to their successes in the uniquely realistic medium of television. Curiously, this approach to liminality tends to minimize the transformative effects of the transition on both the character and the spectator, precisely because the liminal space is normalized and naturalized. It is of interest here that while in the rest of *Oklahoma!* this diegetic approach is generally what the show uses, the "Dream Ballet" provides an opportunity for the show to reject the normalization and naturalization of dance at other moments in the show, like in the previously discussed "Kansas City." The "Dream Ballet," in providing an alternative space for dance to happen both literally and structurally, also makes room for the transformation that Laurey, the character, experiences as she blossoms into Curly's lover, and the simultaneous transformation the audience experiences in watching the ballet transpire.

At the other end of the spectrum, some musicals deal with liminality by creating entirely unrealistic contexts for the show (either as a whole or in part—like the "Dream Ballet" described above), in which breaking into dance numbers is not out of place, but actually reinforces the notion that the piece has departed from realism. The most frequent way choreographers achieve this is in fantasy or dream sequences in musicals. When they are not diegetic in their approach, as is most common, this is the way musicals usually function on film or on television. Jane Feuer posits that these dream worlds are necessary, particularly for the mediated musical, because they hold "at bay the imaginative excess to which musicals are prone."[16] The film version of *Chicago* (2002) takes this fantasy sequence idea to the extreme, effectively having every number function as Roxie's dreams in an otherwise realistic world. On stage, *Spring Awakening* on Broadway deliberately rebelled against realism, as noted above, blithely mixing periods and styles and employing Bill T. Jones's entirely unrealistic choreography to reinforce the disconnect from one another the characters feel. Certainly the dream ballet is also a prime example of embracing fantasy in Broadway dance, at least for one number. Within a relatively realistic show like *Oklahoma!*, for example, the dream ballet gave choreographer Agnes de Mille the freedom to employ an entirely different means of storytelling. As noted above, de Mille used the separate dancing chorus, common at the time of *Oklahoma!*'s premiere, and dream doubles for the leads to perform the ballet, which was not only practical, but also creatively reinforced the idea that the sequence was a fantasy, happening outside the realm of the relative reality of the rest of the show. In fact, it made justifying why Laurey no longer speaks but dances even clearer, since this isn't the real Laurey at all, but a dream double who operates under different conventions. Modern-day triple-threat performers, as in the Susan Stroman–choreographed, Trevor Nunn–directed 2002 Broadway revival, make dance doubles unnecessary, but that change fundamentally alters how dance functions in musicals. For example, when Laurey, the character, is a spectator watching the ritual of the dream ballet, as she was in de Mille's original ballet, she is transformed by her viewing experience of this liminal ritual, but when Laurey is a participant in the ritual enacting her marriage and her beloved Curly's death, she is still transformed by the liminal experience, but in a fundamentally different way and without the relative distance of spectatorship. When Laurey experiences her new femininity, and her sensuality, and her deep attraction to and love for Curly when she dances her own role in the ballet, the character, in a dream state or not, is changed by having had those experiences.

Between these two extremes of backstage musicals and fantasy pieces rest musicals that aren't particularly story driven and rely on conventions for and approaches to dance common in early, preintegration musicals. These shows take on a revue quality, since the plots tend toward the simple and dance works in these musicals precisely because they are not as tightly constructed (in liminal terms, the borders are more fluid). In reality, these exist somewhere between the first two approaches, with choreographers creating numbers that use elements of the diegetic approach to performance, because even the characters accept that they do not need to ignore the audience (embracing revue conventions), mixed with elements of the unrealistic approach (simple or even sometimes implausible plots). While musicals written before *Oklahoma!* even in revival often rely on this third option, newer shows with an old-fashioned feel—like *Crazy for You* (1992), *Thoroughly Modern Millie* (2002), or *The Drowsy Chaperone* (2006)—have also found success with this approach.[17]

These approaches consider ways, particularly in the writing process, to address challenges in the transitions involving liminality and dance. But what of those shows that don't effectively use those approaches listed above? How best can choreographers and director/choreographers grapple with the challenges those transitions present? The simple solution that most choreographers turn to is to manufacture diegetic functions for the dance—one that often pushes the musical toward an integration aesthetic. First, choreographers can create a storyline for the dance itself, the most common of which is a "dance off" (a variation of which Rick Altman calls "the challenge dance") that makes the sequence a competition in movement prowess between two individuals or two groups and is perhaps most famously executed in "The Barn Dance" in the original (film) version of *Seven Brides for Seven Brothers* (1954).[18] This inherently gives the dance, examples of which also include "America" from *West Side Story* and "Shoeless Joe" from *Damn Yankees*, a diegetic function because the characters know they are dancing since they watch their rival(s) dance and respond accordingly with movements that escalate in complexity—this is the ritual of the challenge. The other approach choreographers commonly take also manufactures a diegetic function, this time by having the dancers reintroduce another mode of communicating back into the dance, generally speech. Typically, this employs ad-libbed noises and dialogue, which effectively break down the divide between the dance break and number as a whole, since both now use movement and voice to convey the message. This approach is diegetic because the noises indicate that the characters know that they are dancing, and they are now dancing in the context of the story. The dance break in the Kathleen Marshall–choreographed "Too Darn Hot" from the 1999 revival of *Kiss Me, Kate* on Broadway is an excellent example of this approach.

BEST PRACTICES

Of course, these late-stage Band-Aids reiterate the fact that problems with liminal moments involving dance are best addressed during the creation process of a new musical (or during the revision process, with a revival/revisal), ideally using a complete creative team that employs a choreographer or director/choreographer. For creators of musicals, making conscious choices about what mode of communication will be used when and being clear about what the dominant communicative mode will be can provide a framework for most effectively incorporating dance into the musical. Also, being cognizant of the role and function of dance in the musical during the creative process can help the creators and future directors and choreographers of musicals to navigate their liminal spaces. Successful navigation of the liminal spaces related to dance in a musical can provide a platform for transformation for the dancing characters and for the viewing audience. Indeed, like Laurey in Oklahoma's "Dream Ballet," whose character is transformed, or "unbound," as Turner might argue, by her dream ballet, characters in musicals who dance can find their identities expanded to include expression of their innermost selves through their bodies.[19] In turn, audiences who view this dancing, which can deal with its liminality either through a gradual transition or an abrupt eruption, can likewise find themselves transformed, ideally by being drawn into the musical experience.

Creative teams often try several tactics to successfully navigate the liminality of dance in musicals, typically using one of three approaches: using dance with a diegetic function (as in integrated musicals), using dance in a deliberately unrealistic way (as in postintegration musicals), or using dance in some combination of the two (as in preintegration musicals). For musicals with a less clear approach to dance written into their structure, choreographers and director/choreographers most often try to manufacture a diegetic approach to dance sequences. All of these approaches require careful handling of the shifts between the various modes of communication in a musical, and specifically require thoughtful analysis of how dance is used in the musical and how the liminal spaces will be addressed. The great care that these dance moments require in their construction is indicative of the vital space that dance has taken as the home to the physical gesture of the musical. Musicals are the sum of their disparate parts, to be sure, but effectively communicating through the language of dance in the musical can shape a truly unique performance experience, which, unlike any other art form, can allow a character to develop and even evolve through words, and music, and most visually and perhaps, most viscerally, through the action of dance.

NOTES

1. Graham Wood, "Why Do They Start to Sing and Dance All of a Sudden? Examining the Film Musical," in *The Cambridge Companion to the Musical*, 2nd ed., ed. William A. Everett and Paul Laird (Cambridge: Cambridge University Press, 2008), 306.
2. Victor Turner, *From Ritual to Theatre: The Human Seriousness of Play* (New York: Performing Arts Journal Publications, 1982), 84.
3. Erika Fischer-Lichte, *The Transformative Power of Performance: A New Aesthetics*, Trans. Saskya Iris Jain (New York: Routledge, 2008), 176.
4. Fischer-Lichte, *Transformative Power*, 148.
5. Ibid., 177.
6. Ibid., *Transformative Power*, 179.
7. Ibid., *Transformative Power*, 177.
8. Jane Feuer, *The Hollywood Musical* (Bloomington: Indiana University Press, 1982), 8.
9. Turner, *From Ritual to Theatre*, 47.
10. Fischer-Lichte, *Transformative Power*, 178.
11. Ibid., *Transformative Power*, 177.
12. Feuer, *The Hollywood Musical*, 9.
13. Scott McMillin, *The Musical as Drama* (Princeton, NJ: Princeton University Press, 2006), 8.
14. Fischer-Lichte, *Transformative Power*, 148.
15. Wood, "Why Do They Start," 306.
16. Feuer, *The Hollywood Musical*, 68.
17. Dates reflect the premieres of these shows on Broadway, though perhaps because of the period feel of each show, their gestation in each case has been somewhat drawn out: *Crazy for You* (1992) recycled much of its material from *Girl Crazy* (1930),

Thoroughly Modern Millie (2002) began life at San Diego's La Jolla Playhouse in 2000, and *The Drowsy Chaperone* (2006) sprang from a Canadian bachelor party in 1997.

18. Rick Altman, *The American Film Musical* (Bloomington: Indiana University Press, 1987), 171.

19. Turner, *From Ritual to Theatre*, 84.

CHAPTER 6

"Love, Let Me Sing You"

The Liminality of Song and Dance in

LaChiusa's Bernarda Alba *(2006)*

MATTHEW LOCKITT

Song is expected in a musical. From my seat in the darkened auditorium I eagerly anticipate it. Characters interact, engaged in conversation. In my seat, I wait. New information is revealed complicating the dramatic situation. Then it happens; something exciting and theatrical is occurring. The sound of music intrudes, pulsing under their conversation—a precursor to that inevitable moment when one of the characters will stop talking and start to sing. This is what I have waited for, why I am here. From my seat in the auditorium I register this shift at a visceral level. In my body I feel the character's drive, or emotional pulse. And depending upon the context and execution, the absurdity of someone bursting into song is not only thrilling, it can become the most natural expression of a dramatic moment. I am captivated by this heightened theatrical sensibility, the aptitude to articulate specific dramatic moments through song. And yet for others this fundamental characteristic, that which makes a musical *musical*, is a point of contention—the very thing that detractors of the form are averse to. Writers in creating these moments construct transitions to bridge the gaps between speech and song, while performers discover ways of navigating the leap from one to the other. According to director and choreographer Rob Marshall, "the biggest challenge of doing a musical is figuring out conceptually how to make it work, because you have to solve the biggest problem of all: why do people sing? Why is there music?"[1]

As a practitioner, I find myself engaging with questions like those raised by Rob Marshall. However, rather than justifying song "conceptually" (I accept that a character within a musical is going to sing),[2] I am motivated to identify the dramatic catalyst for song, and to understand the subsequent action that occupies the character throughout the course of the number. Liminality, as a state of transformation, can be utilized to address the function of song and dance, and their relationship to the book of the musical within a theoretical and performative context. The action of these gestures may be interpreted via the appropriation and application of the concepts of the liminal and the liminoid as theorized by Victor Turner. To illustrate, consideration will be given to the ways in which Michael John LaChiusa mediates both character and audience through these transitions in his musical *Bernarda Alba*. Recent musical theater scholarship interrogates the relationship between book and number; the lyrical and musical repetition inherent in song creates moments of suspension temporarily halting the progression of the plot.[3] The subsequent debate, as we well know, positions the disjunctive aesthetics of Bertolt Brecht against the integrated conception of Richard Wagner. Yet neither model adequately addresses the placement of song or articulates the dramatic function of a number. Granted, Scott McMillin acknowledges that song tends to mark "turning points" or moments of "recognition," at which juncture "the plot is suspended for the time of the number."[4] But this does not account for the dramatic action a character engages with through the act of repetition.

In contrast to McMillin, who argues that song suspends plot, director and teacher Aaron Frankel suggests that "a show song is a heightened action springing from a dramatic context, and as a result reveals character, develops situation, forwards plot. It lands somewhere else from where it started, it makes a difference."[5] Practitioners identify song as a space of movement, of action—the opposite of suspension. Composer and lyricist Jason Robert Brown recognizes a comparative difference in the structures of pop songs and songs written for the theater. The former "are about establishing a mood, sustaining it, and finishing with it," while "good theater songs go from one end of an idea to a different place."[6] A tension thus exists between the perception of scholars and the intention of authors: a tension between suspension and action.

Perhaps the challenge for many musical theater scholars who also work practically with the form is to reconcile these conflicting perceptions. To achieve this, a theoretical model able to acknowledge the repetitions inherent in the lyric, melody, rhythm, and harmony of song, while simultaneously accounting for the dramatic action and the transformation of character through the song, is required. But is it possible for such a model to provide a mutual language that can be shared by scholars and practitioners as a tool for both analysis and rehearsal? Before being able to pursue this complexity any further, it is important to address the role of song within musical theater.

THE FUNCTION OF SONG

Musical theater utilizes two primary song forms. One of these McMillin identifies as "diegetic" song[7]; the other he terms the "out-of-the-blue" number.[8] The diegetic song is a tangible song that exists within the "universe"[9] of the musical during which the consequent suspension of plot is comprehensible as the characters are either engaged in, or witnessing, the act of performance.[10] By contrast, the instances of "people opening up and starting to sing"[11] out-of-the-blue emerge from the dramatic situation as direct expressions of character, and are commonly referred to as "book songs." Where the "diegetic" song is of the world of the book, the "book song" is of the book itself.

It is these out-of-the-blue songs that are at odds with the supposed suspension of plot as a result of the repetition of the structural elements of song: lyric, rhythm, melody, and harmony. Rather than song being exclusively a moment of one or the other, perhaps it is a juncture in which suspension and action coexist. McMillin only observes the structural components founded on repetition; he does not account for what is happening *within* the repetition. What is occurring beyond what McMillin terms "the spirit of repetition and the pleasure of difference"[12] is fundamental to understanding a given character in a specific situation. On a dramatic level, what motivates the authors to engage a character in the structures of song, in a state of *active suspension*? Erika Fischer-Lichte, in her book *The Transformative Power of Performance*, states, "when oppositions dissolve into one another our attention focuses on the transition from one state to the next. The space between the opposites opens up; the in-between thus becomes a preferred category."[13]

Fischer-Lichte identifies the liminal space that emerges when dichotomies "collapse."[14] In this case, the opposing energies of suspension and action collapse, or merge. This results in what Raymond Knapp refers to as a state of "suspended animation," slowing the movement of the book.[15] This merging of structural *suspension* with a specific dramatic *action* results in the opening of a liminal state. The gap, or "threshold,"[16] that exists at the point when speech transforms into song may be perceived as a liminal moment. However, Gustavo Pérez Firmat acknowledges a broader conceptualization: "According to Turner, liminality should be looked upon not only as a transformation between states but as a state itself,"[17] "a place of habitation."[18] To explore the notion that song is a space a character actively inhabits for a period, the two aforementioned models of liminal theory (the liminal and the liminoid) will be applied to the two outlined song types (book and diegetic song) respectively. Turner developed his liminal model of social drama as a mechanism to analyze dramatic events within indigenous communities. Alternatively, his conception of the liminoid state offers a means of addressing the liminal-like suspension that occurs in postindustrial leisure activities. Turner perceives a differentiation in attitude defining these two theoretical states: "Optation pervades the liminoid phenomenon, obligation the liminal."[19] Therefore, the four-stage process of Turner's social drama (breach, crisis, redress, restoration / acknowledgment of schism) will be employed to explicate the out-of-the-blue song as an *obligatory* dramatic action. The analysis will focus on the sewing circle sequence that opens the second act of *Bernarda Alba*, and a group of songs I term the "sister's suite." Throughout this sequence Magdalena sings a faux-folk tune that will subsequently lead us to a discussion of the diegetic songs as *optional* liminoid moments of choice.

LIMINAL PHASES: "OUT OF THE BLUE" OR "OBLIGATION"?

Bernarda Alba concerns a widow who mothers her five adult daughters with an oppressive hand in order to protect them from the world and men. Retained by their mother within the shuttered house for the period of mourning, the women occupy a ritual liminal state during which their lives are symbolically suspended.[20] Turner depicts liminal spaces as "suspensions of quotidian reality, occupying privileged spaces where people are allowed to think about how they think, about the terms in which they conduct their thinking, or to feel about how they feel in daily life."[21]

This ritual suspension of the quotidian reality allows the women the space to think about and to work through their process of grief. This frames the dramatic action of the musical within an overarching liminal context. Additionally, the concept of liminal suspension extends to the experience of attending the performance of the musical. With regard to her aforementioned proposal that a state of liminality occurs "when oppositions dissolve into one another," Fischer-Lichte continues: "Again and again we have seen that the aesthetic experience enabled by performances can primarily be described as a liminal experience, capable of transforming the experiencing subject."[22] Fischer-Lichte acknowledges a number of potential binaries at play. Among these is that of the performers and audience, who, as the house lights dim, merge into the experience of that single act of performance as it occupies the auditorium for a time. The "viewing subject" experiences a receding of their quotidian reality to the periphery of awareness for the duration of the performance before returning to the everyday via the threshold of the theater foyer.[23]

Alternatively, the description that Turner offers of the liminal state may be interpreted as a metaphorical hermeneutic parallel to the structure of the musical. Read within this context, the world of the book comes to represent the quotidian reality of the characters, their everyday actions, while song and dance emerge as the privileged suspensions of that reality, an honor to which not all characters are privy. Within this hermeneutic structure, the two song forms suspend this reality in different ways. Furthermore, the two liminal models conceived by Turner reveal the particular qualities inherent in each of these performative gestures.

Within the sequence under scrutiny, the liminal is manifested in the form of soliloquies as the women engage with their inner concerns. Four of the daughters—Angustias, Magdalena, Martirio, and Amelia—gather with Poncia, the housekeeper, to sew. Adela, the youngest, sleeping late, is absent. Throughout the sequence, mini dramatic events rupture the microcosmic society, creating a series of liminal phases. LaChiusa pronounces these ruptures through the deliberate disjunction of the songs on a structural level, signifying the emotional displacement of the characters as they momentarily disengage from the quotidian world of the house.

Applied to these potentially problematic out-of-the-blue numbers, the process of social drama accounts for the preceding gap as well as the dramatic action of the song itself. First a "breach," either physical or verbal, political or ethical, must occur. This breach instigates the second phase, "crisis": What do I or we do about it? This phase leads to a period of "redress," the third stage; the circumstance is investigated, various positions are considered, and the crisis is worked through. Eventually, the final stage is reached as a decision is made; either one of "restoration" to the immediate world, or "acknowledgment of schism," resulting in a form of separation from the community.[24] In this application the breach is not necessarily a negative occurrence, as the word may imply. Rather it equates to what Tracey Moore and Alison Bergman refer to as "The Moment Before [...] an event or a trigger that creates the need for song."[25] The resulting crisis instigates a process of negotiation, or consideration, conveyed through the process of redress (an active engagement with the reiterations of song) leading to the final decision phase.

As the women sew, Magdalena attempts to "liven up the atmosphere" with a "depressing" little folk tune; LaChiusa weaves "Magdalena," an a cappella faux-folk song, through the scene as a structural element to bind the five individual stories together.[26] The nighttime visitations of the suitor Pepé el Romano dominate the conversation. Angustias, the older, wealthy half-sister, is betrothed to Pepé, for whom all of the sisters seem to hold a torch. However, his serenades are not intended for Angustias alone, and the other women know this. Angustias is the first to enter a liminal state.

Envious of Angustias, and aware of Pepé's inclinations toward Adela, Magdalena incites the breach:

MAGDALENA: You've always been known for your great beauty.
ANGUSTIAS: Thank god, I'm getting out of this hell.
MAGDALENA: *Are you sure?*
MARTIRIO: Let's change the subject.[27]

The attempt by Martirio to avert the topic, and Amelia's suggestion to let some air into the room, indicates the tension resulting from the newly opened breach. Angustias is confronted with a crisis, a dramatic question requiring an answer. The liminal state as Turner defines it is one of "obligation,"[28] and Angustias is obligated to address her inner crisis: "what if Pepé doesn't love me and I cannot escape this house?" LaChiusa manipulates the temporal space as Angustias enters the third stage of the process, the period of redress: the realm of repetition. (In each of the liminal states of this sequence, the women become a Chorus supplying rhythmic and vocal support.)

"Angustias" is strophic in form, with a dialogue insert between the two stanzas. Each section is melodically identical and can be broken into four smaller units of thought: (1) the facts; (2) "I don't understand"; (3) Pepé's song; and (4) the truth. As Angustias moves through the repetition toward a decision, LaChiusa charts her progression through shifts in tone of lyric and harmonic development.

A gentle introduction of repeated open fourths in a short/long rhythm suggests the beat of the "heart" Angustias is attempting to hear. The Chorus of women rhythmically layers the space with flamenco *pitos*[29] while giving voice to the continuous mantra Angustias repeats in her head, but is yet to acknowledge in her heart. Angustias begins by laying out the facts:

> My lover's song is sung so sweetly.
> (I can't hear him in my heart).
> At my window singing gently.
> (I can't hear him in my heart).
> And I should be a happy woman.[30]

The melody repeats for the first two phrases, suggesting two possible intentions: an attempt to find comfort in the consistency of the facts and a hesitancy, or reluctance, to move forward toward the truth. However, the third phrase unsettles the established melodic order leaping to a high C on "should," extending the range by a second. This admission of confusion, or introduction of doubt, "I don't understand," allows the melody to open out and carry her forward.

The third unit of thought, in which LaChiusa has Angustias describe the way Pepé's song rises and disappears into the night, is an extended phrase that ushers forth in a single breath. The melody, reflecting the text, ascends chromatically. Yet LaChiusa anchors the ascending line to the root E-flat, building tension through the oscillating, ever-widening leaps. The gravitational pull of the tonic reveals her attempt to remain firm, resisting the inevitability of the truth, while the rise and fall of the melodic line also mimics that of anxious breathing as the phrase propels Angustias to admit, "But I can't hear him in my heart."[31] LaChiusa positions this realization around the dominant pitch of B-flat, not the certainty of the tonic-centered mantra of the Chorus. On the key word "heart," Angustias surrenders to a short, flamenco-inspired melisma. The melisma is part of the flamenco singer's "search for expressive force,"[32] a technique considered to be "one of the more effective ways of exploring feelings."[33] Angustias, vocally exploring the notes around the unresolved fifth degree of the scale, expresses the inexpressible. LaChiusa gives Angustias a moment's pause to listen, before repeating the phrase at the lower, tonic-centered pitch of the Chorus. This lower pitch implies a quieter coming-to-terms with this long-denied truth, a truth that the Chorus echoes.

Although Angustias has admitted that she is unable to hear Pepé in her heart, she has neither accepted (acknowledgement of schism) or rejected (restoration) the truth. Therefore, Angustias is unable to leave the liminal phase even though LaChiusa returns the women to the sewing circle. LaChiusa continues the syncopated pulse of the introduction as underscore, marked rhythmically by the heel of the foot, with an added tongue "cluck" on the fourth beat.

The conversation resumes where it left off; the liminal state occurring in the space between the lines of dialogue.

AMELIA: Let's get some air in here.
(*Angustias gets up and goes to the door.* [First chorus])
Martirio: Last night I couldn't sleep—it was so hot.[34]

Inevitably, the conversation returns to the night visitations; Poncia reports hearing Pepé two and a half hours after Amelia believes he retired. Angustias, denying the accusation, experiences a further breach and returns to the state of redress. LaChiusa intensifies the underscore to indicate this shift, replacing the purely rhythmic pulse with the reintroduction of the syncopated, harmonic ostinato of the heart, followed by a restatement of the rhythmic *pitos* pattern. Magdalena attempts to gain Angustias's attention, but fails: "She's ignoring us."[35] LaChiusa again manipulates the temporality revealing the liminal sphere. Angustias resumes the redress of her thoughts, working toward a resolution, as the words of the chorus once more echo in her heart.

It could be argued that the repetition of strophic form occurs primarily to meet the requirements of song structure. Further, Carolyn Abbate suggests, "the dialectical tension between narrative metamorphosis and structural repetition is itself a poetic device" designed to focus "the reader-listener to fix on the meaning of the words and not their sound: to listen to the story."[36] However, when we are faced with our own individual crises, we will often reiterate the issue to ourselves or to confidants until we are able to reach a suitable, or functional, solution: the decision to reintegrate or accept the irreparable rift. The same is also true if we are overtly excited about something. This is often an obligatory process that consumes our mental attention until we have moved through to a resolution. This is the same process in which Angustias is engaged; theatrically heightened repetition of melody, rhythm, and harmony aid her.

The acknowledgment that she cannot hear Pepé alters her perception. Although the melodic repetition reflects the four units of thought identified earlier, Angustias no longer maintains the romantic image of him "singing gently." Now, Angustias, recalling the facts more honestly, admits:

> My lover's face is cloaked in shadow.
> (I can't hear him in my heart).
> Very near yet very distant.[37]

LaChiusa develops this tonal shift, thickening and darkening the harmonic texture, while increasing the degrees of dissonance. This maturation of the harmonic color and imagery move the repeats beyond mere restatement; Angustias has changed.

"And I should be a happy woman" is the first direct quote of lyric and melody.[38] Angustias's restatement of this phrase requires consideration. This begins to encroach upon the domain of the performer and the variables of interpretation. Actors are encouraged to listen actively and to discover their lines anew each time they deliver them; the characters have never said these particular words before. A similar sense of discovery is applicable to the lyrics, and to a degree the melody, if song is to remain a dramatically active space. Angustias, in her efforts to reconcile her inner conflict, is articulating these thoughts for the first time. But to reiterate, song is structural repetition and a character engaged in song will inevitably repeat thoughts. Therefore, a character should be either expressing a fresh perspective, deliberately reiterating a point, or holding onto something with each restatement.

Angustias sings "And I should be a happy woman" twice.[39] The first reveals an attempt to address the second thought unit, "I don't understand." This may be the first time Angustias has recognized this uncertainty. However, given the facts and her change of perception, the reiteration of this statement should result from a different intention. The development of the accompanying texture suggests an increase of emotion. Filtered through the sensibilities of an individual performer, the line may be an acknowledgment of the freedom Angustias risks losing; or perhaps it is a frustrated assertion, "I am the one who is betrothed; I should be happy."

Inevitably, the melody resumes its oscillating chromatic ascension related to the now offensive serenade. Angustias recognizes the difference between being sung to, and sung for; "it's not for me, it's not for me," she repeats. The Chorus finally join voices with Angustias as she adamantly declares: "And I can't hear him in my heart," once more extending "heart" into a melisma. The slight change of lyric from "but" to "and I can't" demonstrates the progression from surprise to acceptance. She returns to the tonic-centered pitch to repeat the central phrase, implying total acceptance of the situation—if LaChiusa had allowed her to resolve on the E-flat. Rather, he manipulates Angustias to a more ambiguous conclusion, the unresolved fifth degree of the scale, while the women provide the tonic base.[40] Although Angustias understands her predicament, she is not resolved in accepting it. Therefore, rather than acknowledge the irreparable schism of her situation, Angustias chooses restoration, to continue with the engagement as though nothing has changed. A loveless marriage is preferable to a life stuck in the house of her mother. This choice, motivated by her desire for freedom, ultimately heightens the dramatic stakes and impacts the ensuing conflict of the drama. Her decision reached, Angustias is once again able to participate in the quotidian world where the sisters continue their attempt to gain her attention.

During this number the temporal plane oscillates between the "real time" of the house, the contracted, yet protracted time of Angustias' thought process (through which the viewing subject gains insight into the character), and the actual time of the performance experienced by the viewer. The information conveyed through the soliloquy reveals the complexity of the situation, while the music provides an emotional pulse, "the character's heartbeat,"[41] and the flamenco inflections augment the atmosphere. These elements combine to enhance the narrative experience for the reader, in much the same way that contemplative or descriptive passages do in fiction.[42] LaChiusa thinks "in terms of songs, that's the reason we do musicals. Why are we there if we're not going to hear a song? It's much different from a play."[43] But it concerns more than just hearing a song; it is about the level of narrative information relayed through the song. Roland Barthes proposes that there are two primary aspects to narrative structure: "functions" and "indices."[44] Song, considering the layers of information it is able to transmit, may reflect the qualities Barthes associates with the latter aspect. This narrative level refers "not to a complementary and consequential act [those qualities belonging to functions] but to a more or less diffuse concept which is nevertheless necessary to the meaning of the story: psychological indices concerning the characters, data regarding their identity, notations of 'atmosphere,' and so on."[45] These elements reflect those used to describe the narrative information conveyed during "Angustias," above: character, emotion, and atmosphere. However, an important function of the song is that Angustias makes a decision by its conclusion, a decision that acts in "a complementary and consequential" manner. Her decision to acknowledge schism has consequences for the remainder of the action. Therefore, the song can also be categorized as a "function."[46] Similarly, a song portraying a dramatic exchange between two or more characters, unlike the internal soliloquies in *Bernarda Alba*, may, depending on the variables, be more function than index.

Next, Amelia and Martirio, respectively, find themselves negotiating the obligatory repetitions within the liminal. Having discussed "Angustias" in detail to provide a template, I consider "Amelia" and "Martirio" in brief, indicating the key stages. The women primarily converse about men, and the breach for all of them results from this talk of men. However, each encounters a different crisis and reaction to their breach. Naive Amelia experiences embarrassment at the talk, recalling the first confusing flushes of lust, while Martirio scrutinizes the scorn she receives for her appearance.

In contrast to the anguished realization Angustias is required to negotiate, Amelia blushingly enters into a daydream. Her crisis, or dramatic question, is implicit within her lyric: "What was that feeling?"[47] Amelia recollects a chance encounter with a boy, playing his drum made of sheepskin. The members of the Chorus slap their thighs, providing the percussive beats of the drum; the Maid and the Servant gently tease Amelia.

"Amelia" is reflective of the meanderings of a daydream, consisting of five sections, the fifth a short reprise of the first. Section A (mm. 1–11) introduces Amelia, establishing her sweet, innocent nature. The B section (mm. 12–20) concerns the boy. The repetition of incomplete thoughts, "But today—The boy—Today the boy," suggest her nervousness.[48] Section C (mm. 21–35) introduces the drum, the Chorus repeating variations of "Ta-rum-pum!" in imitation of both the drum and her pounding chest. The drum "bursts" releasing into section D (mm. 35–40), two sequences of "Amelia" being called, returning her to the brief reprise of the opening statement, as she asks the question, "what was that feeling?" twice more.[49] Although there are small repetitions within the short sections, the absence of larger stanzaic repetitions suggests a free-form daydream.

The song also resists the notion that a character must reach a decision by the final cadence: Amelia remains none the wiser. LaChiusa acknowledges this inconclusive ending by having Amelia finish on a high E, the unresolved fifth degree of A major. He virtually removes the accompaniment, leaving Amelia exposed, suspended on the unresolved question over a sustained open fifth.

"Amelia" bears no consequence for the dramatic action, but provides an atmospheric counterpoint to the numbers around it. The song is what conductor Lehman Engel terms a "charm song": "the subject matter of the lyrics is light, [...] the musical setting is generally delicate, optimistic, and rhythmic."[50] Although no resolution is reached, Amelia is still obligated to enter the period of redress, overwhelmed by the curiously pleasant recollection of the boy. Interestingly, unlike Angustias, Amelia appears to be distracted in "real time," or longer. At the conclusion of her reverie, the conversation has progressed; LaChiusa drops her (and the audience) into the middle of Poncia telling the story of how she met her husband.

If the talk of men sets Amelia off into a charming diversion, Martirio confronts her demons. Maltreated at a younger age, with a collapsed opportunity of marriage, her breach results from the continuous discussion of men and husbands. Martirio confronts a very personal crisis—her physical self: "Am I any less than other women?"

"Martirio" has a relatively straightforward ABA′ structure. The two A sections relate directly to how men respond to her physical appearance; the B section concerns her yearnings. Martirio enters her phase of redress on the attack. Melodically, the A section is built on a series of repeated notes set to primarily monosyllabic words: "spit," "curse," "mock"; even the first syllables of accented words, "*howl*ing" and "*bitch*es," possess percussive qualities.[51]

LaChiusa softens the lyrics for the B section as Martirio muses over the words she might receive: "If I were beautiful They'd speak in the language of lovers."[52] He partners this with a lyrical melodic line that rises and falls, contrasting the earlier percussive repeated notes. Martirio realizes that although she may not be attractive like her sisters, she is still human and deserves to be loved. This forms the release, with LaChiusa giving her two extended melismas emphasizing the word "love" (mm. 37–52).[53]

Knowing that this is not her reality, Martirio returns to a melodically varied A′ section. LaChiusa restructures the melody to build momentum as she lists her faults in quick succession. However, her resolution to the tonic suggests a form of acceptance. Restoring herself within the community of the house, Martirio is motivated to protect at all costs the love that she knows, the unity of the family. Magdalena intrudes, singing her folk tune, which indicates a return to the house.

According to Fischer-Lichte, "the collapse of the opposition between art and reality and of all binaries resulting from this opposition transfers the participants into a liminal state."[54] This state may emerge when performers or audience members encounter a particular dramatic circumstance, and the boundaries between art (the dramatic event) and reality (their current life situation) blur to create an overt emotional, perhaps cathartic, response resulting from the identification with the material. For instance, someone consistently unlucky in love may connect to Martirio's plea or Angustias's acknowledgment of unrequited love. Similarly, viewers may blush at the memory of first meetings, an experience akin to that of Amelia's. The affect, resulting from the blurring of fact and fiction heightened by the application of music, may go some way to explaining the levels of visceral experiential pleasure gained by attending musicals.[55]

The final liminal turn of the sequence is "Adela." The song is ABCB in structure (verse, chorus, dance, chorus), and again, the four liminal stages are active. However, the primary focus of the analysis for this number will be the choreographic text created by Graciela Daniele, to ascertain how dance continues the process of redress.[56]

The breach occurs as Martirio indicates that she is aware of Adela's indiscretions with Pepé. Caught, Adela confronts her crisis: "How do I escape this life?" LaChiusa indicates this yearning with the tempo marking "Freely."[57]

"Adela" is a paean to independence. Through the chorus, she announces her intention to discard the black of mourning for her green dress, in which she will publicly dance in the arms of Pepé. In one respect, the dance represents this intention; yet, if read on a symbolic level, the sequence develops the liminal process. The verse preceding the chorus establishes her fears ("I won't be locked away like you") and her wants ("I want to know desire").[58] The "fears" share the same rigid, syncopated theme; the "wants" are rhythmically relaxed and conversational. Through dance, Adela further explores the tensions between her "fears" and "wants," kinetically continuing the process of redress.

Utilizing references to traditional flamenco dance combined with conventional Western choreography, Daniele creates a dialogue between the two styles, revealing a young woman caught between the traditional and the new. Daniele appropriates techniques, including *pitos* (clicking) and *zapateado* (stamping), as well as distinctive flamenco postural attitudes. Metaphorically, the flamenco represents the house and the order (or rather the oppression) Bernarda subjects her daughters to within it. Beyond providing atmosphere, LaChiusa manipulates the flamenco dramaturgically:

> It might sound chaotic, flamenco, when you hear it live, but it's very tightly organized. There's not one missed beat. There's no room for improvisation in flamenco, absolutely no room for it. But it goes out of control at the end of *Bernarda Alba* when they are pounding on the door, Actually what they are pounding on is the flamenco beat gone awry, to chaos.[59]

The dance negotiates these ideas of order and restriction, and the collapse of these structures. Robin Totton observes the "downward" nature of flamenco,[60] while Western dance strives for elevation. The Western elements, the layout, hitch-kick, and plié, for example, seem to react against, or erupt out of, the flamenco. At times, Adela appears caged, the choreography prowling in and around the seated Chorus, rather than occupying an open space. The heightened physicality also demonstrates the expression of an otherwise repressed sexuality. At the conclusion of the dance, she stands, arms extended overhead, reaching for something; yearning for elevation.

As the refrain returns, her decision is made to pursue her life and love: acknowledgment of schism. Yet Adela appears less assured, the tempo is slower, and the voice is exposed over a sparse accompaniment. This may result from a disquiet concerning the consequences of her decision or remorse at leaving her sisters. Maybe it is simply relief that a choice is made. Nevertheless, her commitment to this decision ultimately leads to her tragic end. Perhaps then, it also foreshadows this turn of events.

Magdalena, singing her folk tune, dovetails with Adela. But rather than return the women to the quotidian world, LaChiusa supplies a polyphonic coda, the women layering the liminal with their thoughts:

MAGDALENA: My pains, Mother, are not pains of hunger.
AMELIA: Sweet Amelia, no one ever spreads rumors of you.
ANGUSTIAS: And I should be a happy woman! I can't hear him in my heart.
MARTIRIO: I deserve my love!
ADELA: I won't give up and die like you! My heart can't hold a lie[61]

Suddenly, in unison, they proclaim the a cappella refrain Magdalena has sung throughout. The orchestra provides harmonic resolution, bringing the sequence to a close and returning the women to reality.

During this sequence the sisters negotiate the opposing energies of action and suspension, resulting in alterations to their physical and mental being. "Such transformations," Fischer-Lichte suggests, "create psychological, affective, energetic and motoric changes to the body."[62] These changes are manifest as liminal moments of song: Music and rhythm amplify the heartbeat of the character, while energy levels increase to support the symbolic act of "singing" and the motoric engagement with dance. The viewer also registers the affect of these transformations. Physical chemical reactions to the varying stimuli alter the mood and energy of the observer, echoing those being enacted/represented by the character/performer.[63]

Although "Magdalena" is integral to this sequence, Magdalena is not subject to the same dramatic or liminal forces as her sisters. Experiencing a breach, they are obligated to move through a process of redress, in an effort to attend, and resolve, a personal crisis. Of the decisions reached, Angustias (to reintegrate) and Adela (to segregate)most affect the dramatic action. Although the transformation in Martirio is slight, her decision to reintegrate reveals her subsequent motivation and attitude toward Adela. Amelia contradicts the rule that "characters are different at the end of the song (sometimes very subtly) than they were at the beginning," remaining unresolved.[64] The model of social drama, applied to the out-of-the-blue number, dramaturgically accounts for the liminal qualities of song. A character is not engaged in random expression, but obligated to work her way through the four-stage process. Alternatively, Magdalena does have a choice. This is evident in how "Magdalena" is utilized by LaChiusa.

LIMINOID PHASES: DIEGETIC SONGS OF CHOICE

The diegetic song is an act of performance within the quotidian world of the musical; the sisters in *Bernarda Alba* are aware of Magdalena singing. Conversely, she is not privy to their liminal vocalizations.[65] While her sisters are obliged to enter the liminal state of song, Magdalena chooses to sing at will. Granted, LaChiusa dictates when the "performer" must sing the refrain, but the character, within the moment, sings for the pleasure of singing. However, the number still creates a form of suspension within this world: "a pause is a pause even when the characters hear it as a pause."[66] Thus, the diegetic song occupies an alternative liminal sphere, the optional space Turner terms the "liminoid."[67]

Turner developed this alternative concept to address the liminal-like phenomena that arose within postindustrial society as work and leisure became independent of each other. The liminoid "resembles [the liminal] without being identical."[68] While the liminal occurs in the suspension of daily routine via an event of social interruption, the liminoid is present in the suspension of "life" through an engagement with "those genres of free-time activity, in which all previous standards and models are subjected to criticism, and fresh new ways of describing and interpreting sociocultural experience are formulated."[69] Turner identifies the liminoid in the works of "poets, philosophers, dramatists, novelists, painters, and the like."[70] These works offer avenues through which societal standards may be questioned and experience interpreted. To enter a state of liminoid suspension, a person chooses to, perhaps, read a novel or attend a play. This conception adjusts the earlier depiction of performance attendance as a liminal experience. Rather, as performance is no longer associated with the state or social obligation, to attend it is an act of choice: the liminoid.

The diegetic number mimics liminoid-like qualities and can provide potential spaces of criticism and interpretation. An act of performance within the "real" world of the musical, the diegetic song possesses the ability to comment on the events of the plot and the situation of the characters contained within that world. Consider the tongue-in-cheek warning presented in "Life upon the Wicked Stage" from *Show Boat* (1927), the relevance of "The Small House of Uncle Thomas" to the themes of *The King and I* (1951), and the social comment contained within "Over the Moon," Maureen's performance art in *Rent* (1996).

In *Bernarda Alba*, the diegetic numbers are primarily faux-folk songs. According to Bruno Nettl, "we are frequently told that all folk music accompanies other activities, that it never fills a role of entertainment, that it does not provide simple enjoyment. Of course this is not the case."[71] Within the world LaChiusa has created, these songs belong to an "oral tradition."[72] The primary dramatic function of the diegetic numbers within *Bernarda Alba* is to provide pleasure for the characters, as well as the audience.

The Maid, the Servant, and Poncia sing to make their work bearable. Demonstrating free will, the Maid resumes singing "On the Day that I Marry" after Bernarda has told her to be silent. This time, Bernarda allows the singing to continue as tribute to her dead husband.[73] Later, the sisters playfully impersonate the suitor Pepé, singing his serenade "Love, Let Me Sing You." Structurally, this song is expository: it introduces Pepé and establishes character; the version Amelia sings is sweet, while Martirio transforms it into a habanera. Moreover, the number anticipates the songs that are to follow as the women sing about "every feature, every part" of love:[74] unrequited, new, spurned, and forbidden. Dramatically, the women sing it for the pleasure of the game. This idea of *play* is an important quality that separates the liminoid from the liminal.[75] Likewise, the songs accompanying the activity of physical work bring an element of enjoyment to the menial task.

Further, the diegetic song can serve a thematic function, providing comment and observation; in the liminoid, "models are subjected to criticism and new ways of describing and interpreting sociocultural experience are formulated."[76] In *Bernarda Alba* the folk songs connect to the *thematic* core of the piece, referring to aspects of love, marriage, and sexuality. "One Moorish Girl" concerns those who find themselves "plucked," foreshadowing the tragic event about to unfold;[77] "On the Day that I Marry," referencing youth and purity, emphasizes what Bernarda has lost but also what she desires to protect, what is at stake.

The song "Magdalena" operates on each of these levels. Magdalena *chooses* to sing, bringing a form of *pleasure* to the work she is engaged in. The song also provides a level of *comment*, particularly through the refrain:

> My pains, Mother, are not pains of hunger.
> My pains, Mother, are the pains of love.[78]

However, when the sisters reprise the refrain in unison, it takes on a new life. LaChiusa observes:

> Magdalena doesn't have an inner life until the very end when all the girls reprise
> Magdalena's song, which by that point has a whole different feeling to it all. The

beginning of it all, it's just some folk song she's singing to liven up the atmosphere. But at the end, the folk song itself takes a journey, or should. So the folk song itself becomes a sixth sister in the room, if you will.[79]

The "whole different feeling" to which LaChiusa refers results from a transformation of the liminoid to the liminal. The refrain transcends its diegetic origins as it "appears to pass across the boundary between the phenomenal and the noumenal [...] beyond realistic song to that other music surrounding" the sisters as each comes to the realization she suffers the pains of love in her own way.[80] Yet the women cannot admit it. Incapable of completing the statement, they do not voice the word "love," while the orchestra rises to its harmonic resolution, suggesting quiet acceptance.

RESTORATION OR ACKNOWLEDGMENT OF SCHISM

Song is inherently repetitive. This is undeniable. The structural reiterations built into song have prompted musical theater scholars to challenge the accepted precepts of "integration" theory: song and dance progress plot and develop character. Rather, it is suggested that disjunction occurs, in which song suspends plot "in the spirit of repetition and the pleasure of difference."[81] Conversely, practitioners claim that song is "heightened action"[82] moving "from one end of an idea to a different place."[83] The tension between these schools of thought (suspension and action) creates a breach, the impetus for this body of research. The resulting crisis of thought offers a series of questions: Is it possible to reconcile these opposing perceptions? Is there a theoretical model able to simultaneously acknowledge the repetitions inherent in the lyric, melody, rhythm, and harmony of song, yet account for the relationship between song and the book, and the transformation of character as a result of the "action" of song? Does such a model provide a mutual language that can be shared by scholars and practitioners as a tool for analysis and rehearsal?

The effort to reconcile the dual concerns of the scholar-practitioner presented its own phase of redress, resulting in this chapter, which is also built on repetitions. The restatement of ideas and of language is fundamental to the act of laying out evidence and constructing the argument. Yet despite these reiterations, the discussion builds momentum, moving the reader "from one end of an idea to a different place." The writing itself is a performative gesture that affects a transformation in the reader, who is either convinced by the argument (a form of restoration) or rejects its thesis (acknowledgment of schism).

Likewise, the performative gestures of song and dance work to effect similar transformations in character and narrative, performer and viewer. The two primary song types satisfy different dramaturgical needs, and the analysis or interpretation of a given number should account for the song's structural function. A character singing a book song is occupied in a very different activity than one performing a diegetic number. The book song is a process of negotiation, of repeating and developing ideas, in the search for an answer. The character is obligated to engage in this process in an *effort* to reach a decision, to resolve an issue. The emphasis on "effort" implies work. Furthermore, LaChiusa demonstrates through Amelia that a conclusive end may not always be achieved. The four-stage liminal process of breach, crisis, redress, and restoration/schism encompassed in the social drama model provides a theoretical frame that adequately accounts for the dramatic action of song. Most importantly, it requires that a dramatic question be asked, the crisis, enabling a process of enquiry and debate to follow, the phase of redress. It is this phase that justifies an engagement with, and necessitates, the structural repetition of song.

In contrast to the active necessity of the book song, the diegetic number is one of choice. The diegetic song is of the world of the musical, and is one in which the characters are able to derive pleasure through the act of singing. It also provides a platform for comment and observation. These are both qualities of the liminoid.

However, the musical is a slippery form, and songs have the ability to defy categorization. A song may possess diegetic music, but a nondiegetic lyric. A diegetic song may transform into a book song, while a book song may present itself in the guise of diegetic number. Director and choreographer Rob Marshall justifies song conceptually by placing liminal moments within a liminoid frame: a stage. Further, while the liminal numbers in *Bernarda Alba* all reveal personal internal transformations, many songs in the wider repertoire are about effecting a form of transformation in others, either individuals or groups. There are also songs that are neither purely diegetic nor book; many opening numbers fall into this gray area. These theoretical models require further testing against the range of songs in the musical theater that are beyond the scope of this chapter.

While song and dance effect specific changes in the characters within the drama, the viewing subject also experiences transformations of varying degrees as a result of these gestures. Although viewers may not be able to read the liminal structure without an awareness of the four stages, they do register the active process at a certain level. The transition from speech to song or dance is not merely observed, it is felt. The combinations of word, music, and movement effect physical changes to the viewing body. Combined with a dramatic context, this may result in a sense of identification inducing an emotional response. Or perhaps the perception of a character is swayed as sympathies shift. Until Adela's liminal turn, she is shown as selfish and insensitive. LaChiusa then allows the viewer to *hear* her. These may affect viewers in a variety of ways, but they do produce a series of smaller transformations within the larger liminoid experience of the performance.

The liminal and the liminoid models presented within this chapter are able to dramaturgically reconcile the tensions between suspension and action. They supply a theoretical framework for the analysis of the relationship between the book and the number, accounting for the impetus of song, the dramatic arc, and the repetition. They also offer a language that can be utilized within rehearsal and performer training. These theories of the "liminal" provide the basis for a mutual language that scholars and practitioners can share.[84]

NOTES

1. Rob Marshall, "Director's Commentary: Rob Marshall and John DeLuca," *Nine*, directed by Rob Marshall (Los Angeles: Weinstein Company / Relativity Media, 2009), DVD, 114 minutes.
2. Tracey Moore and Alison Bergman propose that "When we 'act the song,' singing is just another given circumstance." Tracey Moore and Alison Bergman, *Acting the Song: Performance Skills for the Musical Theatre* (New York: Allworth Press, 2008), viii.
3. Scott McMillin, *The Musical as Drama* (Princeton, NJ: Princeton University Press, 2006), 6–10.
4. Ibid., 41. See also Millie Taylor, *Musical Theatre, Realism and Entertainment* (Surrey: Ashgate Publishing, 2012), especially chapters 3 and 4, for a more inclusive and complex reading of these issues.
5. Aaron Frankel, *Writing the Broadway Musical* (1977: reprint, New York: DaCapo Press, 2000), 81.
6. Jonathan Frank, "Spotlight on Jason Robert Brown," *Talkin' Broadway*, 2000, online. Available: http://www.talkinbroadway.com/spot/jrb1.html. February 20, 2012.
7. McMillin, *Musical as Drama*, 102.
8. Ibid., 112.
9. Gérard Genette, *Narrative Discourse Revisited*, trans. J. E. Lewin (1983; reprint, Ithaca, NY: Cornell University Press, 1988), 217–18.
10. Joseph P. Swain refers to the diegetic song as a "prop song"; see Joseph P. Swain, *The Broadway Musical: A Critical and Musical Survey* (New York: Oxford University Press, 1990), 47. Carolyn Abbate terms this "phenomenal performance"; see Carolyn Abbate, *Unsung Voices: Opera and Musical Narrative in the Nineteenth Century* (1991; reprint, Princeton, NJ: Princeton University Press, 1996), 5.
11. Marshall, "Director's Commentary."
12. McMillin, *Musical as Drama*, 8.
13. Erika Fischer-Lichte, *The Transformative Power of Performance*, trans. Saskya Iris Jain (2004; reprint, New York: Routledge, 2008), 174.
14. Ibid., 176.
15. Raymond Knapp, *The American Musical and the Formation of National Identity* (Princeton, NJ: Princeton University Press, 2005), 7.
16. Victor Turner, *From Ritual to Theater: The Human Seriousness of Play* (New York: PAJ Publications, 1982), 41.
17. Gustavo Pérez Firmat, *Literature and Liminality: Fesitive Readings in the Hispanic Tradition* (Durham, NC: Duke University Press, 1986), xiii.
18. Ibid, xiv.
19. Turner, *From Ritual to Theater*, 43.
20. See Arnold Van Gennep, *The Rites of Passage* (Chicago: University of Chicago Press, 1960).
21. Victor Turner, *The Anthropology of Performance* (New York: PAJ Publications 1988), 102.
22. Fischer-Lichte, *Transformative Power*, 174. My students often relate in class and reflective essays how the experience of attending a musical transforms their state of being; sometimes this affect can be life changing.
23. These liminal experiences follow the three-stage ritual structure outlined by Van Gennep. See Van Gennep, *Rites of Passage*, 11.
24. Victor Turner, "Are There Universals of Performance in Myth, Ritual, and Drama?," in *By Means of Performance*, ed. Richard Schechner and Willa Appel (New York: Cambridge University Press, 1990), 8–9.
25. Moore and Bergman, *Acting the Song*, 72.
26. Michael John LaChiusa, interview by author, audio recording, New York, June 24, 2011.
27. Michael John LaChiusa, *Bernarda Alba: Libretto* (New York: Rodgers and Hammerstein Theatricals, 2007), 21. My emphasis.

28. Turner, *From Ritual to Theatre*, 43.
29. Robin Totton, *Songs of the Outcasts: An Introduction to Flamenco* (Portland, OR: Amadeus Press, 2003), 195.
30. Michael John LaChiusa, *Bernarda Alba: Piano-Vocal Score* (New York: Rodgers and Hammerstein Theatricals, 2007), 48–49.
31. Ibid., 49–50.
32. Totton, *Songs of the Outcasts*, 37.
33. Juan Serrano and Jose Elgorriaga, *Flamenco, Body and Soul: An Aficionado's Introduction* (Fresno: California State University, 1990), 57.
34. LaChiusa, *Alba: Libretto*, 22.
35. Ibid., 23.
36. Abbate, *Unsung Voices*, 71.
37. LaChiusa, *Alba: Score*, 50–51.
38. Ibid., 51.
39. The line is repeated three times if we take into account the contrapuntal coda LaChiusa places at the conclusion of "Adela" as the finale to the "sisters' suite." LaChiusa, *Alba: Score*, 69–72.
40. Ibid., 53.
41. Michael John LaChiusa, "Interview by Ira Weitzman," *Lincoln Center Theater*, March 13, 2006, online. Available: http://www.lct.org/showMain.htm?id=178. December 7, 2012.
42. Carolyn Abbate also refers to Barthes's narrative structure: Abbate, *Unsung Voices*, 41. Millie Taylor acknowledges a parallel between the narrative structures of the musical and the novel: Taylor, *Musical Theatre*, 119.
43. Michael John LaChiusa, "Interview by Thomas Cott," *Lincoln Center Theatre*, November 17, 1999, online. Available: http://www.lct.org/showMain.htm?id=95. December 7, 2012.
44. Roland Barthes, *Image, Music, Text*, trans. Stephen Heath (New York: Hill and Wang, 1977), 91–97.
45. Ibid., 92.
46. Varying degrees of both qualities may simultaneously occur: "a unit can be of two different classes." Ibid., 96.
47. LaChiusa, *Alba: Libretto*, 24–25.
48. LaChiusa, *Alba: Score*, 54.
49. Ibid., 57.
50. Lehman Engel, *The American Musical Theatre*, rev. ed. (New York: Macmillan, 1975), 108. Cohen and Rosenhaus elaborate, suggesting that "the defining element of a charm song is, of course, that it makes the character singing come across as charming"; Allen Cohen, and Steven L. Rosenhaus, *Writing Musical Theatre* (New York: Palgrave Macmillan, 2006), 95–96.
51. LaChiusa, *Alba: Score*, 58.
52. Ibid., 59.
53. Ibid., 60.
54. Fischer-Lichte, *Transformative Power,* 176.
55. This blurring may also occur at the recollection of known tunes in jukebox musicals. See Taylor, *Musical Theatre*, 149–65.
56. Michael John LaChiusa, and Graciela Daniele, *Bernarda Alba*, directed by Richard Stucker, Mitzi E. Newhouse Theater, performed April 5, 2006, Theater on Film and Tape Archive, New York Public Library for the Performing Arts, Lincoln Center, videocassette [Beta], 89 min. I am grateful to Patrick Hoffman and the staff of the Theater on Film and Tape Archive for allowing me to view *Bernarda Alba*.
57. LaChiusa, *Alba: Score*, 63.
58. Ibid, 63–64.
59. LaChiusa, interview by the author, New York, June 24, 2011.
60. Totton, *Songs of the Outcasts*, 54.

61. LaChiusa, *Alba: Score*, 69–72.
62. Fischer-Lichte, *Transformative Power*, 179.
63. Millie Taylor explores recent neuroscientific analysis of the affects of music and dance on the brain. See Taylor, *Musical Theatre*, 91–94.
64. Moore and Bergman, *Acting the Song*, 87.
65. Carolyn Abbate refers to this as "the fissure between the sung [...] and phenomenal song." Abbate, *Unsung Voices*, 148.
66. McMillin, *Musical as Drama*, 105.
67. Turner, *Ritual to Theater*, 43.
68. Ibid., 32–33.
69. Victor Turner, *Drama, Fields and Metaphors: Symbolic Action in Human Society* (Ithaca, NY: Cornell University Press, 1974), 15.
70. Ibid., 17.
71. Bruno Nettl, *Folk and Traditional Music of the Western Continents*, 3rd ed. (1965; Englewood Cliffs, NJ: Prentice-Hall, 1990), 12.
72. Ibid., 3–5.
73. According to Abbate, an overt acknowledgment of the awareness of singing "forces us to deal explicitly with ourselves as listening subjects, for we—the audience—are mirrored by the rapt listeners onstage." Abbate, *Unsung Voices*, 85.
74. LaChiusa, *Alba: Score*, 31–39.
75. Turner, *From Ritual to Theatre*, 55.
76. Turner, *Drama, Fields*, 45.
77. LaChiusa, *Alba: Libretto*, 44.
78. Ibid., 20.
79. LaChiusa, interview by the author.
80. Abbate, *Unsung Voices*, 119.
81. McMillin, *Musical as Drama*, 8.
82. Frankel, *Broadway Musical*, 81.
83. Frank, "Jason Robert Brown," 1.
84. I am especially grateful to Mr. Michael John LaChiusa for giving an hour of his time so that I could interview him about *Bernarda Alba*. I would also like to thank Dr. Stuart Grant and Dr. Maryrose Casey for their guidance, and Daniel Dinero, Brett Clark, Maeva Veerapen, and the anonymous reviewers for their valuable feedback on this chapter.

PART FOUR

Performativity as Identity

As we have seen, songs and dances are extremely complex performance texts that relate in paradoxical and challenging ways to the narrative (or other) frameworks within which they are performed. They can also be perceived as generative and fluid, in a constant interaction with the external world outside the theater, so that the vocal and physical gestures of performers respond to and rewrite the identities they perform. Often performers will ostensibly mask their own identity to project the identity of a character in the fictitious world of the drama. On the other hand, there are many instances of song and dance in which the performer effectively remains him- or herself in the act of performance. Either way it is not the body of the character but that of the performer that is corporeally enacting the song and dance, though this is not to say that the performance of self is a simple or even stable act. Indeed, the act of performance, in framing that self within a performative dimension, enacts a marked play of identity. Sometimes, as we have seen in the examples from *The Voice UK* (2012), an element of that identity is crystallized or confirmed in the performance, as it is with Tom Jones's enactment of his own celebrity (the "character" of Tom Jones the star); at other times, an element of identity is *achieved* through the rite of passage of the performance, as it is with Leanne Mitchell (the *becoming*-star).[1] Either way, and fundamentally, performance performs some element of identity.

Rather than assuming that character identity, or indeed performer identity, is communicated through story, plot, or dialogue, the following chapters reconsider songs and dances as behaviors enacted in the body and voice through which characterization and cultural identity can be performed. This part, therefore, explores the ways in which songs and dances are gestural languages of the body through which identities are constructed and deconstructed, written and rewritten in a generative and interactive flow.

There are many performances by Jennifer Holliday of "And I am Telling You (I'm not going)" from *Dreamgirls*[2] available on YouTube. Most are filmed as concert performances outside the theatrical context from which the song derives and in which Holliday established a "version" of the song. The version discussed here, however, is a recording of her singing the song as the character Effie, filmed at the 1982 Tonys, at which the musical won six awards.[3] In this version there is a scene and group conversation that leads into and contextualizes the song; the solo section begins at 3'33" of this recording. What is astonishing in this performance is the way in which Holliday locates the song within a history of African American soul and gospel singing by her choices of ornamentation (rising glissandi in particular, but also turns, transforming vowels, and wide jaw-based vibrato) and the occasionally harsh, shouted, or growled vocal timbres. Clearly the song is written in this musical genre, and her performance of it extends the musical performance with a vocal performance of a genre within time, place, and context. But her performance as this character and in this situation also transgresses and exceeds the framework of the genre. The character's context is that she has been replaced in her relationship and in the singing group, and her anger, despair, and frustration are all revealed in the ways she transforms the gospel/soul vocal sounds into expressions of deeply felt emotions. The soul growls become the excessive growls of rage, the gospel shouts transform into desperate articulations of pain and hurt. What can be perceived in this performance is the normative framework of gospel/soul ornamentation and timbre alongside the transgressive excess of the overlaid emotion of the performance of character. But the emotion is not separate from the vocal performance; instead the vocal performance and the genre are transformed or exceeded by other expressions within an identifiable contextual framework. The demonstration of petulance, tenderness, anger and sobbing all feed into the re-articulation of this moment of identity and this transgression of genre. The normative and the transgressive interact within the performance revealing the performativity of identity as re-constructed and discursive. And then one might listen to Holliday singing the song in another context and discover the accretions of performances that extend the vocal expression and its interpretation still further, always repeating sedimented expressions through a framework of cultural knowledge to reveal a politics of identity generation and regeneration.

Jennifer Hudson's performance as Effie in the film version of the show, of the same song and its antithesis in the show "I am Changing" (figure 9), adds further layers to an audience's reading of this character. Identity here is performed through the musical genre, African American musical heritage, the narrative of Effie's becoming throughout the show, previous characterisations and performances of this material, and Hudson's own developing performance of vocal identity. Each of these provide opportunities for normative expression and transgressive excess.

Judith Butler theorizes identity constitution not as the expression of subjectivity but as the performance of social norms that are always already repeated and sedimented. In this way the representation of identity involves socially normative performances. "By stressing performative citationality, Butler allows us to see how [Victor Turner's] theory of ritual may be generalized to understand both transgressive and normative performance."[4] The transgressive is revealed in the excessive, the exorbitant, or the parodic variations of repetition. Thus the transgressive and the normative are not opposed to each other but are neighbors, and performativity can be both discursive *and* embodied. So she argues that performativity "describes this relation of being implicated in that which one opposes, this turning of power against itself to produce alternative modalities of power, to establish a kind of political contestation that is not a 'pure' opposition, a 'transcendence' of contemporary relations of power, but a difficult labor of forging a future from resources inevitably impure."[5] This raises the question of how one recognizes the power that is opposed rather than

Figure 9 Jennifer Hudson, who played the role of Effie in the film version of *Dreamgirls*, sings "I am Changing." Photo courtesy of Dreamworks SKG/Photofest.

that which is promoted, and the response is that knowledge and power are linked in instances of performativity, as in the example above and in each of the chapters that follow. The examples below are both normative and transgressive, and the discussions and analyses reveal the intricate relationship of these two states.

First, Kathryn Edney explores how tap dance, minstrelsy, and the performance of Gregory Hines in *Jelly's Last Jam* (1992) signifies, critiques, and exceeds normative expressions of African American identity to reveal the absence of blackness on the contemporary musical stage, and to reassert the right of African Americans to represent themselves and their histories in performance. Next, Jessica Sternfeld identifies how character identities are queered or othered by their association with Broadway musical songs, and argues that this queering reveals a normative heterosexual politics that is transgressed by the performances of the character Kurt and (to a lesser extent) Rachel in *Glee*. Finally, Judith Sebesta reflects on the performance of masculinity in dance and reveals the ways it has been transformed in contemporary musicals to reflect a postmodern ironic pastiche of styles and genres, revising and rewriting masculinity in a constantly transforming and reconstructing discourse of performativity as identity.

NOTES

1. Deleuze and Guattari write of the transformative processes of becoming rather than being static identities.
2. Music by Henry Krieger, lyrics and book by Tom Eyen (1981).
3. Online. Available: http://www.youtube.com/watch?v=kC_u_q-iND0. December 13, 2012.
4. Jon McKenzie, "Genre Trouble: (The) Butler Did It," in *The Ends of Performance*, ed. Peggy Phelan and Jill Lane (New York: New York University Press, 1998), 222.
5. Judith Butler, *Bodies That Matter: On the Discursive Limits of "Sex"* (New York: Routledge, 1991), 241. Cited in ibid., 228.

CHAPTER 7

Tapping the Ivories

Jazz and Tap Dance in Jelly's Last Jam *(1992)*

KATHRYN EDNEY

Americans like to claim jazz, musical theater, and tap dance as belonging to, and originating in, the United States. Of course, such a formulation ignores the basic histories of how these different modes of popular entertainment evolved within the United States, but the rhetoric is powerful and nearly self-sustaining. As a stage musical that could not exist without jazz music or tap dance, *Jelly's Last Jam* (1992) should thus be American three times over. By all reasonable standards it should be a staple within the canon of the American musical stage, but it is not. Most likely this omission is because of the other uniquely American aspect of the show: it focuses exclusively on the history of African Americans.

Jelly's Last Jam is the stylized biography of the jazz composer and pianist Jelly Roll Morton. Its creator, George C. Wolfe, combined jazz music and tap dance to confront the place of African Americans both within the history of the United States and on the musical theater stage. The musical brings together multiple strands of African American performance history, overlaying the history of jazz music with dance as epitomized in the original Broadway production by tap dancers Gregory Hines (as the grown-up Jelly) and Savion Glover (as a youthful Jelly). African American playwright-director Wolfe actively reworked African American performance traditions within the conventions of the American musical theater stage to render the history of African Americans concrete and physical through tap dancing, a form of dance historically associated with African Americans, but conventionally represented in Broadway musicals and American films by white performers such as Fred Astaire. An examination of the ways in which Wolfe, Hines, and Glover extended the established conventions of musical theater reveals that they combined a particular form of dance—tap—with a particular form of music—jazz—in order to embody the historical experiences of African Americans and to stake a particularly African American claim for the history of the American musical.

Dance and music intertwine in multiple ways throughout *Jelly's Last Jam*. Hines's and Glover's dancing replicated the process of jazz composition: rhythmic music composed by feet pounding out rhythms when performing on stage night after night, just as Morton composed his jazz music in nightclubs and bars. The musical clearly established a relationship between Hines's dancing and Morton's piano playing, yet some theater critics wondered how the two forms related to one another, and so questioned the wisdom of representing Morton's musical ability through Hines's dance.[1] But such critics missed the crucial connections between the history of jazz, the history of tap, and Hines's mode of performance. As a dancer, Hines was a distinctive rhythm tapper who used "hard, roughed-up, low-to-the-ground, free-flowing, funky rhythms" that marked a clear shift away from the smoother, and more polished, style of his predecessors.[2] He was known for his improvisations—what he called "improvography"—and for his percussive phrasing that deployed "intonation and volume [that were] amazingly varied."[3] As a rhythm tapper, Hines composed music with his feet, and indeed was well known for creating a "density of sound" that had real emotional weight behind it.[4] Hines's control over rhythm and his infusion of new rhythms into tap replicated, in a different mode, the ways in which the real-life Morton reshaped American popular music with his vision of jazz.[5]

Jelly's Last Jam's prologue begins with African drumming under a jazz piano. Pianos are percussion instruments, with hammers striking strings just like feet tapping and striking the surface of the stage. Throughout the rest of the show, feet and piano as percussive instruments together refer back to the African drums heard during the prologue, connecting African American forms of creative expression—jazz and tap dance—back to their African roots. Above all else, tap dancing "is percussive rhythms and the floor is the instrument which is played by the feet." As performed by African Americans, tap is traditionally performed as a kind of "rhythm-jazz" with a focus on improvisation, attitude, and musicality; indeed, according to dance scholar Sally Sommer, "tap dancers consider themselves percussive musicians and will describe their feet as a set of drums."[6] The feet of the dancers and someone else's fingers on the keys of the piano echoed each other musically and physically in a form of call-and-response that has historically been a key aspect of African American performance. But the call-and-response was not only a metaphoric reference made between piano and feet; the call-and-response performance tradition was physically enacted between Hines and Glover in their dance routines together.

JELLY'S LAST JAM

The plot of *Jelly's Last Jam* is relatively straightforward. Ferdinand de Menthe "Jelly Roll" Morton, from the Creole elite of New Orleans, is given the opportunity to revisit his life in the moment suspended between life and death. His limbo takes the form of a ghostly jazz club called the Jungle Inn, and his guide is the Chimney Man. Morton seeks to misremember, reinterpret, and rewrite his past, refusing to acknowledge the ways in which the African side of his heritage helped to shape his music. But the Chimney Man and a chorus of African American club members angrily refuse to let him perform this erasure. Only if Jelly can acknowledge his racial heritage and let go of his nostalgia for a particularized, whitewashed past will he be able to obtain an honest and honorable peace in the afterlife. Nor will he be allowed to take his place within the long line of ancestors and descendents who form the thread of African and African American history and collective memory.[7] Morton, who wishes to tell his biography as something that is divorced from both African and African American traditions, must come to terms with the debts he owes to those cultures. While the message from Wolfe would seem to be targeted directly at African Americans, it is also the case that the playwright was commenting on the ways in which African American performative forms in "mainstream" culture—and on Broadway in particular—are often universalized, "whitewashed," and thus erased.

Wolfe was well aware of the earlier history of black theater, and more particularly of black musical theater, when he agreed to write *Jelly's Last Jam*.[8] At the time, he was most famous, or even infamous, for having written the off-Broadway play *The Colored Museum* (1986). Comprising a series of eleven vignettes, or museum exhibits, *The Colored Museum* uses biting satire and blatant stereotypes to reveal the history of the African American experience; as one reviewer noted, "among other things [the play] makes it impossible to watch *A Raisin in the Sun* with a straight face ever again."[9] Throughout his career, Wolfe has been adamant that the divide between black and white musical theater, as perpetuated on Broadway stages and in musical theater scholarship, is a pervasive problem that must be resolved:

> since the very beginning, black people have been involved in musical theater. Some would say that the minstrel show is the grandparent of the Broadway musical. [But] no black people are mentioned in [books about musical theater] until at the end of the book—or at the back of the bus, if you will. All the black musicals are clumped together in one chapter. So, you turn one page and there's *Shuffle Along* (1921), and you turn another page and there's *Ain't Misbehavin'* (1978), and you turn another page and there's *The Wiz* (1975).[10]

Despite his concerns with musical theater's politics and with its tendency toward "mindless giddiness," Wolfe is nonetheless a fan of American musical comedies such as *Hello Dolly* (1964), *West Side Story* (1957), and *On the Town* (1944) because it is possible for such shows to use song and dance to express emotional truths that often cannot be found elsewhere.[11] Wolfe's relationship with musical theater is thus complicated. A fan of the form, as a black man he nonetheless recognizes that it is rare for anyone like him to be represented on the mainstream musical theater stage. He decries the de facto segregation that has historically existed, and still currently exists, within the theater, but his early directing and writing projects for the stage typically reflected an exclusively African American perspective. And Wolfe is very aware of the strange position he holds within American theater, which may be in part what drew him to the possibilities that *Jelly's Last Jam* presented because it represented how "the power of American culture, of black American culture, exists not in its purity but in its contradictions."[12] For Wolfe, the life of the Creole Jelly Roll Morton as told through a black musical that deliberately employed tap dance embodied those contradictions of history whereby African Americans are at once the source of "American" culture and erased from the history of that culture.

Broadway theater seemed especially forgetful of its own history throughout the 1990s, and, as David Savran notes, this forgetfulness manifested itself in terms of a surfeit of theatrical ghosts. Shows as diverse as *Jelly's Last Jam*, *Angels in America: Millennium Approaches* (1993), and *Ragtime* (1998) all featured apparitions. While ghosts were hardly new within theater—just think of Hamlet's father and Emily from *Our Town* (1940)—Savran found this rise of the undead to be a particularly revealing manifestation of the American zeitgeist. He argued that the ghosts flourished in reaction to both the excesses and the forgetfulness of American society during the 1980s and to the fears and uncertainties of the 1990s. The Cold War was ending, the millennium was approaching, old world orders were crumbling, and live theater used ghosts as a means to manage these unsettling historical changes. Indeed, because theater as a form is itself based on impermanence and disappearance, the stage has always been an effective place in which to address fears that the present is not like the past.[13]

The ghosts in *Jelly's Last Jam* are particularly contentious. Not only is the title character, Jelly Roll Morton, a self-deluded ghost with warped memories who must be taught that while history cannot be changed, it can be more clearly understood, but the show as a whole is also haunted by the tap-dancing ghosts of all-black revues, by the ghoulish smile of blackface minstrels, and by the "golden age" of Broadway musicals. Playwright-director Wolfe confronted all of these lingering phantoms by refusing to be nostalgic. For him, there was never a "golden age of the Broadway musical" because musicals repudiated their historical debts to African American culture, and there is very little to celebrate in terms of the racism that made all-black revues necessary and minstrelsy possible.

Producers Margo Lion and Pamela Koslow-Hines laid the foundations for *Jelly's Last Jam* in the 1980s. Lion had the idea that a musical could be written about Morton; Koslow-Hines was searching for a show that would suit her then-husband, dancer-actor Gregory Hines. After a long series of starts and stops that included problems in securing funding, finding and keeping a librettist and a composer, and a change in direction for the show from a revue format to a narrative-driven musical, Wolfe was brought on as the show's new author in 1987.[14] Under the sponsorship of the Mark Taper Forum in Los Angeles—which has, since 1967, helped to fund playwrights as they develop new and often controversial works[15]—*Jelly's Last Jam* finally premiered on February 21, 1991. The show broke box-office records during its initial two-month run.[16] But this first incarnation remained tentative, and Hines declined the starring role. Instead, Morton was played by Obba Babatundé, best known for his Tony Award–nominated portrayal of C. C. White in the original Broadway production of *Dreamgirls* (1981). Although most Los Angeles reviewers recognized that *Jelly's Last Jam* was still a "work in progress," all were impressed by Wolfe's ability to tell Morton's story, both as a playwright and as a director.[17]

Before reopening in New York on April 26, 1992, *Jelly's Last Jam* underwent multiple changes: the majority of the second act was completely jettisoned, a section on Morton's childhood was compressed, and the character of Jelly's mother was eliminated.[18] Moreover, Gregory Hines was sufficiently confident of the shape and tone of the revised production that he was now willing to star in it.[19] Hines's participation was essential; producers Lion and Koslow-Hines were well aware of the financial risks involved in producing a musical on Broadway and appreciated that an all-black musical posed additional problems. As a "mainstream" star known to audiences beyond Broadway, Hines's presence would go a long way to guarantee profitability and so attract the necessary funding.[20]

The addition of Hines as the star meant that unless substantial revisions were made in subsequent productions, *Jelly's Last Jam* would always have a strong element of dance, and tap dancing in particular.[21] Tap dancing—and the long history of African Americans with tap—added another layer of storytelling to the musical: a history embodied. Historically, jazz music and tap dance are tangibly linked: tap dance developed "in direct relationship to jazz music—sharing its rhythmic motifs, polyrhythms, multiple meters, elements of swing, and its structured improvisation."[22] The addition of Hines's and Glover's black bodies performing tap dance forced a consideration of what kinds of stories tap normally told, and what those stories might mean within a musical explicitly concerned with history and its circulation.[23]

Hines had considerable control over how he embodied Jelly Roll Morton on the stage. He was able to rechoreograph the dance numbers featuring his character so as to emphasize tap dance, leaving the ensemble numbers to be choreographed by Hope Clarke.[24] While such autonomy over the choreography may have been appropriate for Hines as a star, it was highly unusual for a dancer within a Broadway musical, who is normally told "where to go" and "when to step."[25] Throughout his career, Hines consistently positioned tap, a vernacular form of dance, to be as viable and artistically "highbrow" as concert dance. Indeed, he was credited during the 1970s and 1980s for spearheading a resurgence of tap dance as a visible and viable form of African American dance. He integrated his formal training from Henry LeTang with informal lessons gleaned from venerable tap dancers such as Harold Cook and Charles Cook, and incorporated funk and rock rhythms into his dancing style in ways that captured the imagination of younger dancers, including Savion Glover.[26] As a black dancer who refused to give up tap dancing or to position it as a lesser form of dance, Hines was thus engaged in a political move similar to Wolfe's in terms of placing a significant value on African American cultural forms.

TAP DANCING AND BLACK IDENTITY

Dance historian Thomas DeFrantz has asked, "do dancing black bodies always dance black?"[27] The issue for DeFrantz is that even as black dancers, such as himself, use the activity of dancing in their construction of a multivalent black identity, an identity that is both "coherent and always changing," that construction takes place within two distinct spaces. Within the social space of black vernacular dance, a space that is nonetheless accessible to outsiders, dancing connects the black dancer in positive ways to other black bodies. Within the public and overwhelmingly white spaces of performance venues like concert halls and theaters, the black dancer no longer engages in a form of call-and-response, but instead "offers stylized movements as objects to be casually consumed by immobile spectators."[28] How, then, could tap dancing in *Jelly's Last Jam* effectively communicate with its predominantly white, Broadway audience the history embedded in tap dance?

In terms of the structures of musical theater, Hines's dancing in *Jelly's Last Jam*, defined at one point in the script as "as exuberant as it is emotionally raw,"[29] continues when the songs of the musicals can no longer contain and adequately express the emotions of his character.[30] It functions as an emotional release and is emotionally revealing. But Hines as a dancing Jelly Roll Morton not only reveals Morton's inner emotional self, the percussive mode of dancing aligns the character with Africa through the Yoruba proverb that says secrets are revealed through drumming and dancing.[31] Morton's secret, the one he unsuccessfully attempts to hide throughout most of the musical, is that his heritage includes Africa.

But it is not just the ethnic connections between Morton and Africa that are exposed through tap dancing. The white producers of *Jelly's Last Jam* initially expressed some veiled reservations about including tap dancing within their production because of what it might signify to audiences: a racist, stereotypical representation of black Americans.[32] The use of tap dancing as the primary mode of dance within *Jelly's Last Jam* obviously has much to do with the choice of Hines as the star, but once Hines moved into the role, tap formed a part of the reflexive commentary Wolfe had structured into the show about the history of musical theater. As the former blackface performer Eddie Leonard noted, "musical comedy [dancing] technique is not so different from that of minstrelsy," although eventually show dancing incorporated more and more ballet and "concert dance" into its repertoire as the genre moved toward musical plays.[33] While tap dancing did not fully disappear from the musical stage, it was certainly moved off to the side. Just as Fred Astaire and Gene Kelly popularized their own version of tap dance on film without fully acknowledging its dark roots, on stage the form was linked either to black vaudeville performers, such as Bill "Bojangles" Robinson, whose contributions to the evolution of show dancing was downplayed in favor of blackface performers like Leonard or choreographers like Agnes de Mille.[34] Tap as used in *Jelly's Last Jam* was a way to reveal, as Wolfe saw it, the open secret concerning the complex racialized origins of musical theater.

The history of tap dance in the United States, like that of musical theater, is rooted in racial and national hybridity, and as with musical theater, in the popular discourse the contributions of African Americans to the form are often forgotten or swept aside. Most scholars agree that the origins of tap can be traced to the complex of cultural interactions that occurred between English, Irish, and African dance traditions as these immigrant groups crossed and recrossed paths within the United States, with many of the most fruitful seeds of tap being planted during the nineteenth century. Not coincidentally, many of these paths crossed as minstrelsy and a distinctively American form of musical theater were developing.[35]

African American tap dancers were not completely forgotten by history, but on the few occasions when they were remembered, it was generally in terms of the movie relationship Robinson had with child star Shirley Temple.[36] The black male tap dancer was rendered sexless, subservient, and left dancing for laughs. A tap-dancing white body recalls an elegant Astaire or an athletic Kelly, but a tap-dancing black body recalls an ever-smiling "Bojangles" or Jim Crow and his jumps.[37] *Jelly's Last Jam*, by pairing two black men representing points on a continuum between past and present, thus worked to recall a different history of tap dance, one not predicated on a black man transmitting his knowledge to a little white girl, but of one generation of African Americans passing down a specific tradition to another.[38]

Tap dance has long incorporated "the challenge" as part of its history of establishing who the better dancer is, as a means of passing down steps from one generation to another, and as a way of advancing the form.[39] Hines and Glover, as Jelly and Young Jelly, created the spaces for specifically African American forms of call-and-response through their improvised tapping in the number "The Whole World's Waiting to Sing Your Song." This number occurs in the first act just after the older Jelly has revisited his childhood home and has recognized how "the Creole way" of his female relatives had stifled his creativity.[40] Hines's Jelly then takes his younger self out into the streets of New Orleans to expose him to life as it exists outside of the formal parlor and to persuade him(self) that by breaking the rules of the household, his music will be heard by the world.

In this narrative and performative context, Hines and Glover engaged nightly in an improvised dialogue of persuasion and competition. As Hines characterized it, "in our number together, we're always trying to top each other. The other night, I felt particularly energetic and went up on both toes and held it. Then [Glover] looked at me with a smirk and went up on one toe. I just wanted to choke him!"[41] Although the primary audience for *Jelly's Last Jam* was white and stationary,[42] there is nonetheless the sense that, at least during certain moments in the musical, Hines and Glover were performing for each other first and foremost. In so doing, they did not just participate in a performance of *Jelly's Last Jam*, but also in a history of African American performance traditions that includes call-and-response, competitive one-upmanship, and the tap dance tradition of passing down steps from one performer to another, in equal measure.

HISTORICAL MEMORY THROUGH SONG AND DANCE

While "The Whole World's Waiting to Sing Your Song" enacts a tradition of transmitting historical memory through song and dance, *Jelly's Last Jam* also engages with the ways in which tap and African American culture have been overwritten and repurposed by white interpretations and performances. These negative histories recalled by tap are fully exposed during the act 1 closer, "Doctor Jazz," when Hines as Morton is confronted by a line of eight black dancers who highlight his Otherness. At the end of the first act, with Jelly isolated from his friends and lover, it first appears that he will perform a defiant solo number that will allow him to once again stake his claim as the singular composer of jazz music. Hines is featured alone on a bare stage, where he is pinned by a white spotlight as he begins to sing, his shoulders slightly hunched forward, a gesture typical of Hines's performative body language. But by end of the first stanza of the song, the rest of the stage lights come up to reveal what is behind Jelly; a so-called "Chorus of Coons."[43] The eight Coons are men dressed in red doormen's jackets, caps, and white gloves. Their mouths are grotesquely exaggerated with the sign of the minstrel performer, bright white lips. As Jelly continues singing about "his" glorious music, the music increases in intensity and Hines's singing becomes frantic as the chorus joins him in song, jeering him on. The number finally culminates in an angry tap dance routine led at the front of the stage by Jelly, who cannot shake off the parody of a chorus line that mockingly mimics his every step until it becomes unclear who is copying whom. By forsaking his African and African American heritage, and the ways in which knowledge was productively passed down from generation to generation—as demonstrated in "The Whole World's Waiting" number—Morton is doomed to have his knowledge stolen and implicitly erased.

Chorus lines typically support the star performer; the anonymous dancers are there to make the lead performer look good.[44] Strictly within the narrative confines of *Jelly's Last Jam*, the chorus line in "Doctor Jazz" performs precisely the opposite function for the lead dancer. They make Jelly look like a race traitor who has sold out his talent, turned his back on his friends, and joined their ranks of minstrels. Structurally, this scene serves as the counterpoint to the opening jam at the Jungle Inn. Instead of a diverse group of African Americans calling forth Jelly from limbo with their song and muted African drums, it is Jelly who has angrily conjured up the Chorus of Coons, a chorus that first derisively repeats his self-aggrandizing lyrics, and which then has the final note in the song. Jelly is finally rendered speechless and struck still by the blackface minstrels who shout "it's Doctor Jazz!" as the scene freezes and goes to blackout before the intermission. The normal relationship between chorus and star is flipped on its head, substituting the collective for the individual.[45] But it is precisely the lesson that Morton—and the predominantly white audience—need to learn; that the collective knowledge of African Americans contributed to the creation of "his" music that Morton insists has no black roots, and which many whites proclaim to be "universal."

At the end of act 1, Morton is no longer even nominally in control of his own story; "Doctor Jazz" sets up the narrative arc for the second act when Morton's life falls apart completely as he keeps attempting to assert his individual version of the past over a collective telling of that past. Hines's tap dancing, although emblematic of the type of control the star had within the production, also signifies back to the centrality of the Chimney Man / Esu-Elegbara and the powerlessness the character of Jelly has over the narrative he thinks he is telling. In Yoruba mythology Esu-Elegbara is "a highly accomplished dancer, a mask-in-motion"; and ultimately it is he who controls the tales within *Jelly's Last Jam* by refusing to let Jelly hide in his nostalgic reimaginings of his story.[46] The interchangeable members of the unchanging Chorus of Coons with their white lips and red jackets will always, and vindictively, return unless Jelly productively engages with history instead of trying to erase it.

Because the Coons are African Americans in blackface, they form a part of Wolfe's wider critique of African Americans who chose to neglect their own history and pander to the expectations of white audiences. The character of Jelly in Wolfe's version of Jelly Roll Morton's biography is guilty of precisely this kind of forgetfulness both when he claims to have invented jazz and when he rejects his oldest friend for being too black. However, viewed in the wider frame of the history of the American musical stage, the Chorus of Coons also highlights the degree to which blackness is used as a stereotype on the Broadway stage; the contributions of African American artists to Broadway are reduced to a single, dancing image of anonymous figures ironically contained within an all-black musical play. They immediately recall an entire history of representations of blacks by whites, a recollection that is difficult to imagine being performed through any dance form other than tap.

The second act flies through a series of events designed to illustrate the fall of Jelly Roll Morton. Jelly's constant denial of his African heritage comes to its logical conclusion when he sells his music, and thus his authentic voice, to Tin Pan Alley.[47] As a direct consequence of this choice, Jelly is reduced to mimicking the music played by Jewish Tin Pan Alley music vendors. He has become a member of the Chorus of Coons; while before he synthesized his music from the authentic sounds of African American streets and bars, in the second act he figuratively puts on blackface and mechanically repeats the musical expectations of Tin Pan Alley to make easy money. As a result, his jazz music is soon left behind by African American composers—Duke Ellington and Count Basie, for example—who did not sacrifice their creative integrity for white approval.[48] In a series of four numbers, "Good Ole New York," "Too Late, Daddy," "That's the Way we do Things in New York," and "Good Ole New York / Door Slam," Morton's music is marginalized more and more until it is reduced simply to the sounds of Hines's tap dancing feet as he circles around the stage fruitlessly searching for a door that will not slam in his face, until even his feet are stilled and the live production of music and of call-and-response is replaced by a radio and its one-way broadcast.

Alone in a New York apartment, and after his experiences in Tin Pan Alley, Jelly listens to a radio quiz program where a woman whose speech patterns mark her as a white American must answer the question "Who invented jazz?" Her choices are Paul Whiteman, W. C. Handy, and Jelly Roll Morton. The woman selects the self-proclaimed King of Jazz and Gershwin interpreter Paul Whiteman; according to the radio announcer the correct answer should have been W. C. Handy, the one person named in the quiz who did not misappropriate black music.[49] Morton has thus suffered the one fate he feared the most: he has been forgotten by history.

The idea of what should be considered "authentic" jazz is considerably confused within *Jelly's Last Jam*. "The message" is not the messenger; as a form of folk music, jazz does not have any one "author" but instead comes from anonymous black folk who contribute different pieces of their songs to the larger whole. Yet when Jelly moves on to New York only to find himself and his music obsolete, *Jelly's Last Jam* has no problem with citing jazz greats Louis Armstrong, Duke Ellington, and Count Basie as singular jazz artists. Indeed, during the musical's prologue, the Chimney Man calls up Armstrong, Ellington, Basie, Bolden, and Bechet as key messengers.[50] And once Jelly admits to his hubris at the musical's end, he is included in the roll call of greats to the sounds of a New Orleans jazz funeral coupled with the return of the African drums. These drums, which throughout the musical have signaled danger and distress to Jelly, by the end are something he welcomes hearing. Their final, non-threatening manifestation demonstrates Jelly's acceptance of his blackness and his acknowledgment of the connections between himself and Africa. But the collective, communal ending does not entirely erase the idea of individual stardom achieved by Ellington, or indeed by Hines and his superlative dancing.

Musical theater occupies a precarious space, located between highbrow and lowbrow, dramatic and musical expressions, a liminal space with which *Jelly's Last Jam* engages through its content and structure. Jelly's life was lived between two world wars, during an era in the United States when African Americans were no longer slaves but still not quite full citizens. The life of Jelly Roll Morton is restaged in limbo—the Jungle Inn—and the show ends with him placed in the middle of a long line of ancestors and descendents dancing toward the door seen at the show's prologue. Wolfe's all-black musical is not a plotless revue, and yet some version of the music used in *Jelly's Last Jam* existed prior to the show, and the musical is, like a jukebox musical, a celebration of the music of an individual composer.

Morton's ultimate redemption is thus perhaps not a capitulation to the "Broadway happy ending," as many reviewers of the show maintained, but is instead a realization of Morton's deep roots in an African past that Hines's dancing body performed during the entire show. It is possible that Morton's final acceptance by the Chimney Man simply replaces one form of Broadway nostalgia for another. Wolfe's narrative, with its reliance on African motifs, signals a longing for a return to an idyllic African past, and evokes a powerful homesickness for a place most African Americans have never visited. But by insisting on the African roots of the American musical through tap dancing and music, the show is historically linked to the minstrel stage, to the first world-famous African American dancer, William "Master Juba" Henry Lane, who made his name during the early nineteenth century, and to all who followed him, including Bert Williams and George Williams, who costarred in the back-to-Africa musical theater landmark *In Dahomey* (1903).[51]

CRITIQUING BLACKFACE IN MUSICAL THEATER

Jelly's Last Jam deliberately restores blackface, the model of white misrepresentations of blackness, not just to critique this practice but to reassert the right of African Americans to perform themselves and their histories on the stage. Further, by openly performing this ghostly/ghastly representation that most audiences would rather forget, as the Chimney Man says, "to relive n' recreate that which was,"[52] *Jelly's Last Jam* recovers the historical link between blackface and musical theater, forcing a reevaluation of musical theater, the absent presence of blackness on the musical stage, and whether the American dream for individual success is worth more than the success and history of a community. In this way, and through the use of tap dance, the show questions one of the central tenets of the "golden age" American musical: the desirability of the American dream. But at the same time, although the resolution is not reached with Jelly achieving his goals during his lifetime or in the resolution of his romantic difficulties, *Jelly's Last Jam* still manages to end on essentially the same note that has dominated many American Broadway musicals since *Oklahoma!* For all of the commitment to an honest assessment of America's cultural history, in the finale *Jelly's Last Jam* adheres to one of the classic conventions of the musical theater formula: the ideal of a coherent and harmonious community. That said, it is clear that *Jelly's Last Jam*'s focus on performing a coherent *African American* community identity, one that has a recognizable past that allows Jelly Roll Morton to take his place in a long line of dancing ancestors, is unique. Such a focus was only possible in the combination of performing jazz music and tap dance, two cultural forms with their roots in Africa and black America, and which have historically been the means through which African American identities have been constructed on stage and off. As embodied by Gregory Hines pounding out his "improvographies" on stage, with Savion Glover there to challenge him, and set against a Chorus of Coons ever poised to usurp his rhythms, the use of tap dance was thus fundamental to recreating the character of Jelly Roll Morton.

NOTES

1. For example, Richard Hornby commented, "The problem, however, is that Hines is primarily a dancer (though he sings and plays piano as well) and Morton was not. This could be confusing [. ..]. Maybe Hines will dance roles as Fats Waller or Duke Ellington or—who knows?—Martin Luther King, Jr." Richard Hornby, "Musicals Revived," *Hudson Review* 45: 3 (1992): 456. Wolfe discussed the connection between jazz, tap, and African American history in Nell Cox, *Jammin': Jelly Roll Morton on Broadway* (New York: PBS, 1992), videocassette.
2. Katie Rolnick, "Gregory Hines: America's Ambassador of Tap," *Dance Teacher* (2010): 248–49. Online. Available: http://www.dance-teacher.com/content/gregory-hines. December 7, 2012.
3. Anne Kisselgoff, "Baryshnikov and Feld Rejoin Forces," *New York Times*, March 9, 1995, C13.
4. Constance Valis Hill, *Tap Dancing America: A Cultural History* (New York: Oxford University Press, 2010), 277.
5. Gunter Schuller, *Early Jazz: Its Roots and Musical Development* (New York: Oxford University Press, 1986), chap. 4.
6. In general, rhythm tap is different from the white tradition of tap, which moved away from complex rhythmic structures and toward smoother choreographed moves, à la Fred Astaire. Sally Sommer, "Tap Dance and How It Got That Way," *Dance Magazine* 72: 9 (1988): 56, 59. Cheryl Willis, "Tap Dance: Manifestations of the African Aesthetic," in *African Dance: An Artistic, Historical, and Philosophical Inquiry*, ed. Kariamu Welsh Asante (Trenton, NJ: Africa World Press, 1996), esp. 146 and 149 (quotation). Savion Glover is also acknowledged as a "musician with his feet": Kellee Rene Van Aken, "Race and Gender in the Broadway Chorus," Ph.D. diss., University of Pittsburgh, 2006, 234.
7. More than one critic pointed out the similarity between the plot of *Jelly's Last Jam* and *A Christmas Carol*.
8. Kentucky Network, "George C. Wolfe," Annenberg/CPB, 1996. Online. Available: http://www.learner.org/resources/series55.html. December 12, 2012.
9. Will Nixon, "Profile: Playwright George C. Wolfe," *American Visions* 6: 2 (1991): 50, referring to a 1991 PBS production. Wolfe subsequently directed *Angels in America* (1993) in New York, an event that rather shocked him because "generally in this country, if you do one thing, that is the one thing you do. [. ..] If you direct stories about black people, that's all you do because that's all you're 'allowed' to do. Which is

not to say that you would want to do anything else, but there's definitely this pigeon-holing dynamic." He later pointed out that "since *Angels in America* and [becoming artistic director of] the Public Theater, I am no longer discussed as being black in the press." The phenomenon he brings up happened after *Jelly's Last Jam*. Charles H. Rowell, "'I Just Want to Keep Telling Stories': An Interview with George C. Wolfe," *Callaloo* 16: 3 (1993): 605, 607.

10. Lawrence Thelan, *The Show Makers: Great Directors of the American Musical Theatre* (New York: Routledge, 2002), 212. It is important to note that Wolfe, born in 1954, experienced the segregated American South while growing up in Kentucky. In an excerpted essay for the *New York Times*, published in response to the Los Angeles riots, Wolfe highlights the cognitive dissonance he experienced by being "extraordinary" in his black community and "insignificant" in the white community. "Defining Identity: Four Voices," *New York Times*, May 24, 1992, E11.

11. Indeed, Wolfe critiques megamusicals because the emotions triggered by the musical content tend to be "machinelike." Thelan, *The Show Makers*, 214–16. He also directed a revival of *On the Town* in 1998.

12. Rowell, "I Just Want to Keep Telling Stories," 608–9, 619; Kentucky Network, "George C. Wolfe."

13. David Savran, *A Queer Sort of Materialism: Recontextualizing American Theater* (Ann Arbor: University of Michigan Press, 2003), chap. 3 in particular.

14. Marty Bell, *Broadway Stories: A Backstage Journey through Musical Theatre* (New York: Limelight Editions, 1993), chap. 4, gives the show's production history from Lion's point of view; he also records that, at one point, playwright August Wilson was slated to write the book for the musical, but his unfamiliarity with the genre of musical theater proved to be a major stumbling block. Originally, jazz musician Butch Thompson had been hired as a music consultant for the show, but he left the production while Wolfe was still writing the script, because he thought Wolfe had taken too "political" a turn: William H. Youngren, "Unfairly Convicted: A Current Broadway Show Has It Wrong about Jelly Roll Morton," *The Atlantic* 272: 1 (1993): 98–103; Sylvie Drake, "Stage Review: 'Jelly' Struts Its Stuff at Mark Taper," *Los Angeles Times*, March 8, 1991, 1; Jennifer Johnson-Spence, director, "Episode 185/186: ATW's Working in the Theatre: Production: *Jelly's Last Jam*," http://www.cuny.tv/audiovideo, American Theatre Wing, CUNY TV, January 1, 1992.

15. Plays that started at the Taper include *Children of a Lesser God* and *Angels in America* (*Part One—Millennium Approache*s). Drake, "Stage Review."

16. Michael Elkin, "'Jelly' on a Roll; Jewish Women Part of Black Musical's Success," *Jewish Exponent* (Philadelphia), August 21, 1992, 9X, 147; William H. Sun and Faye C. Fei, "The Colored Theatre in Los Angeles," *TDR* 36: 2 (1992): 173.

17. Drake, "Stage Review."

18. The advertising representative for the show, Rick Elice, noted that the New York version was changing right up until the previews. That the musical went through revisions and changes is not unusual, although its long incubation period—almost ten years—and the husband/wife dynamic of Koslow-Hines and Hines means that the precise production history for the show will likely always be rather murky. In an online interview Wolfe noted that considerable changes were made between Los Angeles and New York, as he figured out that the Chimney Man was a central rather than peripheral figure within the musical. Johnson-Spence, "Episode 185/186"; Kentucky Network, "George C. Wolfe."

19. In an interview with *Ebony* magazine, Hines made it clear that he and author Wolfe initially had significant creative differences regarding the shape of the musical. Those differences needed to be resolved before he agreed to star in the show Wolfe wrote. It is also the case that Hines at one point intended to direct the show that became *Jelly's Last Jam*, but it is unclear when this was the case and at what point Hines changed his mind. Laura B. Randolph, "*Jelly's Last Jam* and the Pain and Passion of Gregory Hines," *Ebony* 47: 11 (1992): 116–19; Bell, *Broadway Stories*.

20. Bell, *Broadway Stories*, suggested that Babatundé simply did not have the charisma to hold *Jelly's Last Jam* together, but the reviews of the Los Angeles production do not bear out the claim. It is true that significant changes to the libretto were made between Los Angeles and New York, changing the character arc for Jelly and perhaps resulting in the need for a recast. However, Bell's take on the abilities of the Tony award-winning Babatundé seem calculated to elevate Hines by denigrating the previous actor. Also Drake, "Stage Review."

21. The amount of dancing caused some problems when Hines stepped down as the star and when the touring production finally came together in 1994. Maurice Hines, Gregory's brother, took on the role of Jelly Roll Morton for the tour, to mixed results. David Patrick Stearns, "*Jelly's Last Jam* on a Rocky Tour Road," *USA Today*, November 21, 1994, 6D.

22. Hill, *Tap Dancing America*, 12.

23. Brenda Dixon Gottschild, *The Black Dancing Body* (New York: Palgrave Macmillan, 2003), 120–30, discussed how Hines and Glover revolutionized tap by dancing to both pop and hip-hop musics and by appearing in film (e.g., *Tap*, 1989) and television (esp. *Sesame Street*).

24. Judith Sebesta, "Introduction," in *Women in American Musical Theatre: Essays on Composers, Lyricists, Librettists, Arrangers, Choreographers, Designers, Directors, Producers and Performance Artists*, ed. Bud Coleman and Judith Sebesta (New York: McFarland Press, 2008), 1–8, has noted that critical histories and biographies of female choreographers are sadly lacking. As far as I can tell, apart from a small flurry of profiles on Clarke on the occasion of being the first African American woman to direct a production of *Porgy and Bess*, nothing very substantive has been written about her or her choreography. She was also referenced once in a *New York Times* article regarding the state of dance in the 1992 season. Rebecca Morris, "Hope Clarke (choreographer) (People)," *American Theatre* 11: 10 (1994): 53–4; Anna Kisselgoff, "Dance View; Dance and Song Are Cheek to Cheek on Broadway," *New York Times*, July 5, 1992, B1.

25. Robert Sandla, "Meet the Hunnies and a Honey," *Dance Magazine* 68: 11 (1992): 76–77.

26. Sally R. Sommer, "An Appreciation; Gregory Hines: From Time Step to Timeless," *New York Times* August 14, 2003. Online. Available: http://www.nytimes.com/2003/08/14/arts/an-appreciation-gregory-hines-from-time-step-to-timeless.html?pagewanted=2&src=pm. December 7, 2012.

27. Thomas F. DeFrantz, "Foreword: Black Bodies Dancing Black Culture—Black Atlantic Transformations," in *EmBODYing Liberation: The Black Body in American Dance*, ed. Dorothea Fischer-Hornung and Alison D. Goeller (New Brunswick, NJ: Transaction Publishers, 2001), 11–16.

28. DeFrantz, "Foreword," 13.

29. George C. Wolfe, Susan Birkenhead, Jelly Roll Morton, and Luther Henderson. *Jelly's Last Jam* (New York: Theatre Communications Group, 1993), 69.

30. Dance often functions as a form of psychological/emotional exposition in many post-*Oklahoma!* musicals. Indeed, the critical acclaim in 1943 for Laurey's dream ballet in *Oklahoma!* popularized this mode of using dance in Broadway musicals as a means of expressing the inner self: Laurey cannot sing about her confused feelings between Jud and Curley, so she voicelessly works out the problem—her secret desires—within the dream ballet. While in the original production the actors who portrayed Laurey, Jud, and Curly were played by dream versions of themselves: professional modern dancers who substituted their bodies for the bodies of the singing actors. Arguably, the use of new performers to portray "dream Laurey" et al. heightened the dreamlike, uncanny effect of the ballet. In modern productions, these substitutions generally do not take place. In part, the reasons for this shift are relatively simple: it is more cost-effective to cast "triple threats" in the roles of Laurey, Curly, and Jud than it is to triple the number of performers for one number. However, it may also be the case that maintaining the bodily continuity between "real life" and

"dream" emphasizes the emotional turmoil Laurey is attempting to process because her bodily integrity is maintained.

31. Willis, "Tap Dance," 147

32. The comments by the producers were made after *Jelly's Last Jam* had premiered on Broadway; they were speaking retroactively about the concerns they had prior to the show's opening. What is interesting about the group interview is how no one is willing to explicitly state what, precisely, tap dancing represented. There is no other way to put it: they tap dance around the subject of racism. Johnson-Spence, "Episode 185/186."

33. Robert Berkson, *Musical Theater Choreography* (New York: Backstage Books, 1990), 23.

34. Richard Kislan, *Hoofing on Broadway: A History of Show Dancing* (New York: Prentice Hall, 1987), 32–33; Berkson, *Musical Theater Choreography*, 34 (quoting Eddie Leonard); Carol Clover, "Dancin' in the Rain," *Critical Inquiry* 21 (1995): 722–47.

35. Hill, *Tap Dancing America*, 1–3.

36. Ann duCille, "The Shirley Temple of My Familiar," *Transition* 73 (1997): 10–32.

37. Linda G. Tucker, extending Lhamon's theory of "lore cycles," names this process of misrepresentations "white lore cycles" whereby images of the black man as criminal/clown constantly recycle through white popular culture. Linda G. Tucker, *Lockstep and Dance: Images of Black Men in Popular Culture* (Jackson: University Press of Mississippi, 2007), 44–48.

38. Of course, within the narrative of the show, Jelly is transmitting knowledge to his younger self, but within the performative context of *Jelly's Last Jam*, Hines and Glover represented two different generations of African American dancers.

39. Hines even argued that the tradition of the tap challenge was a distinctively masculine trait of this genre of dance. Jane Goldberg, "Talking Tap with Gregory Hines: A Cutting Session," *On Tap* (2008), 8. Online. Available: https://www.tapdance.org/images/up/File/ONTap/19.2_OnTap.pdf[AU: The URL does not lead to a web page or a file. Please check and correct it.]. December 7, 2012.

40. The gender politics of *Jelly's Last Jam* are too complex to address here; however, it should be noted that the musical deals exclusively with how the cultural contributions of African American men have been erased from mainstream white history. It ignores the ways in which African American women are also excluded from mainstream history.

41. David Patrick Stearns, "Hines Taps his Deeper Talents; 'Jelly' Role Earns Him a Tony Nod," *USA Today*, May 29, 1992, 1D.

42. Approximately 13 percent of the audience for *Jelly's Last Jam* was African American. While such a percentage of African Americans in the audience was relatively high for a Broadway musical during the 1990s, it likely did not change the overall performative experience for Hines and the rest of the cast. Johnson-Spence, "Episode 185/186."

43. In the PBS documentary *Jammin'*, Kevin Ard, one of the actors who portrayed a "Coon," expressed that "to put on white lips . . . was a very hard experience." He took a very long pause before articulating that the process was "hard." Wolfe et al., *Jelly's Last Jam*, 68; Cox, *Jammin'*.

44. Aken, "Race and Gender in the Broadway Chorus," 10.

45. Reversing the order of importance between the chorus and the star is not new; *A Chorus Line* focuses on the anonymous dancers behind the (never-seen) star performer. Wolfe explicitly references *A Chorus Line* when discussing the impact of the "Chorus of Coons." Cox, *Jammin'*.

46. Henry Louis Gates Jr., *The Signifying Monkey: A Theory of Afro-American Literary Criticism* (New York: Oxford University Press, 1988), 20.

47. The Tin Pan Alley segment is problematic. The ethnicity of the music men is not explicitly acknowledged, but they perform a kind of Jewishness, adding an unfortunate layer of anti-Semitism to the sequence.

48. To be clear, the idea that Morton sold out whereas other African American composers did not is Wolfe's contention, not mine.

49. Even though he always acknowledged that he transcribed what others had created, Handy is often known as the "Father of the Blues." This modesty may be why Wolfe used him as the answer to the quiz, as it trumps Morton's hubris. Ted Gioia, *The History of Jazz* (New York: Oxford University Press, 1997), 19; Wolfe et al., *Jelly's Last Jam*, 83.

50. Wolfe et al., *Jelly's Last Jam*, 3.

51. Sommer, "Tap Dance and How It Got That Way," 58.

52. Wolfe et al., *Jelly's Last Jam*, 13.

CHAPTER 8

"Everything's Coming Up Kurt"

The Broadway Song in Glee

JESSICA STERNFELD

Only on the television hit *Glee* would one find a "diva-off" between two characters wherein they challenge each other to sing "Defying Gravity" from the musical *Wicked*. One character embraces the challenge since she knows (with annoying over-confidence) that she has the power for it; the other hopes to do well but in the end throws the contest on purpose, fearing that his status as a gay boy will become all the more public should he successfully sing this belted show tune associated with a female role. She conquers through a Broadway song; he retreats, backing out of the spotlight to protect his family from shame, despite his ability to sing the song and his desperate need to prove it. Examining the role of the Broadway show tune within the context of *Glee* (and several other television series) reveals the special place given to theater songs. Almost exclusively the domain of the characters Kurt and Rachel, and often carefully separated from the on-screen "real life" of the characters and their diegetic performances, Broadway songs and singing become marginalized, rendered both powerful for their ability to express earnest emotion at peak times, as well as dangerous in their cultural implications and therefore carefully boxed off. The identity Kurt performs when he sings is meant to be read as heartfelt and liberating, but instead repeats a stereotypical, narrow identity that is awkwardly laid upon him.

As the stories in *Glee* (which premiered in 2009) unfold, high school girl Rachel Berry (played by Lea Michele), the most talented and the most annoying of the McKinley High School show choir, searches for her birth mother. Being raised by a pair of men, she unfailingly refers to as "my two gay dads," she longs for a connection to her mother and fantasizes that she might be Broadway diva Patti LuPone or Bernadette Peters. She later turns out to be Broadway diva Idina Menzel, although Menzel is playing a character: the coach of a rival high school show choir. Before that revelation, Rachel hears her mother's voice for the first time when she receives a cassette tape (in the episode "Dream On," May 18, 2010). The voice on the tape sings "I

Dreamed a Dream" from Schönberg and Boublil's musical *Les Misérables* (1985), and in a fantasy sequence, Rachel joins the mother she has not yet met on an empty stage in an empty theater, and they sing an imaginary duet. Both wearing black and staring straight out into the vacant auditorium, they remake the fallen Fantine's song of lost love into a lament for having never known each other. The lyrics make far more sense coming from world-weary Shelby (Idina Menzel's character) than Rachel, who makes her magical appearance with the nostalgic line, "then, I was young and unafraid," an odd sentiment from a high school girl. But the message is exceedingly clear: both women have faces twisted with emotion, crying as they sing (or, accurately, lip-sync to the prerecorded track), sinking to the ground and holding on to one another without ever making eye contact. They look remarkably alike, and indeed sing similarly, with strong, loud, belting voices that strain and reach (successfully, although possibly with pitch adjustment in the studio) for the high notes. As the number ends, we return to reality: the screen cuts to Shelby crying in her car as rain pours, and then returns to Rachel in her bedroom, crying as she listens to the tape come to a close, harmonizing with her mother's voice on the last few notes.

The setup and delivery of this song are a bold exception to *Glee*'s norm. On the show, nearly all of the songs are diegetic: they're sung in public, for an on-screen audience of at least one other character. Many songs take place in rehearsal or performance, and even those that are meant to show a character's actual feelings are public displays first and foremost. The club's teacher, the earnest Mr. Schuester (Matthew Morrison), encourages students to express an emotion to the class through a song or share their feelings with someone else in a duet, teaching them repeatedly that singing can help them understand, convey, and work through their problems. The students enact his teaching dozens of times, telling each other that they have something important to express and have chosen a special song through which to share. For example, our hero, football player Finn (Corey Monteith), sings the rock ballad "I'll Stand By You" to display his feelings about his cheerleader girlfriend Quinn (Dianna Agron), who is pregnant. Whether on a literal stage or not, virtually all of the songs are performances for an on-screen audience, with those spectators, as we shall see, serving as stand-ins for the viewers at home, broadcasting to us how we are meant to react to the songs. Despite their teacher's attempts to explain the communicative and healing powers of singing and performing, the students choose songs that only sometimes express a feeling they can relate to. This doesn't mean the show's creators don't take advantage of the medium of television to "open up" (that is, use changes of setting, montages, and other visual effects that television or film naturally provides but that live theater often can't), or engage in what musical theater scholar Raymond Knapp calls "Musically Enhanced Reality Mode"; there are indeed visual violations of the natural or possible, when rehearsal morphs into costumed performance in mid-song, for example.[1]

But even the cut-together or far-too-well-rehearsed performances are still diegetic performances, almost all of the time, on *Glee*. Given this tendency, *Glee* is usually not a musical in the most fundamental sense. The defining characteristic of a musical—that characters express their feelings through song—virtually never happens in this show. Instead, the characters sing pop songs, and very occasionally show tunes, as performances or as fun diversions. Like a jukebox musical, *Glee* shoehorns already-known songs into the plot, often on the flimsiest of pretenses, so that the cast can cut loose and jump around to a favorite tune. Like a music video, the songs are heavily mixed and processed, removed entirely from the audio and often the visual frame of the rest of the story and signaling clearly to the viewer that the song was prerecorded by the actors, and the songs stand alone as three-minute performances. Like classic backstage musicals, the songs are almost always understood as performances for the rest of the cast, the actual song or its meaning often irrelevant, which is certainly natural enough on a show about a performing group.

All of these solutions for injecting songs into this broad "dramedy" of a TV show accomplish the same thing: they avoid the essential musical theater ingredient, that someone sings his or her own feelings. The moment when a character transitions from speech to song in a book musical, or from linking musical material to a set number in a sung-through or megamusical, or from recitative to aria in an opera, makes musical theater special; in very few art forms can there be a change of communicative medium in mid-performance. This moment of transition also makes many, many people exceedingly uncomfortable. For a character to break off from the action of a play, walk downstage with eyes lifted to the balcony, and begin to sing an earnest, anthemic song is downright embarrassing for those who don't love and accept the absurdities of musicals. As discussed elsewhere in this volume by Mary Jo Lodge and Matthew Lockitt, it's this aspect of the musical that makes people giggle, because it feels so intimate and so broadly theatrical at the same time. Raymond Knapp explains this discomfort by positioning musical theater as one of the most seemingly inauthentic, performed, obviously fake arts, as opposed to other music genres (like rock, jazz, and the blues) that, thanks to decades of critical commentary, have laid claim to a perceived authenticity. This sense that rock or jazz musicians are somehow more authentic or personal than other performers (especially those playing roles, as in musical theater) is itself a socially constructed opinion that has become "true" simply by repetition, but the dichotomy remains strong. To watch a rock star emote bears none of the discomfort or perceived artificiality of watching an actor emote in a role. Knapp notes that the collaborative and commercial elements of musicals add to their perception as contrived and inauthentic; this is art created by committee, so how can it be heartfelt? Of course this social tendency fails under scrutiny; all music is created by groups or at least influenced by social norms and aesthetics, and all performances are constructed or intentional in various ways.[2]

The writers of *Glee* clearly sense the potential for discomfort in its viewing audience, and seek to mediate the transition from speech to song, thus avoiding any embarrassed or disdainful reactions when *Glee* threatens to become a musical. Choosing to make almost all of the songs diegetic[3] may seem like a savvy choice by the writers in an age when musicals are increasingly becoming viable pop culture commodities. I would argue that it is, in fact, a cop-out motivated by fear of rejection by a larger audience than the true musical can ever have. The book musical may no longer reign, but that liminal moment when speech morphs into song, or when action freezes and reflection takes over, exists in any musical (or opera) with a plot, from *The Marriage of Figaro* (1786) to *Oklahoma!* (1943) to *Wicked* (2003). It is precisely this moment of transition, when a musical reveals itself as a musical, what Mark Steyn calls the "major pleasure of the musical play,"[4] that *Glee* seeks to avoid—most of the time. What are the reasons for this avoidance of song as self-expression, of being taken for a musical? And when *Glee* does have a musical-theater moment, who presents it, and how? Only two characters regularly give in to this intimate/theatrical mode of self-expression, and having the technique be limited to and defined by them makes a bold statement about the dangers of letting actual musical theater run rampant on television. The show controls and boxes off musicals, almost always avoiding a moment of genuine and personal (yet ridiculously over the top) expression like Rachel's duet with her mother.

Glee is not alone in this avoidance. Similarly, the television series *Smash* (2012) frames almost all of its performances either as fantasy or as on-screen rehearsal or performance. Another example of the avoidance of the transitional moment dominates the film version of *Chicago* (2002), in which director Rob Marshall sidesteps the issue by having nearly every musical number take place in Roxie's head; no one in the real world sings, the numbers are simply a coping mechanism for her apparently fractured mind. Critics hailed it as a clever solution to a problem that should not really exist; it's not a problem that people in musicals launch into song unless the audience refuses to accept it as a fact of the genre, and the assumption underlying an on-screen product like the film version of *Chicago* or the show *Glee* is that their audiences won't accept it. And since the 1960s, when the musical became supremely uncool and old-fashioned in the world of pop culture, the moment of transition to song seems to rank high among the "problems" with the genre. The enormous new surge in musical theater sometimes embraces the genre's norms, but often—especially on film or on TV—avoids this particular one by forcing the music to be diegetic, or framing the numbers as flights of fancy, or substituting pop songs for show tunes, or using all of these strategies.

TV MUSICALS, SHOW SONGS, AND GENDER

The idea of having to justify singing on TV is nothing new. Think for a moment about your favorite TV dramas, comedies, or sci-fi shows, in which there has been one episode that, for probably absurd reasons, included singing. *Grey's Anatomy* (2005), *Scrubs* (2001), *Buffy the Vampire Slayer* (1997), *Chicago Hope* (1994), *Xena: Warrior Princess* (1995), and many others have presented one-time episodes in which the cast sings, and always because someone is in a coma, under a spell, or otherwise having a complete break with reality. Of course this makes sense in a show when singing is not the normal mode of communication, but what about when it is? Why do these shows not embrace the simple musical theater axiom that people sing when they talk?

Cop Rock, a television series that ran for half a season in 1990, attempted to face this issue head-on. It was a police procedural—cops would receive a case, hunt down criminals, have a trial—in which various members of each episode's cast would sing (cops, judge and jury, street gangs, victims). Most scholars speculate that it failed for several reasons, including the lackluster musical material and the failure of the songs to further the plot. But I would argue that the real reason was the extreme discomfort an audience watching a cop show felt when characters began to sing. That's just not what happens in this genre, and it made the audience squirm, giggle, resist, and mock. Television scholar Ron Rodman argues that many shows are formed by combining genres; even an obvious cop show example, like *NYPD Blue* (1993), included a significant dramatic and ongoing component focused on the detectives' personal lives, merging police drama with nighttime soap. Audiences can even accept singing if it's explained as fantasy—like the brain aneurisms or magic spells in the one-time episodes, or the fantasy world of the British series *The Singing Detective* (1986), which, like *Cop Rock*, blended the police procedural and the musical, but took place entirely in the imagination of the main character, an invalid writer. As Rodman summarizes, "It seems viewers were ready to accept singing as interrupting the narrative if it is fantasy, but not with ordinary 'folks'"[5] —hence the infamous failure of *Cop Rock*.

So on TV, singing needs to be justified, rendered safe by the distance of fantasy, or by the frame of the diegesis. There is one other way that people can sing on TV, and that's if they sing familiar pop/rock music. If a character can passably render a performance of someone else's pop song, the audience will buy it, since it lies distant enough from a musical both in style and intent (that is, it's not an expression of anything internal). In Disney's made-for-television surprise hit movie *High School Musical* (2006), the cool athlete can sing because he sings vapid pop songs that reveal nothing about himself and he certainly doesn't wear costumes or learn to dance; in *Glee*, the cool athlete can sing for the same reasons. Finn the football player sings rock songs by the Doors or Rick Springfield with earnest, untrained enthusiasm that reminds us again and again that he is not a theater person. His voice, although somewhat high, is high in a way acceptable in rock music—with gravel, pitch-bending, and plenty of growling assertiveness. He is a mainstream male, an athlete, a regular straight guy who likes rock music. Thus he is perceived to be expressing himself in an "authentic," socially acceptable, heteronormative way, with the safe distancing of covering other people's earnest songs.

The notion that boys can only sing on TV if they sing manly songs in a rock style is reinforced by an unlikely example: the irreverent cartoon series *South Park*. The show's creators, Matt Stone and especially Trey Parker, are trained in music and experienced in the language of musical theater, and exhibit their (admittedly mocking) affection for the genre all the time—if their earlier work hadn't proven their experience and expertise in this genre, their 2011 hit Broadway musical *The Book of Mormon* certainly does. Although *South Park* is known for making fun of all sorts of minorities and social groups, the message usually boils down to a common-sense message of acceptance. But as television scholar Sean Nye points out, when it comes to gender and musical genres, the show reinforces a sexism by repeating the notion that men sing rock songs (driving, macho, real) and women sing pop (cheesy, annoying, fake) and show tunes (silly, dramatic). Nye notes, "when male stars are ridiculed, this often occurs by portraying them as effeminate or gay, thus implying that they fail as real men," as in the cases of episodes featuring cartoon versions of Kenny

G, Michael Jackson, and the Jonas Brothers.[6] In the episode "Elementary School Musical," when *High School Musical* catches on at South Park Elementary, our lead boys Stan, Kyle, and Cartman don't understand why it's popular and are horrified by its style.[7] Stan, Kyle, and Cartman—like Finn on *Glee*—are not theater people and would never speak through its music. Finn is already embarrassed by singing as it is; the only way to try to maintain his macho image is to sing without dancing (or by dancing poorly) and choosing songs that can't hurt his credibility as a man. And even that doesn't always work. His status as quarterback of the football team doesn't save him from being bullied and harassed by his own teammates because he dares to sing.

Why is it that boys don't want to sing, or if they do, must sing a rock song that won't hurt their standing as males? A study of elementary school pupils by three sociologists revealed, not surprisingly, that boys are socialized to exhibit toughness.[8] The sociologists point out that the opposite of toughness is not defined generally as wimpiness—it's specifically labeled as femininity, or homosexuality, and boys are constantly on the lookout for this supposed weakness. Along with toughness comes a mandate to exhibit "coolness," which involves "assuming suitably detached postures and attitudes. [...] They act cool in distancing themselves from things they used to like, but are now defined as feminine or nerdy. They act cool by repressing emotionality."[9] The key here is repressing emotionality to avoid seeming feminine. Self-expression through music is shoved to the side, left for girls and for boys labeled as gay. Hence Finn, like Cartman and his friends, is trained *not* to be a theater person lest he risk social annihilation.

But Rachel *is* a theater person. She knows the musical theater canon, and although she sings many pop songs alone or with others, her voice is theatrical, her style of choice is Broadway, and her goal in life is a Tony award. In the population of the glee club—all dorks to the rest of the school to a certain extent because they like to sing—she is the dorkiest, because of her taste in music, and because she expresses herself directly through theater, not abstractly by covering pop songs that kind of relate to her life.

This is not to say that the creators of *Glee* are self-loathing theater people; they clearly love Broadway and lavish plenty of attention on unlikeable, loud, controlling, self-satisfied Rachel, played by a young Broadway veteran Lea Michele. But they also know their audience, which is mainstream America. My anecdotal research on discussion boards and chat rooms reveals that although plenty of fans know theater and, for example, were excited to see Broadway star Kristin Chenoweth on the show, the vast majority are fans of the show because of its humor, its "It's okay to be different" message, and its catchy and familiar pop songs. People on Internet discussion boards asked what "Rose's Turn" and the "Hot Honey Rag" were, but everyone knew the songs by Kanye West, Cee-Lo Green, Aerosmith, Lady Gaga, and Journey.

Statistics about song choice strongly support the idea that the creators are targeting a pop-oriented audience. The average episode features four or five pop songs, and perhaps one show tune, if any. Every episode featuring the work of a single artist has focused on a pop star—Madonna, Britney, Justin Bieber, Michael Jackson—with three exceptions: one when the club tried but failed to mount *The Rocky Horror Show* (1973), a rock musical, and twice when some members performed in productions of

West Side Story (1957) and *Grease* (1972) independently of the glee club. When an episode does feature a show tune but not a show, it is almost always performed by Rachel or Kurt Hummel (played by Chris Colfer), the gay member of the club with a very high and sweet voice (containing no rock-style dirt and indeed barely any chest power at all) and a character who vacillates between biting cattiness and weeping insecurity.[10] Rachel's penchant for musicals seems to be biological—not, apparently, the product of being raised by two gay dads, but rather the result of being Idina Menzel's character's daughter, a fact she realizes when she hears Menzel sing live, and the truth revealed in Menzel's theatrical voice (as she performs "Funny Girl") draws Rachel to her like a beacon—or a spotlight. There is nevertheless a gay subtext to Rachel's audience appeal, since she aligns herself with Broadway divas who are icons in the gay fan community.

A GAY BOY SPEAKS THE LANGUAGE OF BROADWAY

Kurt's leaning toward musicals is apparently a result of his orientation, although this is never said directly. It's simply understood that a gay boy speaks the language of Broadway, and when he feels the need to express his emotions, he doesn't simply perform pop songs like the other characters, he sings Broadway. His orientation has been a major focus of the story thus far; in the first three seasons of the show, he came out, grew increasingly comfortable with his identity, developed a crush on straight football player Finn, got bullied so badly that he transferred to a fancy all-boys' academy, fell in love with a boy there whom he then dated, and transferred back in triumph over the bully (who turned out to be a closeted and suicidal homosexual). Kurt's father Burt (Mike O'Malley), a butch single dad who works at a tire store, struggles to accept his son, not so much for his orientation, but for his interests; he can't relate to Kurt's decorating style, devotion to his skin care regimen, or musical taste. He defends Kurt repeatedly to those who would bully or insult him, but can't relate to his son.

This distance between them reaches an extreme (one of many) in a first-season plotline when Burt begins spending time with Finn, the football player, whose mother Burt is dating. Kurt actually engineered this romance between the two single parents to get closer to Finn, a manipulative maneuver that borders on stalking at several points. In the episode "Laryngitis" (May 11, 2010), he realizes his plan has backfired and led to his father having the kind of comfortable, guys-hanging-out close relationship with Finn that Kurt fails to have.

In a move exceedingly rare on *Glee*, but absolutely the norm in a musical, Kurt expresses his feelings of jealousy and anger by sliding from speech to song. Like Rachel's fantasy about her mother, Kurt's expression of his feelings transforms the visual element and gives him a performance venue—but no audience. The venue is an empty stage, just like Rachel's, and just like the one used for the staging of this song in its original context—for this is "Rose's Turn," from the 1959 musical *Gypsy* by Styne and Sondheim, with a few choice words altered. In that musical, an unfulfilled middle-aged mother lives out her show-biz dreams through her daughters, until one abandons her and the other stumbles into a successful career as a stripper. The woman, Momma Rose, is left on the sidelines, furious and jealous and lonely.

Kurt's embodiment of Rose's pain begins as an integrated book musical number would, with dialogue sliding into song. We find Kurt walking down the school hallway hand in hand with fellow show choir member Brittany, an air-brained cheerleader whom Kurt attempts, for part of this one episode, to date, in a failed effort to fit in and butch up. When Burt tells Kurt he plans to spend time with Finn that night, eating hoagies and watching motocross, Kurt looks pained and asks, "Didn't you ever think that that might be something I might want to do with you?" Burt, not yet understanding Kurt's sense of betrayal, promises to spend time with him later and walks off. Underscoring sneaks into the scene, as Kurt gazes down the hall after his father and takes up Rose's lyrics: "All that work and what did it get me? Why did I do it? Scrapbooks full of me in the background. Give 'em love and what does it get ya?" Kurt delivers an abridged version of Rose's long number, skipping the part that would surely be hardest to fit into this scenario, when Momma Rose repeatedly cries out "Momma!" He also changes a few words: "I had a dream. I dreamed it for you, Dad [...]. If it wasn't for me, where would you be, Miss Rachel Berry?" The reference to Rachel does not make much sense, but perhaps suggests that Kurt is but a supporting player to Rachel the diva; it also fits nicely in the spot where the lyric "Miss Gypsy Rose Lee" would otherwise be. By this point the visual imagery has been transformed by Kurt's outpouring of emotion. His outfit, earlier a baseball cap, T-shirt, and hoodie as part of his attempt to pull off a macho John Cougar Mellencamp song and look like a cheerleader's boyfriend, is instantly replaced by a stylish, slim-fitting shirt, an exceptionally long silk scarf, and his signature side-swept hairstyle. He magically appears on the vacant auditorium stage, and just as Rose reveals the lightbulb marquee that declares her name, the curtain behind Kurt rises to reveal "KURT" spelled out hugely. "Everything's coming up Kurt!" he belts, "everything's coming up Hummel!" The melody sits high in his range, but he actually uses a voice heavier and more chest-centered than usual, even growling with gusto, and then audibly switching into his falsetto in a few places (in the line "if it wasn't for me" in the opening passage, for example) when a higher passage requires it. His momentary jubilation turns to desperation as he cries "for me!" repeatedly and adds a growl to the final note's fall-off.

This is as close to an actual book musical as *Glee* has ventured to date. Speech becomes song, song becomes theater, for only this kind of emotional and performative excess can express Kurt's feelings at this moment. The scene after the song even follows the model of *Gypsy*; Kurt, like Momma Rose, thinks he's alone, but one witness—Burt instead of Louise—has heard the song and understood the pain and jealousy and regret that created it. Like Momma Rose, Kurt is slightly deranged at this point, railing and angry and a little bit monstrous. His dream seems simple enough—he wants his father's love and a normal relationship with him, just as Rose wants a life in the theater and respect from her daughters—but the lengths to which both characters will go to achieve these goals are at times frightening and creepy. Rose eventually encourages her daughter Louise to become a stripper rather than face a life outside the theater; Kurt has encouraged his father to date as a means for Kurt to be near Finn, whom he apparently hopes to convert.

Kurt could have sung any number of songs of frustration or loss here; musical theater provides him with dozens of choices, and so does the world of pop music, for that matter. But the writers handed Kurt "Rose's Turn," which surely is meant to play on the fact that the song, and the role of Momma Rose, is one of the most coveted by aging Broadway divas—it's the role every belter wants to play, and the role has as big a reputation in the gay theater community as the divas themselves. Kurt, by "choosing" this song to express himself, aligns himself with Ethel Merman, Angela Lansbury, Tyne Daly, Bette Midler, Bernadette Peters, and Patti LuPone. Stacy Wolf points out the series of associations the role of Rose carries with it, when she examines what each actress brought to it: Angela Lansbury demonstrated Rose's "slender tie to sanity" when she continued to bow after the applause had died down for "Rose's Turn"; Tyne Daly brought "monstrous fierceness"; Bette Midler was "ghosted by her campy star persona." Together, these associations are what "laminates" the performer (Kurt, in this case) onto the character he plays. "Gender and sexuality are envoiced and embodied in the person of the actor playing the character," Wolf argues, which in this context suggests that Kurt is somehow fusing his own identity as a (young, gay, exaggeratedly flamboyant, angry, lonely) male with that of the crazed would-be diva he seems to admire.[11]

I also see an even more direct logic to Kurt's appropriation of this song. Musical theater scholar D. A. Miller speculates that Rose undergoes a transformation during this number. He says that Rose can never command the stage as her performing daughters do because although she is a mother, she is not a woman; here her singing becomes screaming, and "Rose's Turn" "turns Rose into a boy, any one of the million male child wannabes grown pale and puny in their basement prisons, and whose futile, foreclosed perspective now howlingly commands the stage."[12] Miller explains that for Momma Rose to call out "Momma!" repeatedly is to recast herself as a child, a lost little boy.[13] So, when Rose reveals herself as a boy, she and Kurt unite as one.

But on a broader level, it matters less that Kurt sings a song that fits his orientation than that he sings a show tune and that he presents it as it would be presented in a musical—as a means of self-expression, not as a diegetic rehearsal. Kurt performs directly to us, not to his classmates on the screen, and is accompanied by a magical, invisible music source, which he is apparently creating as he rants. Scholar Heather Laing notes that "this pleasurable illusion of spontaneous, improvisatory composition still works when the song is not original to the film, and may already be well known to audiences from the popular song repertoire, or even previous musicals."[14] So it doesn't matter one bit that Kurt sings an incredibly well-known song meant for a middle-aged woman in an unrelated story; this is his personal moment of self-expression that can only be facilitated by the slide from speech to heightened self-generated singing that a musical can provide.

But as multilayered as we theater scholars may find this scene, most *Glee* viewers don't know what show this song is from, who sings it, or what cultural baggage weighs it down. For most, Kurt simply goes all theatrical, belting out a show tune with his usual mix—both bitchy and vulnerable, chesty and breathy. And he does it again, in a later episode (season 2's "Born This Way," April 26, 2011): in virtually the only other example of a full musical theater number presented as a character's internal feelings, Kurt delivers "As If We Never Said Goodbye" from Andrew Lloyd Webber's 1993 musical *Sunset Boulevard*, to mark the occasion of his return to McKinley High School (his old performing venue) after being away at the prep school for several months, like Norma Desmond returning to the film studio. In *Sunset Boulevard*, Norma Desmond is an aging former star of silent film, who has become a lonely and apparently psychotic agoraphobic, when a young man barges into her life and inspires her to try again. When she delivers this song, she is returning in what she thinks is triumph to the movie studio; just after this song, we will learn the pathetic truth, that acclaimed director Cecil B. DeMille just wanted to borrow her vintage car for a film. But we already know during this song that Norma is deluded, that she'll never work again, that she has already lost touch with reality, that no one is paying attention to her.

Kurt's return to his old stomping ground involves none of this tragic or twisted backstory; he sings sincerely just as Norma does, but the television viewing audience is surely not meant to bring its knowledge of Norma's insanity and imminent humiliation. What in the context of *Sunset Boulevard* is an eerily and inappropriately cheerful and heartfelt testament to a life the singer will never get back, is on *Glee* apparently simply cheerful and heartfelt. Despite the radically different context, the staging of the number on *Glee* parallels the staging in *Sunset Boulevard*, as Kurt wanders through a particularly fake series of stage sets: students painting pieces on the stage, making "waves" by pushing and pulling a wooden cut-out of wave shapes, echoing quite literally the lyrics "I don't know why I'm frightened. I know my way around here. The cardboard trees, the painted seas, the sound here." Later he sits in front of a backstage makeup mirror, and also appears in front of his classmates in their rehearsal room, performing (as is rarely the case for Kurt but so common for everyone else) diegetically.

As with "Rose's Turn," with "As If We Never Said Goodbye" Kurt sings a number meant for an aging diva, and delivers it with complete sincerity and relatively believable emotional ties—and again, he's the only character besides Rachel who sings theater songs in a theater way, although in this case he *also* sings in the classroom for his friends. But are we meant to understand the baggage that this song brings with it? The melody, by tune master Lloyd Webber, is falsely lush here—this shimmery, soaring theme (the heavenly nature of which is reinforced on *Glee* by a harp that we see in the classroom but never hear) is meant to sound like the deluded inside of Norma's mind. In Lloyd Webber's show, the music after this will return to earth, dissonant and conversational and much more realistic, but we don't get that contrast here. So is Kurt delusional? The students in the classroom tell us how to feel: they are receiving his message with beatific smiles of affection and warmth, in full acceptance of his sincerity and earnestness. But anyone who knows the story knows that for Norma, it will all go horribly wrong, and that this song is a false oasis of psychotic peace before the storm hits (leading Norma to snap completely and become a murderous lunatic). For anyone who knows musicals, there is no way to separate the deluded middle-aged diva from Kurt's ostensibly heartfelt youthful emotions; thus he again becomes a queen stand-in, a monstrous pathetic woman rendered on TV as a pink-cheeked and light-voiced boy.

Judith Butler has argued that there is in fact no essence of the self, only a series of oft-repeated performative gestures and habits, through which one continuously performs one's identities. Gender, far from being a biological imperative, is in Butler's reasoning a performance undertaken every day; Nikki Sullivan explains:

> In her seminal text, *Gender Trouble*, Judith Butler argues that gender is neither natural nor innate, but rather, is a social construct which serves particular purposes and institutions. Gender, she says, is the performative effect of reiterative acts, that is, acts that can be, and are, repeated [...]. Rather than being expressions of an innate (gender) identity, acts and gestures which are learned and are repeated over time create the illusion of an innate and stable (gender) core.[15]

If we accept the idea that Kurt is attempting to perform his identity for the world, and indeed for himself so that he understands who he is, he has been directed by society toward (Butler would not say that Kurt chooses it consciously) a particularly effeminate, insecure gay boy who relates most strongly with the loud divas of Broadway stories, taking on those women's pain and indeed their voices. But in this case, "society" is the writing team of *Glee*; for Kurt, they have chosen these modes of expression, and they argue through their choices that Kurt sings these Broadway roles because they most authentically allow him to perform his identity. James Loxley notes that performances (such as those on a stage) are generally—but wrongly—understood to be safer for and more distant from the spectator, since on-stage (or on-screen) performances are just pretend; the viewer knows the actor is acting, so that whatever disturbing transgressions he or she might be presenting, they aren't real. We have "a conception of performance or acting as distinct from and lesser than 'reality' or 'real life'";[16] thus, I would argue, allowing we viewers to dissociate from (and even cheer for) Kurt in a way that many would not do if we met him (in all of his loud, high-voiced, fashionably shocking glory) on the street. The medium of a musical within a TV show provides double distance, giving the audience the ability to relax when faced with a musical theater performance that would surely shock in "real life."

Manipulative cheerleading coach Sue Sylvester (Jane Lynch) sums up the role of the show tune in the world of *Glee* perfectly when she deflates in one sentence these extramusical meanings we might want to attach to the show tune. She flatly returns us to my earlier point that show tunes shed the baggage of their original contexts and simply represent the unlikeable, the laughable, the uncool in a pop music world. She drily says to Kurt one day, "So you like show tunes. Doesn't mean you're gay. It just means you're awful."[17] Only Rachel and Kurt, with their penchant for unnecessary drama, speak the language of show tunes—and yet only they, among all of the regular characters on the show, are given the chance to sing without performing, to express without an audience other than the viewers at home. The minds behind *Glee* may spend four-fifths of their musical material catering to the pop audience, but they also know that the unique trick a musical can pull off, when speech becomes song and life becomes theater, is occasionally the only maneuver that will satisfy.

Unfortunately, this embracing of what a musical can do does not translate into a central place for Kurt's means of self-expression. By the end of the show's third season, we can see more clearly the roles of pop and theater music and what has become the marginalization of Kurt. Despite much focus on him as a character, he virtually never sings in public. In the first three seasons, the glee club attended seven public competitions. At each of these fully staged and costumed performances for packed houses, the group sings two or three numbers, and out of all of these songs, not one of them gives Kurt a solo line or featured moment. It seems that Mr. Schuester is suppressing Kurt, generally agreed to be among the top few singers in the group, to feature Rachel and Finn over and over again. The two sing heteronormative pop songs, the African American R&B singer Mercedes (Amber Riley) steps from the back line to wail some high notes at the end, and Kurt sways in the background at every performance. When the boys of the club performed Michael Jackson's "Man in the Mirror" in competition in season 3, every boy came forward with a solo except the one who doesn't sing, and Kurt—who appeared in the back row with the girls. If ever there was a male singer who suited Kurt's range, it's Michael Jackson. Is the show implying that Kurt is not a man, so he isn't qualified to sing the lyrics? Even in the safety of the rehearsal room or empty auditorium, Kurt is rarely featured in a group number—with one notable exception. In the episode "Born This Way," Mr. Schuester gives the kids an assignment: to wear a T-shirt expressing a challenging or societally stigmatized quality about themselves that they have had to embrace. They sing Lady Gaga's "Born This Way" while displaying the aspects about themselves that others may shun but that give them strength and pride, and Kurt, at long last, is given the chance to solo in a group number—and a pop one at that. Even if this is yet another gay anthem sung by a female diva (the song is quite explicit in its embracing of all orientations and lifestyles, although the most on-point lyrics about homosexuality are inexplicably cut in the shortened *Glee* version), at least it's not "awful" show music.

Kurt opens the performance of "Born This Way" standing center stage, with uncharacteristically spiky hair (in deference to the pop style, perhaps, or the wildness of Lady Gaga's look) with an amusingly aloof expression and a cocky attitude in his body language. "It doesn't matter if you love him," he recites with drama in Gaga style, "or capital H-i-m." His classmates reveal his T-shirt proclaiming "LIKES BOYS." (Other declarations of embracing their stigmas include "FOUR EYES," "BAD ATTITUDE," and "CAN'T DANCE"—of course Finn's T-shirt). Kurt, center stage, leading the song, and declaring his orientation, is almost immediately eclipsed by several girls (Mercedes and classmate Tina) who chime in to do the actual singing. Kurt, neither the strongest nor weakest dancer in the group, quickly fades into the crowd, emerging again only when the spoken portion of the song returns: "Don't be a drag, just be a queen," he raps. "Rejoice and love yourself today, 'Cause baby, you were born this way." He slides back into the group; his voice becomes instantly inaudible on the soundtrack.

This message of embracing your differences is undoubtedly meant with sincerity, and it works; *Glee* has raised awareness for all forms of difference among teens. But it is impossible to ignore that Kurt's voice ends up used, once again, as a stand-in for a diva icon and then, because the rest of the group is there, quickly gets suppressed; he raps, but does not sing, his lines about loving "him" and being a "queen," and then his voice is heard no more. Instead Mercedes wails, Rachel takes the stage despite announcing only seconds earlier that she would not, and Kurt ends up swaying in the background. Maybe someday, he can sing in public. And maybe he can sing a song that isn't meant for a female icon of the gay community, which has been the case with every one of his solos and duets to date.[18]

Rounding out Kurt's first three seasons and the seemingly unshakable commitment the writers have for making sure we all understand Kurt's inability to express himself in any other way than as a flamboyant champion of the gay show tune, Kurt performed "Not the Boy Next Door" from the Peter Allen "bio-musical" (as Kurt explained it) *The Boy from Oz* (1998) in the episode "Choke" (May 1, 2012). The song served as his audition for a (fictional) performing arts college in New York called NYADA (the New York Academy of Dramatic Arts); gaining admission is his (and Rachel's) overarching goal throughout the season. He had planned on performing "The Music of the Night" from *The Phantom of the Opera* (1986), which would have marked a significant change of pace for him, since that is a song performed by a man in an (admittedly twisted) bid to woo a woman. The song is set in a typical tenor range, and Kurt sounded perfectly at home performing it with his natural counter-tenor. But it's clear in rehearsal that it doesn't suit him: he wildly overacts, with grand gestures and insincere delivery, and the whole performance is meant to make viewers understand that he's not comfortable with the song. He can't perform the role of heterosexual, or baritone. He ponders whether putting sequins on his cape would help. The song is "too safe, it's too predictable," he tells boyfriend Blaine. "I need something fresh, I need something edgy, something completely unpredictable." When he announces that he'll be singing "The Music of the Night" to the woman running the audition (Carmen Tibideaux, played by Whoopi Goldberg), her bored reaction inspires him to ponder out loud that she probably hears that song a lot. She confirms this, but for Kurt to bring a song like "The Music of the Night" to a non-theater audience watching Kurt on television would not have been at all predictable or repetitive. We have never seen him sing a song like that—playing a role that isn't him, singing something not written for a female diva or gay icon. So he does what is purported to be the unpredictable thing—he becomes predictable Kurt. "I've decided to go in a different direction," he tells the auditioner from the stage. "Something that's a little more out there, but much more me." He rips off what turns out to be a tear-away tuxedo to reveal a black silk blouse and gold lamé pants, and delivers "Not the Boy Next Door" with more dancing, hip thrusting, shoulder rolling, and pelvic gyrating than he (or anyone) has ever done on *Glee*. The camera angles emphasize his crotch and often shoot from hip level out into the auditorium. He throws himself around the stage in his campiest performance by far, and ends with a spectacularly high G5.[19] "A bold choice, young man," says the intimidating auditioner. "I congratulate you on taking such a risk today."

So are the writers encouraging Kurt to be himself, by giving not only the chance to express himself through song, but by having those songs be ones that we are meant to understand suit his persona? Was his song choice a risk? Or are they reinforcing the reading of his character as a kind of drag queen, unable to sell a song unless he pretends to be a woman—and a campy theatrical woman at that—or an extremely flamboyant gay icon? Most see a message of acceptance and an embracing of gay culture, but it can also be read as placing this boy in a very small box; someday, it would be liberating for him and for viewers to see him sing a show tune or a pop song originated by a straight man, and if he wants to sing it an octave higher to suit his range, so be it. If the message is that they were all born this way, let him be who he is: a gay boy with a high voice who uses theatrical songs to express himself.

The larger message behind Kurt's song choices seems to be that, in essence, boys and musicals automatically equal homosexuality, and that the stigma attached to the musical must somehow be boxed off safely to one side or fought against with fantasy or pop music. Rachel represents another side of the same stereotype; while Kurt aspires to embody the loud-mouthed diva, Rachel is already there, with her huge belting voice, her abrasive manner, and everyone's repeated references to her Jewishness, her big nose, and her other traits that align her with all of her heroes. Thus *Glee* pulls off an impressive, but socially problematic, feat: by putting show tunes into the mouths of these two characters, the writers essentialize and trivialize what a musical is, while purporting to support equal rights and the freedom of self-expression. For most viewers, it may feel liberating and inspiring, but it is reductionist and stereotyping, that only these two characters speak the musical language of Broadway and use it to perform their identities.

Interestingly, it seems the writers of *Glee* may have heard this plea, for in a more recent episode, Kurt addressed his tendency to perform a flamboyant, showy version of himself head-on. Unfortunately, the moment, which delivered exactly what I have called for above—Kurt singing a less culturally loaded song in a seemingly honest way—was undermined immediately afterward. In the episode "Swan Song" (December 6, 2012), Kurt hopes to audition again for NYADA, the performing arts college that Rachel is now attending. He visits the office of auditioner Carmen Tibideaux, who mentions that she saw his second audition submission on video, an acoustic version of Wham's "Wake Me Up Before You Go-Go." Clearly he has not yet learned that he'll be perceived as sincere if he lets go of the exaggerated homosexual references. She tells him that she thought the same thing after both auditions: "Here's a very talented young man who knows how to sell a number, but who is devoid of complexity and depth." At a showcase at the school, where Rachel has just brought the house down, Tibideaux springs the opportunity on Kurt to audition yet again. He panics, having only a few minutes to prepare, and wonders if he should do "Wishing You Were Somehow Here Again" from *The Phantom of the Opera*, or "With One Look" from *Sunset Boulevard*, both women's songs from Andrew Lloyd Webber (read: cheesy, insincere) musicals. Rachel says those won't work for this crowd (one wonders why not, they are a far more musical theater-oriented crowd than at his high school back in Ohio) and that the goal is to show Tibideaux who he really is.

He opts for "Being Alive" from Sondheim's *Company*, which nearly fulfills the call: it's a song originated by a man, not a diva or gay icon, and although the character who sings it has a somewhat unclear sexual orientation (despite his many girlfriends, the character of Bobby has an awkward conversation about homosexuality and many scholars have speculated that his commitment phobia stems from his possibly unresolved orientation), the song is at base about taking the bold step of committing to a partner. Kurt simply stands and sings, without stage business, staring sadly into the middle distance and crying by the end. The implication is that he is thinking about his own troubled relationship with boyfriend Blaine. He dares, in other words, to be himself—or at least to perform the role of himself, expressing vulnerability in a way that is, while no less theatrical or performative, certainly less broad—and it works. He is accepted into the school. But he sets up the performative nature of his delivery before he begins: "I'm Kurt Hummel," he tells the crowd, "and I'll be auditioning for the role of NYADA student." So the lesson he has learned here is not necessarily to be himself, but to act as if the calmer, less theatrical mode of performing he's been instructed to use is himself. This discovery about how to give spectators this other side of his persona could well mark a maturing of Kurt's performance abilities, and indeed his personality as well, because he concedes in this episode that he has previously hidden behind flashy costumes and props, a sort of sideways reference to his reliance on diva songs.

Just a few episodes later, though, as Kurt's trajectory seems to continue to carry him out of the small box his song choices and Mr. Schuester's directorial choices had him in, Rachel puts him right back in it. In the episode "Diva-Off" (February 7, 2013), Kurt and Rachel face off again, as they did with "Defying Gravity" several years back. In a showdown set up by their fellow NYADA students, they (by luck of a draw) both sing "Bring Him Home" from *Les Misérables*, a song not particularly appropriate for either of them, sung by an older man to a young man toward whom he has developed paternal feelings. The students declare Kurt the winner by a small margin. Rachel must finally admit that Kurt is just as talented, that he is no longer an imitation of her but a performer in his own right. To rekindle their friendship, she invites him to join her at an audition for her favorite musical, *Funny Girl*. Undermining every bit of the work these more recent performances have done to pull Kurt out of the small box of the gay musical theater diva wannabe, Rachel shoves him right back in when she teases, "You'll make an amazing Fanny Brice." Once again, Kurt is rendered a drag queen, bound to lose this inappropriate audition to the clearly more suited Rachel, making him again a gay boy who seeks outlet in the language of the Broadway diva.

THE AWKWARDLY HIPBROW MUSICAL

Although it adds a layer of confusion to the situation, it is important to remember that there are two levels of performance happening on *Glee* (and similar musical shows or films): the performances like those discussed above, wherein a character shifts from what we are meant to perceive as his or her "real life" to a performance of a song, but also, always, the performance being presented by every actor on the screen. As with any theatrical endeavor, everything we see is a performance by actors, and because *Glee* includes singing (whether it be a blatantly performative, theatrical musical theater song or a seemingly authentic rock or pop song), the show perpetually struggles to find its balance between being a regular TV show (appealing to a vast audience, accepted as an authentic, or at least realistic, story) and being a musical (appealing to a smaller, more specialized set of viewers, and therefore loaded with expectations about performative posturing). David Savran applies the term "hipbrow," a play on the much-discussed middlebrow status of the musical, to the show *Rent*; it applies remarkably well to *Glee* as well, since both seek to balance artistic integrity with trendy commercialism. Savran describes *Rent* as being "derivative of so many different sources [...]. It reveals the fact that so many U.S. cultural productions that aspire both to hotness (especially to the youth market) and to a measure of artistic seriousness require the simultaneous deployment of a standardized, easily recognizable formula and a mystique of authenticity (or realness)."[20] *Glee*, with its performative theater moments leaping out of its overly stylized trendy texture, is well defined as hipbrow, which "trades at once on anonymity and uniqueness, predictability and a radically chic pose."[21] In other words, *Glee* attempts to be contemporary, appealing to young people, and special, while also being broadly acceptable and predictable enough to maintain a large audience. The show itself performs its identity, balancing with awkward precariousness between mass appeal and hip eccentricity, a balance especially tipped toward the dangerously unappealing and limiting (and thus quickly reigned in and suppressed entirely in on-screen public situations like competition scenes) when it becomes a musical thanks to Kurt or Rachel.

On *Smash*, like *Glee*, one can see the medium of TV struggling with the conventions of the musical, and awkwardly trying to justify the basic feature of the genre: people sing. But discussions about *Smash* have also raised the issue of how to sell musicals to mainstream audiences, burdened as they are by the potential spread of homosexuality, and somehow protect viewers from it and from the automatically implied cast of loud-mouthed divas and their fanboys that come with musicals. Like *Glee*, *Smash* features several gay characters, including composer Tom (Christian Borle) and sometimes—although his orientation is a point of much speculation—assistant Ellis (a character dropped after the first season, played by Jaime Cepero), but the presence of gay characters is not the threat. It's the presence of musical theater. One journalist picked up on the unspoken threat of sung, performed ideas of homosexuality that both *Glee* and *Smash* seem to feel the need to box off into safe zones. In a feature article about *Smash* in *TV Guide*, the author opens with this description: "As anyone who's read the copious critical raves knows, *Smash*—the most *faaabulous* show that's not on Bravo—is all that and an orchestra seat." There are no less than three homophobic slurs in this single sentence: the swishy rendering of the word "fabulous" (a term, even without the extra letters, already associated with gay male culture),[22] the reference to the Bravo network with supposedly gay-friendly programs like *Real Housewives* and *Project Runway*, and the saucy twist on the "all that and a bag of chips" expression. The article then goes on to list the show's redeeming features for those put off by the fabulousness (read: gayness): the producer is Steven Spielberg, the creator also started *NYPD Blue*, and the plot is a "stage-door soap."[23] Watching *Smash*, like *Glee*, struggle so hard and so awkwardly against being a musical, distancing itself from both the homosexual shadow and the concept of people who sing, is exhausting. Just sing.

NOTES

1. Raymond Knapp, *The American Musical and the Performance of Personal Identity* (Princeton, NJ: Princeton University Press, 2006), 67.
2. See Raymond Knapp, "Performance, Authenticity, and the Reflexive Idealism of the American Musical," in *The Oxford Handbook of the American Musical*, ed. Raymond Knapp, Mitchell Morris, and Stacy Wolf (Oxford: Oxford University Press, 2011), especially 410: "In contrast with the hard-won authenticities of the classical canon and the projected authenticities of jazz and rock, musicals offer instead a multi-authored, highly collaborative, eclectic, star-driven commercial product in which roles are performed in the most artificial of modes: the glitzy glitter of song and dance, often with an admixture of camp. And these products are sustained not by artists steeped in a revered tradition but by a full gamut of performers, from Broadway casts performing the same routines every night, to musical neophytes lip-synching to playback that may or may not include their own voices, kids in high schools, college and community groups, and really anyone who might want to sing or dance along to a cast album. How much further from the paradigms of authenticity can you get?"
3. Performances understood as performances by the other characters on the screen.
4. Mark Steyn, *Broadway Babies Say Goodnight: Musicals Then & Now* (London: Routledge, 1999), 103.
5. Ron Rodman, " 'Coperettas,' 'Detecterns,' and Space Operas: Music and Genre Hybridization in American Television," in *Music in Television: Channels of Listening*, ed. James Deaville (London: Routledge, 2011), 53.
6. Sean Nye, "From Punk to the Musical: South Park, Music, and the Cartoon format," in Deaville, *Music in Television*, 156.
7. Nye explains that the boys see this trend of boys singing in musicals as "a crisis of masculinity and a horrible betrayal of the traditions of rock." Ibid., 158.
8. Patricia A. Adler, Steven J. Kless, and Peter Adler, "Socialization to Gender Roles: Popularity among Elementary School Boys and Girls," *Sociology of Education* 65: 3 (1992): 173.
9. Ibid., 183–84.
10. Very occasionally, another character sings a show tune as a means of self-expression; Tina (Jenna Ushkowitz) sang "I Don't Know How to Love Him" from *Jesus Christ Superstar* in a wildly uncomfortable effort to woo her gay classmate Blaine; and the high-strung, mostly one-dimensional character of Mr. Schuester's love interest, guidance counselor Emma Pillsbury (Jayma Mays) has twice used Broadway to deal with her confusion about love and marriage, singing "I Could Have Danced All Night" from *My Fair Lady* when she realizes she has feelings for Schuester, and more recently singing "Getting Married Today" (with him in the groom's role) from *Company* as she flees her wedding to him. She is fundamentally a nonsinging character, but in rare circumstances reverts to Broadway in moments of confusion and panic, presenting the songs as in a musical.
11. Stacy Wolf, "Gender and Sexuality," in Knapp, Morris, and Wolf, *Oxford Handbook of the American Musical*, 220.
12. D. A. Miller, *Place for Us: Essays on the Broadway Musical* (Cambridge, MA: Harvard University Press, 1998), 118.
13. Ibid., 119.
14. Heather Laing, "Emotion by Numbers: Music, Song and the Musical," in *Musicals: Hollywood and Beyond*, ed. Bill Marshall and Robynn Stilwell (Bristol: Intellect, 2000), 8.

15. Nikki Sullivan, *A Critical Introduction to Queer Theory* (New York: New York University Press, 2003), 82. See also Judith Butler, "Critically Queer," and Jay Prosser, "Judith Butler: Queer Feminism, Transgender, and the Transubstantiation of Sex," in *The Routledge Queer Studies Reader*, ed. Donald Hall and Annamarie Jagose (London: Routledge, 2012).

16. James Loxley, *Performativity* (London: Routledge, 2007), 142.

17. From the episode "Laryngitis."

18. Kurt's featured moments in *Glee's* first three seasons include Beyoncé's "Single Ladies"; "Defying Gravity" from *Wicked* in a contest with Rachel (he loses); Lady Gaga's "Bad Romance" with the girls of the glee club; "Baby It's Cold Outside" (the girl's part) with boyfriend Blaine; Barbra Streisand and Judy Garland's "Get Happy / Happy Days Are Here Again" with Rachel; and Momma Rose's "Some People" from *Gypsy*. As mentioned above, he once attempts to sing "Pink Houses" by John Cougar Mellencamp in an effort to butch up, but fails to sell it. In an episode devoted exclusively to the music of Michael Jackson, Kurt's only featured moment is in the corny ballad "Ben," sung by Michael as a child. He does a duet with his boyfriend Blaine on Pink's "Perfect," a very hip rock ballad, but Pink has a strong gay following and the context is that he's trying to tell classmate Santana to be comfortable with her newfound homosexuality—thus his orientation is still on display. When the high school puts on a production of *West Side Story*, Kurt delivers Barbra Streisand's "I'm the Greatest Star" from *Funny Girl* as his wildly inappropriate audition for the male lead of Tony. The teachers and students in charge of the production don't cast him because he can't act manly enough on stage, which his audition proves.

19. G5 is "soprano" G, an octave and a fifth above middle C.

20. David Savran, *A Queer Sort of Materialism: Recontextualizing American Theater* (Ann Arbor: University of Michigan Press, 2003), 45.

21. Ibid.

22. For one reading of the word "fabulous" in this loaded context, see John Clum, *Something for the Boys: Musical Theater and Gay Culture* (New York: St. Martin's Press, 1999), 5.

23. Damian Holbrook, "Making a Smash," *TV Guide*, February 6–19, 2012, 25.

CHAPTER 9

Angry Dance

Postmodern Innovation, Masculinities, and

Gender Subversion

JUDITH A. SEBESTA

In 2002, I saw the original Broadway production of *The Full Monty*, eager, I must admit, to enjoy the display of men onstage that its premise, adapted from the original film, promised. But enjoyable as that display was, I marveled more at what seemed to be an unprecedented number of "manly men" in the audience; later, I published an essay in *Studies in American Culture* analyzing masculine identities of both the performers in, and spectators of, that movical (a stage musical adapted from a film), as well as what had been deemed by numerous observers at the time as a post-9/11 return of "traditional" masculinity in America, particularly the working-class masculinity exuded by the heroes par excellence—firemen, soldiers, and policemen, particularly—of Ground Zero and its resultant wars.[1] While some might argue that this trend is now firmly entrenched in our contemporary cultural imaginary—Tommy Gavin of *Rescue Me* (2004), Raylan Givens of *Justified* (2010), and Captain America of *Marvel's The Avengers* (2012) are just a few characters in current television and film that come to mind—a shift seems to be occurring that signals an acceptance of a spectrum of masculine identities on the musical stage, particularly in relation to choreography. Dance affords, in some very material ways, the opportunity to display the male body—its muscularity, sexuality, and general physicality—in action, potentially engaging and activating not only dynamics of masculinity (in the performers), but also dynamics of desire (in the audience).

Contemporary dance in Broadway musicals engages and activates these dynamics, reflecting a greater range of masculinities than ever before, influenced by modern dance and then even more by the increasing fluidity, hybridity, and performativity of identity in postmodern dance. It will be necessary, in order to lay a foundation for this exploration, to briefly define the concepts of masculinity and postmodernity as they relate to performativity, as well as how these concepts have influenced chore-ographers, beginning in ballet and then moving through modern dance and beyond, including how some have reified and others have subverted traditional notions of masculinity specifically and gender more generally. Then, a focus on two musicals—*Spring Awakening* (2006) and *American Idiot* (2009), prefaced by briefer consider-ations of *Billy Elliot* (2005) and *The Book of Mormon* (2011)—will point toward a future in theater dance and, eventually, American culture, in which the performance of gendered identity is open to myriad possibilities.[2]

STAGING MASCULINITY

Studies attempting to define and explore the limits and ranges of the masculine have proliferated over the past twenty-five years or so, sometimes in conjunction with the study of what historically has been perceived as its opposite, the feminine. Peter N. Stearns's *Be a Man! Males in Modern Society* (1990) and Michael Kimmel's *Man-hood in America: A Cultural History* (1996) are now classic texts that worked to decon-struct masculinity in relation to male identity,[3] but scholars quickly began to realize that masculinity exists on a spectrum of identities and certainly is not limited to those who identify as "male." Earlier attempts to define the masculine had codified its characteristics as including such concepts as aggression, physical strength and prowess, serving as the "breadwinner," and enjoyment of sports, both in participa-tion and spectatorship; for most of these writers, masculinity studies was code for "male heterosexual masculinity studies" and virtually ignored the implications for female, transgendered, and/or homosexual or bisexual identities in such codifica-tion.[4] More recently writers have rejected such limiting, essentializing perspectives for more inclusive ones in such works as *The End of Masculinity* (1998), *The Masculin-ity Studies Reader* (2002), *Masculinities and Culture* (2002), *Masculinities* (2005), and *Performing American Masculinities* (2011).[5]

The authors of these works and others during the past decade argue that "mascu-linities" is more appropriate than a singular "masculinity" and agree that gendered identity is cultural, not biological; many follow the earlier lead of Judith Butler to acknowledge the performative nature of masculinities, recognizing that in this performance, it had become difficult historically to separate masculinity from the oppression of women, and there has been an attempt to recoup the positive aspects of masculine identity. This has been accomplished largely through the aforemen-tioned stretching of the concept of "masculinity" to include a spectrum of identities. John MacInnes in *The End of Masculinity* was one of the first to suggest that at the end of the twentieth century "we are witnessing the emergence of a more fluid, *brico-lage* masculinity"; he also recognized the demise of the belief in masculinity as a gen-dered identity specific to men.[6] Still, Russell West, in *Subverting Masculinity*, astutely points out that "it is more and more clear that the splintering of versions of mascu-linity to be witnessed today in Western societies does not necessarily signify the end of male hegemony, although it may signal the bankruptcy of hitherto monolithic forms of masculine habitus and their images."[7] There also has been a recognition of gender as relational; in other words, one can only define and categorize "masculine" or "feminine" in relation to each other and to other identities in between. As R. W. Connell in *Masculinities* argues: "Masculinity as an object of knowledge is always masculinity-in-relation."[8]

These assertions are crucial to this study, as is the foundation of these theories within postmodern thought. Although it is difficult to define, postmodernity is no longer a contested condition, but it is worth giving a brief overview of its general characteristics in order to then explore postmodern dance. Postmodernism as a category apart from modernism developed first within the field of architecture; it is not necessarily a break from modernism but a "hypermodernism"—a continuation of modernity, taken to the nth degree. As an aesthetic and critical stance, postmodernism is shaped by nostalgia, intertextuality, a suspicion of singular "truths" and grand narratives as explanation for phenomena, pastiche, deferment of meaning, self-reflexivity, parody, focus on process over product, embrace of digital technologies, and fragmentation. Postmodernity recognizes that most forms of identity involve at least some performativity and cultural construction beyond mere biological imperatives. Even more pertinent for this project is how postmodernism has shaped and affected contemporary dance, particularly in how it has led artists to reject essentialist notions of supposed "inherent" imperatives in dance forms and the identities of those who perform them. Postmodern dance as distinct from modern has been identified by historians as originating with the work of such performers as Yvonne Rainer and Steve Paxton at the Judson Church in New York City's Greenwich Village circa 1962. Their dances, and others under this umbrella, often were created through group effort; emphasized rehearsal/process over performance/product; utilized found space; privileged pedestrian, everyday movement and gesture over "traditional" dance technique, as well as looking to sports as a significant source of movement; incorporated contact improvisation; blurred spatial boundaries between performer and spectator as well as distinctions between high and low art; and radically juxtaposed bodies, objects, styles, and so on. Like the modernists before them, these artists worked to subvert normative assumptions about dance and embraced multiple interpretive possibilities while often choreographing a struggle between/among opposing forces.

DANCING MALE

Although postmodern dance can be seen, in many ways, as a continuation of experimentation and innovation by modernist choreographers, in one specific way the two diverge: their representations of masculine identities.[9] During the early to mid-twentieth century, modern choreographers and their dancers tended to conform to traditional markers of the "masculine" and "feminine," many of which were holdovers from the balletic technique in which most of these artists were trained. The feminine, created for the supposed male gaze, was marked by such characteristics as yielding, an averted gaze, verticality and high arabesques, quick jumps, sweeping arm gestures, a supple spine, and display of emotion. The masculine was characterized by aggressive pursuit of the female, split jumps, multiple pirouettes, overhead lifting and other displays of strength, direct gaze at the female or audience, and stoic lack of emotion. Some historians point to inherent physical differences as being at the root of variance in ballet technique for men and women, that, for example, the "wider pelvis and greater torso flexibility in women and greater height and upper body strength in men" have led to separate and inherent techniques.[10] In traditional ballet as it developed through the nineteenth and twentieth centuries, this has meant that typically, women dance en pointe, engage in high leg extensions and fluidity of arms, and in general are subtle and graceful. On the other hand, male dancers take control of the space (and often of the female dancer), showcasing their strength through jumps, leaps, and support of the ballerina in gravity-defying poses and lifts (the male dancer defies gravity unassisted). Indeed, nineteenth-century ballet became "so concerned with the display of female bodies that male charac-ters became almost an impossibility (or reduced to [...] mime and choreographic support-work)."[11] Of course, such essentialist notions have been complicated more recently by such work as Mark Morris's The Hard Nut (1991); the cross-dressing Les Ballets Trockadero de Monte Carlo, an all-male company (founded in 1974) that performs excerpts from classical ballets replete with tutus and pointe shoes; or Bill T. Jones and Arnie Zane's gender-bending riffs on George Balanchine's classically feminine Serenade, Ritual Ruckus (How to Walk an Elephant) (1985).

Of course, traditionally "feminine" and "masculine" choreographic markers are not just performed signifiers of gender, but they are also performative enactments. Where the encoded reading of power or grace might point to associations we have with cultural gender traditions, the enacted gestures of power and grace are not so acculturated, so female bodies can be powerful and male can be graceful. Histori-cally, though, the classical male ballet dancer has been in a double bind: expected to engage in traditionally powerful, masculine activity but always already inherently feminine, and thus less powerful, for engaging in ballet in the first place—and sub-ject to assumptions regarding inherent sexual identity that may not always be accu-rate. Attitudes toward male dancers varied depending on location, but, as Deborah Jowitt puts it by way of example, while men ballet dancers in nineteenth-century America weren't denigrated, as they were in France by such influential critics as Théophile Gautier and Jules Janin, for being all too unappetizingly and stolidly male in a gossamer world, they were largely ignored. It's not clear exactly when the charge of effeminacy first began to be leveled at male dancers, or when a boy studying ballet might be labeled a sissy (a term not always a euphemism for homosexuality). But tap dancers, black or white, largely escaped the labeling.[12]

Indeed, a classic denunciation of the male ballet dancer is this 1838 statement by the aforementioned critic Théophile Gautier: "Nothing is more distasteful than a man who shows his red neck, his big muscular arms, his legs with the calves of a parish beadle, and all his strong massive frame shaken by leaps and pirouettes."[13]

Ever since ballet developed in Italy and France from the intermezzi and ballet du cour of the late Renaissance, ballerinas have become the focal point, which is rather ironic considering that male monarchs, like Louis XIV in France, often danced at the center of court dances. Indeed, increasingly, the male dancer's raison d'être became to support and showcase the female dancer, mirroring the male gaze of the creators of the dance, as well as that of the (ideal) male spectators—and the accepted convention became that the female dancer simply looked better (more balanced and/or gravity defying) when the male dancer supported her. In a traditional pas de deux (particularly in Russian ballets), for example, each dancer often has a solo pas: the male crosses the stage commandingly and aggressively with spectacular jumps; the woman performs smaller steps in a smaller area. According to Adrian Stokes, "her partner guides and holds her. And he—he then watches her *pas* with upraised hand, he shows her off. He has the air of perpetual triumph, and when the time comes for his own variations he bounds, leaps, bounces and rejoins the ballerina in the wings amid applause. Such is the abstract of the *pas de deux*, the crux of ballet."[14]

The strident masculinity of the male dancer in ballet (and other forms) in the nineteenth and early twentieth centuries may have developed to counter the perspective that men who danced were gay (effeminacy being equated with homosexuality). As Burt Ramsey suggests:

> to enjoy the spectacle of men dancing is to be interested in men. Because there was no acknowledged distinction between ballet as aesthetic experience and ballet as erotic spectacle [...] the pleasures of watching men dancing became, in the mid-nineteenth century, marred by anxieties about masculine identity. The male ballet dancer came too close for comfort to the blurred and problematic line that separates [...] necessary and approved homosocial male bonding from forbidden homosexual activity.[15]

Ramsey points out that representing sports and fighting became acceptable choreographic technique to depict male dancers.[16] As with any performance historically, the spectator is presumed to be male, and his dominant male gaze a heterosexual one, thus abnormalizing the presence, even suggested, of homosexuality either onstage or off.

The shift of centrality from the female dancer in ballet to male began with Sergei Diaghilev's Ballets Russes in Paris in 1909. He produced such dances as Michel Fokine's *Le Spectre de la Rose* (1911) to showcase the talents of his lover, Vaslav Nijinsky. As Lynn Garafola put it, the new male roles danced by Nijinsky and others in the twentieth century were "heterodox," meaning that "they transgressed rigid categories of masculine behavior."[17] Although he wore costumes, designed by Leon Bakst in his work with Ballets Russes, that pushed the boundaries of conventional male dress (a bejeweled brassiere in *Scheherazade* (1910); skirts and "nipped in" waist in *Narcisse* (1911) and *Le Dieu Bleu* (1912)), his choreography was, by all accounts, conventionally masculine, with strength and agility, athletic jumps and leaps, a bold spatiality, and skilled partnering of female dancers. But there were certain sensual and even androgynous elements in his dance that helped to push ballet forward to a greater range of masculinities.

In spite of Nijinsky's stretching of boundaries, the primary creators of modern dance, such as Ruth St. Denis and Ted Shawn, Doris Humphrey, Charles Weidman, Martha Graham, and Agnes de Mille, tended to adhere to traditional dichotomies of masculine and feminine. Still, their innovations in other areas would provide a solid foundation on which postmodern choreographers would build. The rounded movements and gestures of ballet could now be replaced with angular shapes, and the pointed toe often gave way to the flexed foot. Furthermore, these artists no longer concerned themselves with concealment of effort, eschewing the balletic tendency to appear as if gravity had no effect on the dancer. Indeed, the play between gravity and our ability to defy it became a hallmark of Humphrey and Weidman's work:

> For Humphrey, the "drama of motion" lay in the struggle to resist the pull of gravity, in the ecstasy or the tragedy of complying, in the suspended moment before equilibrium was regained. The theory gave rise to the many swings, falls, rebounds, and tilts that identified the work of the Humphrey-Weidman company, to the arcs that a slow, falling gesture traced on the air and the oppositional pull of limbs with which a person thrown off-balance tried to avoid collapse.[18]

Graham's contraction and release was a corollary technique, built on the act of inhaling and exhaling. In general, modern dance tended to communicate, through its vocabulary, a dialectic of struggle and conflict, but it did not usually subvert historical stereotypes of masculinity and femininity.

From the beginning, postmodern choreographers resisted patriarchal hierarchies in dance, exploring the terrain between the poles of gendered identity; a shared goal, according to Deborah Jowitt, was often "to free the dancer from the tyranny of rules, ideals, and 'technique.'"[19] An emphasis on everyday movement and gesture tended to erase differences between the masculine and the feminine; sports provided inspiration for male and female choreographers alike. If they explored the terrain of gendered identity, it was often to subvert stereotypes by employing cross-gender markers and technique. Democratization of dance has been key. The early postmodern dances of Merce Cunningham featured mixed-gender companies dressed in unitards, replacing romantic narrative with chance processes. Others like Yvonne Rainer and Steve Paxton engaged in male-male and female-female partnering in addition to the more traditional male-female, applying, according to Janice LaPointe-Crump,

> contact partnering in rhythmically rich phrases founded upon ordinary or vernacular movement vocabulary, basic locomotor skills, democratic relationships and asexual imagery. Dancers sought to represent a neutral, natural body. Maleness and femaleness may have been the undisguised context, but they were not the subjects of the dance. [...] Rainer's *Trio A* (1968) [...] was intended as a "clean-scrubbed" dance to emphasize a nongendered, natural body.[20]

A newer generation of postmodern choreographers has continued this subversion of gender dichotomies. Molissa Fenley, for example, looks less like a ballerina than a triathlete, her body powerfully muscled in order to create the patterns of nonstop, energetic steps of which her dances are comprised. Acrobatics were a hallmark of Bill T. Jones's work with his late partner Arnie Zane and their company; dancers of both genders lifted, vaulted, and dove through space in displays of athletic prowess.

Mark Morris is perhaps best known for such role-reversing, parodic ballets as *The Hard Nut* (1991), a 1970s-set version of the classic Petipa *Nutcracker* (1892) that LaPointe-Crump asserts "presents a startling alternate view of traditional gender constructs, while using humour to raise serious questions of identity and agency."[21] The work of all of these artists, and others, suggests that masculinity is not a singular, limited ideal tied to any given sex or gender, but instead that masculinities are pluralistic, social, and cultural, contingent on context and constantly shifting.

CONTEMPORARY BROADWAY AND THE NEW ANGRY DANCES

Until the twenty-first century, musical theater choreographers tended to adhere to a fairly traditional separation of masculine and feminine dance vocabularies onstage, following in the footsteps of the aforementioned modernists—or they have been modernists themselves, as in the case of de Mille. While innovative in her integration of dance into the plot of *Oklahoma!* (1943) and other shows, her choreography incorporated dance styles in which the men differed considerably from the female characters, exemplified in the "Dream Ballet" at the end of act 1, with its classic lifts; strong, aggressive cowboys who are grounded; and light-on-their-feet, yielding pioneer women. When choreographers subverted patriarchal gender expectations of their audiences in movement, it was usually to comic effect, as in the cross-dressing metatheatrical number "Honey Bun" in *South Pacific* (1949), choreographed in the original Broadway production by director Joshua Logan. A hallmark of Michael Kidd's choreography became a strident, acrobatic masculinity; in such film musicals as *Seven Brides for Seven Brothers* (1954), the brothers are marked as always different from brides in their tumbling, gymnastic dance styles alone. Jerome Robbins, who went further than any musical theater dance choreographer had up to the late 1950s with his complete integration of song, story, and dance in *West Side Story* (1957), did move musical dance a step closer to more complex masculinities (and femininities), blurring the boundaries between his vocabulary for male and female dancers. For example, women and men often mirrored each other, performing similar moves at the same time onstage, as with Tony and Maria in "Dance at the Gym"; in "America," women refused to yield space to the men. It was a dancing duel of sorts, and women held their own when onstage with men at such moments; however, they did not engage in combat via dance, their movements were usually less aggressive and grounded and tended toward the sexy, with an emphasis on the hips and butt, and they were sometimes relegated to the background. Indeed, even with a spatial balance of power between the male and female groups throughout, "America" ended in a classic manifestation of masculine power with a male/female lift, a strong visual reinforcement of traditional gender relationships.[22]

That image is, generally, indicative of the stasis that has existed in communication of gendered identities through musical theater dance—until recently. During the past decade, a shift has occurred that seems to signal an embracement of a spectrum of masculine identities on the musical stage. This pushing of boundaries has ranged from an acceptance of traditionally feminine dance styles and vocabularies for male dancers to a subversion of gendered expectations for female dancers whose choreographers embrace more masculine markers in their vocabulary, and much in between. *Billy Elliot* (2005) has become a classic case of subversion of traditional masculinity, particularly in its rather extreme manifestation vis-à-vis working-class masculinity.[23] In the show, based on a film of the same name, the title character struggles to gain acceptance for his love of ballet from his working-class father and brother in 1980s northern England amid the backdrop of a clash between out-of-work union members and police. Peter Darling's choreography is grounded in both ballet and modernism: ballet is used in more metatheatrical moments when Billy is taking classes, auditioning, or performing this dance form considered too feminine within his family and the larger cultural context; Darling incorporates the modernist techniques of contraction and release and fall and recovery when Billy is expressing his grief, frustration, and angst in response to the death of his mother, gender expectations, and familial/working-class conflicts around him. As modernist choreographers like de Mille and Robbins incorporated techniques like fall and recovery and tension and release into musical theater dance, it was done (famously) to further the story and character. Emotions were of course communicated, but this was not the primary modus operandi of such techniques. Darling shows that these techniques can be used purely to communicate emotion, not necessarily to further the action—and perhaps to show that displays of emotion are as acceptable as displays of more traditional masculine characteristics.

This angst and use of modernist technique to express it comes to a head in the act 1 climax "Angry Dance," in which Darling utilizes a fairly traditional masculine vocabulary for Billy's dance: athletic, aggressive—even violent—percussive, and grounded movement punctuation by obscene finger gestures, guttural vocalizing, and acrobatics. George Rodosthenous, in his article "*Billy Elliot The Musical*: Visual Representations of Working-Class Masculinity and the All-Singing, All-Dancing Bo[d]y," argues that Darling's choreography "has an acrobatic edge to it and makes it a muscular and dangerous activity. It is full of anger and quasi martial-arts qualities and expresses Billy's restlessness and affinity with dance." He even suggests, insightfully, that the show ushers in a new genre, the "athletic musical...which allows for the athletic body to be celebrated, admired and looked at purely for its strength, muscular energy and beauty."[24]

In a way, though, "Angry Dance," and the show in general, foreshadows what is to come: a pastiche of styles that eschews easy categorization, both in terms of dance genres (modernism, tap, ballet) and gendered identity (as the dance reaches its climax, Billy cannot resist a pirouette or two and at one point is supported by another male dancer who thrusts his arm through a piece of scenery and across Billy's torso; throughout, Billy executes powerful vertical moves punctuated by abject drops to floor, his body yielding briefly, and finally, as it lies prone and splayed).[25]

Thus it is really through postmodern dance (or dance that might be more accurately labeled "contemporary" but that clearly is influenced by postmodernism) that gendered identity in dance in musicals has become untethered from past restraints. Its hallmark of pastiche has ensured that choreographers can draw on multiple dance styles within each show to evoke pluralistic identities. This technique is best

Figure 10 Josh Baker as Billy in "Angry Dance" from *Billy Elliot*. Photo by Alastair Muir.

Figure 11 Kaine Ward as Billy in *Billy Elliot*. Photo by Alastair Muir.

exemplified in Casey Nicholaw's freewheeling choreography for *The Book of Mormon* (2011). Here African dance and militaristic marches are juxtaposed with Martha Graham–like Americana, soul, and hip-hop. Characters tend to share the same dance vocabulary regardless of gender, particularly polyrhythm infused numbers like "Hasa Diga Ebowai." And Nicholaw clearly does not view dances by all-male ensembles as a reason to return to traditional markers of masculinity; "Turn It Off," for example, in which the young Mormon missionaries express the need to repress confusing desires like "gay thoughts," is an ironic—given the subject matter—campy, show-stopping number replete with a tap dance break and images of "orientalism" à la Ruth St. Denis.

Gendered equality in dance vocabularies is a common technique to subvert traditionally masculine characteristics in not only *The Book of Mormon* but also *Spring Awakening* (2007). Bill T. Jones, as mentioned above, has embraced the erasure of gender differences before in his choreography, and *Spring Awakening* is no exception. In order to counter the rigid strictures and traditions of Victorian life in *Spring Awakening*, Bill T. Jones brilliantly infused the choreography with his own brand of postmodernism, as the teenagers explore the limits of their sexual and intellectual freedom in late-nineteenth-century Germany. Early in the musical, Jones suggests an adherence to traditional masculine ideals in "Bitch of Living"; sung and danced by all the young men in the cast, the number expresses their frustration—not unlike in "Turn It Off"—at repression, particularly sexual. The dance vocabulary is reminiscent of that in "Angry Dance": percussive, pulsating, and aggressive, with lyric implications of masturbation expressed through gesture, hands gripping and pumping phallic microphones in the air above the lap and feet beating and stamping to that rhythm. As the number climaxes, the teenagers leap about, jumping on chairs and around the space. But much of the choreography for both girls and boys is less reflective of lyrical meaning. Instead, Jones lays evocative but abstract choreography on top of the dancers' bodies; it might outline a body part or pulsate a rhythm but does not necessarily tell a story or directly correlate to a character trait. "Mama Who Bore Me" is a litany of everyday gestures traced around the girls' body parts and through the air; they appear almost as semiotic signs. In "Totally Fucked," the arms of the dancers flail in violent, urgent movements around their own bodies, and at times the entire company bursts into chaotic jumps reminiscent of a mosh pit.

Equality of choreographic expression runs throughout the show in a variety of repetitive techniques, such as the incorporation of chairs into the dancing, the laying on of hands, and the use of technology. Both male ("Bitch of Living") and female ("Mama Who Bore Me") performers stand, jump, or dance on chairs, a move that can indicate power, sensuality, or both. In the latter number, girls straddle the chairs; in "My Junk," they dance around Hänschen as he masturbates, jumping up and down, arms flailing in full-body extension of Hänschen's freedom in sexual release, jumping again on the chair after he stands up. The ritualistic, sensual laying of hands on one's own body occurs throughout, as mentioned above; one particularly effective example is in "Touch Me," in which all of the principal performers march in a circle around the stage, their hands moving in a litany of symbolic gestures across their head, torso, and pelvic region, climaxing in the same gestures performed as they stand in a straight line downstage. In "The Mirror-Blue Night," as Melchior rises on a platform suspended above the stage, he maintains a wide stance while clenching outstretched fists, bringing them up to cover his face, then circling them around his torso, body, head, and so on. Then the ensemble echoes the dance on the floor around him. These movements are repeated, first by Melchior and then the others, in "Totally Fucked"—but at increasing speeds. Here the gestures are not done in unison by the ensemble but as a kind of canon/round (same movement but started at different times), a show of both solidarity and individuality. And finally, in a postmodern embracing of technology and Brechtian technique, Jones regularly and anachronistically incorporates handheld microphones into the choreography—they become the phallus in "Bitch of Living" as well as in "The Word of Your Body" when Hänschen and Ernst sing into and fondle a single microphone (initially held by Ernst but then gripped by both as the former seduces the latter), and in "The Dark I Know Well," the girls support themselves at microphone stands as they sing of abuse at the hands of elders, occasionally demonstrating that abuse by stroking the stand.

Generally, Jones's choreography is not extensive, but it effectively, if abstractly, undergirds both the narrative and the characters while evoking gender equality (although the equality is more about the lack of power shared by *all* young people in the society, whether boy or girl).[26] The visual effect of the dance, gesture, and movement is one of fragmentation and chaos as well as simultaneous but seemingly disconnected movement. The latter reflected, for me, the turmoil in these young people's lives from lack of information and broader education due to the German Victorian society's attempts to strictly order and control them; the simultaneity suggested a display of solidarity among them. And, like the modernist techniques employed by Darling, Jones's abstract choreography taken as a whole seems, at times, pure emotion instead of action; rather than a linear narrative, it performatively suggests parallels between the Victorian teens' anger and angst and the disconnect and disaffection young people may feel in contemporary, postmodern society, acted out in aggressive (traditionally masculine) ways.

Steven Hoggett, with *American Idiot* (2010), seemed to embrace a similar postmodern choreographic aesthetic, although his was steeped in the neopunk/grunge movement out of which grew the composers'—members of the rock group Green Day—music. Neopunk and grunge draw on the punk rock movement of the 1970s, with its suspicion of musical virtuosity, adoption of a nihilistic attitude, overtones of anarchy, and frustration with mainstream music (and by association, culture). Hallmarks of the movement in the fast-paced, ninety-minute *American Idiot* included moshing and thrashing, head banging, fist pumping and explosive movement of limbs outward, jumping, air guitar, acrobatic displays of strength, athletic flying around the stage on trapezes and wires, and percussive use of hands and feet against objects, the stage floor, and other dancers (slam dancing). The overall effect is one of environmental theater, with the choreography executed on a much greater variety of spatial levels than in *Spring Awakening*, and asymmetricality (as opposed to adopting the symmetry of much of Jones's work); however, as in *Awakening*, aggression, repetition, everyday movement, and lack of technique also pervade the movement.[27]

But beyond such postmodern traits, both male and female performers execute these traditionally "masculine" hallmarks equally. The choreography is not gender neutral as much as equal-opportunity masculine. Female characters like Whatsername and Heather as played by Rebecca Naomi Jones and Mary Faber in the original production were suggestive of postmodern choreographer/dancer Molissa Fenley: athletic, lean, and muscular (more so than the male leads in the show in the case of Jones).

Hoggett does occasionally separate the performers by gender, as in "Dearly Beloved" and "Favorite Son," in which a girl group dances and sings around a performer clad only in boxers, dressing him in a military uniform by the end of the song. In "Letterbomb," Whatsername and the rest of the women sing and dance on the raised platform in a tight group, the primary movement in isolated jerks of their arms and shoulders. Even segregated, though, the female performers tend to engage in more traditionally masculine choreography: the balletic aerial dance in "Extraordinary Girl" is highly acrobatic and athletic, and at the end of the number the nurses (female) dance between the hospital beds—aggressive punk head-banging mixed with arabesques and kicks. But more often than not men and women dance the same choreography. For example, in "Jesus of Suburbia" the three principals (all men) play air guitar on a high platform while the ensemble (men and women) crouch, stomp, kick, and jump in unison around them on the stage floor.

Hoggett's choreography seems a near-direct throwback to classic postmodern dance described earlier in this project, with such characteristics as privileging pedestrian, everyday movement and gesture over traditional dance technique; looking to acrobatics and sports as a significant source of movement; blurring spatial boundaries between performer and spectator; and radically juxtaposing bodies, objects, styles, and so on. Like Jones, for example, Hoggett incorporates objects into the movement in *American Idiot*, as when a grocery cart is flown in and out of space through the performers. In "Holiday" the scaffolding is pulled down to become a bus and the performers move in, on, and through it. The most "conventional" musical theater dance is used in "Favorite Son" and in "Last of the American Girls / She's a Rebel," which incorporate rough pirouettes by both men and women. But the less conventional numbers, with more pedestrian movement, include "Are We the Waiting"; while Tunny gets a military physical, underwear-clad, gun-toting (mimed) men and women march in an ominous chorus line behind him. In general, Hoggett's dancers are more earthbound than Jones's; in "St. Jimmy," for example, the performers repeatedly fall to the floor, pounding it with fists, and the choreography remains low as the dancers stay on their knees and move in unison, pantomiming shooting heroin in the arm as St. Jimmy leads Johnny into his first drug experience. In "Give Me Novocaine," soldiers lie prone on the floor, flopping and flipping from back to stomach. This stylistic choice suggests characters more realistic and less optimistic than those in *Spring Awakening*; in that show, the dance suggests a reaching out for a way to either change or escape the restrictive society, while in *Idiot* the characters seem more grounded and accepting of their place in contemporary America, even as they struggle to learn how best to negotiate it in a world of war, drugs, angst, technology, and chaos.

Billy Elliot, *The Book of Mormon*, *Spring Awakening*, and *American Idiot* are all such high-energy shows that I left my viewings of each with the impression that only young people could perform them (particularly the latter two). Indeed, although they have quite a few differences among them, including fairly disparate musical styles (even given the pop/rock creators of three of them), all four shows feature stories built around young (tween, teen, and young adult) characters in various degrees of angst and disaffection. The context of that angst may differ—working-class 1980s England, Mormon Utah and conflict-torn Africa, nineteenth-century Victorian Germany, contemporary drug-ridden America—but within each of these contexts the young people struggle against repression and cultural constraints and expectations and long for escape from them, dreaming of a better life and world. One could say this about the characters in *West Side Story*, even within that milieu of ethnic and economic strife within Hell's Kitchen in mid-twentieth-century New York City. Indeed, the shows examined here are direct descendants of *West Side Story* in both their subject matter and their dance. The depiction of teenagers and young adults in musicals was not new in 1957, but until the brilliant integration of song, story, and dance in *West Side Story*, the full range of complex emotions felt by teens had yet to be expressed in a musical. Jerome Robbins was a pioneer in his ability to brilliantly choreograph the anger and frustration of the Jets, Sharks, and their families/girlfriends with percussive movements and gestures and consistent use of contraction and release/fall and recovery, and these techniques are mirrored in much of the choreography of the four shows examined here, while they often move beyond those techniques or push their boundaries. But perhaps more importantly, musicals, like *West Side Story* and the others examined here, that have libretti/stories that revolve around young people allow for an organic use of innovative techniques that mirrors the youths' rebellion against the mainstream, societal norms and expectations, and limitations. The creators of these shows engage in a similar rebellion. They are part and parcel of a postmodern world that questions easy truths and grand narratives to explain the world around us, and a part of that is a refusal to accept traditional dichotomous gendered identities and an embracing of their often fluid, performative nature.

But as Martha Graham stated, "Nothing is more revealing than movement"; an acceptance of a range of masculinities on the musical stage might signal a larger cultural movement of acceptance offstage as well.[28] Dance offers the opportunity not only to *read* culture but to *write* it, and, more significantly, *perform* it, as well. Dance, more than any other performing art, is action. Judith Butler, in her arguments on the performativity of identity, states that gender can be conceptualized as a "kind of becoming or activity"; perhaps, then, dance offers the real potential for material change in our perception of, and constitution of, masculine identities.[29]

NOTES

1. Martin F. Kohn coined the term "movical" in "The Celluloid Source: Movies Provide a Well of Inspiration for the Musical Stage," *Detroit Free Press*, March 17, 2002; also see

Judith Sebesta, "From Celluloid to Stage: The 'Movical,' *The Producers*, and the Post-modern," *Theatre Annual* 56 (2003): 97–112.

2. This analysis of all four shows is based on multiple viewings of the musicals during their original Broadway runs.

3. Peter Stearns, *Be a Man! Males in Modern Society*, 2nd ed. (New York: Holmes, 1990); Michael Kimmel, *Manhood in America: A Cultural History* (New York: Free Press, 1996).

4. Bruce Traister provides an excellent overview of the historiography of masculinity studies up to 2000 in his cheekily titled article "Academic Viagra: The Rise of American Masculinity Studies," *American Quarterly* 52: 2 (2000): 274–304.

5. John MacInnes, *The End of Masculinity* (Buckingham: Open University Press, 1998); Rachel Adams and David Savran, eds., *The Masculinity Studies Reader* (Malden, MA: Blackwell, 2002); John Beynon, *Masculinities and Culture* (Buckingham: Open University Press, 2002); R. W. Connell, *Masculinities*, 2nd ed. (Cambridge: Polity, 2005); Marc Edward Shaw and Elwood Watson, *Performing American Masculinities: The 21st-Century Man in Popular Culture* (Bloomington: Indiana University Press, 2011).

6. MacInnes, *The End of Masculinity*, 6.

7. Russell West and Frank Lay, eds., *Subverting Masculinity: Hegemonic and Alternative Versions of Masculinity in Contemporary Culture* (Amsterdam: Rodopi, 2000), 22.

8. Connell, *Masculinities*, 44.

9. What follows is only a partial overview of the longer, more complex history of masculinity in modernist dance.

10. Janice LaPointe-Crump, "Of Dainty Gorillas and Macho Sylphs: Dance and Gender," in *The Dance Experience*, ed. Myron Howard Nadel and Marc Raymond Strauss, 2nd ed., 159–72 (Hightstown, NJ: Princeton Book Company, 2003), 161.

11. Karen Henson, "Introduction: Divo Worship," *Cambridge Opera Journal* 19: 1 (2007): 5.

12. Deborah Jowitt, "Dancing Masculinity: Defining the Male Image Onstage in Twentieth-Century America and Beyond," *Southwest Review* 95 (2010): 228–29.

13. Théophile Gautier, *The Romantic Ballet* (London: C. W. Beaumont, 1947), 24.

14. Adrian Stokes, *Tonight the Ballet* (London: Faber & Faber, 1942), 81.

15. Burt Ramsey, *The Male Dancer: Bodies, Spectacle, Sexualities* (New York: Routledge, 1995), 38.

16. Ibid., 70–71.

17. Lynn Garafola, "The Travesty Dancer in the Nineteenth Century," *Dance Research Journal* 17: 2 and 18: 1 (1985–86): 39.

18. Deborah Jowitt, *Time and the Dancing Image* (Berkeley: University of California Press, 1988), 165.

19. Ibid., 313.

20. LaPointe-Crump, "Of Dainty Gorillas," 170–71.

21. Ibid., 164.

22. I am relying on the film version for this analysis, not having seen the original Broadway choreography, unlike the shows I analyze below. However, since Robbins choreographed both versions, I believe that it is safe to make generalizations about the stage dance based on that in the film.

23. For a discussion of working-class masculinity and the musical, particularly as it relates to *The Full Monty*, see Judith Sebesta, "'Real Men' Watch Musicals: *The Full Monty* and Post 9/11 Masculinity," *Studies in American Culture* 31: 1 (2009): 1–12.

24. George Rodosthenous, "*Billy Elliot The Musical*: Visual Representations of Working-Class Masculinity and the All-Singing, All-Dancing Bo[d]y," *Studies in Musical Theatre* 1: 3 (2007): 286–87.

25. And of course, the strident masculinity in the show is also balanced by an embracement of the more traditionally feminine by Billy and other characters, namely Michael, in the campy cross-dressing number "Expressing Yourself," with its shoulder

shimmies, pelvic thrusts, voguing, and short, mincing steps. (Voguing is a style of dance characterized by model-like poses integrated with angular, linear, and rigid arm, leg, and body movements. The style first arose in Harlem in the 1960s as "presentation" or "performance" dance; it was co-opted, renamed, and popularized by Madonna in the 1990s.) However, this number brings us back to the conceit of relegating such gender subversion to the comic and metatheatrical à la "Honey Bun."

26. Not all critics agreed with me regarding the effectiveness of the dance; for example, Mary Jo Lodge in *Theatre Journal* argues that "a major disconnect, for example, was in the incorporation of Bill T. Jones's choreography, which, while technically thrilling, often seemed utterly unsuited to the situations at hand." Mary Jo Lodge, "Review of *Spring* Awakening," *Theatre Journal* 60: 3 (2008): 460–62.

27. *Los Angeles Times* writer Sylviane Gold recently labeled Hoggett the "anti-dance choreographer." Sylviane Gold, "Steven Hoggett is the Anti-dance Choreographer," *Los Angeles Times*, April 10, 2012. Online. Available: http://articles.latimes.com/print/2012/apr/10/entertainment/la-et-steven-hoggett-20120410. December 11, 2012.

28. Quoted in N. Barletto, "The Role of Martha Graham's Notebooks in Her Creative Process," *Martha Graham: Choreography and Dance* 5: 2 (1999): 54.

29. Judith Butler, *Gender Trouble: Feminism and the Subversion of Identity* (New York: Routledge, 1990).

PART FIVE
Performativity as Context

If an emphasis on the performativity of identity calls organizing structures (texts, narratives) into question, it also challenges the internal dynamics of those structures (characters, events, and situations), and performance is revealed as performance. This may suggest a disabling stripping away of performative potential, though in fact the freeing-up of materials can offer extraordinary creative possibilities through which the experience of performance is highlighted, as Peter Brook's celebrated assertion in *The Empty Space* (1968) claimed, and as John Cage's bold 4'33" (1952) testified.

In a post-Brookian and post-Cagean world it its clearly possible to engage with these abstracted performance events, and our next three chapters do this in exploring the concerts of Laurie Anderson, the sound installation *Lowlands* (2010) by Susan Philipsz, and the performative writing of Samuel Beckett. Each of these creates environments of densely textured sound and imagery whose reception challenges our expectations, and whose experience becomes immersive. In their own ways, however, these pieces also alienate their participants, thereby creating a tension between immersion and alienation that only true gestures of performativity—like the gestures of song and dance—can enable.

In fact, Brook and Cage have only been so revolutionary because they startled expectations and confronted assumptions about what "theater" and "music" should be—very Western assumptions steeped in traditions of literacy and supported by centuries of Western practice demanding a particular engagement of the audience. In other cultures, practices differ, and the experience of the performative encounter can more commonly be interactive, participatory, or immersive. Even in Western cultures, performative practices that bypass theater conventions are prevalent, though they may not be called "theater" or "music" and they may exist in conditions less understood as performative.

The pageants of the Olympics opening and closing ceremonies seem to offer an intermediary experience between theater convention and performative immersion. Here the public are distinct from the performers, though the capacity for inclusion and the experience of the event-space can—as with the experience of sport itself—be powerfully emotional and corporeally overwhelming. Even if the experiencers are not themselves choreographed into proceedings (as spectators at the London 2012 Opening Ceremony were, using preissued lightboxes to create interactive participation), the emotive pull is often so overwhelming that the crowd cannot help but interact, tapping feet, swaying arms, or singing along.

But where the festival of narrative and song at the 2012 Olympics opening ceremony emphasized Britain's oral and literary heritage and relied on tropes of Western theater and music, the ceremony at Beijing in 2008 presented a subtly different idiom of stadium theater that reflected a very different cultural landscape. In London, Kenneth Branagh *played* the character of Isambard Kingdom Brunel, the stage set *represented* a pastoral British landscape, and the narrative *related* the progress of technology through Britain's history. In Beijing, a wholly different set of assumptions created of its ceremony a more abstract performance event. Zhang Yimou and his colleagues, the choreographers Zhang Jigang and Chen Weiya, treated the stadium as a blank canvas—very appropriately, as it happens, since one of the themes of the ceremony was to reflect the invention of paper. In this empty space a visual spectacular unfurled using massed phalanxes of performers whose bodies formed moving patterns and pictures in the grandest of mass spectacles.[1]

Without narrative content per se, this ceremony was able to galvanize the materials of performance—bodies, voices, space, time, movement, and mood—into a markedly different show: 2008 drummers beat traditional Chinese drums in regimented lines; 897 performers created an enormous moving type-press; hundreds of bodies choreographed into visual patterns made images of the Silk Road, the Yellow River, and a bird of peace (see figure 12). This, then, was a physical ceremony using bodies in space ("lots and lots of conscript labour," as *Guardian* columnist Tim Dowling put it):[2] a dance-show rather than a musical play. The few concessions to song included the performance of nine-year-old Lin Miaoke, who mimed to a prerecorded track a portion of "Ode to the Motherland," the singing of the national anthem, "March of the Volunteers," by a choir of 224 performers, and the performance of the Olympic theme song "You and Me" by British singer Sarah Brightman and Chinese singer Liu Huan.

Yet stripping away the trappings of drama to create spectacle like this with its visual and sonic excess does not mean creating phenomenological experience in a vacuum; on the contrary, this sort of performance is deeply embedded in a variety of contexts that impact significantly on our experiencing of the event and that inculcate us in their implicit rhetoric. The Beijing ceremony, however abstract, was rooted in the ideologies of the Olympics and the cultural particularity of China, emphasizing and using Chinese traditions within the performance, celebrating the virtuosity of individuals, and bringing enormities of people (the world) together. Otherwise similar pageants or displays of synchronized movement carry completely different connotations that are themselves dependent on a context: Leni Riefenstahl's images of mass rallies in Nuremberg (1934) are difficult to separate from the historicity of Hitler's rise to power;[3] the staged flash-mob of one hundred girls dancing to Beyoncé's "Single Ladies" in central London (2008) is firmly embedded in ideologies of commerce, gender, and sexuality;[4] the logistical trick of having thousands of school-children flash-mob a similar routine in Eindhoven (2011) to promote awareness of humanitarian disasters is cynically immersed in the charitable sector's ideologies of cuteness and guilt;[5] and even the staging of a mass dance to "Radio Ga Ga" as

Figure 12 The bird of peace in the Opening Ceremony of the 2008 Summer Olympics. Photography by Etherled. ©Etherled.

recreational activity by inmates at the Cebu Provincial Detention and Rehabilitation Center in the Philippines (2007) is redolent with messages of rehabilitation and the palliative power of song and dance.[6]

In each of these the performance event projects its ideology and the performers become ambassadors, self-identifying with that rhetoric. Both of these acts—the projection of an ideology and the identification of the individual—are performative statements. Without the particulars of conventional structures like narrative, the rhetoric or ideology may be less evident, but the power of gestures like music and dance, in which these performative statements are made, can overwhelm audiences with the rhythms and emotions of enchantment: we are immersed in sound and excitement, we tap our feet and clap our hands, and we become complicit in the rhetoric of the event.

In this way the power of the performative is that it invites us to self-identify, and the defining elements of performance for all participants are marked as expressions of identity and presence—performer identity, audience identity, the immediacy of the here-now and the marking of this ephemeral moment as a significant recollection.

In different ways, the three chapters in this section explore these ideas of identity and presence, considering three performance pieces in which identity and presence are themselves challenged. In exploiting the performative gestures of physicality and vocality they make use of the immersive power of song and dance; however, they also each deconstruct these expressive forces, breaking—even while maintaining—the spell. Ainhoa Kaiero Claver explores the way in which performance artist Laurie Anderson uses live and mediatized performance to challenge the authority of identity and presence; her performative persona is an ambiguous refraction of character and self, and her performative presence is compromised in an unsettling dislocation of voice and body. A similar dislocation of the voice from the body occurs in Susan Philipsz's *Lowlands*, which Zeynep Bulut considers: here voice(s), environment, and experience combine to both augment and deny the immediacy of presence. Finally, in Fiona Shaw's performance of Beckett's *Happy Days* (1961), the identity of the individual is threatened, as Marianne Sharp discusses. Baffled by an impenetrable stream of language and disabling physical demands, the identity of character and theatrical performance give way and the mechanical frailties of human performance emerge.

NOTES

1. In all, 14,000 performers participated in the Beijing ceremony, compared to London's 7,500 (plus 40 sheep, 12 horses, 3 cows, 2 goats, 10 chickens, 10 ducks, 9 geese, and 3 sheepdogs).
2. Tim Dowling, "The Armchair Olympics: It Begins!" *The Guardian*, July 27, 2010.
3. Online. Available: http://www.youtube.com/watch?v=v6WMXd8ZqmM&feature=related. December 5, 2012.
4. Online. Available: http://www.youtube.com/watch?v=OLj5zphusLw. December 5, 2012.
5. Online. Available: http://www.youtube.com/watch?v=FFtzqqgE3kA&feature=related. December 5, 2012.
6. Online. Available: http://www.youtube.com/watch?v=lAVVVMcTShQ&feature=fvwrel December 5, 2012.

CHAPTER 10

Deconstructing the Singer

The Concerts of Laurie Anderson

AINHOA KAIERO CLAVER

In 1986, the American singer and performance artist Laurie Anderson directed the concert film entitled *Home of the Brave*, based on a performance of her 1984 *Mister Heartbreak* tour.[1] One of the songs performed in the show, "Talk normal," parodied large rock concerts where most of the audience have no direct access to the musical performance and must follow it on live screen images located above the stage. At the beginning of the performance there was an image of Anderson's head, on a big screen behind the musicians, speaking in her usual or standard voice. After a few moments, Anderson's body appeared on the stage and she started singing using an electronic varied-speed filter that made her voice sound like a Smurf. The ironic equation became immediately clear: because her standard voice corresponded to the big screen image, her smaller body size on the stage was equated with the Smurf's voice.

This correspondence between the size of her visual image and the size of her voice, manipulated at the level of the speed, revealed the imaginary construction of her body in the show. In fact, her "normal" voice mediated by the microphone was just another image created by a technological text programmed at a standard speed. It was an illusory body presence constructed at the level of the sign. It was the means by which the technological text creates a sense of immediacy and intimacy with a body that is primarily absent: in a large mass concert, the performer's acoustic voice and expressive face represent a completely remote and inaccessible event, a gap.

Laurie Anderson's concerts explore these electronically mediatized performances developed in contemporary high-tech societies. Her multimedia performances reproduce the entertainment industry's set structures (rock concerts, TV shows, etc.) and question the mythical construction of her own image. Anderson develops different strategies in order to deconstruct the illusion of a genuine lyrical voice and reveal the mediatized nature of her pop star identity. Her use of technology (electronic voices and minimal music) serves therefore to break the illusion of an intentional and expressive gesture emanating from a resonant body, and to present instead the musical flow as a fictional time programmed by a textual mechanism.

THE RECORD AND THE VOICE WITHOUT A BODY

Since her first performances in the 1970s, Anderson has worked with recorded voices and music. Her approach to the music is primarily conceived from the experience of recorded sound, as shown by *Jukebox* (1977), one of her first musical works, consisting of an exhibition of texts, photographs, and recorded songs composed by Anderson and played in a jukebox.[2] In her subsequent works, Anderson has developed this conception of a recorded voice detached from its living acoustic source and rendered in dead plastic boxes such as telephones, radios, phonographs, or music boxes. In many performances, her favorite instrument, the violin, is detached from the acoustic sound it produces and transformed into a box that reproduces recorded alien voices. This is the case with Anderson's most well known conversions of the violin from an acoustic instrument into a sound reproduction apparatus: the "viophonograph," where the violin is converted into a phonograph; the "tape bow violin," where the violin functions as a tape player; or the digital violin that stores different sound samplers.[3]

The modified violins of Anderson's performances—like other music boxes such as phonographs, radios, or tape players—store and render sounds without a body. They have a close relationship, in this sense, with an enigmatic ready-made created by Marcel Duchamp, entitled *With Hidden Noise* (1916).[4] In this ready-made there is a box that contains a hermetic inscription on the front side and encloses an object that we can hear but cannot see. The object enclosed in the box is a mystery, a fundamental gap or a nonpresentable source, that we can only conceive but never experience. The same is true of the electronic voices delivered by technological equipment (radio, telephones, etc.): they are traces left by a missing body that we can only imagine. Following Roland Barthes's ideas about photography as a corpse and applying them to the nearby domain of phonography, it can be argued that electronic voices are just the present image of a body that has already gone.[5]

The electronic voices that speak to us everywhere—through loudspeakers, records, radios, answering machines, and so on—are thus just imprints, signs of an absent body. Technology allows a definitive alienation of the voice from the body and turns it into a marketable sign that enters a circuit of exchange. Taking the sonorous imprints of an electronic apparatus as a point of reference, we try to reconstruct a missing body and a personality. In a story told in the *Stories from the Nerve Bible* tour (1992), Anderson speaks about her experiences with a Ouija board whose textual words seemed to revivify a voice with a marked personality.[6] The electronic voices (a dead textual residue) arouse our desire for a missing living body that we can only imagine and dream about (as with an erotic telephone line). Electronic technology in radios, records, telephones, and so on fills and covers up the absence of a real body, creating a sensuous voice-image (a fetish) that seems to whisper in our ear. In the erotic communion with this imaginary body, we forget the fact that it is just a fantasy of proximity and intimacy based on some dead electronic traces.

Anderson's song "O Superman" (1981) materializes the rupture of this fetishistic communion, making us hear the dead and anonymous nature of the electronic voices delivered by technology.[7] In this song, Anderson appears as a kind of automaton that reproduces different electronic voices: a telephone call from her mother, the answering machine with the recording of her voice and the official speeches of a "Voice of Authority" (as she calls it)[8] broadcast by the media. The polyphonic machine-tone of all these voices breaks any illusion of personal intimacy, alienating her own voice, making her mother's voice sound unfamiliar and revealing the terrifying anonymous side of the power text machinery.

The electronic voices we hear in the media are determined by stereotypical linguistic and cultural codes that render the idea of different sexual, racial, and social identities: the voices of men and of women; the voices of black and white people; the voices of different social strata as identified by different accents or ways of speaking. In her performances, Anderson reproduces all these typified voices and archetypal identities inscribed in the electronic media text: news, films, talk shows, songs. Anderson plays with a deconstruction of all these archetypal personalities, showing their imaginary condition as signifieds generated by electronic signs. This is the case with the classic corporate man and his "voice of authority" that Anderson emulates using an electronic filter. Anderson avoids any illusory identification with this emblematic personality, by showing the textual machinery that makes possible its imaginary construction.

THE IMAGINARY CONSTRUCTION OF OUR OWN INNER VOICE

The imaginary identification with the electronic voices delivered by the media contributes to a shaping of our own inner voice. In an interview with Nicholas Zurbrugg, Anderson asserts that her father's voice was modeled on Jimmy Cagney, Bob Hope, and Abraham Lincoln (the latter as a textual voice in documents).[9] In this sentence, as in all her artistic trajectory, Anderson shows her alignment with Derrida's ideas about the linguistic configuration of our inner voice.[10] Derrida sees the origin of an illusory psychological interiority of the voice in the fact of hearing oneself speaking from within. The microphone and recorded sound allow us, on the contrary, to hear our speaking voice from the outside, as a coherent image generated by external signs. When we speak, we think we are externalizing the internal thinking of an inner voice. But, according to Derrida, this internal sense is actually our identification with a signified created in the movement and combination of linguistic signs. In many experimental songs and performances, Anderson uses recording technology in order to show how the sense of a sentence is composed thanks to the external movement of signs. For example, in the song "Late Show" (1986), from the film *Home of the Brave*, Anderson plays a prerecorded spoken sentence on the tape bow violin, shaping and completing, gradually, word by word, with the forward and backward movements of the bow, the sense of an inner expression: "Lis/Listen/Listen to/Listen to my/Listen to my heart beat."[11]

The idea of an inner voice shaped by an external linguistic device connects with Lacan's concept of a symbolically mediated subjectivity.[12] Merleau-Ponty's phenomenological philosophy sees a fundamental (preconceptual) unity of the body expressed in our intentional gestures. Lacan's psychoanalytic theory, on the other hand, conceives the body as an original state of fragmentation. A child has no real sense of a unitary body, of having her or his own personal body, and is driven by blind alien impulses over which she or he has no control. So in the beginning, there is a gap concerning the sense of having one's own body. This fundamental gap is, however, compensated by a symbolic (linguistic or sign) system that creates a coherent and unitary image of one's self. Lacan exemplifies most of his concepts using visual metaphors: the body is reflected and composed in pictures, mirrors, screens. The gaze (as an external or impersonal impulse) is framed and centered by a screen—such as a mirror—that renders a coherent image of one's body and of the world around it. The gaze identifies itself with the internal point of view of this picture, delivering a unitary vision of one's self. Thus the total identification between the gaze and the internal point of view of the reflected body produces the imaginary sense of an inner "I."

The screen can be any sign system that reflects and articulates the chaotic blind impulses of our body into a coherent unitary picture. This is the case of language, discourse (as a language exchange with others), and narration (as a specific kind of discourse). Narrations, the raw material of Anderson's performances, are in this sense a privileged medium for self-construction. One's daily actions are thus composed into logical plots that depict a coherent portrait of oneself.[13] The complete identification with this imaginary self-portrait can hide the fact that it is a symbolic construction. As Anderson points out, it can also mask the fact that this is only one way of understanding the actions of our daily life, which could always be explained differently and composed in another way.[14] The central opacity of our body impulses, this central gap concerning ourselves, opens indeed the possibility of constructing our self image from different and infinite points of view. Each image will always be partial, just one coherent version that fills and covers up a central absence or a gap. The irruption of another point of view that explains and sees things differently can defocus and deconstruct the coherent vision we had of ourselves, as if it were another screen reflecting from a different angle some aspect of our body that we hadn't contemplated before.[15] The infinite rewriting of one's own image is thus part of our symbolic exchange with others.

The same screen device could be applied to the configuration of an inner expression or voice. Electronic technology (with the microphone and the recording) allows us for the first time to hear our voice from the outside, as a coherent image created by a sign system. Applying the schema of Lacan's mirror device, speaking—or singing—would be a blind impulse framed and articulated by a linguistic or a musical system. Both the linguistic and the musical systems are conceived as textual screens that compose a coherent expression. Musicologists such as Naomi Cumming and Lawrence Kramer agree in seeing tonal music as a frame that depicts a coherent expression by centering our hearing.[16] The sense of an inner voice emerges when we identify our speech act with the internal point of audition framed by the sentence. The subjective and the musical voice are just the imaginary result of a total identification of our speech act with the coherent expression we hear.

This identification between the speaking and the hearing (the act, according to Derrida, of hearing oneself speaking from within) can be broken by the use of technology. In an early performance from 1974, "As: if," Anderson speaks out of synch with a prerecorded voice that reproduces the same text.[17] This time delay between the act of speaking and the act of hearing our reflected voice (as if it were an echo in a phone call) desynchronizes our speech from the audition, alienating the sense of the voice and making it sound like an empty shell (that is, a dead sign). In other words, this strategy allows us to hear our voice from the outside, as a dead image created by a sign device (the screen).

The aim of Anderson's concerts and performances is precisely to deconstruct the illusion of an inner voice and an inner body, the sense of a psychological interiority of the self. For this purpose, she creates a distance from the imaginary dimension in order to see the symbolic dimension (the screen) that is masked. She destroys the total identification between the gaze and a coherent vision, and between the speech and a coherent audition, showing the screen that is in between. The framed vision and the framed audition are defocused in order to allow the gaze and the ear to see and hear the screen that adjusts what is represented/expressed. Thus, Anderson plays with the visual screens that regulate the relationship between the gaze and the vision. And she also plays with aural screens, primarily the microphone-loudspeaker system located between the utterance and the ear, in order to render different possible images of her voice.

ELECTRONIC DOUBLING, LOOPS, AND THE NARRATIVE VOICES

In Anderson's songs, the presence and immediacy of her singing voice is revealed as something imaginary. She uses different strategies, principally what Lawrence Kramer calls "narrative effects,"[18] in order to make us hear that the voice and the gesture we are listening to are just the result of a technological editing process. But what are these narrative effects that Kramer refers to? They primarily concern the elaboration of literary works. Here the musicologist is following a distinction drawn by Paul de Man between the level of the story (the reported action) and the level of the textual process (the action of narrating or reporting). While reading a book, we experience a kind of mimetic effect that makes us identify completely with the story level as if it were actually happening. The narrative effects are all those strategies that render the textual process or the reporting activity problematic, in order to break our identification with the story and make us aware of its imaginary construction. Among these strategies are constant interruptions, digressions, and repetitions of the textual production, which displace and render difficult our identification with the narrated events; and the noncoincidence of different narrative agents' discourses (the different points of view of the character, the narrator and the implicit author), which prevents the story's events from being clearly established.

The application of these narrative effects to music implies a complete deconstruction of its primary dimension as a one-level discursive activity.[19] Music is thus compared to a narration and doubled in the two dimensions of a reported story (the musical gesture as a fictional discourse) and a reporting activity (technological editing as the actual discourse). The single agent of the discourse, the musical voice, is equally deconstructed and duplicated in the different agents of a narrative structure: the voice of the character of the song, the voice of the performance persona (as a fictional narrator), and the textual voice of the sound engineer. Anderson accomplishes these narrative effects by making use of an electronic doubling of her voice.

The song "La langue d'amour" from the film *Home of the Brave*, for example, begins with an introductory performance of Anderson telling a story about a woman seduced by a snake (the story seems to be an original retelling of the biblical story in Genesis). From the beginning of the performance, there is a kind of identification between the character of the snake and the gestures and seductive voice of a narrator dressed in a silver costume and black gloves. When Anderson begins reporting the words of the snake there is an electronic doubling of her voice that reveals the two layers of the narration: the words of the snake's character and their reporting by a narrator. The song "La langue d'amour" starts immediately after, reproducing the hypnotic singing of the snake. The lyrical "I" of the song assimilates the snake's character and the female voice of the performance persona in the same gesture. This musical voice is thus an emblem of a female eroticism that connects the sensuous body of musical stars with the hypnotism of a snake. Anderson, however, destroys our identification with this mythical voice through the extension of the electronic doubling. The imaginary voice is therefore defocused and deployed in its constitutive textual layers or narrative agents: the snake's voice, the performance persona's voice, and the textual voice of the sound engineer. At that moment, we realize that our focus on the snake's sensuous voice prevented us from hearing the other narrative voices that compose it.

The narrative effects used in "La langue d'amour" reveal not only that the snake's discourse is a report, but that Anderson's voice is also an imaginary entity reported by an electronic text. In most of the songs from the album *Bright Red* (1994),[20] Anderson uses reverb effects that make her voice sound distant. The reverb is a delay filter that simulates the sound resulting from the reflection of a voice source by surrounding walls and objects (it is a kind of room simulator). The reverb effect concerns not the instantaneous direct impression of the voice, but the temporal delays related to the spatial distances of the room. Consequently, these temporal delays render the traces of a past utterance: they make us hear different reflections of a gesture that is already gone. Anderson explores this idea in a project from 1976, "Some Experiments," where she uses two microphones that try to translate back into words the sound waves created by a past conversation in a room.[21] Technology is here employed in order to amplify the sound traces left by an absent body.

In the song "Tightrope," from the album *Bright Red*, Anderson exploits reverb effects that make her voice sound ghostly, as if it originates from a remote source, lost in distance and in time. Her voice sounds like the echo or the trace of a body that long ago disappeared. The electronic voice is equated with a textual imprint—or a fossil—that reports and renders the image of a past life. This impression is confirmed by the lyrics of the song: Anderson speaks in absentia, as if she were dead or in a dream. In fact, she reports a dream in which all her life was rearranged in a theme park after her death. The narration and the textual-electronic voice that performs it are thus conceived as a kind of funeral monument.[22] The lyrics from the chorus seem like an epitaph that recalls her absent body: "Remember me is all I ask. And if remembered be a task, forget me."[23] This chorus intensifies the reverb effects, making us hear Anderson's voice as a spectral image composed by multiple echoes: it is the emblem of an absent or inaccessible being.[24]

So in these reverb effects her apparently current singing is revealed to be an image created by multiple sound reflections of a past utterance. In several songs, Anderson extends the reverb effect to a loop treatment of her voice. As another delay filter, the loop treatment contributes to displaying the imaginary nature of her voice and the fictional character of its musical gesture. In loop sequences, her singing voice is shown to be an imprint (or sign), decomposed in the numerous recorded traces of an utterance already disappeared. The loop strategy is analogous to the defocusing procedures of minimal music, one of the main influences on Anderson's work, especially the music of Philip Glass.[25]

American minimal music deconstructs the tonal frame that focuses our hearing on a central point: the present gesture. According to Naomi Cumming, tonal voice-leading (as outlined by Schenkerian analysis) contributes to the framing of a present musical gesture with a meaningful purpose.[26] Naomi Cumming sees the musical voice as a semiotic or textually constructed entity. Tonal voice-leading thus concentrates the different textual layers of a score in the audition of a unitary single gesture deployed in the present. Minimal music, on the contrary, deconstructs this tonal frame, defocusing our hearing, undoing the sense of a musical present gesture, and allowing us to hear the numerous textual layers or voices hidden underneath. The main idea is to desynchronize the musical gesture into its constituent textual layers, thus revealing its fictional nature.

Most of Anderson's songs use such minimal music strategies in the accompaniment. In her performances, the repetitive process activated from a violin or an electronic keyboard disintegrates the sense of a current and effective gesture deployed by a present voice. The present musical discourse, its developing gesture, is then defocused in the movement of many electronic layers or sound recordings of a past utterance. The procedure is similar to the external visualization of a zoetrope, an old precinema device for moving images. In the zoetrope device, our gaze is concentrated on a keyhole that frames the animated movement of a picture. When we defocus our gaze, away from the keyhole, and see the zoetrope from the outside, we perceive that it is just a fictional gesture generated by the rapid passing of successive images through one point. At that moment we realize that what actually moves is not the designed gesture, the picture, but the images that compose it. The zoetrope allows us to visualize the circular movement of a device that makes images pass, creating the effect of a fictional gesture.

If the zoetrope shows the movement of the images, the visualization of a phonograph or a tape player illustrates the circular movement of soundtracks. The musical gesture is thus revealed as an internal fictional movement based on the actual passing of different electronic traces through a point. Anderson's playing of the viophonograph and of the tape bow violin clearly shows this production of an imaginary musical gesture, due to the external movement of sound imprints. But in her songs, the repetitive loop sequencing of sound images makes us hear, and not only see, this circular mechanism.

The hearing of the recording medium itself (such as the noises produced by the needle in contact with the sound imprints) or of the apparatus's circular movement is analogous to the narrative effects that foreground the textual process and break our identification with an imaginary voice. This strategy, used frequently in electronic music, is clearly shown in the song "Scatterheart" by Björk. In this song, from the album *Selmasongs* (the soundtrack of Lars von Trier's film *Dancing in the Dark*, 2000), an instrumental melodic line is accompanied by the rhythmic sounds of a turning disc, thus revealing the recorded and imaginary condition of the musical gesture.[27] Similarly, the melodic loops in Anderson's songs are usually accompanied by a rhythmic sound reproducing the circular movement of a mechanical device. In the song "Speak My Language" from the album *Bright Red*, the melodic line advances at the same time that it is enclosed in the circular repetition of a machine that generates the sound of jolting of a phantasmal train. The current flow seems simultaneously to happen and not to happen, as it is finally revealed to be a simulacrum produced by the continual reproduction of past musical facts.[28]

THE FACTORY OF REPRESENTATION

In all these examples analyzed, Anderson breaks our identification with her auratic voice and body, showing the technological screens that produce, as the different layers of a narration, her imaginary presence. Anderson appears on stage as an imaginary product, a mask, and at the same time as the person who controls, backstage, the editing of her own image. She is the engineer in charge of different textual, photographic, and sonic screens that allow her to narrate and fabricate her own identity.

In her multimedia performances, Anderson uses her life and body as the raw material for a technological narration of herself. But her body and daily life experience as a real person are missing: they are just fragmentary material that she reflects and rearranges in diverse textual, photographic, and audio narrations that depict a more or less coherent portrait of herself. Taking her body and personal experiences as a starting point, Anderson designs a character for her songs and stories and, simultaneously, defines the star text of her own public image as a celebrity (a secondhand fictional character). The latter is a text that exceeds the limits of a fictional performance and embraces the media coverage (on disc covers, in TV shows, etc.) of her public image as a real performer.[29]

Anderson plays ironically with this star text, creating different versions of herself: in the video *What You Mean We?* (1986), for example, she creates several digital clones that replace her in her promotional commitments. In all her TV and stage performances, Anderson interposes different screens and filters, aimed at protecting herself from the audience's gaze and controlling the image she shows. In this way, Anderson plays with our gaze, directing our vision and audition toward some aspects of her body and voice, and then replacing them with other aspects she had previously left in the dark. She thus performs a kind of striptease that reveals the fetishistic nature of a star image that fills (always partially) and covers up the absence of a real body.[30] A conscious performance of the entertainment industry's voyeuristic-fetishistic game is, in fact, one of Anderson's aims.

Hence Anderson performs on the stage the symbolic discourse that articulates and simultaneously conceals itself behind art entertainment images. In this sense, she follows the conceptual art tendency to foreground the institutional game of the art industry (museums' exhibiting rules, etc.) that usually remains in the shadows. In particular, Anderson brings onto the stage the backstage factory of visual and aural fetish images, that is, of capitalist phantasmagorias or commodities. Laurie Anderson appears thus as a corporate label, as an image created by a collectively managed factory. More than as a traditional artist, Anderson conceives herself as an anonymous worker (a no-body) who produces the emblematic image of an earlier economy of representation. Following Walter Benjamin's ideas about the masking of new industrial techniques behind earlier forms of production, we can argue that the music industry simulates and conceals itself behind the auratic dimension of an earlier representational game.[31]

According to Frederickson, the change from an economy of representation to an industrial mode of production took place in nineteenth-century opera (in particular Wagner's operas) and concerts.[32] First, there was a social technology that rationalized musical performance, submitting musicians' bodies to a technological time in order to produce a specific aesthetic effect. Frederickson describes a gradual process whereby a musical performance that originally developed according to a body gesture and tempo was gradually alienated from the body and coordinated by more efficient technological timings and procedures that completely subjugated the performers. This rational process is equivalent to the introduction of new industrial techniques into factories, which replaced the ancient methods of production by hand. The arrival of mechanized recording technology is, according to Frederickson, the logical culmination of this process. Similarly to the cinema, the bodies of the performers are dismembered into many specific tasks, submitted to the fragmentations and repetitions of the recording process, and then definitively concealed behind the image of a mythic performance. As in just one more industrial factory, the fragmented gestures of the workers make sense and compose a unitary coherent body only in the final construction of an imaginary product, that is, in an alienated commodity.

Anderson's multimedia concerts perform the backstage factory of a contemporary mythic representation. This is clearly staged in her film-concert entitled *Home of the Brave*. Following Meyerhold's experiments, Anderson appears on stage as a body reproducing mechanical cyclical tasks, wholly incorporated in a technological machine.[33] Her automatic body evokes a cyborg, an integration of flesh and technology, whose movements activate and coordinate a global mechanism. Her heart is the motor of a technological pulse (a metronome), and her repetitive and accurate gestures set in motion different audiovisual sources. At the beginning of the song

"Smoke Rings" from *Home of the Brave*, for example, Anderson performs a conduct-ing dance composed of cyclical programmed movements, which coordinates the sonic production of the other musicians. In many other performances, her arms and body serve as the moving screens that regulate the composition of a visual text: this is the case of the multimedia performance *United States*, where Anderson intercepts and composes an image thanks to the recurring movement of her violin bow.[34]

Moreover, Anderson's body is completed with different technological prosthe-ses, especially recording technologies: she uses headlight glasses that illuminate the audience; video glasses and video bows that record the audience and her own body; microphone, loudspeaker, and recording systems attached to her body movements and her mouth. Her sight and hearing, her sensuous corporal system, is thus com-pletely merged with a recording technology that registers the fragmentary perspec-tives of her body. Anderson's discontinuous gestures are recorded and, at the same time, are the medium that coordinates and composes the audiovisual text of her own image. So Anderson performs a live recording device where the blind acts of her fragmentary body are recorded and composed into a coherent audiovisual text that brings back to her, as with a mirror, the illusory presence of a self.

Her multimedia performances are therefore related to the idea of a mediatized subjectivity, that is, of a fragmentary body that needs a technological sign device to complete itself. The cyborg, as a mutilated body filled with technological prostheses, underscores the postmodern incapacity to keep a distance from the sign: from this point of view, all presence would be already traversed and constructed by the sign. Anderson aligns herself with the poststructuralist conception of a reified human being, in particular with Foucault's ideas about a body absolutely disciplined by mod-ern technologies that generate the illusion of a self or a subjective voice. In turn, poststructuralist conceptions reproduce the scientific-rational notions of a body fragmented and reduced to a force. The worker in a capitalist factory would be this reified human whose body has been wholly dismembered by social and machine tech-nologies, and whose fragmentary gestures can only be combined and acquire mean-ing in an imaginary self provided by commodities.

FROM THE BODY TO THE TECHNOLOGICAL PERFORMANCE

Anderson's multimedia performances reveal the change of music theater from the early economy of representation to the industrial economy of the simulacrum. In the economy of music theater representation—the opera being its greatest example—a character previously depicted by a dramatic and musical text is acted out by a con-crete singer on the stage. Following the phenomenological perspectives of the French philosopher Merleau-Ponty, we can argue that it is the active gesture of a present sensibility—the physical gestures of its voice and movement—that completes and makes sense of a character merely sketched by the signs. This present activity of the body is an intentional gesture that unifies linguistic signs and directs their significa-tion in a particular way. In addition, each sensibility performs a musical character with a completely different style, contributing thus to a constant renovation of the role.[35] So in mimetic acting, the identity archetypes conveyed by literary and musical characters are constantly renewed thanks to the centrality of the body in the performer-audience exchange.

In contrast, in contemporary musical shows mediated by technology and the media, the character and the physical gestures that perform it are depicted by the same electronic design process. In the case of pop stars, their personal gestures and voices are just as much a construction as the characters they perform. Roles and subjective archetypes are not easily renewed, as songs are fixed once and for all in a unique mythical performance and their characters confusingly identified with the designed style of a single celebrity's image. So, in this context, the voice and gestures of the body, far from being the creative source of renewal described by Merleau-Ponty's philosophy, are reduced to the mythic "aura" of a commodity produced by technological means. Laurie Anderson deconstructs this phantasmagorical nature of the body performance, revealing the technological performance hidden underneath it. Rejecting an immediate physical and empathic communion with the audience, she achieves a more conceptual, reflexive, and technological performance that creates a distance from our fetishist identification with archetypal forms of subjectivity and allows us to play with them as multiple symbolic signifiers or masquerades.

NOTES

1. *Home of the Brave: a Film by Laurie Anderson*, directed by Laurie Anderson, VHS (1986; Burbank, CA: Warner Reprise Video, 1990).
2. Laurie Anderson, *Stories from the Nerve Bible: A Retrospective 1972–1992* (New York: Harper Perennial, 1994), 55–61.
3. Anderson, *Stories*, 36–37.
4. Craig Adcock, "Marcel Duchamp's Gap Music: Operations in the Space between Art and Noise," in *Wireless Imagination. Sound, Radio and the Avant-garde*, ed. Douglas Kahn and Gregory Whitehead (Cambridge, MA: MIT Press, 1992), 105–39.
5. See Roland Barthes, *Camera Lucida*, trans. Richard Howard (1980; reprint, New York: Hill & Wang, 1981), 115. Anderson, in many of her performances, expresses this poetic idea of corpse-photography by leaving the silhouette of one of her gestures on a back screen after it has been completed.
6. This story appears in Laurie Anderson, *The Ugly One with the Jewels and Other Stories*, 1995 by Warner Bros. Records, Warner Bros. Records 9 45847-2, compact disc.
7. The song is part of the larger performance *United States* (1981). First released as a single, the song also appeared on her debut album *Big Science* (1982). Laurie Anderson, *Big Science*, 2007, 1982 by Warner Bros. Records, Nonesuch 130428-2, compact disc.
8. See Anderson, *Stories*, 150–51.
9. Ibid., 24.
10. Jacques Derrida, *De la grammatologie* (Paris: Les Éditions de Minuit, 1967), 33.
11. Laurie Anderson, "Late Show," from *Home of the Brave*, 1986 by Warner Bros. Records, Warner Bros. Records 9 25400-2, compact disc.
12. See Jacques Lacan, *Les quatre concepts fondamentaux de la psychanalyse (Sem 11)* (Paris: Seuil, 1973). In this chapter I have followed the application of Lacan's theories to the cinema by Christian Metz, *Le signifiant imaginaire: Psychanalyse et cinéma* (1977; reprint, Paris: Christian Bourgois Éditeur, 2002) and to postmodern performance by Mathew Causey, "The Screen Test of the Double: The Uncanny Performer in the Space of Technology," *Theatre Journal* 51: 4 (1999): 383–94.

13. For a further explanation of the narrative construction of our subjectivity, see Jerome Bruner, "Life as Narrative," *Social Research* 54: 1 (1987): 11–32.

14. See Laurie Anderson and Celant Germano, *Dal Vivo* (Milan: Fondazione Prada, 1999), 244.

15. This situation is clearly shown in a story Anderson tells about her visits to a psychiatrist. Anderson, *Stories*, 84.

16. Naomi Cumming, "The Subjectivities of 'Erbarme Dich,'" *Music Analysis* 16: 1 (1997): 7–11; Lawrence Kramer, "The Mysteries of Animation: History, Analysis and Musical Subjectivity," *Music Analysis* 20: 2 (2001): 153–78.

17. For a further analysis of this performance, see Ainhoa Kaiero, "Technological Fiction, Recorded Time and 'Replicants' in the Concerts of Laurie Anderson," *TRANS: Transcultural Music Review* 14 (2010), online. Available: http://www.sibetrans.com/trans/a10/technological-fiction-recorded-time-and-replicants-in-the-concerts-of-laurie-anderson?lang=en. October 31, 2012.

18. Lawrence Kramer, *Music as Cultural Practice 1800–1900* (Berkeley: University of California Press, 1990), 186–87.

19. According to musicologists such as Lawrence Kramer and Carolyn Abbate, music is a discursive activity located at the antipodes of a narrative statement. Both agree that music is pronounced in the present tense of the first person (the lyrical "I" or the musical voice) who performs the events at the very moment in which they occur. The music we hear is thus a present, effective gesture that questions or provokes a reaction, constituting a veritable speech act (in the sense of J. L. Austin's and John Searle's theory of performative utterances). Music, as the present manifestation of a subjective voice, constitutes, in this sense, the opposite of a textual report that narrates the past actions of a body already absent or gone. For a further analysis of music as a discursive activity see Lawrence Kramer, "Unsung Voices: Opera and Musical Narrative in the Nineteenth Century by Carolyn Abbate," *Nineteenth-Century Music* 15: 3 (1992): 235–39.

20. Laurie Anderson, *Bright Red*, 1994 by Warner Bros. Records, Warner Bros. Records 9 45534-2, compact disc.

21. See Anderson, *Stories*, 52.

22. The relation between the narration and the funeral monument is especially foregrounded in the installation *Dal Vivo*. See Anderson and Celant, *Dal Vivo*.

23. Laurie Anderson, "Tightrope," from *Bright Red*, 1994.

24. This idea of an inaccessible body connects with Laurie Anderson's interest in anonymous "nobodies": buried and forgotten persons (like women or imprisoned criminals) who can only be evoked by a past image or a report.

25. See Fernando do Nascimento Gonçalves, *Fabulaçoes eletrônicas: Poéticas da comunicaçao e da tecnologia em Laurie Anderson* (Rio de Janeiro: E-papers, 2006), 196–97.

26. Naomi Cumming, "The Subjectivities of 'Erbarme Dich,'" *Music Analysis* 16: 1 (1997): 5–44.

27. Björk, *Selmasongs*, 2000 by Elektra, Elektra 62533-2, compact disc. In fact, in the film sequence, the song is used to accompany an imaginary undoing of the events that had occurred previously: the crime committed by Selma against her patron. The hypnotic rhythm makes Selma's imagination enter a dream time where facts are as reversible as a soundtrack.

28. This image evokes the phantasmagorical progress described by Walter Benjamin: a fictional or mythic progress based on the "eternal recurrence of the same." See the chapter "Mythic History: Fetish," in Susan Buck-Morss, *The Dialectics of Seeing: Walter Benjamin and the Arcades Project* 9, Cambridge, MA: MIT Press, 1989), 78–110.

29. See Philip Auslander, "Going with the Flow: Performance Art and Mass Culture," *TDR* 33: 2 (1989): 119–36.

30. This lack is recognized by stars such as George Michael, who observed that "It's not the something extra that makes the star—it's the something that's missing." See

Andrew Goodwin, *Dancing in the Distraction Factory: Music Television and Popular Culture* (London: Routledge, 1993), 117.

31. See Buck-Morss, *The Dialectics of Seeing,* 110.

32. John Frederickson, "Technology and Music Performance in the Age of Mechanical Reproduction," *International Review of the Aesthetics and Sociology of Music* 20: 2 (1989): 193–220.

33. In the 1920s, the Russian and Soviet theater director Vsevolod Meyerhold brought Frederick Taylor's scientific management theories into theater. Taylor's scientific methods were originally conceived to increase worker efficiency in factories. See Steve Dixon, *Digital Performance: A History of New Media in Theater, Dance, Performance Art and Installation* (Cambridge, MA: MIT Press, 2007), 64.

34. See Anderson, *Stories,* 162.

35. For a further explanation of the relation between body and language, see Maurice Merleau-Ponty, *Phénoménologie de la perception* (1945; reprint, Paris: Gallimard, 1976), 211–14. The body as an open performing gesture can renew not only the role, but also the artistic techniques that conform to conventional styles of voice and movement.

CHAPTER 11

Singing and a Song

The "Intimate Difference" in Susan Philipsz's Lowlands (2010)

ZEYNEP BULUT

A fictitious *I* is wandering around the River Clyde in Glasgow. Her voice is spread all around. It is in the air, in the water, on the sideways, on the facade of the building that she just passed by, on that red sweater that she wears. She is singing. As she sings, she fills in and moves through a space. Her voice appears in bits and pieces as moments, as traces, as *I* walk along the bridges, as *I* hear the voices of other pedestrians. *I* follow and sing with her: "Lowlands I heard them say...My Lowlands away." Pause for a second and think where she is. Where is she singing? *I* have caught her voice in the silence of the River Clyde, now lost it in the noise of the others. Where did the "low" of Lowlands go? Where did I leave the "lands" of Lowlands? Who is singing? What made me think that Lowlands would always be there? This is a fictitious River Clyde that I imagined. It is neither familiar nor otherworldly. This is a fictitious *I* that I just voiced, a singing *I* that became more and more present in movement, in the movement of a song. A song is contagious like a virus. In and out of body and language, we can carry and be carried by a song to various physical, social, and imaginary landscapes. What happens when we anonymously sing a song into a particular landscape? How does a song locate, extend, and transform the landscape for us, while being changed by the very landscape itself? What would be the sensory and spatiotemporal play of a song for our performing selves?

Susan Philipsz's famous sound installation *Lowlands* evokes all of these questions. Philipsz won the 2010 Turner Prize for her sound installation, the first artist to win this prize for a sound installation. Controversies arose afterward, as *Lowlands* was considered not a visual work or installation but music. After all, Philipsz was "only" singing. I do not intend to discuss the historical narratives behind this divide between installation work and music in this chapter, but it may be important to reflect on the idea of "just singing" within the changing context of music theater.

In its conventional sense, what comes to mind when we think of music theater is perhaps a Broadway scene, where girls and boys dance and sing synchronically, where singing and dancing are equally choreographed. What we hear in this setting is a series of musical themes and songs—each of which is usually associated with a character—and variations of the songs repeated with different instrumentation in different tempo and dynamics. Take the original 1934 version of the musical *Moulin Rouge*. Constance Bennett sings Harry Warren and Al Dubin's famous song, "The Boulevard of Broken Dreams," in at least three different versions, each time giving a different context and mood to the song, to the words and to the sounds of the words: "I walked along the streets of sorrow, the boulevard of broken dreams [...] Here is where you'll always find me, always walking up and down [...] where gigolo and gigolette still sing a song and dance along."[1] The lyrics of this landmark song provide a strange counterpoint to the story of *Lowlands*, leading us to imagine how singing is never just singing. It is rather a sonic act of walking up and down and all around, an extension of one's self to one's surroundings with a variety of voice and sounds. Contemporary music theater asserts this idea, while highlighting singing as a situation, as an event of sonic, visual, spatial, and performative gestures in everyday life.[2] This is precisely what is at stake in *Lowlands*.

Philipsz sings three versions of an old Scottish lament, *Lowlands Away*, and installs her recording under three bridges in Glasgow. In the form of a spatial projection, her singing voice surrounds, embodies, and transcends the bridges. Bridges have double ends, as Philipsz notes. Over the bridge, there is sunlight, an ongoing presence. Under the bridge, there is water and mystery, a wet echo of the passed. Encouraging us to oscillate between these two ends, Philipsz helps us consider a new definition and function of singing and song: singing as an act of navigation for finding and re-sounding one's embodied voice, and song as a corporeal play of spatiotemporal sounds.

SINGING: FINDING AND RE-SOUNDING ONE'S EMBODIED VOICE

Singing is a form of storytelling. Take some of the great songwriters like Leonard Cohen, Joni Mitchell, Marianne Faithfull, and David Bowie. They all tell little stories, stories that echo, translate, and retell the shared modes of feeling, doing, and being in everyday life. Philipsz's singing is also such a form of storytelling.

Philipsz's sixteenth-century Scottish lament *Lowlands* tells the story of a woman who mourns for the death of her lover, a sailor who was drowned in the water. By singing, she calls and perhaps tries to bring him back to earth from the water. Philipsz's voice reenacts this calling. In a casual way, like a neighbor singing next door, she performs the song. The different versions of the recordings create a canonic effect, through which we hear syncopated superimpositions of tunes. But we still follow the words. Philipsz does not deconstruct words. The way she sings does not necessarily lead us to crystalize the sonic materiality of language. Similarly, she does not literally amplify the sonic environment of the bridges.[3]

Yet, the site-specific installation of her singing echoes the words along with the concrete sounds of the environment, of the bridges. We are then left with the following questions: How does a disembodied singing voice reflect and transform a particular place? Does it create a haunting effect for the people who randomly pass by the bridge? Does it help us perceive a place as continuous and fluid and bond different bodies, times, and spaces? In other words, does a disembodied singing voice function as an audio-tactile string? Suggesting these questions, Philipsz amplifies the very act of singing as involved in hearing, navigating, and re-sounding one's self, and song as a corporeal—embodied—play of spatiotemporal sounds.

Various scholars and thinkers such as Roland Barthes, Jacques Derrida, Steven Connor, Allen Weiss, Mladen Dolar, Adriana Cavarero, and Carolyn Abbate[4] examine the human voice as a physical, phenomenal, cultural, and political strain between the immateriality of language and the materiality of the human body. When it comes to voice, there is always a degree of intangible presence and tangible absence. Even if we see someone speaking in front of us, we cannot perfectly see the source of his or her vocal production. We would still ask where the voice comes from. Yet we would also resonate with the voice and uniquely incorporate it into our own bodies. Such uncertain knowledge is related on the one hand to the ephemeral, approximate, overarching, and surrounding nature of sound, which triggers a "lost and found" play, and on the other hand to the embodied nature of the voice.

The "lost and found" play of sound derives from the impossibility of sonic objectification. Sound has been analyzed both as a physical and as a metaphysical phenomenon. In the special volume of *Differences*, "The Sense of Sound," Rey Chow and James A. Steintrager lay out the major discourses of sound and sonic objectification. Chow and Steintrager initially remind us of the romantic paradigm, which conceptualizes sound as an "indivisible continuum."[5] Due to its ineffable and continuous character, sound is considered almost always lost. This discourse of sound couples the sonic loss with the "sonic capture."[6] The reciprocity—and even the entanglement—between the sonic loss and the sonic capture puts the question of sonic objectification forward: do we really catch a sound, or are we caught by it? Equally, do we really lose a sound or does it really leave us?

One can answer both yes and no to these questions, which implies that we cannot really pinpoint whether the loss or the capture of sound comes first. More significantly, this shows that we are not fully detached or distanced from sound. The bodily involvement, which again comes with the ephemeral yet also continuous and surrounding nature of sound, leads us to investigate the sensory perception of sound. We embody, process, and translate a sound through a multisensory matrix. Given its vibration, sound is a tactile phenomenon. We hear a sound not simply through our ears, but also through our whole bodies. We process a sound through our embodied imagination, translating it into a variety of mingling images and scenes. This is how the way we perceive sound becomes partial, contingent, almost always imagined, open to change and in need of a personal body.

And perhaps this is why the subsequent narratives of sound are somehow in tune with the romantic paradigm of loss. Take the Frankfurt school. Pursuing a Platonic line of thought, Max Horkheimer and Theodor Adorno mention sound as an interruptive and dangerous phenomenon that threatens the mechanical order of a system.[7] Also consider the digitalization of sound. Computerized technologies turn sound into discrete units, which can be multiplied. Nonetheless, the "infinitum"[8] or the mathematical multiplication of sounds still employs the idea of "loss" with its vocabulary, as Chow and Steintrager underline. Terms like "lossy," "degradation," "deterioration"[9] are exemplary of this vocabulary.

The loss of sound informs the question of the disembodied voice. If sound is never fully lost or caught and never fully disembodied or objectified, how can voice be fully disembodied? The voice cannot be fully objectified either. What's more, its disembodiment is more partial and more immediately translated into a reembodiment. Always associated with a body, the voice calls for a direct oscillation between the familiar and the unfamiliar. Its multitude suggests the Freudian uncanny. Take the voices that we hear on the radio or on the phone. We do not see who is speaking, a situation Michel Chion refers to as "acousmatic" in relation to voice-over in cinema,[10] but we tend to imagine a body that is attached to the voice that we hear.

The body that we imagine could be anyone's body, a variety of bodies. We build a bridge between the recorded voice and the live voice, which is the voice that we imagine in our particular physical environment, perhaps in tune with the sounds of our particular acoustic ecology. We attach the recorded voice literally to an imagined body and thus embody it in our own voices. As Allen Weiss proposed in *Breathless: Sound Recording, Disembodiment and the Transformation of Lyrical Nostalgia*, this bridge also implies a connection between life and death.

Such reembodiment informs us about the ways in which we may respond to Philipsz's disembodied voice in *Lowlands*. Suppose that you are walking by the bridge, without knowing that there is an installation under the bridges. You hear the singing voice and the song, with which you could be familiar, especially if you are local to Glasgow. But the way you hear and the place that you are in would affect the quality of singing, the song, and the place itself. Where does the voice come from? And where does it go? Does it ever settle or end?

With the setup of multiple recordings and speakers, one can hear superimpositions between the tunes and the words within the song. Take the chorus. Philipsz sings, "Lowlands lowlands away my John. Lowlands I heard them say. My lowlands away." Three recordings of the slightly different vocalization of this line are played simultaneously. Thus the words overlap, almost echo one another, generating a rhythmical texture. Concrete sounds of the environment beside the River Clyde envelop this texture on the one hand, and punctuate it on the other. Similarly, the pitch, timbre, and dynamic range of Philipsz's singing are in dialogue with the sounds of the River Clyde. None of these musical elements are stable or perfectly crystallized. It is of course true that one can still hear both the melody and the singing voice as distinct from the rest of the sounds. Nevertheless, the setup of the installation attempts to liquidate the musical context. To put it in another way, *Lowlands* emphasizes not necessarily the musical context but the sonic spectrum of the song.[11]

The sonic spectrum encourages us to walk through the pluralities of echoes, which possibly both extend and expand the presumed limits of the bridges. To be more precise, the song penetrates into the place, and the singing voice disseminates into multiple sounds, marking new boundaries and new zones of soundings. One can then attentively hear the timbral, textural, lyrical, rhythmical, and melodic constituents of the singing voice within the place. Walking, one recognizes the sonic, spatial, and performative instances of voicing itself. Walking, one resings such instances. S/he catches an echo and reechoes it.

In this way, Philipsz's voice becomes anyone's voice, an anonymous and singular voice at the same time. What at first appears a haunting and ghostly voice that comes from all over the place can now be found in multiple bodies as fragmented and partial, as tangible, mobile, and negotiable. The partial disembodiment and reembodiment of the voice thus allows us to transform and even liquidate the time and space with a vulnerable and open state of being.

The connection—bridge—between the poles such as life and death, water and earth, presence and absence, fantasy and reality, private and public can then come into being. The story of the song is embedded in this connection. Let us recall the last line of the lament: "My love is drowned in the windy Lowlands." Singing the song, the sailor's lover embodies the sailor's voice and attempts to bring him back to earth from the water. Just like the connection or the loss of clear distinction between the poles, the two voices are blended. Their singularities already become multiplied.

In *The Burrow of Sound*, Mladen Dolar explains this situation beautifully. Referring to Kafka's story "The Burrow," Dolar highlights sound at the edge of "oppositions between wakefulness and sleep, inside and outside, dream and reality, location and dislocation, time and space, duration and intermittency, between subject and the Other, reality and fantasy, one and multiple."[12] "The Burrow" is the story of an animal that lives in an underground tunnel to protect itself from its enemies. However, the burrow does not function as a fully contained, closed, or hidden space. On the contrary, it is an entangled space like a web, which has a variety of exits and entries. As Dolar writes, the animal attempts "to keep its enemies at bay," where the burrow's exits and entries become points of "transition, vulnerability and openness."[13]

Within the burrow, there are little and lower sounds that recur rhythmically, singular silences that are one's hearing of one's own bodily sounds,[14] and inaudible and almost haunting noises that the animal both "wakes into and sleeps through."[15] Thus, the enigma—the web—of the burrow remains. The animal cannot perfectly locate where the sounds begin and end.

This impossibility as seen and described in Kafka's "Burrow," Dolar argues, is the "beast," the "animalistic excess," the "super-nature and un-nature" of sound.[16] The animalistic excess of sound reveals both the noise and the silence of the human kind. The embodiment of the beast of sound helps us materialize an existential crisis and relief, a state of awakening and sleep into the world. We cannot escape sound. Even if we close our ears, we cannot shut our bodies down. Our bodies constantly vibrate within, below, or above the threshold of hearing. Sounds grow both onto and into us, enveloping and extending our whole bodies from inside to outside. Such overarching quality breeds the impossibility of the perfect loss or the perfect capture of sound. In short, sound is the "burrow" itself. It leads us to spatial thinking with its multiple exits and entries, as Dolar tells us throughout his whole essay.

This reading is insightful in crystallizing what's at stake in *Lowlands*. As mentioned earlier, the musical context of Philipsz's singing and the architectural aspect of her installation draw attention to the sounds of a particular place, which provide both the exits from and the entries into the matrix of the material culture and imagination of the River Clyde. The piece pronounces singing within hearing, as an act of understanding the spatiotemporal instances of a place.

SONG: A CORPOREAL PLAY OF SPATIOTEMPORAL SOUNDS

Spatial thinking can be understood as a relational constellation or installation of things. Through the movement of sound, we draw a space and navigate a place. "What forms of experience and negotiation are opened up by mobilizing sound's spatial particularity?" asks Brandon LaBelle in *The Site of Sound: Of Architecture and the Ear*.[17] This seems to be a question key to the ways in which one can find him- or herself walking around the River Clyde through the *Lowlands*. Both the mobility and the mobilization of sound can turn the space into a continuous and fluid landscape, a relational and vibrational surface, where there is no clear-cut point of departure, and from where there is no one single straightforward direction. In this landscape, all oppositions—above and under the bridge, the water and the earth, the echoes of the voice and the words of language—may come closer to one another and behave as one another's function.

Like Kafka's "Burrow," the River Clyde becomes a cavity, a complex web of sounds, where one echoes with another by mimicking the disembodied voice's singing while walking. One then pays attention to how both the act of singing and the song are distributed through the place on the one hand, and change the perception of the place itself on the other. Once the singing and the song are mobilized, the spatial sounds of the voice, the atomic units of the words like onomatopoetic sounds, and the voluntary or involuntary bodily noises are amplified. Singing becomes voicing, extending, and transforming a spatiotemporal sound, and song becomes a corporeal—embodied—play of such sounds.

In *Varieties of Audio Mimesis: Musical Evocations of Landscape*,[18] Allen Weiss reminds us of the correspondences—reflections and transformations—between soundscape,[19] landscape, and language. At the heart of this trilogy, Weiss indeed highlights the intersensory composure and representation of hearing. More specific to the sounds of voice and language, he explains how primal speech sounds evoke an imagery of a landscape, how they allow us to internalize the sounds of the whole world into our own bodies, and how with every utterance we throw ourselves back into the world.[20] This is "singing the world,"[21] as Weiss puts it. What one experiences in *Lowlands* is such singing. As mentioned above, guiding us to building bridges between the juxtaposed positions of a landscape, soundscape, and language, it leads us to a multiplicity of states, where we can "sing the world." Walking in and out, up and down, and around is here a necessary part of the singing itself. In return, we can remap the place. Thus singing becomes a tool for hearing the soundscape louder, for navigating and refinding a song through the soundscape, for transforming the multiple exits and entries of the landscape—the bridges—into a zone of resonance, for sounding with the others and then returning to our own selves.

In its literal sense, resonance means a deep echo. In figurative language, it means evoking memories, images, thoughts, and emotions. In physics, it means "the reinforcement or prolongation of sound by synchronous vibration, and a short-lived subatomic particle that is an excited state of a more stable particle."[22] In mechanics, it refers to an "enhanced vibration of an object subjected to an oscillating force close to a natural frequency of the object."[23] Given its sonic spectrum and spatial layout, the concepts of resonance are significant for understanding the ways in which the verbal, musical, and sonic aspects of the song *Lowlands* melt into the spaces in and around the River Clyde.

Within such mise en scène, imagine how one could reembody Philipsz's voice—and equally bits and pieces of the song—in the form of resonance. Can we consider such resonance an "intuition," "a case of hearing in advance," "a carried difference,"[24] in a Derridean sense? If so, can we imagine this difference perhaps in the form of a conflicting and dissonant external voice or in the form of an approving and approved inner voice, yet all and all in the form of the voice of others? My intention is not to give a yes or no answer to these questions here. I articulate these questions to highlight how they gesture to the necessity of revisiting the role of shared vibration in our everyday life. Resonance—and in particular the vibration that we exchange through our embodied voices—informs us about the way we make ourselves and make sense of the world. Veit Erlmann's thought-provoking book *Reason and Resonance* enlightens us about the historical and the scientific roots, the musical and the aesthetic contexts, and the philosophical implications of resonance.

We tend to think that resonance is the opposite of reason, subjectivity is the other of objectivity, and emotion is the obstruction of rationale. Are these dichotomies real dichotomies? Or do they share an "intimate relationship," as Erlmann proposes? "This is where *Reason and Resonance* seeks to break new ground. The book attempts to chart a terrain in which 'understanding' and resonance, hearing and the 'meaning of being,' physics and philosophy enter into complex and intimate relationship with each other," writes Erlmann.[25] Unfolding the false dichotomies, Erlmann initially corrects our immediate reading of Cartesian ideology and explains how the physiology of the ear and hearing is key to Descartes's philosophy of mind and body. As he argues, the concept of resonance, which is interwoven with scientific theories about the physiology of the ear and auditory perception, takes a central part in constructing modern science and philosophy of the modern self. The divide between hearing and listening seems to sit at the heart of this construction.

Discourses are many. As Erlmann also reminds us, sound is not simply understood but also idealized as an impossibly objectified loss in the romantic paradigm. Hearing is both a physiological and a psychological channel, which activates this loss. As embodied, the loss of sound leads to the loss of self. On the contrary, one can revisit the very possibility of "ear training" and of "self-containment" within the discourse of structural thinking. Here the loss of sound—its prolonged reverberation—is usually translated into a failure, a failure that also delivers the chance for learning what it means to listen, the recipe for discovering the authentic self. Since the epistemology of hearing is uncertain and deceptive, the ear needs to be trained to hear "what to hear" in a particular order with a particular amount of attention and intensity. Listening is thus a cultural and cultivated activity, a form of distanced, concentrated, and conscious hearing, which helps one become a subject.[26] Neither an elusively lost echo nor a perfectly controlled echoless medium, a poststructural reading of listening goes beyond the romantic and the structural discourses and underlines the reciprocity between the embodied experience of hearing and the material culture of listening.

Among these narratives, Erlmann concludes with a joint notion, the listener's function:

> I do not dwell much on how a person's inner listening may be socially and culturally conditioned. Instead I focus on what it is about the ear—its structure, its elemental substances, its functioning—that allows such a person to speak of this experience as pertaining to his or her inner self in the first place. And instead of a history of behaviors tied to the ear or a history of ideas representing such behaviors my account of modern aurality is a history of the "listener function."[27]

What is the listener function that the physiology of the ear facilitates? Is it a function of knowing one's self by pricking his or her ear to his or her physical environment? The physical environment consists of both what gets heard within the culture of listening and what gets unnoticed within the multitude of other sounds. The listener's function is then a function of founding the presence of the former in the latter, of integrating self with the world not as one but many, of carrying and circulating an unknown intimacy to another, a Derridean difference again. The unknown is not the magical, not the mystical, not the inaccessible. Quite the contrary, it is physical, and perhaps a matter of sound that we breathe in and out on a daily basis.

NOISE AND JUST *A FRIEND'S VOICE*

Sounds almost always sound similar, neither perfectly the same nor perfectly different. For some the uncertainty and for some others the failure of sound derives from this status. Either way, what sound becomes is an intimate difference, a felt proximity and distance at the same time, "a separation in rapport."[28] What the intimate difference of sound leads us to is a falling. We fall in and out of sounds, just as we fall in and out of love, into one another, into a trap, into water. Falling in and out is a case of vulnerability, a case of being caught and lost in a place. Vulnerability crystallizes spatial thinking. It renders the edges—the edge of tears and laughter, of pain and pleasure, of sanity and insanity, of life and death—the in-between modes of being sensible. A constant openness, a bodily stretch from depth to surface, and thus a commitment to being hurt and remembering, and perhaps a sustained addiction to struggle and pain, vulnerability secures life as a web of unintended affairs. It is not a discourse of fear and isolation, but a discourse of anxiety and connection. Sound both contains and spreads such vulnerability, such a discourse of anxiety and connection. And voice simultaneously internalizes and externalizes sounds. It uniquely performs and realizes them as points of exits and entries, of transition and openness.

Lowlands offers a playground where we can recognize the transition and the openness of the voice. Philipsz's singing voice is like a call, engaging the listener's function. As explained earlier, Philipsz's call gradually but clearly triggers hearing the sounds of the voice. Through the sounds, she carries "the voice of a friend," as Heidegger would posit.[29] The voice of a friend can be a variety of voices. It does not have a particular figure or name. It is anonymous but also singular, containing and being contained in a network of particularities. Derrida's suggestive piece "Heidegger's Ear: Philopolemology,"[30] in *The Politics of Friendship*, tells us the story of "the voice of a friend" at the heart of hearing:

> The friend has no face, no figure. No sex. No name. The friend is not a man, nor a woman; it is not I, nor a "self," not a subject, nor a person. It is another Dasein that each Dasein carries, through the voice it hears, with itself, neither within itself, in the ear, in the "inner ear," inside a subjective interiority, nor far away, too far from the ear, for one can also hear from afar, in an exterior space or in some transcendence, but in its vicinity…[31]

It is just this sort of friend's voice that Philipsz's voice becomes. One could argue the contrary, given the specificity of the context of Philipsz's singing: this is a "she" singing one of our best-known tunes beside our very own River Clyde, one might say. But that would exclude the plural echoes and the "vicinity" of Philipsz's voice. The specificity does not simply come from the given place, time, or tune. The specific unknown that I have termed the intimate difference emerges as we also hear the multitude of other sounds in a friend's voice. The sounds of a friend's voice can carry many other historicized voices, since the sounds pluralize the material figure, name, and contexts. They then help us transform a place into a particular space. This is not an absolutely relative state or an endlessly open interpretation. It is rather a shared and a commonly distributed state that we all contain, exchange, and then probably change. Pursuing the listener's function, hearing a voice, accordingly, cannot simply be hearing what the voice says. Or even, what the voice says is much more layered than what it appears to be. "In any case, what matters here is not what the friend's voice says, not its said, not even the saying of its said. Hardly its voice. Rather what matters is the hearing (das Hören) of its voice," writes Derrida.[32] The hearing of a voice of a friend is an existential mode, "the primary and authentic opening" of Dasein.[33]

Perhaps Philipsz's singing voice unfolds the "hearing of" in a more concrete way. The more we shift our attention to the melodic, rhythmic, harmonic, and eventually sonic contours, the more we embody the sounds of the voice. We hear of the voice of a friend, and embody its call. The call is partial, both yours and mine. The call is performative. It only "evokes,"[34] but does not dictate. It enacts, but does not narrate. It is just a call, which we may be prepared to answer or not. But in any case, we respond. We pass by the bridges beside the River Clyde and resonate with Philipsz's call and with the presence of others. This is how each of us can hear the call. This is how "Dasein carries the friend in carrying its voice."[35] And this is where there is "no ear without friend" or "no friend without ear."[36]

In other words, this is a zone of resonance, of distributed familiarity of sounds among us. Distributed familiarity here addresses the contingent web of sonic affairs that are involved in and shared through the background noise, and which travel underneath and around the voice of a friend. Consider the possible sounds that constitute the voice of a friend in *Lowlands*. The sounds of Philipsz's voice, of the water, of the bridges, of traffic, of footsteps, of someone's speaking voice or of another's humming voice, they could all coincide both with the musical and with the sonic elements of the song. The sounds cannot be added into one another like a mathematical operation, but they can mirror, transform, and multiply one another. Like a familiar noise, the voice of a friend turns the song into a personal labyrinth of concrete—spatiotemporal—sounds. The voice of a friend distributes the song. The more it is resung by other voices, the more the song is distributed. It melts into the background noise and vice versa, and then becomes a "common multiple."[37]

Multiplicity is "not an epistemological monster but on the contrary the ordinary lot of situations, including that of the ordinary scholar, regular knowledge, everyday work, in short, our common project," posits Michel Serres in *Genesis*.[38] Serres draws on the notion of multiplicity at the heart of noise. As he argues, noise is not a phenomenon that we can separate and analyze, but it is a surrounding and grounding state, "a matter of being itself."[39] Sea noise, water, is "the origin," and "the background noise" is the "ground" of the multiple, which we neither fully grasp nor fully avoid.[40] I suggest Serres's reading of noise as punctuation for *Lowlands*. The work situates the song within the web of sonic affairs in everyday life, which we cannot fully grasp or avoid. In doing so, it also enables us to bond different times, spaces, and bodies with an invisible yet audio-tactile string. It crystallizes the song as a call of the voice of a friend, as an intimate difference, an echo carried to a variety of other people and contexts.

In this sense, *Lowlands* exposes us to a theater situation, a music theater, which could also be considered a theater of sounds in everyday life. A theater of sounds allows us to think about singing, voicing, sounding, and moving as functions of song and dance. It stages a variety of things, bodies, and events as involved and performed in material culture. In the recent volume *Theatre Noise: The Sound of Performance*, Lynn Kendrick and David Roesner insightfully underline the significance of noise, the performance of sound in understanding such theater. Kendrick and Roesner write:

> Theatre provides a unique habitat for noise. It is a place where friction can be thematised, explored playfully, even indulged in: friction between signal and receiver, between sound and meaning, between eye and ear, between silence and utterance, between hearing and listening. In an aesthetic world dominated by aesthetic redundancy and "aerodynamic" signs, theatre noise recalls the aesthetic and political power of the grain of performance. For us "theatre noise" is a new term which captures an agitatory acoustic aesthetic. It expresses the innate theatricality of sound design and performance, articulates the reach of auditory spaces, the art of vocality, the complexity of acts of audience, the political in produced noises.[41]

Theater noise is indeed where *Lowlands* leads us. Kendrick and Roesner's description is revealing. It recalls how Philipsz's voice becomes an anonymous yet also an embodied and singular voice, as its verbal, musical, and sonic aspects are distributed in the physical environment. It recalls that such a voice is not limited to a certain name, character, or identity but is a fictitious *I*. It warns how the playfulness of the song—of finding the song every now and then in a variety of time and space, in a variety of bodies and things, and in bits and pieces—is not given or neutral but contingent. It highlights the self-performing, self-reflexive, and precarious presence of sound. It tells how the mingling of all these things generates a noise, an atmosphere, a zone of resonance, which manifests itself again as a voice that speaks and carries an intimate difference.

NOTES

1. "Boulevard of Broken Dreams," *Moulin Rouge*, Twentieth Century/United Artists' production, lyric by Al Dubin; music by Harry Warren (Sydney: J. Albert & Son, c1933).
2. Dominic Symonds and Millie Taylor explain this reading of song and dance in their introduction to this book.
3. For instance, sound artist Jodi Rose literally amplifies the noises of the bridges. Her project, *Singing Bridges*, gestures toward how the resonant frequencies of a bridge can be translated into a song. The bridges sing. Through the sounds of the bridge, one can find a particular voice of the bridge, as Rose proposes. Jodi Rose, "Why Bridges? Why Sound?" in *Site of Sound # 2: Of Architecture and the Ear*, ed. Brandon LaBelle and Claudia Martinho (Berlin: Errant Bodies Press, 2011), 187–95.
4. Carolyn Abbate's *In Search of Opera* (Princeton, NJ: Princeton University Press, 2001), Mary Ann Smart's *Mimomania: Music and Gesture in Nineteenth-Century Opera* (Berkeley: University of California Press, 2004), and Michel Poizat's *The Angel's Cry: Beyond the Pleasure Principle in Opera* (Ithaca, NY: Cornell University Press, 1992). Also see Roland Barthes, *The Grain of the Voice: Interviews (1962–1980)*, trans. Linda Coverdale (New York: Hill and Wang, 1985); Jacques Derrida, *Speech and Phenomena*, trans. David B. Allison (Evanston, IL: Northwestern University Press, 1973); Steven Connor, *Dumbstruck: A Cultural History of Ventriloquism* (Oxford: Oxford University Press, 2000); Mladen Dolar, *A Voice and Nothing More* (Cambridge: MIT Press, 2006); Allen Weiss, *Breathless: Sound Recording, Disembodiment and the Transformation of Lyrical Nostalgia* (Middletown, CT: Wesleyan University Press, 2002); Adriana Cavarero, *For More Than One Voice: Toward a Philosophy of Vocal Expression*, trans. Paul A. Kottman (Stanford, CA: Stanford University Press, 2005).
5. Rey Chow and James A. Steintrager, "In Pursuit of the Object of Sound: An Introduction," *Differences* 22: 2–3, ed. Rey Chow and James A. Steintrager (2011): 7.
6. This is also a key to understanding the impossibility of sonic objectification. Chow and Steintrager convey: "Sonic objectification is almost by default organized through a Romantic paradigm, whereby sonic capture is understood implicitly as the capture of that which is lost. More succinctly put, sound is always capture, and capture is always loss." Ibid., 4.
7. Chow and Steintrager tell us how Adorno and Horkheimer recast the mythology of Odysseus: "Homer tells of Odysseus's encounter with the Sirens, whose alluring sounds have compelled many interpretations over the centuries. Max Horkheimer and Theodor Adorno recast the episode [...]. If Odysseus can hear the Sirens' song, he is also immobilized, whereas the oarsmen, precisely because they cannot hear them, are able to proceed with their task, doggedly and with mechanical efficiency." Ibid., 3.
8. Ibid., 7.
9. Ibid., 4, 5.

10. Michel Chion, *The Voice in Cinema*, trans. Claudia Gorbman (New York: Columbia University Press, 1999). One should also note that, prior to Chion, French composer Pierre Schaeffer first introduced the idea of "acousmatic" within the context of musique concrète, for the sounds that we hear without seeing their sources.

11. One can also argue that this liquidation of the musical context allows us to expand on what musical context is or could be in the first place.

12. Mladen Dolar, "The Burrow of Sound," *Differences* 22: 2–3 (2011): 130–36.

13. Ibid., 113, 114.

14. Just like there is no absolute sound, there is no absolute silence. Dolar articulates this very fact in a poetic way: "silence itself is always populated by infinitesimal sounds, there is the heart and the pounding of blood, there is the sounding presence of one's own body whose limits stretch into the surroundings [...]. Silence is not the absence of sounds, but quite the opposite, the state of the greatest alertness in which sub-sounds emerge, the minimal thumps of both one's body and the ambient surroundings." Ibid., 118. Here we should also recall John Cage, who first anchored the idea that one's body is never fully silent. A relatively silent situation indeed draws attention to one's own bodily sounds.

15. Ibid., 114, 115.

16. Ibid., 120.

17. LaBelle, *The Site of Sound*, vii–viii.

18. Allen S. Weiss, *Varieties of Audio Mimesis: Musical Evocations of Landscape* (Berlin: Errant Bodies Press, 2011).

19. Soundscape (in line with the notion of acoustic ecology) is a term proposed by the Canadian composer and writer R. Murray Schafer. Schafer used this term to articulate the need for hearing the ecological sounds louder within a variety of noise pollution. Weiss also appropriates this definition of the term. R. Murray Schafer, *The Soundscape: Our Sonic Environment and the Tuning of the World* (Rochester: Destiny Books, 1994).

20. In his argumentation, Weiss refers to Connor, *Dumbstruck*, 26.

21. Ibid. Here John Cage's well-known piece *Song Books* is worth mentioning. The solos for voice in *Song Books* urge us to "sing the world." Based on Henry Thoreau's *Journals* and the map of Concorde, Cage instructs the performer to draw a melodic line and project it to his/her immediate physical environment. The melodic line is also inspired by the words from the *Journals*. Cage fragments the words into phonemes or word-like sounds or plays with their typographical representation. In doing so, he encourages the performer to find his or her own spatial imagery, which would inevitably be in dialogue with the soundscape and the landscape. John Cage, *Song Books* (New York: C.F. Peters Corporation, 1970).

22. *Concise Oxford English Dictionary*, ed. Catherine Soanes and Angus Stevenson (New York: Oxford University Press, 2008), 1225.

23. Ibid.

24. By difference, I especially refer to Derrida's notion of auto-affection, which derives from "hearing oneself speak." As Derrida argues, auto-affection is a form of self-proximity, yet the lack of immediacy or synchrony between hearing and speaking also generates a distance, "a spacing." Difference can be considered such spacing, as Derrida proposes: Derrida, *Speech and Phenomena*.

25. Veit Erlmann, *Reason and Resonance: A History of Modern Aurality* (New York: MIT Press, Zone Books, 2010), 12.

26. Erlmann refers to Roland Barthes, Theodor Adorno. and Walter Benjamin. Ibid., 21, 22, 308.

27. Ibid., 23.

28. Derrida explains the intimacy of difference as such: "dif-ference [...] if one takes into account that in the words, difference, then in Greek as well as in Latin, the division or separation is in rapport." Jacques Derrida, "Heidegger's Ear: Philopolemology," in *Reading Heidegger* ed. John Sallis, trans. John P. Leavey. Jr. (Bloomington: Indiana University Press, 1991), 169.

29. Based on Derrida's reading of Heidegger and the ear, I suggest Philipsz's singing as a call, as the "voice of a friend." Ibid.
30. Ibid.
31. Ibid., 165.
32. Ibid., 164.
33. Ibid., 173.
34. Ibid., 166, 171.
35. Ibid.,166.
36. Ibid., 174.
37. Michel Serres, *Genesis*, trans. Geneviève James and James Nielson (Ann Arbor: University of Michigan Press, 1995), 6.
38. Ibid., 5.
39. Ibid., 13.
40. Ibid.
41. Lynne Kendrick and David Roesner, eds, *Theatre Noise: The Sound of Performance* (Newcastle: Cambridge Scholars Publishing, 2011), xv.

CHAPTER 12

Acting Operatically

Body, Voice, and the Actress in Beckett's Theater

MARIANNE SHARP

In 2007, I saw four performances, spaced out across the length of the opening run at the Royal National Theatre, London, of Deborah Warner's revival production of Samuel Beckett's *Happy Days* (1961), with Fiona Shaw as Winnie (see figure 13). I wrote comments about the variety of Shaw's arm movements in my notes and in my initial description of her performance used the phrase "arm opera" to describe what I saw. I further noted the effect on Shaw's voice of some specific actions, for example in the sequence leading up to the exploding umbrella in act 1. In this sequence, the performer is required to hold the umbrella up over her head for an extended period of time. These directions are Beckett's, as are many, but not all, of the arm movements Shaw makes during act 1 of the play. Winnie, of course, comments on the strain of holding it up. The strain of holding up the object that seems to be pulling her upward, high over her head, can be heard in the timbre of Shaw's voice. The strain is actual, representational, and commented upon: it is actual (Shaw is actually holding up the umbrella and this is actually hard work); it is representational (of the desire for flight from that which ties a person—in this instance the ground); and it is self-consciously noted all at the same time:

> I am weary, holding it up, and I cannot put it down. [Pause.] I am worse off with it up than with it down, and I cannot put it down. [Pause.] Reason says, Put it down, Winnie, it is not helping you, put the thing down and get on with something else. [Pause.] I cannot. [Pause.] I cannot move. [Pause.] No, something must happen, in the world, take place, some change.[1]

The speech continues for some time as she begs Willie to "bid [her] put this thing down,"[2] until the "something"—the explosion—happens. In this sense Beckett's composition, or choreography, highlights the duality of the body of the actress as

Figure 13 Fiona Shaw as Winnie in *Happy Days* (2007). © Royal National Theatre.

both real and representational, but it is the voice that bears and carries the desire and containment and travels upward and out toward the audience where Shaw's actual body cannot. The actual strain in the voice of the actress created by the directed arm movements is one example of where we can hear (and see in the tension of Shaw's body) the meeting between the writer and the actress through the medium of the text.

While improvising a potted history of dramatic language at a National Theatre master class, Fiona Shaw described Beckett's writing for theater as the moment when "the text left the actors after God died and nobody knew who they were talking to anymore."[3] Though descriptions of Beckett's work frequently refer to the increasingly pared-down language in his later plays, this partly flippant description says something about Shaw's perception of the relationship of Beckett's texts to the actor or actress performing the work. Not only has the text diminished in a world where lack of aspiration to divinity has a direct impact on the length of a sentence (i.e., where the ultimate interlocutory gesture is aimed via "man" to God, Shaw suggests that the sentence structure and richness of language extends accordingly), but the text, she suggests, is something that is, metaphorically, running away from the actors. Speaking some years later on a similar theme, she explicates this notion further, describing how, for her, Beckett's plays are "not plays, really, they're sort of 'end-of-line,' and the energy of the writing leaves the stage and jumps into the listeners' heads."[4] Her suggestion here seems to be that the incomplete sentences somehow create a space for language and thought, and further a kind of transfer of energy in the work for the individual spectator.

In *Happy Days*, the text is reduced to tatters of sentences and stage directions because Winnie is running out of words. What can she do "when even words fail?" Only "gaze before me with compressed lips."[5] The obvious comparison here, for the broken speech patterns in the play, is with Shakespearean language in which the rhythm of the iambic pentameter famously supports the actors' delivery of the text. Shakespearean language, because of the rhythmic drive in the text, encourages a particular kind of embodiment of that text on the part of the performer. But *Happy Days* leaves the actress with a plethora of unfinished sentences and, at first glance, little hope of finding a body-voice "flow" in the work. This is coupled with the actual removal of the actress's main tool from the playing space, that of her body, as it sinks lower into the earth throughout the course of the play. These impositions mean that as the play progresses, by the second act the actress can neither use any props, nor look away from the audience: performing becomes a relentless act made visible for the silent spectator.

Focusing on what I term her "operatic" vocal score, in what follows I examine Shaw's performance as Winnie. My analysis is aided by Julia Kristeva's work on the phenotext and genotext (1984), taken up by Roland Barthes in his essay "The Grain of the Voice" (1977), and Steven Connor's work on "the sob" (2008).[6] I will demonstrate how through a combination of her bodily engagement with the choreography suggested by Beckett's text and her autobiographical relationship to the language in the play, Shaw constructs an "operatic" vocal score that can be characterized as an extended sob. This eventually produces a moment of pure "geno-song" that communicates with the individual spectator via a "chora-like" performance energy.[7]

PLAYING WINNIE

Winnie has been played by a number of established actresses. What several of these actresses share, in terms of their documented experiences of performing Winnie, are stories of the extreme difficulty of working on this role. Of the British actresses who have played the role, Brenda Bruce, Peggy Ashcroft, and Billie Whitelaw all found the process of rehearsing Winnie profoundly excruciating in some way.

Whitelaw has written explicitly about this in her autobiography. She describes how the experience of working on Beckett's texts produced lasting physical "scars" on her body.[8] She found that two seasons of performing *Not I* (1972) aggravated and inflamed her spine and neck;[9] *Footfalls* left her with a twisted spine;[10] and *Happy Days*—which she had found very difficult to learn—sent her into "a kind of terrible muscular spasm through tension."[11] In Whitelaw's descriptions of performing Mouth in *Not I*, the speech patterns themselves cause such an excess of energy to be produced by the performer as she attempts to embody the text that they actually appear to throw the literal body of the performer into crisis in a way that is extreme in comparison to many other kinds of play texts.

In *Happy Days*, it is the body and its speech-noise, even as it disappears into the earth, that is the marker of existence. S. E. Gontarski has described the language that Winnie uses as "little more than noise," tatters of sentences "redolent with banalities, clichés, half-remembered literary quotations and mis-quotations," but further notes that the noise has a very clear function: "It is a means of familiarizing the unknown, the cosmic void, a means of ordering and compartmentalising phenomena."[12] In other words, language in *Happy Days* is a barrier to—or a protection against—the "void" of losing oneself, and Winnie's re-presentation of herself to herself through spoken language is a theatrically infused attempt to "stage an adequate presence"[13] and a simultaneous avoidance of emptiness both within and without. This attempt, manifested in the breaks in her language, places Winnie, in Kristevan terms, as "thetic," as she exhibits only a partial articulacy. In what follows I demonstrate how the partial articulacy of Winnie's speech patterns becomes manifested in the sound of the sob: a threshold sound somewhere between speech and song, which opens the way for a more musical, or song-like, articulation of Beckett's text by Shaw.

THE ARM OPERA

Beckett has described the play as "a sonata for voice and movement,"[14] highlighting the sense of the actress's body as instrument, and there is a precision to the structure of Winnie's speech patterns, actions, and silences already written in to the text that makes for an intricate vocal and physical challenge for the actress. Shaw and her director, Deborah Warner, reported a form of crisis in their experience of working on *Happy Days* similar to that of Bruce, Ashcroft, and Whitelaw some years earlier. Warner revealed that she and Shaw had "run away" from the rehearsal room at one point.[15] Elaborating on this, Shaw describes a struggle not dissimilar to that of Whitelaw almost thirty years earlier:

> There's an enormous amount of stage directions which I didn't want to look at and I couldn't learn it, I couldn't learn the speeches because they were all interrupted speech [...] and it was a very hard thing to learn [...] in this instance I could never get beyond the line "that is what I find so wonderful."[16]

She further shared how working on the precise actions in the play felt:

> There are these gestures in the play that are written entirely like music, musical gestures, and we didn't want them to appear like gesture because it seems to me that theatre is a live event and whoever the creatures are who are speaking must somehow represent something to do with the way in which we experience life which is not choreographed in any abstracted way. So our work was really in unpicking these terrible stage directions and making them not appear like stage directions both in my mind and in the action of the play. And that was an incredibly labour-some, slow, uninspiring and uninspired activity.[17]

What Shaw seems to be describing here is something about the process of building up a physical "score" for her performances as Winnie—and a score that, before she can do anything else as a performer beyond functionally carrying out a prescribed choreography of upper body and head actions, has to be meticulously worked out and learned. Describing Beckett's theater texts, from *Happy Days* onward, in terms of musicality is a well-established notion, but it is interesting that Shaw, here, speaks of the stage directions for physical actions—most of which Winnie has to conduct in some way with her arms (at least in the first act)—as "musical gestures." By way of accessing her possible meaning here, there is first the sense that the gestures themselves form their own physical/visual score, creating (for the audience) visual patterns in the performance space with their own rhythms and modulations (See figures 14, 15 and 16). Further and by way of analogy, her overall description seems akin to my experience of learning the piano: you have to learn first what the fingers on one hand must do, then the fingers on the other hand, then your feet must learn when to touch the pedal, and only when all of these movements are ingrained in your body so that you can throw away the sheet music can you actually begin to *play*. This analogy would suggest that as the arm gestures become ingrained in Shaw's body, they eventually enable Shaw to *dance*, but the actions do not read as dance, but rather as physical action(s) that have a connection to Shaw's vocal work that suggests a quality of the operatic.

Shaw's director, Deborah Warner, has spoken eloquently about actors and their vocal work, citing Shaw among a number of established performers. These comments arise in the context of speaking about the differences in directing opera singers and actors:

> It took me a very long time to realise that one could have a relationship [with an opera singer] which was very akin to having a relationship with a very able actor. A very, very skilled actor, so Fiona Shaw, Maggie Smith or Michael Gambon, I feel now are very, very close to a great singer. They are working in as complex a way with their voice. They're not having to hit certain notes but they're having to construct their own score which is a very complicated thing, which you could begin to argue makes acting very much harder than singing. There is no score and they have to write one and they have to exist within the confines of the one that they've written for themselves, which in part is what our rehearsal work is, but actually a very, very accomplished actor is carrying their own score and changing it each night.[18]

So, in this instance, while Beckett provides the choreography and, as far as he is able through his text, the rhythm of the "score" for Winnie, the actress must develop the vocal score herself, in negotiation with Beckett's framework. I use the term "score" here in agreement with Warner's comments. Beckett's text is also a "score," but he does not provide the melody, or tune, for the voice of the performer in the way that a composer does in music. The actress must provide that, and in Shaw's case her "tune" is unique, repeatable even, and can be heard in recordings of her performance as Winnie: though, of course, her "tune" will have varied slightly from performance to performance. The sequence leading up to the exploding umbrella, described at the

Performativity as Context

Figure 14, 15 and 16 Fiona Shaw's "arm opera." Photographs 14 and 15 by Marylin Kingwill, © Arena PAL Images; Photograph 16 © Alastair Muir.

start of this chapter, demonstrates the impact of the arm opera on the materiality of Shaw's "tune."

THE SOB

My aim is now to show how close analysis of Shaw's performance in terms of her body-voice work as Winnie can enable her performance to be characterized as an extended sob. Further, consideration of Shaw's vocal score in relation to Barthes's notion of the "grain of the voice" can open up questions of intersubjective relations in the theater space between writer, actress, and audience. In this writing, Barthes adapts Kristeva's terms "phenotext" and "genotext,"[19] remapping these terms as "pheno-song" and "geno-song." I will begin by outlining Kristeva's descriptions of her original terms, as this will help to situate Barthes's adaptation. Genotext and phenotext can loosely be mapped onto the terms "semiotic" and "symbolic" in Kristeva's work. The genotext is the harder of the two terms to define and relates to the drive-energies of the *semiotic-chora*.[20] Kristeva's description of "genotext" relates to the manifestation of the semiotic in a given text and crucially, she states, "the space it organizes is one in which the subject will be *generated*."[21] Noelle McAfee, working from Kristeva's description, explicates it more simply as "the motility between the words, the potentially disruptive meaning that is not quite a meaning below the text."[22] By contrast, the phenotext

> denote[s] language that serves to communicate [...]. The phenotext is constantly split up and divided, and is irreducible to the semiotic process that works through the genotext. The phenotext is a structure [...]. It obeys rules of communication and presupposes a subject of enunciation and an addressee.[23]

Kristeva suggests, by translating into a kind of metalanguage, that the difference between genotext and phenotext can be conveyed as the difference between topology and algebra.[24] The genotext is a process, and the phenotext is a structure.

Barthes suggests that we can see, in song, the two texts identified and described by Kristeva: "The *pheno-song* [...] covers all the phenomena, all the features which belong to the structure of the language being sung." By contrast, he describes the *geno-song* as

> *the volume of the singing and speaking voice, the space where significations germinate "from within language and in its very materiality"*; it forms a signifying play having nothing to do with communication, representation (of feelings), expression; *it is that apex (or that depth) of production where the melody really works at its language—not at what it says, but the voluptuousness of its sounds-signifiers, of its letters—where melody explores how the language works and identifies with that work.* It is, in a very simple word but which must be taken seriously, the *diction* of the language.[25]

In relation to Beckett's text, Shaw's work on her vocal score (partly impacted upon by the various physical commands in the form of stage directions and demands in the form of restrictions on the body of the actress) might then be described as combining these two "songs," but perhaps aspects of the geno-song are belonging to her body-voice rather than Beckett's text per se because she creates the "melody" and "the voluptuousness of its sounds-signifiers" in relation to how Beckett's language "works."

Thinking of Shaw's vocal score as not unlike the vocal score of a singer can be further supported, as an idea, by the actual range of tones, notes even, identifiable in her speech sounds through the course of the play. While I don't claim to have conducted an exact measurement of her range through a given performance of *Happy Days*, I have identified, at minimum, at least a two-octave range present in Shaw's spoken word-sounds through the performance.[26] In this sense her spoken vocal score can be described as richly melodic and her performativity could be seen as something that finds many parallels with the performativity of song.[27]

This "melody" appears to have been partly constituted in relation to Shaw's autobiographical relationship to the text, accentuated through her own Irish accent. The accent seems to have been, for Shaw, an important way into working with Beckett's text in the context of developing a somewhat autobiographical relationship to the work. Aoife Monks, writing on Warner and Shaw's earlier collaboration on *Medea* (2001), staged first in Dublin and later in London, has asserted that in terms of Shaw's identity as an actress, "when Shaw works in Ireland, she is both encoded as an 'outsider' to Irish theatre, and is seen as *more* Irish than in Britain, by virtue of her accent and birthplace. Shaw is 'almost English but not quite' on the British stage and simultaneously 'almost Irish but not quite' on the Irish stage."[28] In *Happy Days*, Shaw played specifically on, and played up, her Irishness in her London performances, and used this as a means of making autobiographical connections of her own with the text and its inherent speech patterns. This choice undoubtedly impacted on the relationship between language and melody "at that apex [...] of production where the melody really works at its language" in Shaw's performance.[29]

Both she and Warner have, differently, spoken of autobiography in the context of working on this piece. Warner noted that "it may not be true of all of Beckett's plays, but it did seem to be true of this—I felt we were rehearsing the rather dark place from which, perhaps, he wrote this play [...] and it just got darker and darker and darker."[30] In this sense, she appears to have felt that they somehow accessed something of the author's experience of "creating" as they recreated the piece for themselves, further indicating Shaw's work as the creator of aspects of the vocal score. Shaw's process was aided after a visit to their rehearsals made by Roger Mitchell, who had assisted Beckett on the 1979 production with Billie Whitelaw, and following which experience she "started to find footholds for the role from my own life."[31] She further acknowledges that as the opening of *Happy Days* got closer, though she "[has] never been one to solve art through biography," she found herself reading Knowlson's biography of Beckett and

> was delighted to find that Beckett's prayer as a child had the same ending as the prayer in the play, and that he, too, had memories of the womb—as Mildred in the play has. These now felt like emotional truths rather than intellectual constructs.[32]

In this sense Shaw appears to have found something helpful for the process of constructing her score through making these connections that in some way began to function as the connections "actors need to invent [...] between seemingly foreign bodies," in the wake of "the distance between things, between people, that makes Beckett's writing sing."[33] She continues with these connections between Beckett's text and her own life (not unusual as part of an acting process) with reference to her Irishness, but specifically in the context of language:

> Being Irish: it does benefit it remarkably. I think if it had been the famous Albanian playwright, Samuel Beckett, I'd have much more difficulty [...] of course, because it's not just written in the English language, it's written in a sort of suburban city Irish [...] and I come from just outside the city of Cork and Beckett's from outside the city of Dublin and in that way he sounds, you know, his voice in the play, or in the writing, sounds remarkably like my upbringing.[34]

In this way, Shaw claims an ownership of the speech in the play in terms of how much the sounds she will make are like the sounds from her own life. Interestingly, the use of an Irish accent in the English version of *Happy Days* is something that several actresses, who have played the role of Winnie, have commented upon.

In an interview with Katharine Worth, Peggy Ashcroft reports how she told Beckett that she knew how Winnie's voice should sound: "Oh, how?" he replied, "Like you," she said. Further she "found there were all sorts of little turns of speech that seemed to come more easily in an Irish rhythm."[35] Rosemary Pountney has proffered a similar response to playing Mouth in *Not I*:

> We had decided upon an Irish accent because (in a note subsequently deleted from the manuscript) Beckett had suggested that "any" might be pronounced "anny" and "baby"—"babby", as though he had an Irish voice in his head while writing the play. Despite the deletion (made, presumably, since it both set the piece too specifically in Ireland and might prevent a non-Irish actress attempting the role) [...] I felt convinced that it was an Irishwoman with whom we had to deal.[36]

Pountney has suggested, however, that using an Irish accent (as a non-Irish woman) trapped her "in a certain vocal cadence" and that she felt "strait-jacket[ed]" in terms of pace and accent in a role that demanded "extreme vocal flexibility to give it life."[37] Elsewhere Pountney has critiqued Peggy Ashcroft's Winnie, describing Ashcroft as "at first rather disappointing,"[38] citing a similar issue. She suggests that Ashcroft's difficulty was "largely vocal." The great flexibility of her voice "was flattened and deadened" in the attempt at the Irish accent, resulting in a straitjacketed "non-accent," which meant Ashcroft was unable to fully convey Winnie's fluctuations in mood.

Though, no doubt, there are actresses who could manage the accent[39] and the rhythm and the unfinished sentences of Winnie's speech patterns, it might seem from these descriptions by actresses that there is a strong connection between grounded vocal flexibility in a role and speaking in one's mother tongue. Perhaps this is the case more so in a piece like *Happy Days* where the speech patterns are functionally awkward for the actress because of the interrupted nature of the "essentially monological" text.[40] Diction, intonation, colloquialisms, and rhythms of speech are significant factors in production of identity whether actual (in daily life) or actually doubled in theatrical performance. The identification, or not, of the actress with her mother tongue, in the instance described by Pountney here, seems potentially to produce a vocal score that is "out of tune" with itself and hence less resonant, less operatic (in the sense of richness and flexibility) than it has the potential to be for the audience. Hence, for Shaw, this autobiographical identification she makes with Winnie's speech appears to have a potentially significant impact on the possibilities for auditory reception of the performance and to create the conditions in which something identifiable as Shaw's "geno-song" might become manifest.

During the course of the play the interrupted speech patterns are paralleled by another kind of vocal interruption. In my first of four visits to *Happy Days*, Shaw seemed to begin almost to cry at points in the performance but then pull back and not actually cry, so that there was a sense of something bubbling under the surface that broke through the spoken language at points. In notes taken during my second visit to the performance (February 12, 2007) I had written: "[Shaw's] eyes watering—20 mins in," and that around "25 minutes in [there were] momentary tears." In the Royal National Theatre's archived, recorded version of *Happy Days*, there was eye watering, from Shaw, at around the same time. These moments, on closer inspection of Beckett's text, actually correspond with first a stage direction and then a description of what is happening given by Winnie. The first reads "to your golden...may it never... [*voice breaks*]...may it never,"[41] and the second

> All I can say is that they are not what they were when I was young and...foolish and...[*faltering, head down*]...beautiful...possibly...lovely...in a way...to look at. [*Pause. Head up.*] Forgive me, Willie, sorrow keeps breaking in.[42]

In both of these extracts, Winnie is remembering a former time, when she was younger, loved, perhaps. The memory, the time gone, lost, seems to cause a physical break in her voice. The appearance and subsidence of these momentary sobs—and they were sobs, a kind of momentary "bubbling up," rather than cries or the more extended wail—seem to be borne upward and out of Shaw's body as if the "grain" here is the memory as present in the fibers of the body. Returning to Barthes, it is

> something which is directly the cantor's body, brought to your ears in one and the same movement from deep down in the cavities, the muscles, the membranes, the cartilages [...] as though a single skin lined the inner flesh of the performer and the music [s]he sings.[43]

This sense of a "something" that is "breaking in" develops through the course of Shaw's performance, prompted by Beckett's stage directions, but executed in terms of the "diction" that is Shaw's geno-song work. This "breaking in" can be seen to function as a kind of crescendo from the early memory of the man with whom Winnie shared a first kiss in a toolshed ("though whose, I cannot tell. We had no tool-shed, and he most certainly had no tool-shed")[44], through to the peak of the "happy day" when Willie comes crawling toward her in his wedding suit and Winnie's song is finally sung. The aside about the toolshed comes early on in the play, and Shaw pronounces this memory as a kind of quizzical aside to herself, spoken in a low tone. This is in stark contrast to the traumatic memory that surfaces toward the end of act 2, when Winnie tells the story of Mildred:

> Suddenly a mouse... [*Pause.*] Suddenly a mouse ran up her thigh and Mildred, dropping Dolly in her fright, began to scream—[*Winnie gives a sudden piercing scream*]—and screamed and screamed—[*Winnie screams twice*]—screamed and screamed and screamed and screamed till all came running, in their night attire, papa, mamma, Bibby and old Annie, to see what was the matter... [*pause*]...what on earth could possibly be the matter. [*Pause*].[45]

Shaw's screams here, and also the pitch at which she speaks the first part of this extract, are produced from her body at roughly two octaves above the early memory of a kiss. The Mildred story, or memory (we don't know which) is usually interpreted as some kind of displaced sexual trauma, the climax of which is interrupted by the shower/cooker story and returns as a kind of reprise to the climax of that story. Lawley suggests that this story "re-imagines the play's other theatrical relationship—that between Winnie and her enemy, the bell—in terms of a gross sexual violation."[46] Winnie's screams, first one, then a burst of two, are like the external interruptions of the bell, but they come trilling from within: from the gut, through the larynx: Shaw's body here becomes "a threshold between self and other, internal and external."[47] The screams, however, coming in controlled bursts, never become the more excessive wail. They are somehow like the letting off of steam, a release of some pressure (like the whistle from an old steam kettle)—the sound doesn't reach the point of explosion. It is the peak of the extended sob, but there is still a withholding at work.

Steven Connor has written eloquently about the nature of the sob:

> The sob enacts a sense of rising constriction, a desire for utterance so intense that it seems to fill and block the means of it. [...]. Sobbing has become a mode of utterance, though it is the utterance of the unuttered, the venting of the fettered. Novelists will often have their heroines speak "with a barely surpressed sob," but a sob is already a suppression, a contraction or holding back of articulation. In the sob, the overcoming of the voice is itself overcome, as it becomes part of the armoury of the voice. Sobbing can therefore become a kind of discipline, an exertion as well as a contortion.[48]

In Shaw's performance it wells, chokes, rises, subsides, rises, and subsides again and again but never becomes a full-blown cry, reaching its wavelike height at the scream: moving between words, below, around, through the words of Beckett's text. The structures for this to occur are, of course, written into Beckett's text, but one only has to compare the vast difference between the vocal score—specifically the rhythm, pitch, and volume of both the screams and other moments—of Whitelaw's Winnie, or others, to recognize that there remains a vast scope for body-voice creation by the individual actress performing this role.[49] It is possible to locate, in this moment of Shaw's "disciplined" withholding of what could easily become a cry, a kind of distillation of what is occurring through the course of the performance in the relationship between audience, actress, and text.

In this moment, there is a kind of collapsing of actress and character at work. However much Shaw may or may not have felt herself to be emoting at this point in the play, as an audience member I felt sharply conscious that as much as this scream was representative of the surfacing of Winnie's traumatic memory, it also read as the peak of her frustration of being now neck-deep in earth: but Shaw's as much as Winnie's. Through the second act, Shaw has something in her mouth that makes her oversalivate through her now partly blacked-out teeth. The result is that her speech is infused with the sound of spittle and she makes partly gargling noises as she speaks. The effect of this is that it appears to be very difficult for Shaw/Winnie to talk: it appears as though she is drowning as the earth is swallowing her up, but it looks actual and not acted, as it's clear that Shaw is genuinely finding speech difficult and that subsequently when Winnie finally cries, "My neck is hurting me,"[50] that Shaw's neck is, or must be, hurting by this point. Of course, Shaw may not actually be in pain, but Whitelaw's descriptions of embodying Beckett's texts would suggest that, to produce the extraordinarily energized vocal performance that Shaw gives while negotiating severe bodily restrictions, she probably is. The controlled screams are physically arresting (in my experiences of watching the performance)—moments that might be (arguably) posited in vocal terms as pure geno-song. In his introduction to Kristeva's *Revolution in Poetic Language*, Leon Samuel Roudiez describes (some) writings by Antonin Artaud as "unblended genotext," suggesting they are those "in which language becomes partly unintelligible; that is, an unmediated physical presence."[51] In a similar way, the sound-language of Shaw's vocal score in itself somehow exceeds representation (whether or not Shaw's actions are actually representational). It rather becomes the "thing": pure body, translated as sound, or "unblended" geno-song, capturing the physical presence of a body in pain fighting to exceed its own pain through "disciplined withholding." This notion is not unlike a phenomenon in musical theater. The "money note" is a term used by industry practitioners to denote a particular kind of "belting" sound that a performer may choose to use, for example, at the end of a song. The sound is somewhere between speech and song and is characterized by the materiality of the performer's body overriding the sense of melody and pitch of the note.[52]

THE AUDIENCE

In terms of how this works in and on the audience, Warner and Shaw both noted how getting the play to "work" in rehearsals had been an impossible task and how it was only after the previews that they discovered that "the missing character in the rehearsal room was the audience."[53] Shaw further noted her excitement, from her vantage point on the stage, at seeing and "hearing all the silent heads thinking loudly, themselves, writing their own plays,"[54] and Warner confessed that what she enjoyed the most about her production in performance was watching the audience responses—which she claimed were diverse—through the course of the play. She related an anecdote to explicate this:

> I had one very interesting experience where a friend came with a friend of his, who I didn't know, and my friend had laughed all the way through—possibly too noisily—and his friend had, indeed, cried all the way through, and they were sitting side by side, and I think that the fact that this play allows that is just extraordinary, and very, very exciting: I've not had an experience quite like that.[55]

Warner's description here is commensurate with my experience of sitting with different people in four different audiences (during the four separate performances I had four quite different emotional experiences in watching the piece). It suggests that the performance, particularly the final section involving the screams, followed shortly afterward by Winnie's song, was producing a range of visible, physical responses among audience members. For me this section was, variously, painful and funny, terrible and exhilarating to witness. The pain that Shaw is (or appears to be) experiencing, as Winnie, in this final section translates into a range of really-felt, visceral experiences for audience members. Perhaps this can be explained in part by synesthetic audience responses and by the excess energy Shaw is generating by attempting to express so much while being physically restrained. But her vocal score—the extended sob—overall combining aspects of the pheno-song and geno-song, is the operatic tour de force that allows this experience to materialize for the individual spectator. This raises the question of whether the withholdings at work in the sounds of the sob are, like Beckett's unfinished sentences, that which leaves space for spectators to experience their own subjectivity, somehow by the performer withholding their own.

SPEAKING BY HEART

Shaw acknowledged, in the acting master class cited at the start of this chapter, how as an actor you can harness the "onomatopoeic sensation" of certain vowel sounds and "you can find an enormous amount of meaning by allowing the vowel to come through your body."[56] Giving an example of how this idea manifests itself in other descriptions of our sensory relation to speech, she described a phrase from Gaelic, "the idea that you should *speak by heart*, though it's often very difficult to find where your heart is."[57] She appears to have engaged this idea in the musicality at work in her voice in *Happy Days*, characterized by the extended sob. In Shaw's usage here, "heart" seems to stand in for a possible, but unnameable location from where the vowel sounds that can "come through your body" can emanate. Vowel sounds, like the sob, are threshold sounds: they are not speech, but they point to the possibility of enunciation. The "onomatopoeic sensation[s]" of vowel sounds ("o-o-o-o; a-a-a-a") are like the underside of language and linguistic utterance: they are sounds reminiscent of the babble of infants before they have fully entered into language, they are the sounds of chora-energy in speech or song. It is perhaps worth noting that, as Gontarski highlights, Winnie's song, too, at the close of the play, "comes bubbling up not from the mind, but from the heart."[58] After the hard "a" sounds in Shaw's screams in the Mildred speech ("Ah! Ah! Ah!"), which felt, to me as an audience member, like sound-punches, it is not long before Winnie finally sings her song. She gurgles and gargles as she sings because of the spittle produced by whatever is causing her to oversalivate. This heightens and extends the vowel sounds in the line "it's true, it's true, you love me so," so the audience experience a kind of rhythmic "ooo, ooo, oo, oah, eee, ohh" that sounds a little like someone "happily" drowning: Shaw's voice and song become performative gestures throughout the final stages of the production. The sound reminded me of Robert de Niro's performance as Max Cady at the end of Scorsese's 1991 remake of the movie *Cape Fear*, where he is attached by his feet to a sinking boat and continues to sing through the water until he is completely swallowed up. Cady was singing to God. In the same master class, Shaw has located Beckett's writing as coming "after God died and nobody knew who they were talking to anymore."[59] To whom, then, is the speech directed in Shaw's performance?

The gurgled vowel sounds and the sinking back into the hole in the ground that is now made watery by Shaw's vocal score—and also represents a kind of sanctuary from the glaring white lights of the setting for *Happy Days*—suggest that Winnie, like Mildred and like Beckett, who both have memories of the womb, is falling back (in)to an absent mother, not unlike the "tiny little thing [...] before her time" of Mouth in *Not I*.[60] "After God died," it seems that Shaw/Winnie's literal "no-body" was talking or, more accurately, singing to Mother, whose "impossible body" becomes replaced by those of the audience.

At the end of this performance analysis, it seems less than clear how to fully distinguish between Shaw's work and Beckett's. It is as though in the composition of the work, the "sonata for voice and body,"[61] Shaw's actress-knowledge—here a "how to" knowledge—of developing a vocal score becomes manifest in the geno-song of the performance, providing "that apex (or that depth) of production where the melody really works at its language—not at what it says, but the voluptuousness of its sounds-signifiers, of its letters—where melody explores how the language works and identifies with that work."[62] In the operatic speech act that is the performance, Beckett's choreographic and linguistic structures provide the pheno-song, but the two become interwoven as Beckett's language works through Shaw's body (the range of movements in the "arm opera" paralleling and helping to produce the range of Shaw's vocal modulations) and Shaw's body works on Beckett's language. Through their location of the audience as the impossible body of the (M)Other via the extended sob, Shaw's "dance" (arm opera) and "song" (vocal modulations) become performative gestures that reconfigure the audience-performer relationship as an uncanny return to the (lost) memory of our primary connectedness to another human being.

NOTES

1. Samuel Beckett, *Happy Days* (London: Faber and Faber, 2006), 153.
2. Ibid.
3. Fiona Shaw, "NT25: Masterclass with Fiona Shaw," master class at the Royal National Theatre, London, March 8, 2002.
4. Deborah Warner and Fiona Shaw, "Platform: Deborah Warner and Fiona Shaw on *Happy Days*," public discussion at the Royal National Theatre, London, February 27, 2007.
5. Beckett, *Happy Days*, 147–48.
6. See Julia Kristeva, *Revolution in Poetic Language*, trans. Margaret Waller (New York: Columbia University Press, 1984), 86–90; Roland Barthes, *Image-Music-Text*, trans. Stephen Heath (London: Fontana, 1977), 179–90; Steven Connor, "De Singulatu: The Life and Times of the Sob," paper presented at the "Breaking Voices" Symposium, London College of Fashion, June 7, 2008, online. Available: http://www.bbk.ac.uk/english/skc/lectures.htm. October 22, 2008.
7. See Kristeva, *Revolution in Poetic Language*, 86–90; Barthes, *Image-Music-Text*, 182.
8. Jonathan Kalb, *Beckett in Performance* (New York: Cambridge University Press, 1989), 147.

9. Billie Whitelaw, *Billie Whitelaw . . . Who He?* (London: Hodder and Stoughton, 1995), 131.
10. Kalb, *Beckett in Performance*, 147.
11. Ibid.
12. S. E. Gontarski, *Beckett's "Happy Days": A Manuscript Study* (Columbus: Ohio State University Libraries, 1977), 18.
13. Paul Lawley, "Stages of Identity: From Krapp's Last Tape to Play," in *The Cambridge Companion to Beckett*, ed. John Pilling (New York: Cambridge University Press, 1994), 103.
14. Whitelaw, *Who He?*, 151.
15. In a "Platform" talk at the National Theatre during the run of their production, having acknowledged that the rehearsal process was difficult, Shaw related how at the "peak" of the difficulties, Warner had exclaimed: "What is the opposite of an epiphany?—because I'm having one." Warner and Shaw, "Platform," 2007.
16. Warner and Shaw, "Platform," 2007.
17. Ibid. I interpreted here, in the context of Shaw's speech, that she was implying that the stage directions were "terrible" to work on, not that she was referring to the quality of the stage directions in themselves.
18. John Tusa, "The John Tusa Interviews: Deborah Warner," BBC Radio 3, 2001, online. Available: http://www.bbc.co.uk/radio3/johntusainterview/warner_transcript.shtml. December 12, 2012.
19. Kristeva, *Revolution in Poetic Language*, 86–89.
20. For a fuller discussion of the semiotic-chora see Kristeva, *Revolution in Poetic Language*. Noelle McAfee provides a helpful description of the Kristevan chora as "the psychical space in which the infant resides and expresses its energy" (*Julia Kristeva*, Critical Thinkers Series [New York: Routledge, 2004], 24). It is the space of the prelinguistic, what Jaques Lacan terms "the Imaginary," and where the infant does not yet recognize itself as a self, separate from the mother.
21. Kristeva, *Revolution in Poetic Language*, 86, emphasis in original.
22. McAfee, *Julia Kristeva*, 24.
23. Kristeva, *Revolution in Poetic Language*, 87.
24. Ibid.
25. Barthes, *Image-Music-Text*, 182, emphasis in original. Kristeva does not hyphenate genotext and phenotext, but Barthes hyphenates geno-song and pheno-song. I have hyphenated, or not, according to whose terms I am referencing.
26. In addition to the four theater visits I made to this performance, I have watched/listened to another of Shaw's performances in *Happy Days* an additional three times, plus repeated certain sequences, on film at the National Theatre Archive, to familiarize myself with Shaw's (slightly varying) vocal score.
27. I use the term "melodic" here in the general sense of "melody," and not in the technical sense of, e.g., harmonic scale differentiation.
28. Aoife Monks, " 'The Souvenir from Foreign Parts': Foreign Femininity in Deborah Warner's *Medea*," *Australasian Drama Studies* 43 (2003): 33.
29. Barthes, *Image-Music-Text*, 182.
30. Warner and Shaw, "Platform," 2007.
31. Fiona Shaw, "Buried in Beckett," *The Guardian*, January 23, 2007, online. Available: http://www.guardian.co.uk/theguardian/2007/jan/23/features11.g21 http://www.theguardian.com/theguardian/2007/jan/23/features11.g21. December 20, 2008.
32. Ibid.
33. Ibid.
34. Warner and Shaw, "Platform," 2007.
35. Quoted in Linda Ben-Zvi, ed., *Women in Beckett* (Urbana: University of Illinois Press, 1990), 12.

36. Rosemary Pountney, "On Acting Mouth in *Not I*," *Journal of Beckett Studies* 1 (1983): 83.
37. Ibid.
38. Rosemary Pountney, "*Happy Days* at the National Theatre," (1976), online. Available: http://www.english.fsu.edu/jobs/num01/Num1Pountney2.htm. December 20, 2008.
39. In Pountney's 1976 review, in which she critiques Peggy Ashcroft's performance as Winnie, she also notes how "Winnie's fluctuations in mood [were] so deeply moving in Madeleine Renaud's performance" (ibid.). Renaud played Winnie in the French premiere in 1963 (which actually opened in Venice and then moved to Paris) and was, reputedly, during the 1960s, Beckett's favorite Winnie up to that point. Renaud would, of course, have been performing Beckett's French version of the play and was, presumably, performing in her own accent.
40. Lawley, "Stages of Identity," 88.
41. Beckett, *Happy Days*, 14.
42. Ibid., 20.
43. Barthes, *Image-Music-Text*, 181.
44. Beckett, *Happy Days*, 143.
45. Ibid., 165.
46. Lawley, "Stages, of Identity," 97.
47. Anna McMullen, *Theatre on Trial: Samuel Beckett's Later Drama* (New York: Routledge, 1993), 11.
48. Connor, "De Singulatu."
49. Whitelaw's screams in the "Mildred" speech, for example, are almost the antithesis of Shaw's. Whitelaw's screams are tiny, barely audible yelps.
50. Beckett, *Happy Days*, 165.
51. Kristeva, *Revolution in Poetic Language*, 5.
52. The powerful effect of experiencing this separation of the voice from language is at the heart of the notion of "jouissance," discussed elsewhere in this volume by Carlo Zuccarini.
53. Warner and Shaw, "Platform," 2007.
54. Ibid.
55. Ibid.
56. Shaw, "NT25," 2002.
57. Ibid., my emphasis.
58. Gontarski, *Beckett's Happy Days*, 12–13.
59. Shaw, "NT25," 2002.
60. Samuel Beckett, *Not I*, in *Complete Dramatic Works* (London: Faber and Faber, 1986), 376.
61. Whitelaw, *Who He?*, 151.
62. Barthes, *Image-Music-Text*, 182.

PART SIX
Performativity as Practice

Perhaps a reappraisal of the performative encounter makes challenging demands on the experiencer (to use Robin Nelson's useful terminology).[1] The performances discussed in the previous part on Laurie Anderson, Susan Philipsz, and Samuel Beckett certainly do, destabilizing comfortable, complacent modes of listening and watching. Equally, the performative density of a theater that is physically and vocally rich also demands a multithreat performer. We have used this phrase deliberately, because it calls to mind the idea of the "triple-threat" performer who is multiskilled in singing, acting, and dancing for the Broadway stage. The idea of the triple-threat performer has become the dominant conception of what a "fully trained" performer in music theater might be, though of course the actual training approaches engaged in preparing for the paradigm of the Broadway musical are very specific, targeting a particular sound, idiomatic styles of movement, and, often, a devotion to a psycho-physical (Stanislavski-based) acting technique.

The following three chapters explore various practical approaches to performance, all considering styles very different from the Broadway aesthetic. One writes from the perspective of the performer herself, one considers training approaches, and one considers the way in which choreographic interpretation mediates the relationship between performance and text. What becomes clear from these various explorations of practice is that the development of technique—performance competence—is only one aspect of performance preparation. As we have seen throughout this collection, the affective dynamics of performativity, difficult to grasp though they may be, are fundamental to performance, and in many ways it is the development of a mastery over these dynamics—a *performative* competence—that accounts for those moments when performance transcends the mundane.

The Blue Man Group has enjoyed success internationally since it was founded in 1987 (figure 17), and its franchise has extended to around a dozen different performance troupes at various points: each has three blue, mute performers and each production blends music, dance, technology, and humor to create an undeniably entertaining show—"untrammeled infantile sensuality, the pre-verbal joy of goo and finger painting [...] a post-modern romp in a lunatic nursery school,"[2] as the *New York Times* put it. In one routine, the characters pour different colored paint onto big drums which they then pound in a frantic tattoo, causing the vibrations of the drum skins to spray globs of paint in all directions; in another routine—usually

Figure 17 A Blue Man plays drums on stage during a live concert performance in Miami. Photo by Katseyephoto. © Katseyephoto.

the finale of the show—the Blue Men leap into the audience and dance between spectators on the armrests of the chairs as loud music from the live band fills the air and the audience pulls rolls and rolls of toilet paper over their heads. The effect is overwhelming, baffling notions of propriety and convention, and walloping the senses with delightful excess: one can only giggle and join in.

There are undoubtedly specific skills in which these performers have trained—they are by turn musicians, dancers, mimes, and circus performers, and some of their routines impress audiences for the virtuosity that is shown. Perhaps this technical proficiency draws attention to the "twice-behaved behavior," the reiteration that allows performance and performativity to intersect.[3] On the other hand, the performances really offer a jumble of silly antics whose affect relies to a considerable degree on the brilliant handling of performative energies. In many ways, some of these energies result from key conceptual decisions made at the inception of the Blue Man brand: anonymizing and androgynizing the Blue Man characters creates a dehumanizing effect; inviting playful audience interaction informalizes the conventions of the theater space; behaving childishly and making a mess invokes wonder, exhilaration, and glee. At each moment the performance is both a reiteration and a present live moment, a performance that is rehearsed but that is also provisional and changeable. It is the interaction of the iterations of performance with the live experience—the "is" of performance—that audiences experience, and performers and creators organize.[4] Many of these performative dynamics, skilfully handled, have come from conceptual decisions—such as Susan Philipsz's decisions for *Lowlands*, discussed "as" performance in the previous part—and in this sense what is experienced is the impact of a collaborative performative competence in which the many authorial voices of the production coalesce to great effect. Finding the vocabulary to explain (or teach) what this involves can be challenging: phrases like "working the audience," "comic timing," "reading the house" go some way toward articulating how performers sense the performativity of their acts, though these dynamics often operate sensually, tacitly or by instinct, and are best understood through experience, through the "know-how" of performance.[5]

The Blue Man Group is not necessarily what one would think of as a music theater outfit in a conventional sense, though neither are the performers discussed in the following three chapters (computer programmers, extended vocalists, contemporary dancers, Gardzienice), or for that matter, the previous three (Laurie Anderson, Susan Philipsz, Fiona Shaw). However, it is worth recalling the fact that, to us, music theater is not restricted to a repertoire of canonic texts in a Broadway (or opera or perhaps vaudeville) aesthetic; to us, music theater is a performative landscape whose expressive gestures (its song and its dance) generate its identity through their performativity; increasingly, we can see this as a conceptual methodology to employ for critical study.

In the work of the Blue Man Group (their song, their dance), music and physicality are fundamental to the impact on the audience—like the corporeal and embodied beating of the drum tattoos in Beijing and London, the Blue Man drumming is felt viscerally in both musical and physical terms (to very different effects). The capacity of the music-dance to swamp the whole performance space and for its sounds to invade our whole bodies physically reminds us of both the metaphysical flow of excess and affect in these gestures, and the way that they (which we inadequately *call* song and dance) are mutual corporeal plagues (to use Artaud's phrase). Likewise, the performance work discussed in the following chapters relies fundamentally on the musical and corporeal dynamics of bodies in performance to achieve that performativity. In this, the performers are operating beyond the level of simple performance competence and in a zone where their performative competence can take the lead. Often—as we see with Sabine Wilden's discussion of how choreographers respond to music and convert it into physicalized expression—that "know-how" may be so tacit or instinctive that the artists themselves may not quite be sure or aware of what it is they are tapping into. For them, the performative competence is in trusting their instincts and following the physical responses of their bodies, *giving in* to the performative plague. Sometimes such holistic practice becomes itself the interest of the practitioners—as in the case of Gardzienice, whose work Konstantinos Thomaidis discusses in his chapter. For Gardzienice, the performative possibilities of the body in its expressive gestures of vocality and physicality are the central focus of a laboratory-style exploration, *understanding* the performative. In the first of these three chapters, the performer herself speaks, trading her performative song and dance for the gestures of the written word. Here, Caroline Wilkins discusses her own performance practice, exploring the collaboration of live and mediatized vocal energies and the performative "know-how" of her performance body and voice, *articulating* the performative.

NOTES

1. See Robin Nelson, "Modes of Practice-as-Research Knowledge and Their Place in the Academy," In *Practice-as-Research in Performance and Screen*, ed. Ludivine Allegue et al. (New York: Palgrave Macmillan, 2009), 112–30.
2. Vicki Goldberg, "High Tech Meets Goo with Blue Man Group," *New York Times*, November 17, 1991.
3. This refers to Peggy Phelan's discussion of the development of performance studies in "Introduction: The Ends of Performance," in *The Ends of Performance*, ed. Peggy Phelan and Jill Lane (New York: New York University Press, 1998), 10.
4. The idea of the "is" and "as" of the relationship between performance and performativity derives from Richard Schechner, "What Is Performance Studies Anyway?," in Phelan and Lane, *The Ends of Performance*, 361.
5. Nelson, "Modes of Practice-as-Research Knowledge."

CHAPTER 13

Vox Elettronica

Song, Dance, and Live Electronics in the Practice of Sound Theater

CAROLINE WILKINS

The singer enters in a furor of activity and begins her song, unaware of the slow, deliberate arrival of her counterpart from behind. She catches a glimpse of him from the corner of her eye, maintaining a long high note while fixedly staring at his presence as he is caught in midstep. A moment of suspension; thought communicated not through verbal means but through body language. He interrupts the vocal storyline with electronic sounds; he creeps to the piano during her wild improvisation and removes the microphone. A staged dance occurs between the two as they vie for sonic control of the space. Sometimes one or the other exits as the reins fall from their hands.

Later, the audience witnesses a dance between animate and inanimate forces. Standing vertically on the table like a jack-in-the-box waiting to be opened, the bandoneon is approached cautiously by the singer as she explores its folded body with curious fingers, her chin resting carefully on the top. A song and dance in miniature ensues, as the voice enters into dialogue with the small movements of her hands, producing percussive sounds on the instrument, pulling one end upward in a rush of air. It appears to move of its own accord in a series of curves that unfold and take new directions. It begins its own song and dance in a series of asthmatic sighs, groans, and squeaks, struggling for a melody in between angry chord clusters. The singer responds with cries of astonishment until the interaction takes on anarchic proportions in a visible/audible struggle between the two. Finally, after a manic outburst of scat singing, she is silenced by an uncontrollable bandoneon that shrieks its last high notes and raises vertically to shut the "shutters" in front of the performer's face, blocking her from audience view.

In art forms such as the performance song, exemplified and expanded into "Sound Theater" in this performance of *Zaum: Beyond Mind* (2010),[1] it becomes clear how voice and movement are linked in the integral space created by the body. Their counterpoint is then developed by means of choreography, text, and music, and in cases where the performers incorporate instruments and technologies in their performance, even functional gestures become a sort of "dance" as the instruments create their own "song."[2] Contemporary instrumental theater abounds in examples where gestures of playing become a visual focus, either in synchronicity with, or deliberate separation from, the sonic result. Choreographer Xavier Le Roy, in his *Mouvements pour Lachenmann* (2005), puts live music instrumentalists behind a screen on stage while two musicians play air guitar in front of it, drawing our attention to the physical production of music. Similarly, composer and theater-maker Falk Huebner plays with synchronous differences in his work for a miming saxophonist and prerecorded audio/video tracks, *Thespian Play* (2008–9), where the fragmentation of each element results in a new constellation of the whole. In each case the movements of the performers can be seen as a form of dance, all the more so when separated from any direct sound production.

Perhaps the key to understanding the age-old term "song and dance" lies in its oral definition, meaning "rigmarole" or "commotion"—a means of communication that draws attention to the expressive resources of the body. Deeply embedded in cultural tradition, it stems from our ability to play and finds its source in gesture. Derived from the Latin *gerere* meaning "to wield," gesture expresses feeling through movement, through verbal rhetoric, through visual traces such as drawing, or through a musical figure that contains a distinctive aural shape. Its definition implies a need to communicate that meaning contained within, operating, as it does, on the level of the signifier. "Gesture is statement, expression, communication and a private manifestation of loneliness, a 'signal through the flames' [...], yet this implies a sharing of experience once contact is made."[3]

Shifting the perspective a little further by reintroducing the song, I propose a re-examination of its role in relation to the musical instrument. Traditionally viewed in terms of accompaniment, the latter can, however, enter into another dialogue with the voice, this time as an extension of a performer's body that is capable of producing both sound and movement independently of each other. Thus three elements are potentially at play—the choreographed dance, the music, and the song of the performer. Singers and instrumentalists naturally possess the ability to generate movement as a consequence of technique and musical gesture. By focusing on the performing nature of a body-in-action and its inherent expressivity, the borderlines between musicians, actors, and dancers become porous, stretching any preconceptions of imposed skills and training.

In this essay performance song and dance are placed within the context of "sound theater," a term that embraces material not necessarily notated in the form of a fixed score, encompassing both music and sound in their relation to the staging of a work. Essentially it is a form that has emerged from the increased role of live and interactive electronics in new music theater. Reference is made throughout to observations that occurred during a period of embodied practice as research involving vocal and instrumental interaction with audio technology. A particular connection between song and dance emerges within this context of live performance, one whose borderlines have been challenged by a particular use of technology. Examples from key moments in the resultant work are given, in which comparisons are drawn between the real and the virtual worlds juxtaposed during performance, the voice and instruments providing a vital link in each case. Finally, my approach is summarized as a shift of perspective with regard to new, emergent forms of sound theater.

GESTURES OF PERFORMANCE

Zaum: Beyond Mind takes its title from the sound poetry of Russian Futurists and employs a wide variety of vocal styles in close dialogue with an instrument, the bandoneon (similar to the concertina or accordion), and choreographed movement. Essentially its creation emerged through collaboration between myself and electronics composer Oded Ben-Tal. The piece comprises voice, bandoneon, piano, live/interactive electronics, choreography, lighting, and film (an excerpt from Dziga Vertov's *Man with a Movie Camera*, 1929). Coined by Russian poet Khlebnikov, *zaum* means "beyond mind" and describes experiments in sound symbolism and linguistic creation stemming from Russian Futurist poets of the 1900s such as Alexei Kruchonykh. His *Zaum in Tiflis* (1918) provides the basis for much of the vocal material used in the performance. There is a direct link between the transrational language or *words-in-freedom* of *zaum* and the historical beginnings of electronic music. Both reflect the influence of an increasingly industrialized society on the sonic arts; vocal sound and noise become liberating factors that challenge a former aesthetic based on literary or musical representation. *Zaum: Beyond Mind* explores physical presence and absence, the "undesiring" bodies of voices-off, the animate/inanimate, and the reversal of performer/instrument relationships.

Indeed the performative gestures that occur between its two protagonists—singer/instrumentalist and computer operator—can be interpreted as a kind of "dance" that underlines an element of subversion or provocation in their tragic-comic relationship onstage. A dramatic tension is readable in their physical distance, moments of sudden eye contact, and reactions to the ploys of the other, in a constant struggle for power. The intentions behind each performer's movements become readable through their respective visual presences, whether through playful movements accompanied by deadpan facial expressions or excessive melodrama contained within formalized operatic gestures. A comic "gap" is set up between these gestural differences, the one "real," the other melodramatic. It renders a situation of cross-purposes between the two protagonists in their attempt to share a "dance," one that becomes engagingly clear to the audience.

At this point I focus on the live interaction of song and dance enacted by the main performer, which also incorporates a musical instrument, the bandoneon. There are three scenes in which both voice and instrument play together in gestural dialogue. The first one occurs without the live presence of the latter, the arms and hands of the performer miming instead the act of drawing and closing imaginary air bellows in contrapuntal movement to her vocal line. The visual impact is one of phrasing, of tracing lines in the space that comment, in turn, on that of the voice, like a form of punctuation interspersed with pauses for "breath." The dynamic of movement is suggested by the amount of energy needed for each gesture, but always remains in a relation of independence toward those levels of intensity and volume issuing from the song.

The other two scenes from the work concern the instrument itself, again in conjunction with voice and choreographed movement. Placed, in both cases, on its end—first on a table and later on the floor—this unorthodox positioning of a musical instrument already dislocates it from a normal contextual framework in advance of any interaction on the performer's part. The table scene involves at least a semblance of normal playing position as the bellows eventually extend and contract horizontally along its surface, guided by the arms of the performer while she intones long, sustained notes (see figure 18).

Here visual and aural gestures are deliberately confounded in a dialectical "play" between what is seemingly animate and inanimate. The notion of an instrument that determines its own course of sound and movement evokes a technological separation between machines and humans. The scene reflects a moment of their struggle for power.

A more radical encounter with regard to choreographed movement and voice occurs in the third scene, where the instrument is placed in a standing position on the floor. Again there is the suggestion of a small, puppet-like body occupying a space, viewed, this time, in relation to the larger size of the performer's body as she

Figure 18 *Zaum: Beyond Mind*, Brunel University, Digital Resources in the Humanities and Arts conference (2010). Photo by Neil Graveney.

Figure 19 Choreographic sketches for *Zaum: Beyond Mind*. Caroline Wilkins, 2008–9.

approaches it. Both voice and instrument begin their dialogue of sound and movement as the performer elicits percussive sounds from its keys, wooden frame, and the ridged folds of the bellows, responding with vocal sibilants, fricatives, and the breath. The "dance" continues until instrument and performer-body seem to become an extension of each other, the movement of one propelling the other in a balance of weight and gravity (see figure 19).

Moments of stillness and silence evoke images of a sitting rag doll, the bellows becoming an extension of the performer's legs, or an exotic headdress curved around her face as she lies on the floor. Some movements evoke the multiple intersections of a caterpillar moving in midair as her body folds and unfolds the bellows or her hands guide each end of the instrument and describe small curves. By its very construction, this anthropomorphic instrument suggests an undulating creature filled with air. No wonder, then, that its movement lends itself so well to visual expressivity. A visible line of movement dynamic in the folding and unfolding of bellows is something we also imagine in human bodies dancing, images of which are often captured in photos or in real-time video processing as blurred motion.

FUSION AND INTERMEDIALITY

Mention of a media tool such as the camera leads me to the main concern of this chapter, namely the extension of song and dance by means of technology. During the course of my arguments I explore three issues that have surfaced during the development of the work in question and illustrate how these are exemplified in performance. They concern the degree of fusion between live performance and technology, the interaction between the live voice/instrument and electronics, and the dislocation of voice and body within the technological material. However, before launching into any analysis of the above it seems necessary briefly to outline the electronic tools involved in this piece and the working process involved.

The creative work on *Zaum: Beyond Mind* began by recording sound material from a musical instrument, the bandoneon, that would become the basis for the interactive electronics to be generated during performance. These sound samples were then modified and processed, producing significant changes to their original timbre in order to approximate that of the human voice. Here it is important to note that the term "interactive" suggests an active-reactive relationship between performer and computer, whereby a level of intelligence in the latter that is not present in live electronics is implied. In fact this piece employs both genres, as the vocal and instrumental sources also undergo some live electronic processing in real time during performance. Using a pure data[4] (Pd) program, my colleague Oded Ben-Tal developed a prototype patch that analyzed any live sound issuing from the instrument and reacted accordingly with electronic responses. A second patch, based on the same source, was then created in order to respond to the live voice, both offering an interface that was possible to work with on my part as performer. However, necessary adjustments and expansions of their parameters took place over a long period of collaboration and experimentation, and remain ongoing as we evolve new ideas. Further developments were needed so that a larger scale of electronic responses to the live sources, such as unexpected silences or extensions of timbre, became possible. Our main concern was that both bandoneon and voice should be able to work with the electronics at the same time if they are performed simultaneously. It underpins an aesthetic choice of fusion between the sound sources, so that their separate identities become deliberately blurred.

The microphone can be considered as an instrument of real-time processing, whereby the sound source is altered electronically, to a greater or lesser degree, before it reaches a loudspeaker. In this case the subtleties of extended vocal technique, involving nonpitched, avocal sounds, or air and percussive noise issuing from the bandoneon, can be magnified into macrocosmic proportions in relation to their original source. The traditional role of a singer/instrumentalist shifts from that of providing acoustic narrative toward a more radical, intimate dialogue with technology. In *Zaum: Beyond Mind* this is manifested in moments where the "dance" (choreographed movement with the instrument) takes place along with the "song" (vocal utterances in dialogue with the instrument). Technical difficulties with playing an instrument in unconventional postures are surmounted by developing another vocabulary of extended sound made possible by means of audio technology.

Prerecordings of the instrument, and later the voice, contribute largely to the fused nature of the overall sonic material in this work. Both timbres are modified in order to sound related, but also slightly different, to that of the live sources. These are then relayed either as fixed or interactive sound material during performance. By

Figure 20 Text example of prerecorded voices from *Zaum: Beyond Mind* based on *Zaum in Tiflis* (1918) by A. Kruchonykh, Caroline Wilkins (2010). © Caroline Wilkins.

way of libretto it is the onomatopoeic poetry of the Russian Futurist Kruchonykh—*Zaum in Tiflis*[5] (1918)—that forms the basis for the "song." Spoken originally by my voice, the text is multiplied into virtual sonic extensions that are played back during the course of the piece (see figure 20).

Figure 21 shows a scored example of prerecorded material based on the same words that have been heard live beforehand, thus providing a contextual link for the audience to recognize. Other fixed material includes short sound files of a few minutes, containing more abstract electronic treatments, but whose basis lies nevertheless in an acoustic source. These are put into play with the live performer at key moments that have already been determined within the overall structure, her task then consisting of a one-way response. A link is always maintained between these live and prerecorded components through the use of word repetition, echoes of the same vocal or instrumental timbre, or reiterations of the musical material. Their intertwining serves as a means of recall to the ear.

A different story emerges, however, in the case of interactive electronics. Here, live sonic impulses generated by the voice or the bandoneon are simultaneously heard over four loudspeakers by means of amplification through wireless and contact microphones, while being fed into the computer. The program decides on a range of possible responses, based on a palette of electronic material, which are then distributed among the same loudspeakers and heard by performer and audience alike. Technology thus extends the boundaries of the live into the truly live as the present moment becomes a vertical ground for real-time encounters between

Figure 21 *Zaum: Beyond Mind*, Brunel University, *Digital Resources in the Humanities and Arts* conference (2010). Photo by Neil Graveney.

voice, instrument, and electronic sound, each rebounding from the other's response. The parameters of such interaction are extended by sonic material that goes beyond human capacities. A dislocation occurs, in which the live performer vies with her virtual protagonists.

The creation of a virtual voice by means of electronic processing implies the existence of an imaginary character with its own sonic "body" in the acoustic space. Pieter Verstraete describes this voice as an "imaginary body"[6] that brings with it a sense of its own unique space. Dislocation enables a separation to occur between voice and body, allowing for the coexistence of several personae and the displacement of the singing subject. The "I" of a physical body is no longer the focus. Instead it becomes split into identities that reveal simultaneous facets of their characters imported from other sonic dimensions.

Multiplicity then becomes a key word with regard to the transformation of a live sound source into infinite virtual possibilities. A purposeful separation of the aural/visual doubling that is typical of live musical performance allows for a different perception of each sensory faculty on the part of the audience. Prerecorded or live amplified sound material that does not reveal its acoustic source immediately, either because of its abstract nature or its electronic treatment, poses a question to the listener.[7] One enters into the realm of the acousmatic and a theater of sound. For example, in *Zaum: Beyond Mind* a choreographed scene of "dance" involves the floor movements of a human body "wearing" extended bellows, whose only audible acoustic sound is the release of air. This is surrounded by a wash of electronic sound from the virtual instrument heard over loudspeakers. A deliberate desynchronization between instrument-body and sonic material reawakens the audience's perception. Player, instrument and music become three elements that are independent and yet combined in a new formation. Instrumental playing is suddenly perceived as mime, gesture, or dance. An amplified, electronically treated instrument is heard as if the audience were inside its sonic "body." The same phenomenon applies to voice, gesture, and song. At a decisive moment during the work, live vocal interaction with the electronics is silenced by multiple renditions of words issuing from voices elsewhere in the space. These are virtual manifestations of the performer's voice, clearly dissociated from the visual movements of her mouth. Thus the borderline between the live and the virtual is constantly breached by means of a dislocation of sound from source, engendering a sonic equivalent of multiple mirrors.

DRAMATURGIES OF SOUND THEATER

Vital to a work of sound theater is its role in determining an "observable connection" between the real and the virtual; otherwise, as Todd Winkler points out, "the dramatic relationship will be lost to the audience."[8] The seemingly "magic show" quality of unseen bodies and heard voices certainly offers new dimensions of presence to an audience provided it also includes some points of convergence with the physical, solid world. On this subject composer Jonathan Harvey writes of a "theatre of transformation, [...] an expansion of the admissible" made possible by the seamless application of electronics to live performance.[9] Here the importance lies in maintaining contact between the familiar world of live instrumental/vocal sound and that of technology in order to avoid an effect of alienation on the part of the listener. A use of electronics that manages to retain an audible element of the "body"—through musical gesture—in its processing, is more likely to sustain an audience's interest.

One dramaturgical approach that enlarges on the subject of synchronous differences would be that of Heiner Goebbels. He insists on the bodies of both actor and text as two entities to be considered independently, achieved by dislocating the physical presence of one from the other.[10] By extension, and in relation to the apparent dislocation of the one from the other through technology, I propose the inclusion of the singer/dancer, the instrument, the music, and even the loudspeaker in this list of "bodies." Examples from *Zaum: Beyond Mind* have already been cited that include scenes of separation between the singer and her song, the "body" of the latter represented by virtual voices uttering text-fragments or intoning sounds. The very opening of the work presents the audience with a hidden, unknown "voice-off" calling from the wings. In this case the amplified voice is live and projects its imaginary singing body into the space. The musical instrument is encountered as a body-object in both its silent presence and in its "dance" with the performer that initially appears to elicit no sound. Again, through technology, its music has been transferred to a virtual sound body that is magnified and extended to an enormous degree. Therefore, in terms of prerecorded and interactive sound, both electronic-vocal and electronic-instrumental materials represent the sound-body.

Figure 22 Score page of voice and electronics analysis, *Zaum: Beyond Mind*. Caroline Wilkins (2010). © Caroline Wilkins.

In this work the loudspeaker-body comes into a realm of its own in its unique presence both as a technological tool and as a visual "speaking/singing object." Suggesting a vague similarity to the human form, four of these objects stand, often on small legs, at peripheral points of the space facing each other. The dislocation that has taken place between voice, instrument, and body is now relocated in this physical but also imaginary "body" provided by technology. The four "speaker-singers" enter into a dialogue with each other, exchanging fragments of the protagonist's stories in the form of a delayed echo-response. Of course, as well as providing amplification of the live sound, their role also includes relaying interactive responses, but an essentially theatrical component is introduced by emphasizing their physical presence as coperformers. This is achieved by means of lighting, placement in the space, and direct interaction with a performer. A form of gestural dance takes place as the computer operator approaches each in turn with a microphone, moving it playfully in front of the speaker surface in order to elicit a response of feedback loops—"singing" sine tones that vary in pitch and length. Thus, audience attention is drawn toward a new awareness of the spatial and sonic properties of these technological "bodies." There is a sense of dislocation between the microphone and the loudspeaker, a reversal of roles in which no live acoustic sound is transmitted.

The same approach can be applied here to the "object-body" of a computer that becomes the medium for a virtual singing character—Lazhila—through a dramatic moment of interaction with the live singer as she calls her name. A sonic response, triggered by the performer as she touches the keyboard, causes her to recognize her virtual counterpart in an ecstatic gaze directed toward the screen. The audience registers a connection between live and virtual performers. Visually, the computer occupies a space adjacent to that of the potential "dancer," namely the vertical "instrument-body" of the bandoneon. A nineteenth-century musical object standing on its end and a twenty-first-century digital tool are joined together by technology in the form of a thin line of electronic cable that renders their relationship a little incongruous. Thus the presence of two "object-bodies" onstage, the one producing live, the other virtual sound, defies any tendency to relegate the latter to an offstage position. By nature of becoming part of the stage set they remain visually important within the dramaturgical framework of the piece. By way of contrast there are moments when the live voice/instrument is no longer seen. Its sonic character is transformed into a virtual form by means of electronics. No longer physically on stage as a focus of audience projection, these virtual voices or instruments have the power to evoke a remembered body in that space that actually awards them presence.

The terms "presence" and "absence" have assumed a more complex definition in relation to real and virtual worlds. Derrida situates them within logos and teleology and the role played by deconstruction in ungrounding signification, thus allowing meaning to be indeterminate.[11] Absence would then correspond to the destable self, desire, and lack, whereas presence represents stability, plenitude, and certitude. However, with the dismantling of the liberal, humanist subject in favor of an emergent subjectivity that interacts with intelligent machines, a new configuration occurs between the material forms of absence and presence joined by those based on abstract information—randomness and pattern—in a semiotics of virtuality.[12] Here emergence replaces teleology, the distributed cognition offered by technology replaces autonomous will, and a dynamic partnership of humans and machines replaces a domination of one over the other. Thus absence and presence can be applied in a material sense to our perception of live bodies on stage, but there is no certainty as to whether we can determine the nature of this aural/visual reality when it is combined so intimately with the virtual.

In *Zaum: Beyond Mind* the link between the two, as between the live and mediatized or the immediate and the mediated, is provided by the voice and the instrument. In spite of being transformed from their familiar characteristics of sound into virtual electronic counterparts, timbral traces from both sources are guarded. This provides an audible connection between the two, thus ensuring that the live and virtual enter into a recognizable dialogue. The original timbre or "body" that comprises the live has simply been extended by technology. Its mediatized "double" retains all of the former's essence but offers us an expansion of its capabilities. Mediation is provided by the microphone, altering our perception of the immediate sound of a voice or an instrument. This technological tool renders any intimacy of sound, such as avocal articulations, audible. Sounds are then subjected to live electronic modification that includes the use of filters and equalizers or the addition of echo and resonance—in fact, all manner of alterations that intervene between the sound source and its reception by an audience.

THE MUSICKING BODY

Faced with a mediatized world, we are led inevitably to the key question of embodiment and disembodiment, in particular with regard to the voice that, unlike an instrument, contains its hidden means of sound production within the human body. Given my proposal of an "imaginary body" pertaining to the virtual voice, and underpinned by the "voice-body" or gesture in live vocal performance,[13] I would argue that it remains differently embodied in each case. The virtual voice is not disembodied but rather a *re*-embodiment of the embodied real voice. Virtual technology is embraced without aiming for the "disembodied immortality" of the voice but by accepting "finitude as a condition of the human being."[14] Thus the posthuman singing subject is not split into fragments by disembodied information, but enters instead into a discourse with technology by means of embodiment. As E. Hutchins writes, "human functionality expands according to the parameters of a cognitive system, extending embodied awareness by means of electronic prosthesis."[15] New experiential frameworks are created that remain embedded in a material world of great complexity and allow, in turn, for the emergence of new contexts for the performance song.

Indeed, song and dance are not only articulations of music and physicality, but also active agents that can transform meaning and identity during a performance, altering characters, performers, and audience perception of events onstage. This is achieved by a juxtaposition of real and virtual worlds, a fusion of the live with the mediatized, a play between their interaction, and the use of synchronous differences between "bodies" on- or offstage. In a performance of *Zaum: Beyond Mind* humans are perceived as puppeteers in relation to their musical and technological instruments; the dislocations of mediatization are deliberately exposed by separating function from form, the visual from the aural, and presence from representation. As to the work itself, its starting point remains firmly rooted in the human body, a body that determines certain parameters of control over the nature of the original sound material or the choreographed movement in space, for example. Song and dance manifest themselves in the form of physical gestures within the voice- or instrument-body of, or attached to, the performer. The act of singing or playing an instrument—"musicking," to use Christopher Small's terminology—becomes a form of dance or mime: "to music is to take part, in any capacity, in a musical performance, whether by performing, by listening, by rehearsing or practicing, by providing material for performance (what is called composing), or by dancing."[16] Thus both song and dance become essentially performative gestures, whether in terms of sound or movement, lending a new extension to their former identities within the practice of music theater.

NOTES

1. *Zaum: Beyond Mind* was created by the author in collaboration with electronics composer Oded Ben-Tal during 2009–10. It has been performed at several conferences (including the "Digital Resources in the Humanities and Arts" conference at Brunel University in 2010), festivals (Sonorities, Belfast 2012), venues such as the Rose Theatre, Kingston, and the Cockpit Theatre, London (2011/12) and at Stichting Logos, Ghent, Belgium (2011), where it won an award for best performance of the year.
2. Nicholas Cook explores a similar case with performers of rock music, whose body movements far exceed the demands of music production and become an essential dynamic of the show, working in conjunction with massive sound amplification. Nicholas Cook, *Analysing Musical Multimedia* (Oxford: Oxford University Press, 1998), 263.
3. Peter Brook, *The Empty Space* (London: Penguin, 1968), 57. Brook is referring to Antonin Artaud's famous assertion that performers should be "like victims burnt at the stake, signaling through the flames." *The Theatre and Its Double*, trans. Mary Richards (New York: Grove, 1958), 13.
4. Pure Data is an open source programming language invented by Miller Puckette before the advent of Max MSP in the early 1990s.
5. Alexei Kruchnoyck, "Zaum in Tiflis," trans. Gerald Janacek, in *Zaum: The Transrational Poetry of Russian Futurism*, ed. Gerald Janecek (San Diego State University Press, 1996). Online. Available: http://www.thing.net/~grist/l&d/kruch/lkrucht1.htm. November 27, 2012.
6. Pieter Verstraete, "The Frequency of Imagination: Auditory Distress and Aurality in Contemporary Music Theatre," Ph.D. diss., University of Amsterdam, 2009, 178.
7. Michel Chion, *Audio-Vision: Sound on Screen*, trans. W. Murch and C. Gorbman (New York: Columbia University Press, 1994), 71.
8. Todd Winkler, *Composing Interactive Music: Techniques and Ideas using Max* (Cambridge, MA: MIT Press, 1998), 9.
9. Jonathan Harvey, "The Metaphysics of Live Electronics," *Contemporary Music Review* 18: 3 (1999): 80.
10. Heiner Goebbels, "Text als Landschaft: Librettoqualität, auch wenn nicht gesungen wird," in *Komposition als Inszenierung*, ed. Wolfgang Sandner (Frankfurt am Main: Verlag der Autoren, 2002), 70.
11. Jacques Derrida, *Of Grammatology*, trans. Gayatri Chakravorty Spivak (Baltimore: John Hopkins University Press, 1976), 71.
12. N. Katherine Hayles, *How We Became Posthuman: Virtual Bodies in Cybernetics, Literature, and Informatics* (Chicago: University of Chicago Press, 1999), 285.
13. Verstraete, "Frequency of Imagination," 165.
14. Hayles, *Posthuman*, 5.
15. Ernest Hutchins, *Cognition in the Wild* (Cambridge, MA: MIT Press, 1995), 291.
16. Christopher Small, *Musicking: The Meanings of Performing and Listening* (Hanover, NH: University Press of New England, 1998), 9.

CHAPTER 14

From Ear to Foot

How Choreographers Interpret Music

SABINE WILDEN

From my experience as a classically trained pianist and dancer, I had assumed that there was one "correct and valid" relationship between music and dance, in which the dance mirrors elements of the music. However, after researching and evaluating the results of the studies conducted for my thesis, it became obvious that music and dance can relate to each other in a panoply of ways. Depending on the choreographer's intention dance *can* mirror the music (as with Balanchine's collaboration with Stravinsky), but by contrast, dance and music can be two independent entities (as with Cunningham's collaboration with Cage). Now I realize that there is a whole spectrum of possibilities, and that all of these approaches are valid.

Only a small amount of research has been done in the field of music and dance. In his book *Analyzing Musical Multimedia* (1998), Nicholas Cook emphasizes the idea of a spectrum of possibilities in the music-dance relationship. He discusses how media can relate to one another in a myriad of ways, and he presents three basic models: conformance (in which, effectively, dance mirrors the music), complementation (music and dance are neither consistent nor contradicting) and contest (both art forms are independent entities).[1] Other research studies have primarily focused on audiences' perceptions, investigating whether an audience can perceive the intended relationship between the art forms. This research is important because it demonstrates that viewers are sensitive to the music-dance relationship, but it is limited in that it only focuses on audiences' perceptions. To the scholar interested in music-dance relationships, the choreographer's perspective should also be of interest. Very little is known about how the creators of dance make their movement choices in response to music. How and why is music chosen by today's choreographers? Is it chosen before or after the dance is made? How—other than simply conforming to the musical patterns—do choreographers relate to the music? Which musical features are influential to choreographers when interpreting music with movement? How do choreographers choose which paths to pursue when confronted with ambiguities in the music? Answers to these inquiries result in different strategies and aesthetics.

In order to broaden the understanding of choreographic-musical relationships, two studies were executed for this project. For the first, fourteen professional choreographers from Europe, Brazil, and the United States were asked to participate in a survey. This included general questions about how they use music when choreographing, and specific questions concerning four short musical passages taken from the second movement of Maurice Ravel's *String Quartet in F Major*. Responses from the general questions revealed that choreographers have diverse procedures for incorporating music into their dance creations. In response to the specific questions, however, answers showed a striking consistency in how the four musical passages might be interpreted with movement.

The second study was a choreographic assignment, designed to further analyze the choreographic methods experientially rather than through discussion. Five student choreographers, trained mainly in contemporary modern dance technique, were asked to create and perform a solo dance to the complete second movement of Ravel's *String Quartet*. Choreographers today compose less to classical music, even early modernist classical music, than they once did, making this perhaps an anachronistic choice of composition. Nonetheless, the musical selection seems to be justified due to the *Quartet's* wide range of interpretational possibilities: the change of characters between the quick A part and the extremely slow middle B part—along with the wide range of tempi, the broad variety of rhythmic ambiguities, the extensive exploration of harmonies, varied dynamics, contrasting articulation, and motivic as well as thematic work—make this piece effective and challenging for a listener and choreographer.

All dance performances were videotaped, and each video was analyzed for rhythmic, dynamic, textural, structural, and articulative qualities.[2] Musically ambiguous passages (e.g., those with conflicting meters) were of special interest, as they would potentially demonstrate various ways that choreographers (and presumably listeners as well) could interpret them. In general, choreographers responded to rhythm, meter, mood, melody, dynamics (loudness/softness), structure (phrase beginnings and endings), contour, timbre (e.g., the sound of a violin played with or without mutes), articulation (e.g., the sound when plucked as opposed to bowed), and motivic structure. However, each choreographer prioritized these musical attributes differently.

This chapter can help us understand and learn about the creative act of choreographing as well as about choreographers' various perspectives on the music-dance relationship. Additionally, this chapter contributes to the literature on music perception and cognition: choreographers and dancers are also listeners who happen to act out their structural and emotional responses to music. Listeners often do not only imagine movement when hearing music,[3] but actively engage their other receptive senses,[4] just as audience members often engage their own bodies while watching dancers. Music and performance have a visceral power that stimulates the body of an audience member in various ways.[5] However, bodily responses to music are often not clearly visible for an observer, since music performances (especially for Western classical music) traditionally take place in concert halls. Here, listeners are seated, which gives them little possibility to use their body as a resonator and act out their perception and interpretation of music. Observing listeners in concert halls, thus, only provides a minimal insight into the realm of structural and emotional responses to music.

Following the logic that choreographers are also listeners, one can examine how listeners perceive and interpret music generally by studying how choreographers respond to it, since choreographers can act out their structural and emotional responses to music in the form of dances. After all, choreography and dance can be considered a magnification of the bodily affect we all feel (but often repress) when we listen to music.

THE RELATIONSHIP BETWEEN CHOREOGRAPHY AND MUSIC

One notable research project has sought to explain the relationship between choreography and music. In her book *Moving Music* (2000), Stephanie Jordan analyzes choreographic-musical relationships in the works of three famous choreographers. This research study is one of the most valuable as it gives special attention to dance-music relations. However, the choreographers chosen are not representative, since they were all highly musically trained. George Balanchine, "the musician choreographer *par excellence*,"[6] who founded the New York City Ballet, "studied not only piano but harmony, counterpoint, and composition."[7] Antony Tudor, also a choreographer of ballet, studied piano "at one of the London music colleges" and "[was determined] to learn as much about music as possible."[8] The third choreographer whose work Jordan analyzes, Frederick Ashton, was not as highly trained in music as Balanchine and Tudor, but claimed to "tak[e] [his] lead directly from the music."[9] In a chapter for *Ravel Studies* (2010),[10] Jordan analyzes "choreomusical" relations in *Shimmer* (2004); this work was choreographed by the contemporary modern dance choreographer Richard Alston employing the musical piece Sonatine by Maurice Ravel. Jordan points out that the "reason for focusing upon Alston is his widely acknowledged 'musicality,'"[11] and that "his work is prompted primarily by music."[12] Balanchine, Tudor, Ashton, and Alston are atypical in two respects: almost all of them are choreographers primarily of ballet, and they all stress music as their primary focus or guiding force. Three of the four, in fact, were highly trained musicians, which makes them unusual among contemporary choreographers.

Denominating Balanchine, Tudor, and Alston as "unusual" seems to be ironic. Should it not be expected that a choreographer, who chooses to incorporate music in the act of choreography, is trained musically, just as a chef is expected to know about ingredients? Dance programs at universities in the United States, however, require surprisingly little musical training for undergraduate dance majors, frequently no more than a semester.[13]

Music and dance seem to have been separated to become two different expressive forces. How did this happen? In today's Western culture, university education aims at "specification." Whether students study music or dance, they are usually required to focus on one concentration (a certain instrument, voice, or music theory, or a certain dance technique or choreography). This emphasis often channels students' education to only one dimension. Many would suppose that dance students have to engage not only in their dance education, but equally in the discrete study of music in order to become a "complete choreographer"—outside the students' area of specialization. Balanchine, Tudor, and Alston engaged in and committed themselves to both dance and music. Their degree of musical training thus far surpasses that of the majority of university-trained dancers and choreographers (in the West).

Two terms can be defined, analytical and intuitive, referring to methods of approaching music. Choreographers with extensive musical training have the capacity to be highly analytical in their approach. They can systematically analyze structure, rhythm, and harmonic and motivic elements of a musical score. Consequently, those highly sophisticated musician-choreographers have the competence to translate their musical knowledge into dance movements. Musical training, nevertheless, does not necessarily mean that those choreographers always choreograph analytically; they will often choose to be *intuitive* but may incorporate deep structural concerns as well. Thus, the analytical approach to choreography expands the choreographic possibilities immensely: analytical choreographers can choose whether to choreograph instinctively, emotively, or analytically, or if they wish to combine different approaches—leading to exciting and rather complex relationships between the music and the dance. Besides, their musical acumen can give them insight into the way the less obvious discourse of performativity works. The more choreographers have internalized musical analytical thinking, the more they can spontaneously and intuitively understand music's complexity.

Contemporary choreographers, in contrast, often prefer a more intuitive approach to music. They tend to enter into the choreographic process with a spontaneous, open-minded attitude without preset concepts in mind. Their analysis might not have the intention to be systematic, comprehensive, or theoretically valid in a musical sense. The choreographer's "intuition" is likely a type of engagement with the performative complexity of the music, which finds expression in their choreography. However, it must be supposed that lack of music-specific training might often translate into a reliance on the intuitive at the expense of the analytical. If today's choreographers are more intuitive in practice than Balanchine, Tudor, and Alston, then it follows that an understanding of analytical music-choreographical methodologies may be unrepresentative of the majority of contemporary choreographers. Studies of intuitive choreographic processes are necessary in order to solve the mystery of intuition.

Current research in the field of music and dance either emphasizes the analytical approach to choreography, or it focuses on audiences' perception only, as studies by Krumhansl and Schenck (1997)[14] or Mitchell and Gallaher (2001)[15] demonstrate. Although they can serve as a basic point of origin in the investigation of music and dance relationships, none of them addresses the question of how intuition (or what gets *called* intuition) plays a part in the choreographic process.

A significant work in music-dance research is Paul Hodgins's book *Relationships between Score and Choreography in Twentieth-Century Dance: Music, Movement and*

Metaphor.[16] It is a practical strategy for analyzing choreographic-musical relationships, where Hodgins outlines the shared features between dance and music: rhythm, dynamics, texture, structure, quality, and mime. These parameters are important, because—common to the analysis of both choreography and music—they can serve as analytical tools for my studies. However, the list of parameters is limited in that it excludes performative dynamics such as energy, liveliness, communion, or desire. The reason for omitting those features might be the difficulty of measuring them appropriately; there are no common conventions for notating the performative attributes.

The most relevant research for this project was done by Zohar Eitan and Roni Y. Granot, who set out to investigate "the ways listeners associate changes in musical parameters with physical space and bodily motion."[17] Participants in this experiment were asked to envisage an object that could move around in their imagination in response to musical stimuli. Results showed that dynamics and pitch contour affected motion imagery the most. Dynamics were associated with distance and speed. A crescendo was associated with higher and increasing energy, approaching motion, and an increase in velocity; a diminuendo, on the other hand, related to descending and moving away. Furthermore, pitch contour was related to verticality, in that pitch rise evoked the idea of increasing distance while pitch descent related to decreasing distance. Eitan and Granot have shown that perceivers are sensitive to the music-movement relationship, and that they have an internal movement imagination when confronted with certain musical stimuli. Those stimuli, however, are rather simplistic; it would be interesting to confirm the results with passages from actual music literature.

Since choreographers can be thought of as listeners, the results of Eitan and Granot's study can help explain which musical features lead to which bodily motions. Are choreographers conforming to the same cultural frameworks, though, as do other listeners? Eitan and Granot investigated whether or not musical training has an effect on the imagined object's movement. They found that "in most respects musicians and non musicians relate musical and motional features in the same way," but that "musicians use such mappings more consistently and securely."[18] The same is probably valid for choreographers, who have a more sharpened understanding of music than "customary" listeners have, simply because they use and express music routinely.

CHOREOGRAPHERS' THOUGHTS ABOUT MUSIC

The relation between music and dance cannot be understood in empirical or scientific ways only; it instead calls on urges and instincts. One of those urges is the attempt to explore and enquire without needing to find definitive answers. The research presented in the next section was accordingly intended to go beyond studying "measured" listener responses and instead to examine the creative processes of choreographers themselves.[19]

In the survey, almost all choreographers generally described music as an impulsive force playing an essential role in the dance creation. Responses revealed that music usually illustrated and propelled a work forward. Choreographers mentioned three possible relations between music and their choreography: 1. "dance first—music responds"; 2. "music first—dance responds"; and 3. "independence between music and dance."

In the first relation, choreographers started their working process with the actual movement, a concept for a theme, or an intention for the piece, before looking for suitable music. Choreographer Jennifer Predock-Linnell would "create the dance first, [then] have [a] composer come to rehearsals, ask questions, watch the movement and go from there."[20] Thus, dance is created first, and music is used to embellish the creative idea. Following Cook's three basic models of how differently two media can correlate with one another, the relation "dance first—music responds" could be called conformance, in which the music mirrors the dance.

In the second category, music comes first and inspires the movement. Choreographer Donna Jewell wanted her dance creation to "serve the music and relate deeply to it,"[21] where music had been her first choice. Patricia Dickinson echoed this: "the choreography must complement the music and emphasize the changes in the music."[22] In line with Cook, this relation presents an example for conformance *and* complementation, since dance mirrors the music as well as supplements its specific elements.

Music and dance are considered to be independent partners in a third relation (which could be labeled contest, according to Cook): For Vladimir Conde-Reche, music, dance, lighting, costumes, and the performance space should all be independent entities. "The world around us is like a choreographed work," Conde-Reche says, "that changes daily according to the placement of each layer." Moreover, he mentioned the ubiquitous presence of music: "There is always music. The silence is music."[23] Rahel Weißmann further elaborated on the idea of music and dance as two self-standing entities: audience members would have the opportunity to find their own interpretation within the tension that potentially exists between the two art forms.[24]

All three defined relationships seem to insist on separating music and dance. This could be a culturally learned distinction inherent to the Western practice. Researchers have found that the relationship between musical and physical expression tends to be more homogenous and organic in other cultures. In the Javanese region of Malang, for example, "musicians associate particular drumming patterns with particular movements, and certain compositions with certain dances."[25] Western practice behaves differently, possibly due to the development of "art music" since the medieval era. Establishing and stylizing music and dance as "art forms" might have led to the loss of their natural bonds.

Moreover, choreographers display a tendency to elevate the music's primary function. A reason for this valuation could be that music has an established culture of literacy as well as a stable notation, whereas "'art' choreography is a fairly young phenomenon compared to the thousands of years in which music has evolved."[26] According to Stephanie Jordan, "there are relatively few analyses of dances compared with music. This may well be because dance, an altogether younger, smaller field than music, with a less developed specialist typology, has never been driven by scores and recordings in the same way as music."[27] Many would suggest that the West has become progressively more reliant on documenting knowledge (analyses, scores, and recordings) and less comfortable with bodily practices. Responses confirm this assumption in that choreographers consider music as "safe," whereas dance is somehow unpredictable. This could explain choreographers' tendencies to consider music superior to dance.

Pursuing my original assumption (that dance conforms to music), another question of the survey aimed at finding which musical features influence choreographers the most in their movement choice. When interpreting music, the majority of the participants identified rhythm and mood as the most influential factors (figure 23). The impact of rhythm/pulse was mentioned eight times and, thus, appears to have played the most significant role.

The priority of rhythm could have been expected, since moving along to a steady beat is considered to be "one universal of human music perception."[28] In an evolutionary sense, rhythm can be considered innate to human beings. Biologically, rhythm probably emerged from the motor apparatus. All animals have rhythmic motor programs, such as for example a horse's gallop or a bird's flight patterns; some scholars have speculated that developments in gait (walking upright rather than on all fours) and also in learning language (developing vocal mimicry potential) may have led to a capacity for rhythmical awareness as a result of "gait-mimicry."[29] This could explain why choreographers intuitively consider rhythm to be the most influential factor.

Additionally, "rhythm [is] the main component for the comparison of music and dance," says Stephanie Jordan. For her, "rhythm is an immediate point of contact between the two art forms."[30] This can be observed in many dance classes, where counting eight-beat phrases is common in order to match the music with the dance movement, and in order to provide a simple and understandable framework for the exercise. Thus, music is "reduced" to its rhythm, serving primarily as timekeeper. Dancers are rarely instructed to follow other musical features, such as the dynamics, the form, the articulation, or the melody, since those elements are not easily "measurable" and discernible.

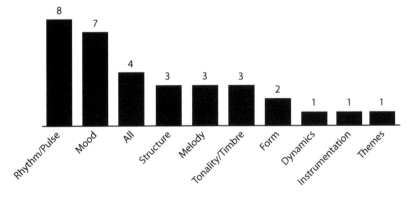

Figure 23 Diagram of musical features by which choreographers are influenced . © Sabine Wilden.

The second most important musical influence for choreographers was the mood of the music. Mood is commonly described as "a temporary state of mind or feeling"[31] trying to convey a certain atmosphere. Mood furthermore represents an abstract and immeasurable factor. With regard to measurability, the main influential aspects, mood and rhythm, can be considered to be antithetic. Although mood seems ephemeral in contrast to clear assessable rhythm, it nonetheless appears to be tremendously important for the reception of music. As suggested by composer Richard Cameron-Wolfe, it is conceivable that mood is even more important than rhythm: "[Choreographers] would not consider the rhythm of a piece [to be of primary importance], if the mood was inconsistent with [the feeling they wished to express]. It is true that choreographers mention rhythm [as influential], but they have already filtered [the piece] through a 'mood censor.'"[32]

Concerning thematic and motivic work, only one choreographer indicated themes, and no choreographer indicated motives as prominent influential factors. This could suggest that the cultural normative demand for content (narrative, character, drama, etc.) seems to be less significant than we might imagine.

Moreover, no choreographer designated articulation as significant.[33] Nevertheless, most of the participants responded emphatically to articulation when imagining movement in response to actual music. This confirms the assumption that most choreographers probably do not consciously choose their movement. Instead, it seems that they are culturally aware of detailed elements within the music, which they instinctively respond to when interpreting music with movement.

CHOREOGRAPHERS' INTERPRETATIONS OF MUSIC

In a second part of the survey, specific questions were posed concerning four short musical excerpts taken from the second movement of Maurice Ravel's *String Quartet in F Major*. Two of those excerpts will be discussed here. The participants were asked to describe what about the music stands out and what possible movements the music suggests.

This section of my studies originates again from my initial thought that dance conforms to music. Taking this path, I have limited my research, but I have also made the results describable since the musical analysis of each excerpt provided a basis to evaluate choreographers' responses.

The first excerpt is the beginning of the *Quartet's* second movement; figure 24 presents the first two measures, though the choreographers did not see the score at any time.

This passage is metrically ambiguous, with possible readings in 6/8, 3/4, and 3/2. Ravel indicates two different time signatures at the beginning: 6/8 and 3/4. In the first measure, the 6/8 time signature can be found in violin 2 and viola: six eighth notes per measure with a dotted quarter note as beat. Violin 1 indicates 3/4, thus, three quarter notes per measure. The first two measures can also be interpreted in 3/2 (three times 2/4). Furthermore, the forte pizzicato marking in all instruments gives the passage a particular character.

Figure 24 Beginning of Excerpt 1, mm. 1–2 from the *Assez vif, Très rythmé*, second movement of Maurice Ravel's *String Quartet in F Major*.[64]

Regarding rhythm, meter, and tempo, almost all choreographers seemed to have a similar and clear perception of the excerpt's "fast tempo, driving pulse, forward motion, and the strong rhythm."[34] Furthermore, choreographers referred to the articulation throughout; five found the "pizzicato/plucked strings/plucking sound" considerable, and four noted the staccato sound. The comments regarding the influencing musical factors confirm the fundamental significance of rhythm. Articulation, however, was not mentioned once when answering the earlier question, whereas it was acknowledged as an important musical influence in response to the actual music.

Moreover, three choreographers had staccato movements in mind in response to the staccato sound they had perceived: "staccato character embedded in a flow of movement,"[35] "sharp, staccato, distal movements,"[36] and "staccato physical accents."[37] The staccato articulation in particular could have led half of the choreographers to imagine fast footwork for this passage, described as "light footed movement,"[38] "sharp footwork,"[39] or "very light, quick footed movement."[40]

The fast tempo of the music was considered appropriately set by similarly fast movement; and accordingly, the energetic mood was reflected in energetic movement: "lots of energy,"[41] "fast allegro jumps,"[42] "fast, ballet movements, and on the beat movements."[43] The overall movement interpretation thus went *with* the music. It seems that most choreographers mirrored the descriptive elements of the music. Only one choreographer, however, would "oppose the fast tempo with extremely slow movement [in a] complete legato."[44]

Although choreographers delineated their movement ideas in different ways, movement choices were surprisingly similar, particularly the described footwork in response to articulation and rhythm. It might be possible that those culturally similar responses are based on acquired if not analyzed musical responses.

The second excerpt deals with the beginning of the scherzo's middle section (figure 25), which contrasts with the A part in many ways: the timbre is different (mutes are used), the tempo is much slower, and both metrical and harmonic structure are highly ambiguous.

Figure 25 Beginning of Excerpt 2, Ravel, *String Quartet*, II, mm. 88–93.

Although notated in the key of B flat major (or G minor), the main theme in the cello seems to be in D minor. Ravel uses a lot of chromaticism in the viola and second violin. In the circled section of figure 25 the global time signature is 3/4, but locally the phrasing slurs give the sense of three bars of 2/4 (i.e., one bar of 3/2).

In addressing the second excerpt, respondents commented less on the music than in the first excerpt. They used a rather descriptive, abstract, and narrative language, suggesting that an attempt was made to interpret the nonlinguistic expression of the music through the semantic codes of language. Most of the choreographers referred to the slow tempo and the harmonic ambiguity by describing this section as a "dreamy sequence,"[45] as "the beginning of something,"[46] or as "adagio, lyrical,"[47] legato, and melodic, revealing a "dramatic"[48] mood. This might indicate that choreographers tried to translate something ambiguous into something understandable. When the participants did not succeed in doing so with easy analogues, they turned to the idea of the "dramatic" mood.

Choreographers had a similar idea of the section's mood. Prevailing attributes were heaviness, sadness, mystery, longing, sentimentality, darkness, somberness, memories, sorrow, or a feeling of wandering. The need for explanation, meaning, drama, and narrative was indeed powerful, as responses showed: for Donna Jewell, "people [are] searching for each other, but then turning away; [there is] a desire for the individual to open oneself but not receiving a connection/communication to do so."[49] To Zoe Knights, the section also evoked the "promise of the arrival of something possibly menacing."[50]

Moreover, the description "slow" predominated: "slower movement, quiet stage,"[51] "slow earthy movement,"[52] or "slowly, tied, calm, and lyrical."[53] As in the first excerpt, the music and the movement interpretation mirrored one another; the slow tempo of the music was considered appropriately set by a similar slow movement. Only one choreographer would choreograph "very fast and dynamic movement to contrast the sentimentality."[54]

Responses to the earlier general questions presented multifaceted approaches choreographers use to incorporate music in their dance creations. However, when choreographers were asked to listen to actual music and interpret it, their responses to the specific questions showed a surprising consistency in the imagined movements. Rather than using musical analysis as a conceptual starting point, choreographers seem to rely on general responses to semiotics in music (i.e., mood and atmosphere). This confirms the results of Eitan and Granot's experiment: when listeners (here the specific kind, the choreographers) are confronted with actual music passages, and when they are asked to imagine a moving object to this music, responses are similar.

ANALYZING CHOREOGRAPHIC PRACTICE

The second study was designed to further assess the various choreographic methods in response to music, this time in a practical environment.[55] Five student choreographers created and performed their individual interpretation of the complete second movement of Ravel's *String Quartet*. This approach had the benefit of not restricting the participants to only one dimension of response, as in a tap-along study; the dancers were free to express their primary reactions to the music in any way they saw fit.

Results of the musical analysis were compared to results of the analyses of all five dance performances.[56] Each choreographic interpretation revealed very different and individual approaches to the music. Dancer A presented a comedic modern dance in which he was also talking to the audience, Dancer B showed a narrative approach, while the other three interpreted the music with more common modern dance movements. In general, choreographers responded to rhythm, meter, melody, dynamics, structure, contour, timbre, articulation, and motivic work. Only those dance interpretations that stand out as notable will be discussed here.

In response to the beginning of the music (fig. 24), one might expect the dancers to have followed the "easier" time signatures of 3/4 or 6/8, which are both stated explicitly in the score. Still, some appear to have heard the passage in 3/2. Dancer B stretched her arm *out* in m. 1, beat 3, and pulled it back *in* on beat 2 of m. 2, repeating the same movement in mm. 3–4; thus, she probably heard the first measures in 3/2.[57]

The most obvious musical event (for almost all choreographers) in Excerpt 1 seemed to have been beats 1 and 1+ in mm. 11–12 (fig. 26). Dancer E, for example, clearly responded to those two eighth notes, first with a *passé*, then with a quick motion into a *grand plié* in second position, moving *out* on beat 1, and back to a fifth position on 1+.[58] Both examples confirm the influential importance of rhythm.

Whatever movement the choreographers chose in response to the first iteration of the second theme in the violin (fig. 27), the choreographers repeated this same movement pattern for the second iteration of this theme in the viola.[59] Such a choice might reflect that choreographers are acknowledging and interpreting thematic work, perhaps even above rhythm. This may be the result of ambiguous rhythm, or it possibly contradicts the answers in responses above (no choreographer considered thematic work to be an influential musical factor in the survey). The complexity of the choreographic process and the paradox of intuitive and analytical methods are again demonstrated.

Dancers' responses to the thematic work additionally suggest that our Western reception of music prioritizes the rhetoric of thematic iteration. Presumably, the

Figure 26 Ending of Excerpt 1, Ravel, *String Quartet*, II, mm. 11–12.

Figure 27 Beginning of the A part's second theme, Ravel, *String Quartet*, II, mm. 13–14.

recognition of themes might take away the performative expression of dance itself and instead turn it into something that is musically (or even linguistically) driven.

In the slow middle section of the *Quartet*'s second movement, it is difficult to describe the dancers' perception of meter. Eitan and Granot revealed that listeners perceive high-level melodic patterns and rhythmic patterns in a slow tempo with greater difficulty than they do with patterns in a faster tempo. This can explain dancers' responses to the second excerpt (fig. 25). While almost all dancers showed a clear perception of meter and rhythm in the *Assez vif, Très rythmé* A part of the work, the slow B part (*Lent*) tempo (quarter = 46) obscured the evidence of the dancers' metrical perception.

Dancer C executed slow *and* fast movements when interpreting the excerpt's music, which did not align with any particular metrical structure.[60] Dancer E's overall slow, fluid, and stretched movement interpretation was in accordance with the music's slow character. Likewise, many of the participating choreographers in the earlier part of the study (Part 2) had referred to slow and fluid movement in response to the second excerpt.

In Dancer E's interpretation of the second excerpt, rising movement corresponded to a rising melody line both in m. 94 as well as in m. 98.[61] This echoes Eitan and Granot once again, whose results showed that a rise of pitch was associated with the imagined object moving away from the listener; dancers use different body parts (e.g., the leg or the arm) to refer to melodic movements.

CONCLUSION

Results revealed that the perceptions and interpretations of music by intuitive choreographers are more differentiated than expected. A variety of musical features can influence choreographers in their movement choices. Rhythm and meter were shown to be of primary influence, followed by mood, dynamics, structure, contour, timbre, articulation, and motivic/thematic work. Although not all choreographers cited those attributes as influential, they did acknowledge them in the actual creation of dances in response to a complete musical piece. Regarding thematic work, for example, choreographers mentioned its influence on their music interpretation only once, whereas almost all choreographers acknowledged the thematic work by choosing similar movement in response to repeating themes in the music.

The responses to the general questions of the study have shown how multifaceted choreographers' descriptions of the importance and the role of music are, and how diversely choreographers incorporate music into their choreographic processes. In the later part of the survey, however, we find the opposite phenomenon: choreographers imagined very similar movements in response to the two musical excerpts. Thus, when it comes to the actual dance creation, choreographers show comparable approaches to respond to musical pieces with movements.

When perceiving and interpreting music, it is very possible that the primary influential musical factors, rhythm and mood, were guiding all choreographers. In some passages of the music, such as the prominent rhythmic event of beats 1 and 1+ in mm. 11–12 (fig. 26), almost all choreographers agreed upon prioritizing the rhythm over other musical features. Thus, even if subconsciously, choreographers imagined similar movements. By contrast, the later study has shown that different musical attributes seemed to be of importance for each choreographer at certain times. This explains the overall variety of choreographic interpretations in response to the complete musical work.

Interestingly, the two major influences in music, rhythm, and mood, are rather differing: Rhythm, defined through its pulse and tempo, is a measurable, concrete factor, whereas mood is a conceptual, abstract factor. This combination of the concrete and the abstract in music could have led choreographers to use a mixture of methods: a culturally acquired analytical approach on the one hand and an intuitive approach on the other hand.

Sometimes, the dance responses showed an inconsistency with traditional music theory analysis: if the dancers had not interpreted the beginning of the first excerpt in 3/2, I would not have seen this interpretative option through my "music theory glasses," since Ravel clearly indicated a 3/4 or 6/8 time signature. Consequently, "unindoctrinated" choreographic responses to music can reveal additionally valid musical interpretations.

Following this train of thought, "dancers offer us a potential truth about music [in which] music forms space and environment in such a way that [. . .] all can become something else."[62] As a result of the choreographer's focus on prioritizing certain musical elements, a dance piece can influence the observer to interpret music differently. Listening to music and watching its dance interpretation redirects the audience's musical interpretation toward that of the choreographer. In fact, each dance interpretation of the music created a different focus for me, as observer and listener.

A final consideration is related to the fact that both studies have included a vast majority of *female* choreographers. This contrasts with the studies conducted by Jordan, which only focused on *male* choreographers. Furthermore, the choreographers included here were more of the intuitive type than the analytical, in that none were highly trained in music theory (their average number of months of music theory training being eight). Future studies could examine the difference between female and male choreographers, as well as analytical versus intuitive, with regard to music perception and interpretation.[63]

I hope that this chapter furthers the field of choreography in relation to music by illuminating not only the multifaceted approaches choreographers use when interpreting music but also the differences between working analytically and intuitively. By understanding the pros and cons of each approach, we have a greater chance of moving beyond the traditional and commonly accepted choreographic patterns and approaches. Dance and music can encourage and suggest interpretations of each other, casting new light through their interactions and collaborations.

NOTES

1. Nicholas Cook, *Analyzing Musical Multimedia* (Oxford: Clarendon Press, 1998), 98–106.
2. My process was somewhat similar to that outlined in Paul Hodgins, *Relationships between Score and Choreography in Twentieth-Century Dance: Music, Movement and Metaphor* (Lewiston, NY: Edwin Mellen Press, 1992), 25–30.
3. Zohar Eitan and Roni Y. Granot, "How Music Moves: Musical Parameters and Listeners' Images of Motion," *Music Perception* 23: 3 (2006): 221–47.
4. Lawrence M. Zbikowski, "Music and Movement: A View from Cognitive Science," draft submission for the symposium volume *Bewegungen zwischen Hören und Sehen* (Forschungsinstitut für Musiktheater der Universität Bayreuth, 2010), 4. Online. Available: http://humanities.uchicago.edu/faculty/zbikowski/pdfs/Zbikowski_Music_and_movement_draft.pdf. October 17, 2012. Here, Zbikowski describes how aural stimuli can cause "certain groups of neurons [mirror neurons] to fire." See also Ivar Hagendoorn, "Dance, Choreography and the Brain," in *Art and the Senses*, ed. David Melcher and Francesca Bacci (Oxford: Oxford University Press, 2010), 499–514. Online. Available: http://www.ivarhagendoorn.com/files/articles/hagendoorn-oup-2010.pdf. October 17, 2012.
5. Michel Poizat's works *La voix du diable* (1991), *La jouissance lyrique sacrée* (1991), *La voix sourde* (1996), and *La société face à la surdité* (2004) give insight into the physical

conditions (e.g., goose-bumps, shiver down the spine, clammy hands, or salivating) caused by the performative voice.

6. Stephanie Jordan, *Moving Music: Dialogues with Music in Twentieth-Century Ballet* (London: Dance Books, 2000), 105.

7. Robert Gottlieb, *George Balanchine: The Ballet Maker* (New York: HarperCollins, 2004), 17.

8. Jordan, *Moving Music*, 269.

9. Ibid., 188.

10. Stephanie Jordan, "Ravel Dances: 'Choreomusical' Discoveries in Richard Alston's *Shimmer*," in *Ravel Studies*, ed. Deborah Mawer (New York: Cambridge University Press, 2010), 166.

11. Ibid., 169.

12. Ibid.

13. Sabine Wilden, "From Ear to Foot: How Intuitive Choreographers Interpret Music," master's thesis, University of New Mexico, 2012), 65–66. Online. Available: http://hdl.handle.net/1928/20796. July 7, 2012.

14. Carol L. Krumhansl and Diana Lynn Schenck, "Can Dance Reflect the Structural and Expressive Qualities of Music? A Perceptual Experiment on Balanchine's Choreography of Mozart's Divertimento No. 15," *Musicae Scientiae* 1: 1 (1997): 63–85.

15. Robert W. Mitchell, and Matthew C. Gallaher, "Embodying Music: Matching Music and Dance in Memory," *Music Perception* 19: 1 (2001): 65–85.

16. Hodgins, *Relationships between Score and Choreography*, 25–30.

17. Eitan and Granot, "How Music Moves," 221–47.

18. Ibid., 240.

19. Purpose, method, detailed results, and findings of this first study can be found in Wilden, "From Ear to Foot," 19–49.

20. Jennifer Predock-Linnell, quoted in Wilden, "From Ear to Foot," 81.

21. Donna Jewell, quoted in ibid., 95.

22. Patricia Dickinson, quoted in ibid., 98.

23. Vladimir Conde-Reche, quoted in ibid., 97.

24. Rahel Weißmann, quoted in ibid., 95.

25. Christina Sunardi, "Making Sense and Senses of Locale through Perceptions of Music and Dance in Malang, East Java," *Asian Music* 41: 1 (2010): 89–126.

26. Richard Cameron-Wolfe, e-mail message to author, February 20, 2012.

27. Stephanie Jordan, "Choreomusical Conversations: Facing a Double Challenge," *Dance Research Journal* 43: 1 (2011): 5.

28. Aniruddh D. Patel, John R. Iversen, Micah R. Bregman, Irena Schulz, and Charles Schulz, "Investigating the Human-Specificity of Synchronization to Music," in *Proceedings of the 10th International Conference on Music Perception and Cognition*, ed. M. Adachi et al. (Adelaide: Causal Productions, 2008), 1. Online. Available: http://birdloversonly.org/docs/Patel.pdf. November 7, 2012.

29. Steven Mithen, *The Singing Neanderthals: The Origins of Music, Language, Mind, and Body* (Cambridge, MA: Harvard University Press, 2006).

30. Jordan, "Choreomusical Conversations," 11.

31. *Oxford Online Dictionary*. Online. Available: http://oxforddictionaries.com/definition/mood?region=us&q=mood. October 30, 2012.

32. Richard Cameron-Wolfe, interview by the author, March 19, 2012.

33. Dynamics and articulation were not mentioned in my question; this could be a reason why nobody referred to those aspects.

34. See participants' responses to Excerpt 1 in Wilden, "From Ear to Foot," 116–19.

35. Weißmann in ibid., 117.

36. Predock-Linnell in ibid.

37. Byron Suber in ibid., 118.

38. Jewell in ibid., 116.

39. Mary-Anne Santos Newhall in ibid., 117.

40. Jim Self in ibid.
41. Vladimir Conde-Reche in ibid., 118.
42. Weißmann in ibid., 117
43. Predock-Linnell in ibid.
44. Martina Morasso in ibid., 116.
45. Conde-Reche in ibid., 125.
46. Self in ibid., 123.
47. Predock-Linnell in ibid., 124.
48. Jewell in ibid.
49. Ibid.
50. Zoe Knights in ibid., 125.
51. Self in ibid., 123.
52. Rachel Germond in ibid., 125
53. Weißmann in ibid., 124.
54. Suber in ibid., 125.
55. Purpose, method, detailed results, and findings of this second study can be found in Wilden, "From Ear to Foot," 50–58.
56. Dancer A was a male undergraduate dance major. A link to his complete performance can be found at: "Dancer A—complete version," *YouTube.com*. Online. Available: http://youtu.be/Oj6EnQ4xZf8. December 8, 2012. Dancer B was a female graduate dance major with a focus on choreography: "Dancer B—complete version," *YouTube.com*. Online. Available: http://youtu.be/C--Ri7CNVFs. December 8, 2012. Dancer C was a female undergraduate dance major: "Dancer C—complete version," *YouTube.com*. Online. Available: http://youtu.be/lzTvsd7BXEk. December 8, 2012. Dancer D was a female graduate dance major with a focus on choreography: "Dancer D—complete version," *YouTube.com*. Online. Available: http://youtu.be/S6mbbc0nKfk. December 8, 2012. Dancer E was a female graduate dance major with a focus on choreography: "Dancer E—complete version," *YouTube.com*. Online. Available: http://youtu.be/SzluLrbG45E. December 8, 2012.
57. "Excerpt 1—Dancer B," *YouTube.com*. Online. Available: http://youtu.be/slVB-jb9n7KA. December 8, 2012. The excerpt is taken from the repeat of the first theme in mm. 40–51, since the video quality was better.
58. "Dancer E—Excerpt 1," *YouTube.com*. Online. Available: http://youtu.be/sC9Pgo-FyKpc. December 8, 2012.
59. "Excerpts 2+3—Dancer A," *YouTube.com*. Online. Available: http://youtu.be/HXQpz6Y6fqc. December 8, 2012. "Excerpts 2+3—Dancer C," *YouTube.com*. Online. Available: http://youtu.be/d050x_XDbj8. December 8, 2012. "Excerpts 2+3—Dancer D," *YouTube.com*. Online. Available: http://youtu.be/xJDyHnn9pjU. December 8, 2012.
60. "Excerpt 4—Dancer C," *YouTube.com*. Online. Available: http://youtu.be/aVsrCk-j7FY4. December 8, 2012.
61. "Excerpt 4—Dancer E," *YouTube.com*. Online. Available: http://youtu.be/Vok-m8m0rwvM. December 8, 2012.
62. James Currie, "Music After All," *Journal of the American Musicological Society* 62: 1 (2009): 187.
63. Drawing a link between maleness and the analytical method on the one hand, and femaleness and the intuitive method on the other is not intended.
64. Maurice Ravel, *String Quartet in F Major* (Paris: G. Astruc, 1905).

CHAPTER 15

Singing from Stones

Physiovocality and Gardzienice's

Theater of Musicality

KONSTANTINOS THOMAIDIS

It is midday in the village of Gardzienice, Poland, in September 2009. This is my penultimate day of fieldwork with Wlodzimierz Staniewski's theater company. After an intensive session of morning acrobatics in the meadows, physical exercises in mutuality, and ensemble singing of Georgian and ancient Greek songs, we rest in preparation for rehearsals, performances, and night running in the forest. The relevant entry from my training journal reads:

> A student from the Academy is playing the violin near a window of *Oficyna*. From inside *Carmina*, I can hear Joanna, Anna, Agnieszka and Maniuszka practicing the dance of the maenads, singing *"Euoi Backhai,"* screaming, shouting celebratory calls. Some fellow-trainees are still trying to get the rhythm of "Hai-Hai-Hai-Ha-Ee-Ha" in their bodies, moving their vase-inspired, two-dimensional choreography in the meadows. Up the hill, contractors are yelling at each other. A few birds are chirping, the breeze echoes in the forest, the stream creates a constant buzz. And Kirca, the energetic dog with the ancient name, barks at the window out of which the sound of a violin emerges. It may be just me, but it sounds as if everybody acknowledges the sounding of the others. In a weird way, it seems that all these sounds are not antagonizing each other and, at the same time, they are not intruding on the calmness of the early afternoon.[1]

Certainly, the excerpt does not claim scholarly accuracy. However, it hints at important themes and recurring preoccupations of the group, such as the sharpened sense of aural perception, the trained attitude of openness toward other(s), and the connections between voicing and the landscape. Building on my recent fieldwork, this chapter examines elements of both Gardzienice's performances and pedagogy as case studies of what I call *physiovocality*. Meanwhile, the overarching aim of my investigation is to formulate a definition of Staniewski's theater(s) of musicality.

In 1976, Staniewski (b. 1950) decided to pursue his vision of theatrical deurbanization and resist the leveling of minority culture resulting from the Communist administration in Poland. He subsequently founded the Centre for Theatre Practices Gardzienice, which is still based in the homonymous village of the Southeastern region. Constantly pushing the boundaries of the avant-garde, the company has cultivated a unique approach to devising, one that is inspired by expeditions to the multicultural Polish borderland as well as abroad. The performances of Gardzienice, which incorporate acrobatics and gestural choreography alongside such complex vocal phenomena as antiphony or dissonance, have been a territory for the exploration of the tensions between the physical and the vocal. Not surprisingly, his pieces have been thus analyzed as either "ethno-oratoria"[2] or "village operas."[3]

In this creative strand, literary sources or playtexts are only a point of departure. The musical and vocal material defines the devising process and the final aesthetics to such an extent that Staniewski has declared directing to be a praxis pertaining to the field of musical composition.[4] In *The Life of the Archpriest Avvakum* (1983), the autobiography of the Russian archpriest and liturgical songs are juxtaposed with Lemko folk songs, whereas in *Carmina Burana* (1990), the well-known codex and the story of Tristan and Isolde are combined with Georgian songs. Similarly, the last period of the company's work, while building on the gestural and vocal depository accumulated through years of traveling, is largely dedicated to the reconstruction of ancient Greek music. Combining academic research with their deep understanding of folklore, Gardzienice has revisited Apuleius's *Metamorphoses* (1998) and Euripides's *Elektra* (2003), *Iphigenia at Aulis* (2007), and *Iphigenia in Tauris* (2011).

Singing in these productions is either homophonic, heterophonic, or in canons; hence the importance of the dynamic interactions taking place between the voices. Although the vocal arrangement often accords with the division of Catholic choirs in high and low, male or female voices, the sound texture is dense and inclusive; registers are frequently blended and strict lines intermix with perceptible breaths, vocal glidings, exclamations, shrieking laughter, and cries. Still, the sounding of Gardzienice performers exhibits a distinct connection to its body source. The release of breath into voicing follows the impulses of the choreographed sequences, gesticulation, or the physical encounters between the actors. The quasi-spoken or semichanted text is performed in a mixture of (mostly) Polish, English, and ancient Greek, with a strong use of facial musculature and an accentuation of consonants. Singing employs spasmodic inhalation, a raised larynx, and gaping mouth—in a combination of technical qualities of folk singing with festive/marketplace imagery. This meticulous examination of vocal and corporal interconnections has consistently been the cornerstone of Staniewski's endeavors, informing his group's balanced investment in both theater-making and the development of a new strand of performer training.

The interweaving of song and dance in Gardzienice's performances is not merely an aesthetic choice. Staniewski frequently admits Bakhtin's (1895–1975) influence on his theater.[5] Staniewski's dialogue with the Russian philosopher's writings is evident in his interest in folk culture, his awareness of historical processes, and the undividedness he perceives between the individual, the community, and the cosmos. Also, Gardzienice's director places distinct emphasis on bodily movements that mingle the high and the low, such as the whirling of the dervishes in *Sorcery* (1980), "which expresses the release of an excess of joy,"[6] or the dance of the maenads in the last scene of *Metamorphoses*. Most importantly, Staniewski's training, in a decisive amalgamation of Bakhtin's polyphony/heteroglossia and the grotesque bodily canon, promotes states of abundance, physical exuberance, and vocal interrelativity, which reject the concept of "the private, egotistic, 'economic man.'"[7]

From the foundation of the company until the radical political change of 1989, the embodiment of Bakhtin's principles and the exploration of grotesque physiovocality were effected via the methodology of expeditions and gatherings. Expeditions were "pilgrimages"/fieldwork in specific communities, especially those of the eastern borderland, during which the group, after an initial "reconnaissance" visit by one or two of its members, journeyed toward the village, trained in the new environment, engaged in conversation or everyday tasks with the locals, and organized gatherings. The latter were events during which Gardzienice performed songs and rehearsed performance extracts and physical sequences, in an attempt to involve the locals as much as possible in a mutual sharing of dances, music, and songs: "Singing," according to Staniewski, "was the most open channel of communication."[8]

In blending everyday labor with the extra-daily exigencies of gatherings, in an atmosphere of reciprocal conditioning, Staniewski discovered the connective tissue of his directing: song, music, and episodic storytelling. The elements of pilgrimage and the intentionally Bakhtinian blending of high and low culture (as exemplified in the impromptu encounter of canonical texts with folk art) were major components of the experience of gatherings. These, in combination with direct inspiration from culture-specific gestures and voice vibrations and the urgency to hone performance skills in an informally competitive situation, contributed to the dynamics of Gardzienice's productions in such a definite way that Staniewski considered his training as taking place at "the 'university' of the countryside."[9] Preserving and transforming the musicality of the encountered ethnic groups, Staniewski's expeditions in the rural culminated in his "ethno-oratorio" performances.

Gardzienice's use of the body and the voice stems from a particular lineage of performance, the Polish student theater of de-Stalinization and the practices of Jerzy Grotowski (1933–1999). Staniewski grew up in Poland in the oppressive atmosphere following Stalin's death in 1953. Upon graduating from the University of Kraków, he joined Teatr STU, an influential group of the early 1970s, which resorted to music and techniques of collage as means to avoid censorship and to support the undercurrent of resistance to the Communist regime. Staniewski performed with the company in the piece *Spadanie* (*Falling*) (1970), and the aesthetics of this work (emphasis on music and exploration of voice and sound, devising techniques, a variety of written sources) was crucial to the shaping of his own creative perspective.

In 1970, he was invited by Grotowski to join his paratheatrical activities, characterized by an attempt to erase the boundaries between audience and performers, a deliberate refusal to create in conventional theatrical settings, and the formation of intimate "meetings," where vocal participation and movements that unleashed sound were paramount. Grotowski promoted a physical understanding of the actor's work cultivated through exercises called *plastiques* and detailed work on gesture, understood as a "*sign*, not a common gesture, [which] is the elementary integer of expression for us."[10] It is here that one can trace the origins of Staniewski's interest in gesture, epitomized in his inspiration from village gesticulations and iconography in *Avvakum* and *Carmina* and Greco-Roman vase painting in the Greek plays.

Furthermore, in terms of voicing, the conceptual skeleton underpinning the pedagogy of Gardzienice has been formed to a large extent in relation to Grotowski's paradigm; the avoidance of prerecorded or technologically modified sounds in performance,[11] the disparagement of vocal improvisation in performance,[12] the cultivation of freedom and spontaneity in the training and rehearsals,[13] as well as the "body first, then voice" principle.[14] All of these can be better comprehended if related to similar concepts in Grotowski's teachings. Thus the following statement by Grotowski could be endorsed by Staniewski as well:

> Being products of different systems of transcription (both in the sense of musical notation and in relation to recording) and not of the oral tradition, Westerners mistake singing with melody. They are pretty much able to sing anything that can be notated in notes. But they are completely unable to notice such things as the vibratory quality of the voice, the resonance of the space, the resonators of the body or the way in which the vibrations are carried through the out-breath.[15]

Differences are noticeable nevertheless. Grotowski, when working on the voice, suggested exercises that address individual needs, while Staniewski's training, as will be analyzed in the following section, highlights the role of the group. Moreover, while Grotowski worked from a detailed anatomical perspective when touching upon resonators,[16] Staniewski, aiming at a similar result of holistic vocal exploration and honing of the vocal imagination, relates the areas of the body to cultures and ethnic groups.[17] Rather than insisting on a physiological concretization of vocal qualities, Gardzienice achieves the vibrations peculiar to each song through imitation and imaginative playfulness. In an informal conversation, Gardzienice expert Alison Hodge recalled that in the mid-1990s the company was experimenting with "very specific sounds from specific regions." In her Gardzienice workshops, Anna-Helena McLean, who worked with the company from 2001 to 2007 and performed the title role in *Elektra*, teaches a step-by-step warm-up of the resonators, moving from the pelvic area to the cranial structures, and attributes the filtering of the harmonics in each resonator to a region or people. For example, the sound around the nasal cavity and the sphenoids is called the "Bulgarian sound" and the open sound at the top of the head "the Ukrainian sound." Staniewski worked in a similar way in the Summer

Intensive 2008, asking invited trainees to share songs and encouraging mimesis of the "geographically proper" vibrations.

Gardzienice's inspiration by the primordial role given to voice by Grotowski's and Bakhtin's examination of folk festivities is further illuminated if related to contemporaneous findings of Polish ethnomusicology. Anna Czekanowska, studying the period of the 1970s and 1980s, concludes that in Poland, folk music in its entirety, comprising both vocal and instrumental genres, has derived from the vocal repertory. This is manifest in the use of such terms as *spiewany* (vocal) when referring to traditional forms, while *techniczny* (technical) stands for more recent and elaborated versions. In a sense, "vocal" is used as a synonym for originality. Furthermore, events that have traditionally been central to the life of the community called for songs; however, and this is quite important to my discussion of physiovocality, out of these collectively valued sung repertories, the most well preserved are those that accompany entertainments such as dances, while ritual song has fallen into decline.[18]

The productions of the post-Communist years revolve around the artistic director's collaboration with composer Maciej Rychly and actor-musicians Tomasz Rodowicz, Mariana Sadowska, and Marcin Mrowca,[19] a group that attempted to access the musicality hidden in the remaining fragments of ancient Greek music, "not in a manner of reconstruction, but of reminiscence."[20] The training principles and core devising techniques of the first period persisted. Still, Staniewski's interest in preserving the physiovocal expressivity of near-extinct minorities developed into an equally ambitious project: the research into the "revival" of the less-documented elements of Greek drama, its physical and vocal resources. In McLean's description:

> We tried from every root to get close to the original. But the more you studied, you realized it is nonsense to try and reconstruct exactly what it was. [...] Initially with Maciej [Rychly], we absorbed the melodies that were left, and looked at the words. Then you created a new melody based on your invention, based on the scales that you have studied, the sounds you think are there, the instrumentations that are signaled in the scores that are left from Ancient Greece. So how do you put new life into it? You go and study today's indigenous cultures, looking for sounds and colours and rhythms and affectations, and, being a musician yourself, you evoke your way of reconstructing this or that song, making lots of different versions. You are not saying any one of these is the right way, but "how about this way?"[21]

In view of the devised performances, this process of embodiment was further informed by Staniewski's research into other remains of the culture (sculptures, ceramics, mosaics, texts), in particular through the work, and personal input, of philologist Oliver Taplin. This led to the creation of musico-theatrical études, the iconograms, which tested the invented vocality through sequences of postures found in vase-paintings,[22] the reconstruction of Greek instruments (see figures 28 and 29), and the development of an "alphabet of gestures," known as *cheironomia*, which joined the expressive gesticulation of ancient Greece to specific musico-textual fragments.[23]

Staniewski's vested interest in physicality and voice is what provides his work with a sense of continuity. The creation of the "dramaturgy of gestures"[24] is a

Figure 28 A reconstruction of a *seistron*-type instrument. Photo: Konstantinos Thomaidis.

development of his earlier work on iconography, in tandem with his commitment to discovering the "archetypal" gestures of the minorities of the countryside. Similarly, music remains the focal point of all activities and dramaturgical choices. Once more, Staniewski's decisions seem to have been dictated by the musical data at his disposal more than anything else. None of the tragedies he staged is analyzed in Taplin's *Tragedy in Action*, Staniewski's main theoretical influence in his work on tragedy. No surviving ceramic pot is directly connected to any of the two Euripidean plays he directed (even though Euripides is, generally speaking, by far the greatest source of inspiration for the vase painters). However, Euripides is the only one of the tragic poets whose music has survived, although in just a couple of short and not easily decipherable fragments.[25] Furthermore, the oral character of musical transmission in ancient Greece, which inevitably drew attention to the acts of listening and memorization, is yet another element with which Staniewski's research can identify.

Consequently, any classification of the group's work as pertaining to either the fading Communist past or the internationalized present is reductive, and does not acknowledge the ability of the company to evade such categorical polarities as Ratajczakowa's "artistic reinterpretation of national symbols versus universal archetypes," Cioffi's "literary versus visual" strands of the Polish alternative theaters, and Taplin's "iconocentric versus philodramatist" approaches.[26] Staniewski overcomes

Figure 29 A reconstruction of a *kithara*-type instrument. Photo: Konstantinos Thomaidis.

such polarities by drawing on the Greek concept of *choreia*, the principle according to which the actors merged elocution, singing, dance, expressive gesture, and character-making into a seamless whole. This aspiration to an all-encompassing acting style informed the reconstruction of the songs. As Rychly, comparing Gardzienice's work with scenes depicted on Attic vases, relates: "That's how musicians really behaved. They did not use to sit hunched over their scores. We see them flying in dance movements. Their entire bodies are alive with music."[27]

Staniewski's work is therefore a significant case study in physiovocality, the uncompromised parallel development of the performer's bodily and vocal technique. A Gardzienice actor is not a triple threat, an actor-singer-dancer who cultivates each discipline separately in order to combine them at later stages of professional development. This, as affirmed by Allain, would be "anathema to their [Gardzienice's] approach."[28] Physiovocal integration in this case is key to every phase of preparation and performing, as song is learned through movement, and choreography is understood as part of a musical composition. Furthermore, the inseparability of voicing and movement is not only a matter of aesthetics. It is historically necessitated (the avoidance of Communist censorship and the need to explore multiple national identities), pertains to a well-defined genealogy (Polish folk music and Grotowskian techniques), relates to performance parallels (student happenings and the Greek *choreatic* expression), and is philosophically articulated (the relation to Bakhtin's marketplace). In other words, Staniewski's suggested paradigm of how voice and body cooperate does not only problematize definitions of the actor; it promulgates a particular cosmology of being. This is why in the following sections I will probe the principles that form the backbone of the company's pedagogy and examine how these, rather than a specific style or aesthetic, have become the wellspring of other theatrical work.

MUSICALITY, MUTUALITY, CHORALITY, AND VOICE AS A BODILY IMPULSE

The training of Gardzienice epitomizes a movement toward both ends of the continuum from artificiality to authenticity, from the open performativity of the twice-behaved to the everyday-ness of the behaved, as encountered in expeditions. Artificiality is cultivated through the attempt to "expand the actor's *instrumentarium*."[29] The actors should be capable of executing challenging acrobatics, energetic dances, or choreographies based on iconography, while voicing poetic texts and a wide range of songs. However, Staniewski, inspired by distinctly local rituals, the directedness of transmission in oral cultures, the Polish concept of *pieknoduch* (aesthete), and the ancient Greek notion of *paideia* (≈ education), searches for the originality of encounter between trainees or performers that will constitute the nucleus of truthful expression in all his attempts.[30] Staniewski has summarized this attitude as being in search of an actor who is "truthfully artificial."[31] Toward this end, the main principles underpinning the training of Gardzienice are those of musicality and mutuality, the emphasis given to the ensemble, as well as the cultivation of an approach toward voice that begins with the actor's physicality.

The origins of these principles can be traced back to Bakhtin's analytical discourse; the unifying force behind the first two is his discussion of dialogue. Bakhtin, being a proponent of dialogism in literary theory and linguistics, extends this concept to his philosophical investigation of the act and the individual's participation in being:

> Two worlds confront each other, two worlds that have absolutely no communication with each other and are mutually impervious: the world of culture and the world of life, the only world in which we create, cognize, contemplate, live our lives and die or—the world in which the acts of our activity are objectified and the world in which these acts actually proceed and are actually accomplished once and only once. An act of our activity, of our actual experiencing, is like a two-faced Janus [...]: it looks at the objective unity of a domain of culture and the never-repeatable uniqueness of actually lived and experienced life.[32]

In other words, Bakhtin suggests that each action partakes simultaneously in the timeless concept of dialogue and the implications emerging in the present, contingent dialogue within the given circumstances; each action is situated within a complex nexus of response-abilities toward the eternal, logical, or moral (in its philosophical meaning) *and* the necessity and liveliness of the moment. Through this prism, each act is axiomatically dialogic and presupposes and cultivates an intricate network of reciprocal connections. This is a useful tool in order to comprehend Staniewski's distinction between a method and a codified training process; the first is closer to "the objective unity of a domain of culture," while the second highlights the importance of a set of principles reinvented in each "never-repeatable" encounter— Staniewski is interested in principles, not systems, and sees each moment of the training as unique and located at the center of mutually influenced lived presences.

Therefore, Staniewski's training should be understood as situated within the tensions between each *specific* dialogue and the *general condition* of dialogue: on the one hand, the concept of the grotesque body, and, on the other, the specific, exuberant, human body; the notion of carnivalesque and the particular festivity; the eternal image of the banquet and the historically specified banquet of a certain people; the ideology of Bakhtinian laughter and the physiologically concrete laughter.

Following this line of thought, it is easier to touch upon the way music is distinguished from musicality within the practices of the group. Music, according to Staniewski, is an abstraction, the codification of sounds into concrete compositions and systems of notation or intellectualized perception. Musicality is the realm of sounds beyond music, the entire array of sounding vibrations that cannot be easily explained, notated, or reduced to our listening and voicing habits. Recent developments in evolutionary musicology have confirmed that "music may be considered as a product of social forces, whereas musicality is principally a biological phenomenon."[33] Contrary to the cultural specificity of music, musicality includes the biological ability to make and perceive any sound. Therefore, in terms of human voicing, music can be understood as the superficial level of melodic and rhythmic schemes. Musicality, on the contrary, provides access to each performer's physiology, each performer's unique bodily imprint as encapsulated in the voice: "Musicality exists only if it is in permanent connection with its source. Musicality speaks about identity, it identifies, it says who I am and what I am doing here."[34]

Staniewski draws on a variety of sources to explain and solidify his concept of musicality: "the psychagogic power the Greeks attributed to music,"[35] the Sami practice of *yoiking*, or the rediscovery of Hellenistic musical philosophy during the Renaissance, among others.[36] *Yoiking* is a voicing practice of the Nordic Sami; Staniewski is fascinated by the subtle nuances of the term "to yoik," which could be considered synonymous with "to sing." "I *yoik* you" is not "I sing about you" but rather "I sing you."[37] *Yoiking* in this sense is a way of connecting to the other, to all manifestations of existence, and materializing them in the act of song. In the light of performativity, it is a vocal act (to broaden and paraphrase Austin's speech acts) that effects "truthful"/daily meetings through the extra-daily means of song. According to Thomas Hilder, an ethnomusicologist who is currently conducting ethnographical research on the Sami people, "[if] I say 'I *yoik* you,' it means 'I make you present through my *yoiking*.' In the same sense, if I want to express that you bring happiness to me, I *yoik* you happiness, and the happiness is present."[38]

In terms of the Western concept of music as extending beyond the level of aesthetics and being a notion crucial to the understanding of the cosmos, this can be traced back to the Neoplatonists and the Neopythagoreans. They distinguished between *musica mundana*, *musica humana*, and *musica instrumentorum*: the first is the music created by the movements of the stars and the heavens, the second allows the coexistence of the bodily and the spiritual elements in the human being, and the third is the instrumental as well as the vocal music.[39] Similarly, Staniewski talks about musicality as *musica vita* (music of life, or life music) and links it to the concept of *harmonia mundi* (harmony of the world), in a Bakhtinian gesture of perceiving at the same time the entirety of the musicality of the world and the interconnections between the musicalities of the individual in their relation to the environment and history. Therefore, in the practices of Gardzienice musicality becomes a sociological and ecological term as well, revealing an ethical stance toward all aspects of the world and human activity: "I am utterly convinced that the earth is musical, that it has musicality and that every part of nature can be musical [...]. When the strings of the earth's musicality break, the earth dies."[40] In this sense, vocal expression is invested with a performative character of cosmological dimensions.

The training of Gardzienice exhibits a tripartite relationship to musicality. The first step is to widen the trainee's perception and sensibility beyond music and toward musicality, as exemplified in the expeditions to "the university of the countryside." Then, the perceived musicality needs to be absorbed in their training practices—the "revival" of the stone fragments illustrating this stage. Finally, for every new performance, new ways of allowing musicality to inform all its aspects should be explored.[41] Staniewski implies that every component of the performance rises from musicality. First, the musical material is learned and repeated, as in an act of allowing a mantra to exert, through its musical structure, a specific spiritual function. Then, out of this deeply embodied musical structure, out of the wholeness of the musical "score" and its choral/group lifeline, the characters emerge: "In this moment, the actor no longer produces the voice—the voice is already a given, functioning somehow like the actor's alter ego; and in this moment, for the spectator, it is as if the space is sounding."[42] Even in performance, the idea of openness and dialogue is applied to the voicing of the actors, whose voice is defined more in relation to their connection to the group and the space than to their individual physicality.

Mutuality,[43] the principle of meeting others, working with them, or simply *being* with them in a deeply collaborative partnership, is also inspired by a variety of literary and lived sources: Socratic dialogue, Plato's idea of shame, "the underlying idea of dialogue and correspondence" of the Polish folk repertoire,[44] the spontaneous interactions encountered in gatherings, Zeami's concept of the "flower," and, once more, the Sami *yoiking*.[45] Of course, Bakhtin's discussion of the grotesque, ever-interactive, and nondelimited body is of paramount importance. Influenced by all the above-mentioned ideas and principles, the training practices at the village of Gardzienice are founded on the concept that the body should not be merely understood as the individualized byproduct of the advent of industrialization, or of the processes that led to what Bakhtin names "the bourgeois ego."[46] The individual physiology is trained toward a state of alertness and responsiveness, which, in a sense, erases its own importance and places the emphasis on what takes place among mutually interacting physiologies. To put it in a deliberately oxymoronic way, the Gardzienice performer's body exists only in coexistence.

The point of convergence between the principles of musicality and mutuality in the practices of the company is the use of the breath. Breathing is not only the mechanical basis of phonation; it becomes the source of the common vibrations of the polyphonic voicing, the foundation of a shared rhythm in morning exercises or night running, as well as the principal form of communication in physical sequences. This understanding of musicality and mutuality as communicating vessels is of paramount importance in my discussion of physiovocality. Furthermore, for the same reason, it is essential to note that mutuality, in its purest form, the form of being in relation to a partner, or even to a transcendental Other, denotes a connection to a whole that is "gay and gracious,"[47] with connotations of happiness: "In Old Church Slavonic the word '*bog*' (god) had three meanings: 'fate-lot-happiness.' Experience [*sic*] shared mutuality gives happiness. Cognition and positive sensation changes into sadness, if we do not share with Another."[48]

This idea of openness and constant interconnection with the members of the group is cultivated through what I term the choral character of all training, performance-related, and everyday activities. The philosophical groundings of the principle lay, once more, in Bakhtin's propositions, encapsulated in his understanding of the festival-type activities of the Middle Ages, hosted by and targeted to the "chorus of the laughing people."[49] I understand the entirety of the group's endeavors as choral encounters, not only because of their all-out, musico-kinesthetic tone, but also because of the primordial emphasis placed on the dynamics of the group at all stages of artistic and noncreative processes. In the performances, the role of the group is stressed to such an extent that Hutera describes Gardzienice as "a collective human flame,"[50] and Niziolek states that in *Elektra* "the theatrical reality becomes polycentric."[51] The omnipresent group, out of which individual characters emerge only to be absorbed by it again, takes in *Avvakum* the role of the mob, in *Carmina* that of the choir, in *Metamorphoses* that of Plato's "family," and in *Elektra* and *Iphigenia* that of the tragic chorus. Solos are used as exceptional dramaturgical devices; even in these instances, the actors react to sounds, provocations, or the spatial configurations created by the group. The idiosyncratic nature of solos in Gardzienice performances urges Staniewski to claim that "parting is a sacrificial ceremony."[52]

The principle of chorality finds, once more, parallels in such sources as the gatherings of the indigenous communities visited during the expeditions, the Bakhtinian notion of carnivalesque, the dithyramb, the tragic chorus, and the antiphonal practices of Mount Athos. Staniewski, inspired by the notion of *zgromadziciel* (gatherer), sees himself as a conductor of the group's choral encounters.[53] Moreover, he often creates an alter ego of a "master of ceremonies" who paces and orchestrates the group's performances from the inside; this is the case with the accompanying violinist in *Avvakum*, the magician Merlin in *Carmina*, and the figure of Euripides in *Elektra*.

In the everyday activities of the group, teaching, administrative, and "housekeeping" tasks are evenly allocated, while students of the academy and workshop performers are encouraged to participate. Thus, in each synchronic cut, the Centre for Theatre Practices is animated by a different "constellation," to use Staniewski's term. Regarding the company's voice pedagogy, the emphasis is mostly placed on group voicing. This is not only the appropriate context to put into practice Staniewski's vision of a new natural, deurbanized environment for theater, but also becomes a means through which spontaneity and expressivity are encouraged within the group and ego-related inhibitions are surpassed.

As for the fourth principle, the *through-the-body approach* to voice, and performing in general, it is important to reiterate that in Staniewski's cosmological understanding of theater, the body is a dynamic aggregation of historically, philosophically, and individually specified forces. The physicality of the actor is molded by memories and archetypes evident in social gestures of indigenous traditions and iconographic paradigms of such ancient cultures as the Greco-Roman antiquity. Through the reassembling of hidden traces of musicality residing in the actor, the body becomes a microcosmic representation of the cosmos and of unity. In its movement toward extreme physical expressivity, the soma reaffirms Bakhtin's topography of the grotesque body; cartwheels and the movements of the clown (the buttocks taking the place of the head and vice versa), considered parallels of the rotation of earth and sky, symbolize the mingling of high and low culture.[54]

Singing and movement, the creation of bodily images and aural landscapes, are inextricable in Staniewski's directing and of equal merit in the creation of the tone for each piece. The transmission of these melodies within the company follows a similar pattern. Rhythm is embodied through touch and stomping, while melody is taught with gestures. Considering the melismatic complexity of the company's songs (both those of the repertory and the material explored in training), gesticulation is an embodied, visually engaging and easily followed pedagogical tool. In the language of these invisible neumes drawn by the performers' hands in the air, movements upward or downward translate into changes of pitch, while movements on the horizontal axis can either signpost duration or volume, depending on the context and the particular moment within the song. On a deeper level, teaching through gesticulated neumes, if compared to reading a score, brings the emphasis to the group. The need for imitation and the subconscious following of the pulsating choral movements of the hands and the arms, especially when done with the speed and high energy of Gardzienice performers, entrain a common rhythm, leave no time for intellectual processing, and immediately establish an embodied relation to voicing.

In terms of the company's research into ancient Greek practices, Wildstein rightly emphasizes the difference between the constructive and expressive kinds of artistic creation, and situates Staniewski's work within the choreatic (expressive) strand, which encompassed dance, music, and poetry in an inextricable whole.[55] Staniewski, in his *Humanities* lecture (2005), relates that the first performers of tragedy sang, spoke, and danced, but due to lack of breath they were unable to sing properly; thus, the separation and discipline-based organization of performing arts, still prevalent in the West, was established. However, Staniewski reverses this tendency and, in his training, acrobatics, running, *cheironomia*, and iconograms become "physical ways of tapping into the voice"—or, to resort to his own terminology, "a song of the body."[56]

These main principles of Gardzienice's training, in tandem with the characteristics it inherited from its Polish folk roots (centrality of the voice, heterogeneity, and tension between strict structure and spontaneity), make it necessary to clarify that such elements as rhythmic patterns, modes, and melodic features are not rigidly conventionalized. These are constructs directly related to music, and, as explained above, musicality is far more important in Staniewski's vision of theater. Therefore, any analysis of these elements in the company's training should be regarded as an attempt to grasp recurrent musical traits rather than to outline unyielding rules. Put differently, the aesthetic codification presented through the performances is often less pressing an issue than the organic embodiment of the principles of mutuality and musicality.

TOWARD A THEATER OF MUSICALITY

This working ethics has found applications extending beyond the rural home base of the company. Through years of long- and short-term collaborations, nationwide and international touring, teaching, demonstrating, and lecturing, a Gardzienice "landscape" has already begun to be formulated.[57] The availability of electronic sources has also facilitated its recent expansion and the establishment and maintenance of a wide network of audiences, scholars, collaborators, artists, and aficionados.[58] Central to this activity is the company's archives department, based at the offices in Lublin. However, tape-recording of voice sessions has not yet invaded the pedagogy, and the use of electronic media in the training room is strictly prohibited. This is not only an outcome of the oral memorization techniques employed in the training. Gardzienice voice training, with its all-body character and the relational physiology as its "grain," to employ Barthes's term, cannot be realized outside the given constellation/ensemble.

My fieldwork with both Gardzienice and several "parts" of its landscape has illustrated that their common denominator is not an aesthetically fixed use of the voice. Each company and artist has developed distinct performance styles and has been inspired by Staniewski in a way that is in dialogue with their own artistic pursuits. The major axis around which their activity develops is formed by the notions of polyphony, expedition, mutuality, and musicality, the training process through which physiovocality is understood on the level of intersubjectivity, and the subsequent attempts to create performance contexts that promote a new understanding of sounding and gathering-type participation. Given that musicality is, to Staniewski's eyes, the most effective path to interconnectedness, "the most open channel to communication," one can see this lineage of productions and practices as attempts to create a "theatre from the spirit of sounds."[59]

CONCLUSION

I cannot deny that there is a certain allure of mysticism in Staniewski's terminology and theoretical formulations. In concluding, however, I wish to return to the main questions of this chapter and, more broadly, of this volume. What is the performativity of singing and gesturing in Gardzienice's case? In other words, what is effected through what is articulated here as physiovocality? In searching for an answer, the densely heteroglossic fabric of Gardzienice's performances and their episodic, abstract, and explicitly choral character point away from the semantics or syntactics of performance as the main agents of performativity. Conveying characters or the meaning of songs and movements does not seem to be Staniewski's main interest. It is in the contexts of voicing, in the vocal pragmatics, to borrow from semiotics, that his core concerns are revealed. His main focus is on processes rather than aesthetics. The anthropological expeditions and long-term training of his company cultivate an ethics of openness, vulnerability, and sensitive listening and voicing. The complex dialogues between the soma and the voice in Gardzienice's pedagogy systematize an embodied understanding of physiovocality as expressive of individual and collective identity. In other words, what the materiality of gesture and singing are designed to effect is the implementation of a specific type of desire, the performer's desire for interpersonal, "I-thou" physiovocal communication.

In the case of the performances, however, I see this desire as less tangible, as the analysis needs to shift from the kinesthetically palpable to a glimpse of something verging on the affective. The spectauditors are not only to partake in the company's intercorporeal principles and ethics; as outlined in the first section, Staniewski wishes to invite them to his broader understanding of the world as musical. If we, capitalizing on Staniewski's accounts as well as related concerns of evolutionary musicology, identify music as a sociocultural praxis and musicality as its biological grounding,[60] then Gardzienice's work is significant in advocating another taxonomy of musico-theatrical performance. Staniewski's pieces and the considerable corpus of his students' and collaborators' work seem more accurately theorized not as music or musical theaters but rather as *theaters of musicality*. This new taxonomy comprises theaters that (aspire to) go beyond employing music as their main expressive means. They inculcate, instead, a systematic belief that all aspects of the theatrical event can be devised, perceived, and comprehended as musical behavior. In this sense, and if Jill Dolan is right in suggesting that theater can make "palpable an affective vision of how the world might be better,"[61] it does not seem unfair to speculate that, for Staniewski, there is only one utopian performative: to give his audiences a glimpse of the world as an undeniably musical one.

NOTES

1. Extract from the author's training logbook, September 11, 2009. Oficyna is the central building in the company's base in the village. Carmina is one of the performance spaces, named after one of the long-standing performances in Gardzienice's repertoire, *Carmina Burana*. "Euoi Backhai" is a newly composed song, inspired by ancient Greek exclamations in celebration of god Dionysus. "Hai-Hai-Hai-Ha-Ee-Ha" is a vocal drill devised by the group.
2. The term was first suggested by Polish critic Leszek Kolankiewicz and is quoted in Alison Hodge, "Wlodzimierz Staniewski: Gardzienice and the Naturalised Actor," in *Actor Training*, ed. Alison Hodge (London: Routledge, 2010), 268–87.
3. Former Gardzienice actor Grzegorz Bral is responsible for coining the term; see Paul Allain, "Gardzienice: A Village, a Theatre, and a Cultural Crossroads," *New Theatre Quarterly* 2 (1993): 48–58.

4. Wlodzimierz Staniewski and Alison Hodge, *Hidden Territories: The Theatre of Gardzienice* (London: Routledge, 2004), 109.

5. See, among others, Wlodzimierz Staniewski, "*Iphigenia at A* . . .: Oxford Lecture," Magdalen College, Oxford, October 26, 2009.

6. Yana Zarifi, "Staniewski's Secret Alphabet of Gestures: Dance, Body and Metaphysics," in *The Ancient Dancer in the Modern World*, ed. Fiona Macintosh (Oxford: Oxford University Press, 2010), 399.

7. Mikhail Bakhtin, *Rabelais and His World*, trans. Hélène Iswolsky (Bloomington: Indiana University Press, 1984), 19.

8. Wlodzimierz Staniewski, "Baltimore Interview with Richard Schechner," *Drama Review* 113: 1 (1987): 137–63.

9. This is quoted in Paul Allain, *Gardzienice: Polish Theatre in Transition* (Amsterdam: Harwood Academic Publishers, 1997), 39.

10. Jerzy Grotowski, *Towards a Poor Theatre*, ed. Eugenio Barba (London: Methuen, 1969), 69.

11. Richard Brestoff, *The Great Acting Teachers* (Lyme, NJ: Smith and Kraus, 1995), 155.

12. Thomas Richards, *At Work with Grotowski on Physical Actions* (London: Routledge, 1995), 21.

13. Grotowski, *Towards a Poor Theatre*, 188–89.

14. Ibid., 151 and 174.

15. I have translated the passage from its transcription in Greek, in Konstantinos Themelis, *Enestos Diarkeias: Synantisi me ton Jerzy Grotowski [Present Continuous: A Meeting with Jerzy Grotowski]* (Athens: Indiktos, 2001), 125.

16. Grotowski, *Towards a Poor Theatre*, 165–66.

17. This dialogue between Grotowski and Staniewski should not be seen as one-way. Shortly after Staniewski left, with the clear intention of exploring the musicality of marginalized ethnic minorities, Grotowski entered his "Theatre of the Sources" period (1976–82). Expeditions to Haiti, Mexico, India, eastern Poland, and Nigeria and the idea of roots became central to his new vision of artistic discoveries, as outlined in Lisa Wolford, "Grotowski's Vision for the Actor," in Hodge, *Actor Training*, 191–208. Also, in 1991, Rodowicz, Staniewski's collaborator, visited Pontedera, Grotowski's base in Italy, and worked with Grotowski on folk songs, as documented in Allain, *Gardzienice: Polish Theatre in Transition*, 55.

18. Anna Czekanowska even contrasts ritual songs with entertainment songs and concludes that "the music of entertainment is definitely Polish," in *Polish Folk Music: Slavonic Heritage, Polish Tradition, Contemporary Trends* (Cambridge: Cambridge University Press, 1997), 103.

19. In 2003 Rychly and Rodowicz cofounded Theatre Association Chorea, so as to explore further their discoveries related to the music of ancient Greece, their "dream of capturing" the "living brilliance" of ancient music, as affirmed in Maciej Rychly, "Untitled Note," in sleeve notes to *Metamorfozy, Music of Ancient Greece*, Universal 5423692 (2000), 9, compact disc.

20. Staniewski and Hodge, *Hidden Territories*, 128.

21. This is an edited section from an extensive interview between Anna-Helena McLean and the author in London, in December 2009.

22. Staniewski and Hodge, *Hidden Territories*, 82–92.

23. See Zarifi, "Staniewski's Secret Alphabet," for a broad contextualization of Staniewski's system of gestures.

24. In Phoebe Hoban, "Euripides in Bacchanal (It's Also One of His Plays)," *New York Times*, April 13, 2005, E7.

25. For a detailed transcription and analysis of the musico-textual properties of the surviving fragments, refer to Egert Pöhlmann and Martin L. West, *Documents of Ancient Greek Music: The Extant Melodies and Fragments Edited and Transcribed with Commentary* (Oxford: Oxford University Press, 2001).

26. The methodological continuum from nationalism to universalism is discussed in Dobrochna Ratajczakowa, "In Transition: 1989–2004," trans. and ed. Paul Allain and

Grzegorz Ziolkowski, *Contemporary Theatre Review* 15: 1 (2005): 17–27. The symbiotic or antagonistic coexistence of the literary and visual strands in Polish theater is the thematic axis in Kathleen Cioffi, "New (and Not-So-New) Alternatives," *Contemporary Theatre Review* 15: 1 (2005): 69–83. Oliver Taplin investigates the icocentric and philodramatist approaches in *Pots & Plays: Interactions between Tragedy and Greek Vase-Painting of the Fourth Century B.C.* (Los Angeles: Getty Publications, 2007), 22–26.

27. See Rychly, "Untitled Note," 12.

28. In Allain, *Gardzienice: Polish Theatre in Transition*, 60.

29. Staniewski and Hodge, *Hidden Territories*, 65.

30. Staniewski is quoted as saying: "In Poland we speak of *pieknoduch*, one who is cultivating his own beauty. I wanted to go into the eye of the cyclone or, if you like, the heart of darkness," in Donald Hutera, "Religion and Ritual," *Glasgow Herald*, May 1, 1989, n.pag. One such figure for Staniewski is the legendary violin player Magur. For the ancient Greek notion of *paideia*, see Giovanni Comotti, *Music in Greek and Roman Culture*, trans. Rosaria V. Munson (Baltimore: Johns Hopkins University Press, 1991); David Binning Monro, *The Modes of Ancient Greek Music* (Oxford: Elibron Classics, 2005); and Wlodzimierz Staniewski, *"Gardzienice" Practising the Humanities* (Gardzienice: Dialog and Institut Teatralny, 2005), CD-ROM.

31. See Staniewski, *"Iphigenia at A."*

32. Mikhail Bakhtin, *Toward a Philosophy of the Act*, trans. Vadim Liapunov, ed. Vadim Liapunov and Michael Holquist (Austin: University of Texas Press, 1993), 2.

33. Barry Ross, "Challenges Facing Theories of Music and Language Co-evolution," *Journal of the Musical Arts in Africa* 6 (2009): 61–76.

34. Staniewski and Hodge, *Hidden Territories*, 64.

35. Comotti, *Music*, 6.

36. Staniewski also quotes Milton in his research for fragments of musicality: "Milton is positive in saying, 'Look for the pieces,'" in Staniewski and Hodge, *Hidden Territories*, 23.

37. See Wlodzimierz Staniewski, *Gardzienice, Poland*, ed. Peter Hulton and Dorinda Hulton (Exeter: Arts Archives, 1993), DVD.

38. Thomas Hilder, e-mail to the author, February 10, 2010.

39. See also Comotti, *Music*, 47.

40. Staniewski and Hodge, *Hidden Territories*, 63.

41. Staniewski understands devising as "musical dramaturgy," and elaborates on this principle in "Carmina Burana: Director's Note," in *Hidden Territories*, Arts Archives CD-ROM, ed. Wlodzimierz Staniewski, Alison Hodge. and Peter Hulton (London: Routledge, 2004). Albert Hunt sees even the visual elements of the performances in close-knit connection to musicality: "the musicality of Gardzienice's theatre language is made up of a highly organized structure of complex images," in "Gardzienice: An Introduction," in Staniewski, *Gardzienice, Poland*, ed. Hulton and Hulton, 3–12.

42. See Staniewski, *Gardzienice* 18.

43. For the most extensive discussion of this principle in the literature, see Staniewski and Hodge, *Hidden Territories*, 72–101.

44. Czekanowska, *Polish Folk Music*, 131.

45. Socrates is well known as a proponent of a dialogic concept of philosophical inquiry. His student, Plato, discusses several aspects of the idea of shame (example given, as an ethics underlying friendship or, in the public sphere, as a motivator of justice), in several of his works, such as *The Apology of Socrates*, *Crito*, *The Symposium*, and *Gorgias*. The concept of Zeami's "flower" has been much discussed and debated; the purpose of the actor is to allow his or her "flower" to blossom. Staniewski proposes this as the obligation of the partner: to make their colleague's "flower" flourish, in Staniewski and Hodge, *Hidden Territories*, 82.

46. Bakhtin, *Rabelais and His World*, 19.

47. Ibid., 474.
48. Staniewski, *Practising the Humanities*, n.pag.
49. Bakhtin, *Rabelais and His World*, 474.
50. Hutera, "Religion and Ritual," n.pag.
51. Niziolek Grzegorz. "Gardzienice: 'Elektra,'" *Le Théâtre en Pologne–The Theatre in Poland* 1–2 (2004): 41–44.
52. Staniewski, *Practising the Humanities*, n.pag.
53. Staniewski and Hodge, *Hidden Territories*, 97.
54. Bakhtin, *Rabelais and His World*, 353.
55. Michael Billington, in his review of *Elektra*, admits that the company reminded him of the fact that Greek tragedy was intended as a "total theatre experience rather than a restrained poetic event," in "Metamorphoses/Elektra," *The Guardian,* February 2, 2006), online. Available: http://www.guardian.co.uk/stage/2006/feb/02/theatre?INTCMP=SRCH. March 10, 2011. A cross-reading of the notion of choreatic expression and Gardzienice's work can be found in Bronislaw Wildstein, "Theatrical Mediations and Dionysian Intoxication: On 'Metamorphoses' by Gardzienice," trans. Agnieska Ginko-Humphries and Carl Humphries, in Staniewski, Hodge, and Hulton, *Hidden Territories*, n.pag.
56. The first formulation of the principle is derived from an interview with Yale voice coach Pamela Prather, who visited Gardzienice in 2008 and worked with performers and trainees. For a discussion of the latter formulation, look at Staniewski and Hodge, *Hidden Territories*, 87.
57. For the most detailed discussion of Gardzienice's influence in the literature, consult Alison Hodge, "Gardzienice's Influence in the West," *Contemporary Theatre Review* 15: 1 (2005): 59–68. See also Dariusz Kosinski, *Polish Theatre Perspectives: Theatre "Out of the Spirit of Music"* 2: 2 (2011). In Poland, companies inspired by Gardzienice or founded by ex-members are Pogranicze (led by Krzysztof Czyzewski and Malgorzata Sporek-Czyzewska), Muzyka Kresow (by Jan Bernard), Teatr Wiejski Wegajty (by Wolfgang Niklaus and Malgorzata Dzygadlo-Niklaus), Studium Teatralne (by Piotr Borowski), Teatr Piesn Kozla (by Grzegorz Bral and Anna Zubrzycka), Teatr Zar (by Jaroslaw Fret and apprentices of the Grotowski Institute) and Theatre Association Chorea (by Tomasz Rodowicz and Maciej Rychly). Companies working in other countries are Double Edge Theatre in the United States (by Stacy Klein), Theatre Gargantua in Canada (by Jacquie P. Thomas), Tanto Theatre in Austria (by Jan Tabaka and Susanna Tabaka-Pillhofer), Stella Polaris in Norway (by Per Borg), Earthfall in Wales (by Jim Ennis), Oyfn Veg in Germany (by Christian Bredholt and Uta Motz), The Quick and the Dead (by Alison Hodge), Moon Fool (by Anna-Helena McLean, Christopher Sivertsen, and Ian Morgan) and Waving Not Drowning (by Andrei Biziorek) in the UK. Also, artists who have been influenced by Staniewski's vision include British director and National Theatre associate Katie Mitchell, Viliam Docolomansky, artistic director of Farm in the Cave, and Yale voice coach Pamela Prather, among others.
58. CD-ROMs, videos, and DVDs of performances, documentaries on expeditions and training, CDs published by the Ancient Orchestra project, and a frequently updated website all contribute to the dissemination of the work. See Staniewski, *Practising the Humanities*; Staniewski, *Gardzienice, Poland*, ed. Hulton and Hulton; and Staniewski, Hodge and Hulton, *Hidden Territories*.
59. Staniewski and Hodge, *Hidden Territories*, 47.
60. See Ian Cross and Iain Morley, "The Evolution of Music: Theories, Definitions and the Nature of the Evidence," in *Communicative Musicality*, ed. Stephen Malloch and Colwyn Trevarthen (Oxford: Oxford University Press, 2009), 61–82.
61. In Jill Dolan, *Utopia in Performance* (Ann Arbor: University of Michigan Press, 2005), 6.

PART SEVEN

Performativity as Community

Building on the ideas developed in the last chapter, of musicality and chorality in the work of Gardzienice, where a group ethos informs all activities, the following part analyzes the dramaturgies and the politics that become apparent when song and dance are performed by groups of people collectively. These performances are also watched/listened to by another group that is interpellated by the first. Arising from a collective expression, the volume or spectacle produced has a greater sensual impact, the texture can be more diverse, and the overall effect more theatrical, as described by Macpherson in his analysis of *Cats*. The effect of 1,000 drummers at the London Olympics Opening Ceremony, the massed voices of the audience participating in the performance of "Hey Jude," the 2008 drummers in rows at the Beijing opening ceremony, and the thousands of Tai Chi performers dancing in unison are all far greater and more spectacular than could be achieved by any single performer.[1] Spectacle is sensually affecting and exciting; spaces and patterns are articulated and altered, the gaps between the bodies are as important as the shapes and gestures of the individual bodies, and the sounds of massed voices produce felt vibrations and stimulating textures.

Conversely, spectacle is less likely to produce the nuanced arguments of drama or an emotional sung characterization in a musical. The spectacle itself can be thrilling, but identification and empathy with performer or character is sacrificed. Large group spectacle valorizes the sense of community cohesion and creates a visual impact, but reifies the bodies of the individual performers who become automata in a Fordist production line (figure 30). Even within spectacle there is diversity, though; groups of performers can be directed or costumed in ways that allow individuality to appear or in ways that celebrate the unanimity and conformity of the group. The corps de ballet can be dressed in identical costume and perform identical steps, the aim of which is to represent a society from which the principal emerges as the single, unique, and identifiably different body. Martha Graham's *Chronicle* (1936) contains a section entitled "Devastation, Homelessness, Exile" that is rigorously designed and performed so that the uniformity in the pathways and groupings is breathtaking.[2] The same is true of massed choirs performing Carl Orff's *Carmina Burana* with the Berlin Philharmonic Orchestra.[3] The massed choral group, whose combined sound organizes a complex and dynamic sensual impact, is subsumed into a coherent foil from which the principals can emerge.

Figure 30 Busby Berkeley famously used massed groups to spectacular effect. Photo: Warner Bros./Photofest. © Warner Bros.

On the other hand ensemble performances can occur in both song and dance; for example, in madrigal or barbershop singing each part is sung by one vocalist. In postmodern dance as described by Sebesta all the performers are treated equally, male and female dancers perform the same gestures, but all participants are also individuals. This alternation between group action and individual gesture can be seen in "Enter Achilles" (1995) performed by DV8.[4] These, chorus and ensemble, are the two types of group performances that are celebrated in the chapters below. Bethany Hughes analyzes the functions of the chorus, while Millie Taylor critiques the politics of the ensemble.

However, it is in group performance that song and dance might also be divorced; song's key gesture is audible, while dance's key gesture is visible. A group of dancers who dance in unison can all be seen individually; their gestures are available to the audience whose members can focus on seeing individual performers if they choose, even though the power of the performance may result from the action of the group. A singing chorus, though they can be seen as individuals, cannot be heard as individuals; in fact choirs and choruses are encouraged to blend their voices into a harmonious symphony. That is not to say that a unison moment is not noticeable within a choral work, but that individual performers are subsumed into the group more completely in their essential gestures than chorus dancers. Spectators and audiences are performatively established through their role in the interpretation of gestures, but more importantly the issue of audibility, or its lack, is the surprising feature that makes communal singing popular as a tool of confidence building and community cohesion.

In the UK "singing in choirs is one of the nation's favorite pastimes with over 25,000 registered choirs and at least half a million members."[5] *Last Choir Standing* (2008) was a television reality competition for which sixty choirs were chosen.[6] Audiences voted week by week until the final three choirs sang for the prize. The winning choir, Only Men Aloud, signed a recording contract with Universal Music. Other documentaries have celebrated the work of the national Rock Choir, which has over 16,000 members in more than 200 towns in the UK, and the government-funded Sing Up program for schools provides training and advice for choir leaders and participants, focusing especially on younger people.

One figure to emerge from this proliferation of community singing has been Gareth Malone, famous for making television documentaries of his attempts to create community choirs in diverse locations. Under his leadership a group of military wives whose husbands were on a six-month tour of duty in Afghanistan came together to sing in a choir that performed at the Homecoming Medals Parade for their husbands and then for the Queen and Royal Family at the Royal Albert Hall during the annual Festival of Remembrance. In a series called *Sing While You Work* (2012), Malone created choirs in four different workplaces, the Lewisham NHS Trust, the Royal Mail, Manchester Airport, and Severn Trent Water Company. His purpose in creating these choirs is to develop community and to improve working relationships, but, as with all reality television programs, the filming does something slightly different. The choir sings as a group, but individuals are heard at auditions, in solos within songs, and in moments of rehearsal. Individuals are also interviewed and become characters within the narrative of the choir and the program. In this way the choir is a choral group that learns to operate as a community, but as it coheres during the development of the choir and program, the group comes to be perceived as individuals by the viewers of the television program. This reflects the discourse between the two chapters that follow: between choir and ensemble, community or community of individuals.

What is clear, though, is that the act of singing together leads participant groups to become a community in a process that extends beyond the rehearsal or performance and leads ultimately to greater empathy.[7] Musical participation aligns expectations, attention, and affective states and has an efficacious effect on social interaction and social action.[8] Community music-making or dancing to music as a group allows participants to experience a temporal framework within which to organize their experiences with the music and with each other, producing entrainment. But audiences are not participants until we factor in the effect of mirror neurons through which the brains of audience members are activated almost as though they were doing the activity themselves. Christian Keyser explains that not only does doing an activity as a group activate the reward areas of the brain and bind the participants together, but that experiencing music and dance as a group could activate the same reward areas.[9] The participants singing "Hey Jude" in the London Opening Ceremony and those watching the drumming at Beijing would both experience entrainment and neural stimulation from being part of those ceremonies as well as from the sensual excess of the sound and gestures of the choral spectacle.

The performativity in the next two chapters derives from the experience of community articulated in and resulting from group practices by the chorus and the ensemble. These chapters articulate these two types of group, but they also articulate the different approaches in this volume. Hughes considers the functions of the chorus as community, responding to the question: how do song and dance function as physical and material gestures, as dimensions or perhaps subsets of music theater works? Taylor, on the other hand, explores the politics of the ensemble and addresses the question of the performance of identity for characters, performers. and audiences within and through the song and dance of music theater. In this way these two chapters not only juxtapose chorus and ensemble but are also complementary in their focus on dramaturgical function or structural politics. Finally, the two chapters encompass a journey from the dramatic work through its performance to the ways in which dramaturgical structure can represent a contemporary politics, forcing contemplation of the wider world. In this way these two chapters also mirror the diversity of the volume as it analyzes works, performances, and contexts through function, identity, and diversity.

NOTES

1. Online. Available: http://www.youtube.com/watch?v=JsDY1Ha83M8. October 17, 2012.
2. From a talk by Catherine Seago entitled "Devising for Dance: A Triadic Perspective," Winchester Theater Royal, October 11, 2012. Photographs of a reconstruction of excerpts from the work by the New School for Liberal Arts (2006) are available at http://www.flickr.com/photos/newschool/sets/72157600169087419/detail/. October 17, 2012.
3. Online. Available: http://www.youtube.com/watch?v=ig1Dx06IDXU&feature=related. October 17, 2012.
4. Conceived and directed for the stage by Lloyd Newson. Adapted for the screen by Lloyd Newson and Clara van Gool. Online. Available: http://www.youtube.com/watch?v=7c9ToyDs3mY. December 21, 2012.
5. Online. Available: http://www.bbc.co.uk/lastchoirstanding/about/about.shtml. September 27, 2012.
6. July 5–August 30, 2008.
7. Ian Cross, "Music as a Social and Cognitive Process," in *Language and Music as Cognitive Systems*, ed. Patrick Rebuschat, Martin Rohrmeier, John A. Hawkins, and Ian Cross (Oxford: Oxford University Press, 2011), 323–24.
8. Ibid., 324–26.
9. Christian Keysers, "From Mirror Neurons to Kinaesthetic Empathy," keynote presentation, "Kinaesthetic Empathy: Concepts and Contexts," Manchester University, April 22–23, 2010.

CHAPTER 16

Singing the Community

The Musical Theater Chorus as Character

BETHANY HUGHES

In the 2012 NBC television program *Smash*, a new Broadway musical is being created and produced.[1] A minor character discovers a coworker has been cast in the show and labels her coworker as part of the chorus. The minor character is corrected and asked to call it the ensemble. Standing corrected, she goes on to liken the distinction between chorus and ensemble to the nonexistent difference between a garbage collector and a sanitation worker. This example of the attitude toward the chorus that exists in contemporary culture is telling. The chorus is seen as something that cleans up a musical, dancing and singing a bit while the important characters change costumes. That is a simplistic and inaccurate definition. The chorus is not a distraction; rather it is a unique character, possessing specific qualities and functions that are impossible for other characters to exhibit. The chorus is a distinct character, a manifestation of community, a connecting force between audience and story.

On October 10, 1947, the newest Rodgers and Hammerstein musical opened at the Majestic Theatre in New York.[2] Coming on the heels of the hugely successful writing partners' productions of *Oklahoma!* (1943) and *Carousel* (1945) as well as in the wake of winning an Academy Award for a song written for *State Fair* (1945), expectations were high for *Allegro*. Running a modest 315 performances, the show had mixed reviews. Critical feedback included phrases such as "excitingly unconventional" and "grave disappointment," while Brooks Atkinson of the *New York Times* declared *Allegro* had "just missed the final splendor of a perfect work of art."[3] *Allegro*'s troubled status is revealed when one considers that as of December 2012 there were 103 licensed productions of *Oklahoma!* scheduled for 2013, whereas there were none for *Allegro*.[4] Even though the production was not a commercial success, it has been praised by such notable Broadway artists as Stephen Sondheim for its forward-thinking inclusion of set design that attempted seamless, cinematic scene changes as well as its iteration of what would later be called the concept musical.[5]

One of the unusual aspects of *Allegro* was its use of the chorus. Rodgers and Hammerstein expanded the role of the chorus to include commentary and narration in the style of a Greek chorus. Because the chorus is unusually foregrounded in *Allegro*, it provides a clear case study to explore what a chorus can do and how it functions. The original Broadway production of *Allegro* will serve as the site of this chapter's exploration and analysis of the musical theater chorus.

Since antiquity the chorus has been recognized as a distinct character. Aristotle wrote of the chorus's importance to successful tragedy in his *Poetics*, stating that "the Chorus too should be regarded as one of the actors; it should be an integral part of the whole, and share in the action."[6] Greek playwrights incorporated choruses into tragedies singing, dancing, chanting, and speaking. A modern musical theater chorus is hardly different; it, too, can be regarded as *one* of the characters. As one of the characters, and one specific kind of character hardly matched in any other theatrical genre, it achieves the simultaneous performance and presentation of community by virtue of its presence on stage. It possesses intimate knowledge of the inner lives of other characters, understands the implications of other characters' choices, and connects to the audience through alternately including and distancing it. The chorus, while consisting of discrete embodiments, displays perpetual congruity with individuals and the community, producing a unique presence that constructs and responds to the world of the musical and its audience.

It is important to note that there is a difference between a chorus and an ensemble in musical theater. NBC's *Smash* might not make a distinction, but an ensemble is distinct from the character of a chorus in a musical. Since the chorus's identity is centrally located in song and the ensemble phenomenon often occurs within song as well, looking to those who study music is wise in trying to form a working definition of both ensemble and chorus. In John Potter's brief discussion of ensemble singing for the *Cambridge Companion to Singing*, he notes that a choir is distinct from an ensemble in the number of persons assigned to a part.[7] In a choir several singers sing one part, whereas in an ensemble only one singer is assigned to each part. Likewise, in instrumental terms one can think of a chorus part as a second violin section in an orchestra and an ensemble member as the second violin player in a string quartet. In this example it is not the size of the whole group or the line being played that differentiates the two, but the number of instruments playing each musical line. Potter's definition is readily applied to the chorus of a musical. The songs or harmony lines sung by a chorus are almost entirely sung by multiple performers, with all members of the chorus, singing at the same time.

Jessica Sternfeld offers another difference between chorus and ensemble. In her book *The Megamusical*, Sternfeld briefly mentions the song "Masquerade" from *Phantom of the Opera* (1986). In a passing comment she states that the song is "the only true chorus number (as opposed to ensembles sung by principal players) in the show."[8] For Sternfeld a musical theater chorus number is, at least partially, defined by an absence of named principal players. While Sternfeld seems to rely on definitions of chorus and ensemble similar to those offered by Potter to inform her comment, her parenthetical observation suggests more. A dialectical relationship between chorus and ensemble is posited by Sternfeld's positioning of the two. It is not the absence of named characters that defines a chorus, which could reduce all roles in musical theater to a binary of using named/unnamed characters, but rather a related opposition on the continuum of groups of people.[9] Some characters are personified by a narrower range of expressions, which increases their specificity, often leading to a name, but that also weakens their ability to represent what a single person cannot contain, a community for example.

In thinking of the chorus in a musical, its affinity for Scott McMillin's definition of "lyric time" is obvious.[10] A chorus rarely participates in dialogue, relying almost exclusively upon song to express itself as a character. Because of this the characteristics of lyric time are located within the chorus. Expansion, doubling, repetition, and its ability to highlight difference and similarity are clear starting points. A chorus sings songs introduced by other characters, in support of and with other characters, and its own songs provide possibilities of repetition and expansion by other characters and itself. In doubling or harmonizing the melody of a song the chorus can enact multiple positions through the sheer number of chorus members singing, even as it might also enact a symbolic joining with another character through shared musical material. A chorus participates routinely in the repetition of musical material, instead of following the cause–and-effect structure of most characters' trajectories in a musical. Instead it is able to perform multiple, discrete identities within a single show. A through line or superobjective, to borrow terms from actor training, hardly exists for a chorus. Because of these unusual characteristics and potentials located in the chorus, the extension of McMillin's lyric time to the chorus can be made. The chorus in *Allegro* is a lyric character that defines, creates, reveals, and contrasts with the characters, story, audience, and itself.

McMillin's conception of the "ensemble effect," a moment of coming together and bursting forth in song or dance that occurs so often in musical theater is just one example of the power of many people joining together as one.[11] Though McMillin focuses on principal and supporting characters joining with the chorus to create the "ensemble effect," it is clear that some of its power comes simply from the number of people on stage doing or singing the same thing at the same time. This power is a characteristic of the chorus; its presence brings the hint or the promise of energy and strength.

The chorus actively creates and participates in congruous relationships with other characters, itself, and the audience. It performs in harmony with other characters expressed through its knowledge of their inner lives as well as its ability to sing their songs. It enacts community through its euphonious singing, showing and telling the personality of the community. It creates a space for intimate connection between the audience and the characters by explaining and commenting through song on the story, characters, and emotions present in the musical. It can act as commentator and narrator, as character or as multiple characters, and it can bridge the gap between stage and audience communities. The chorus in *Allegro* provides many examples of these various, often distinctive, functions.

THE CHORUS AS COMMENTATOR

Many different characters perform the role of narrator or commentator in musical theater.[12] In *Allegro* the chorus fills this role. Narration of plot events and commentary on action are two types of seemingly objective knowledge the chorus offers to the audience, filling in gaps in the story, and moving time forward or back, but always staying outside the action. These moments give the chorus the opportunity to tell the story and to express a seemingly objective viewpoint since narration always reveals a perspective. Importantly, a narrator or commentator might also be unreliable, offering thoughts or ideas that the audience is aware conflict with the onstage actions. This creates a dialectical relationship and challenges the audience to consider the themes being addressed.

The opening moment of *Allegro* shows a woman on a bed and, on the opposite side of the stage, a group of chorus members who introduce the woman, her husband, and the occasion: the birth of their son, Joseph Taylor Jr.[13] After a brief dialogue between the wife and husband (Marjorie and Joe Taylor) the chorus sings again, introducing the protagonist of the musical by describing the infant. This is an instance of narration that establishes the key characters. The chorus explains who people are and what is happening, but it can also provide information that explains how or why something is, or makes a judgment.

The chorus in *Allegro* also holds the role of commentator. The chorus is able to move between narration and commentary on the actions of principal characters, and between directly addressing the audience and addressing the principal characters. In "One Foot, Other Foot" the chorus sings about Joe learning to walk, with words that directly inform Joe of his newly earned freedom and autonomy: "now you can go wherever you like." The song is sung to Joe but it addresses the audience as well. The audience learns more than just who or what happened, but how to interpret the events. The chorus's commentary on the action, stressing the choices that Joe can now make and the ownership that accompanies the ability to choose—"the world belongs to Joe"—focuses the audience on information that prepares them to understand and interpret the rest of the show.

"Poor Joe" is a very short song the chorus sings three times, always commenting on an interaction between Joe and his love interest and eventual wife, Jenny. The first time the chorus sings it, Joe has brought Jenny home from a high school party. She makes herself available for a goodnight kiss, but Joe is unable to recognize this and does not kiss her. This short song describes the basic idea that adult life is complicated; with age comes confusion. The repetition of the exact same song in two other situations, also where Joe is conflicted between his desires for Jenny and for something else (propriety, professional aspirations, family loyalty) is telling. The song serves as a sonic reminder of past situations where Joe faced moments of conflict involving Jenny, and it is repeated at each of these moments of conflict until Joe succumbs to Jenny's influence. Although the same sequence is sung on each occasion, the repetition increases the effect of the commentary, drawing attention to these moments, and in repeating the same musical material reveals for the audience the resemblance between the moments and the motif of inner conflict brought about by Jenny. The commentary and the themes it reveals are thus emphasized through its repetition.

In *Allegro* the chorus also fills a narrative role in relating to the audience the inner thoughts or feelings of other characters. The chorus's special knowledge and access to these inner workings allows it to reveal characters in an intimate way. In act 1 when Joe is away from home studying at college, he is routinely distracted from his studies by thoughts of Jenny, visions of Jenny in reality. "Jenny glides across the stage" as the chorus sings of her home in Joe's heart.[14] The song is just a fragment, a line or two sung at a time. However, these fragments come into play later in the act, when Joe finally declares his love to Jenny. In previous scenes with Jenny, Joe does not speak eloquently or at length. As Joe interacts with Jenny after being away at college, he is moved to express his feelings, encouraged by the chorus as they speak lines from the fragments of song they sang earlier. As the chorus hums underneath, Joe is able finally to sing the fully formed song in its entirety, "You Are Never Away."[15] The chorus displays its prior knowledge of Joe's inner life, in singing fragments of the song in a previous scene as a prequel, while it also enables Joe to sing the song himself, but not alone. In this moment the chorus shapes the action of the scene, demonstrating remarkable power even as it is outside the action. The chorus participates in the creation of this new version of Joe, the Joe who is able to sing beautifully and poetically of his love and unbreakable connection to Jenny. The chorus knows Joe better than he does himself, and teaches him how to sing his self. The chorus sings in harmony with Joe, showing the congruity it possesses with him—or its manipulation of him.

Given the impossibility of discovering how the chorus knows, questions regarding the accuracy of what it knows arise. Does the chorus sing the truth? How can it be determined as truth? To answer these questions one can refer to the role of narrator and the performed events of the musical. Verifying the veracity of the chorus's knowledge occurs through tracing the narrative and comparing it to the claims made or information given by the chorus. In "Poor Joe" the chorus comments on the confusion that comes with age. This can be ascertained as truthful because other characters act out this confusion; Joe desires Jenny, is frustrated by his inability to rid himself of this desire, dates another woman, and eventually acquiesces to his yearnings for Jenny. This circuitous route to Jenny, performed by Joe, is an illustration of Joe's confusion with himself and with his relationships. While the chorus's knowledge is secret, it is also verifiable, tested by the events in the musical and proven by other characters.

THE CHORUS AS CHARACTER

The chorus is an unusual character because it has inside knowledge of other characters' thoughts, and can put thoughts or feelings into characters' minds. It can also present opposing viewpoints either on different occasions or by splitting itself into subgroups and presenting juxtaposing viewpoints. This results from the fact that it is sometimes inside and sometimes outside the events, and that it is comprised of a number of individuals.

The chorus's knowledge is broad, covering the actions of the characters and including personal information about individual members of that community. In contrast, a principal character such as Joe only knows about himself and what he sees through the actions of the plot. He is not privy to the private knowledge of others' desires, feelings, or thoughts in the same way the chorus is. The chorus knows more than a principal or supporting character.

In *Allegro* the chorus performs its knowledge of the onstage community in "Lovely Day for a Wedding." This song, near the end of the first act, occurs as Joe and Jenny prepare to marry. The entire population of Joe's hometown comes together, as they did at his birth, to sing in celebration of a significant life event, marriage. The song joyously expresses the town's feelings regarding the event, performing repetition not through repeated music but through repeated community support and happiness. However, the community reveals more than the joy it feels regarding the event. The first line of the song, "What a lovely day for a wedding! Not a cloud to darken the sky," connects with the scenes immediately preceding the wedding. It also connects with what the chorus knows that challenges the happiness of the event. The scene immediately preceding the song showed Joe returning home from his mother's funeral. His mother's openly stated objection to Jenny as a life partner for Joe and her deeply felt absence reverberate as the chorus sings of nothing darkening the sky during Joe's wedding. As the song continues, Jenny's father divulges his reservations about the marriage, and the chorus repeats his words, gossiping about what might go wrong. Then after a refrain the chorus breaks into two groups, relatives of Joe and relatives of Jenny. Each group chatters within their groups about the mismatch and speaks poorly of the other group. The chorus's knowledge in this situation is broad, knowing all parts of the onstage community. The chorus displays knowledge of an individual character's inner thoughts through the repetition of his words, and furthermore expands his thoughts to show that the community, too, questions the wisdom of the marriage. The chorus is simultaneously for and against the marriage, a dialectical position impossible for any other character to enact in this way. It does not have to make up its mind in the way a principal or supporting character must. The chorus can be of two minds without splitting into separate characters and without impacting on the congruity it holds with both of the represented communities in this scene.

The congruity the chorus expresses can be seen in act 2 of *Allegro*. "Come Home" is largely sung by Marjorie, Joe's mother, who is dead at the time of the song, but the chorus begins it. The song is akin to a vision, with Joe on stage at his desk and the chorus and Joe's father revealed behind a gauze curtain. The chorus sings, "We are the friends that you left behind. You need us, Joe—and we need."[16] This is a marked shift in tone and expression from the "Opening." The chorus is not merely expressing its feelings of longing for Joe, but rather is declaring its knowledge of what it needs and what Joe needs, too. It is not a public expression or speech, but a private communication directly from the mind of the townsfolk to the mind of Joe.[17] The chorus performs the character of the townspeople in such an intimate way because it represents the collective needs of that community and can articulate them from the inside. The chorus's knowledge of the inner lives of characters includes both those inside and those outside of the chorus, both individuals and the community.

Because no other character can understand the plot and actions to the extent the chorus does, it is also uniquely able to identify those who fit into a particular community and those alienated from it. In act 1 of *Allegro*, soon after Joe has gone away to college, a brief song occurs, "Wildcats," in which the chorus represents the college community. A cheerleader introduces it as "The Football Song," and Joe attempts to take part in the performance in his identity as a college student. He fails miserably, not knowing the right time or right words to join; he is glared at by those who know how to perform their inclusion in this society and leaves in shame.[18] Joe is clearly not of this place; it is not home. The chorus illustrates this more vividly than any book scene could by representing that community. The community knows the song, the gestures, and the words, performing them with aplomb, while Joe is surprised, late, and disgraced. The chorus's identification of Joe as an outsider complicates its relationship with him. The chorus has been Joe, voicing his thoughts as an infant; it has known Joe, revealing his own emotions to him. Yet it has also revealed itself as separate from him, commenting on events and choices; it has communicated directly to the audience, singing its difference from the events happening in the narrative.

Another characteristic that a chorus performs is the presence of multiple communities. This means that the chorus in these instances has a multiple presence. Identifiable subgroups of the town are listed in the libretto, including "drunks," "a church choir," and "children," who, during the opening number, in turn reprise previous musical passages describing the baby or introducing new musical material celebrating Joe's birth.[19] The chorus begins this song as a narrator but shifts within it to become multiple characters.

In the title song "Allegro," the chorus joins with Joe, his friend and fellow physician, Charlie, and a nurse, Emily. Joe and his friends sing of the dizzying speed of the life lived by Joe's patients and Joe himself since coming to work at a Chicago hospital. The chorus echoes Emily and joins Joe in singing about the hectic pace of life.[20] When the chorus begins singing, they are not seen but slowly they are revealed upstage of a gauze curtain and eventually fully revealed as the song moves into the "Allegro Ballet."[21] The dance reflects the "confusion and the futility" of Joe's life in Chicago. The chorus performs literal and multiple versions of the frenzied and pointless life that Joe unhappily lives. This moment of physical expansion presents various lives equally as lost as Joe's, but in different circumstances or expressions. It is an act of expansion of Joe's life and a characterization of one aspect of community in *Allegro*.

Joe is incapable of showing the variety of frenzied existences that surround him in Chicago; the chorus is capable of just that. It can enact the multiple selves of the city of Chicago, but these multiple, enacted selves also occur in other songs. "Yatata" in act 2 shows the complexity of the chorus' potential in a musical. The guests at a cocktail party hosted by Jenny and Joe in their Chicago home sing "Yatata." The guests are patients and colleagues of Joe's, fawning over the celebrity doctor Joe works for and desperately seeking attention and medication for their own perceived—and notably hypochondriac—health conditions.

On the surface the bodies of the chorus members perform the guests at the party, drinking, eating, and talking. On the musical level the lyrics and repetition of specific words, including the nonsense word "yatata," perform another function, commenting on the situation. "Yatata" is filled with lyrics such as "Broccoli Hogwash Balderdash," signifying that the communication occurring at the party is worthless.

The lyrics do contain clear sentences, but they either reveal a particularly distasteful moment of narcissism or sycophancy, or explain that the conversation at hand goes on and on but never arrives anywhere. The musical meaning, getting at the subtext of the scene, creates an enacted opposition to the physical event occurring in the scene. Interestingly the characters performed by the chorus are unaware that the words they say act in opposition to the movements they perform. The chorus performs two selves, one that acts and one that sings. But the singing self is ambiguous. Singing together, as the chorus does, is an act of community expression, showing cohesion and congruity with itself as community. However, lyrically the chorus subverts this community, pointing to the cracks in the facade, the moments so blatantly fatuous they cannot be taken seriously. This subversion is intended for the audience, since no character present in the scene on stage understands the lyrics as separate from the bodies' actions. Because of this a third self can be added to the chorus in this number, one that communicates a dialectical subtext to the audience.[22]

The repetition that occurs in "Yatata" is noteworthy. The word "yatata" is heard over 150 times in the song, with the possibility of many more given the measures that are to be repeated while dialogue occurs over them.[23] This repetition both lulls the audience with its droning nature and also draws attention to itself. It is a word spoken and sung but incapable of communicating anything, a signifier without a signified. This futile act of speaking a word impossible to understand becomes a symbol for futility itself, and for the pointless and monotonous lives of the community. In this case repetition overlays the several selves performed by the chorus, demonstrating the intricacy of the communities indicated and expressed by the chorus.

The multiple selves performed by the chorus are notable in other scenes in *Allegro*, too. In "Finale Ultimo" the chorus enacts various populations, including the people of Joe's hometown and the Chicago society inside which Joe practices. This scene is important because it highlights the dialectical relationship the chorus so often articulates in *Allegro*. The chorus performs both ends of the spectrum making demands on Joe, from the perspectives of the city and the small town. The chorus wants Joe to stay in Chicago and to leave Chicago. Two distinct groups, separated by costume, spacing, and set and lighting choices, physically represent these two poles on stage. In performing these communities the chorus does not privilege one aspect of itself, one side of the continuum. All variations within the community are expressed, though not all are equally valued as seen in "Yatata" above. The chorus is inimitably equipped to enact multiple selves in this way. No other character in *Allegro* can enact and honor both sides of an argument in the complex and clear manner the chorus can. Performing multiple selves and creating a dialectic within itself or with other aspects of a scene separates the chorus from other characters and indicates its special potential and function in this musical.

THE CHORUS AS COMMUNITY

The chorus's direct link to and representation of community in *Allegro* is undeniable. By virtue of its component parts and its unified expression, the chorus is the best suited of any musical theater character to play the part of the various communities Joe encounters. But community has a greater symbolic function in musical theater; community is both a destination for characters in a musical and an omnipresent environment for them. Principal and supporting characters move, think, speak, and act within the context of a community, whether it is physically present on stage in the form of the chorus or not. The community embodying the world of a musical possesses unique characteristics including specific knowledge, presence, and multiple potentialities.

How can one understand the chorus as a character who is always and never combined with other characters? Community provides one approach to explore this problem. Community encompasses individuals and also draws attention to each member's difference from the other members. The community is comprised of its members, but any one member does not represent the entire community: only one version of it. The chorus in *Allegro* performs many versions of the community in which Joe lives, one that is not bounded by geography or temporal or spatial conditions. The versions performed, which do not imply they are the only versions of the community possible, explore the world Joe inhabits, always defining him, always enfolding him, always revealing his separation from it. Joe and the chorus acting together perform the complex relationship an individual has with community: it is alternately a home and a prison. One he inhabits organically as an extension of himself; the other is a constant reminder of the space between him and it. Through this enacted ambiguity the contradictory and sometimes antagonistic nature of Joe's relationship to the community can be exposed and explored.

The narrowly located presence of Joe in *Allegro* is highlighted by the widespread presence of the chorus. Joe is always in one place at one time; he may think about others, but he is only present in one. However, the chorus has the potential to be anywhere and any time. The chorus is the townspeople, the students at college, Joe's patients, and representatives of the big-city lifestyle. But they are also on stage speaking to Joe and communicating with the audience throughout the musical. The chorus is not merely located apart from Joe, representing people physically around him at a given time; it is also with Joe, connected to him as an iteration of community. He is part of the community, and so the chorus is a part of Joe. Its presence is felt and seen in multiple locations simultaneously.

In *Allegro* the chorus takes on many roles, as discussed above. It is complex and complicating to the characters and events on stage and reaches into the auditorium, touching the audience and directly implicating them in the performance. The chorus fashions itself as a surrogate for and a guide for the audience. Early in the first act members of the chorus enter and speak in unison, addressing the audience and making them feel that the audience is Joe.[24] The chorus tells the audience members what they are supposed to be thinking, the thoughts of an infant Joe. In this way the chorus forms the audience into a character in the musical, implying that they are also actors.[25] The chorus speaks for Joe; the audience thinks for Joe. Both chorus and audience become Joe. The character of Joe is located in the bodies of the chorus members, the bodies of the audience members, and the body of the actor who will eventually portray the character for the remainder of the musical. This act of incorporating the audience into the principal actor is one initiated and accomplished by the chorus.

In addition to integrating the audience into the protagonist, this act additionally integrates the chorus into the audience. Both are outside the singular body that eventually performs Joe; therefore both are spectators of the character they perform. The chorus is an audience, watching itself. The distance that the act of watching suggests delineates the chorus as both inside the action and events of the musical and outside. The chorus encompasses and is separate; it is present and absent from the community it performs. The audience is, too, present and absent, present in the theater, spatially and temporally located near the actors on stage, but absent from the events occurring.

The audience and chorus share another distinctive quality, secret knowledge. The chorus and audience are privy to information about characters, community, events, and inner lives that other characters are not. Both can lay claim to omniscience, though neither can quite live up to it. The audience witnesses everything there is to see in *Allegro*, but that does not mean it knows everything that could be known. In contrast, the chorus regularly dispenses knowledge of other characters, events, and commentary on both that cannot be traced to its witnessing of onstage action. The chorus knows what has been secret from the audience and, in many cases, the other characters. But the chorus does not witness all the action like the audience. It is not always present and does not know all that happens. The audience's knowledge is secret in that it sees all and yet remains unseen. The chorus's knowledge is secret in that the source of its knowledge cannot be unearthed.

The audience's and chorus's secret knowledge is informed by their privileged access. Both are present at public and private moments. Both witness events in which they are not visibly present, such as when the chorus is upstage of a gauze curtain, but are physically present. Their bodies are not limited by the space and time implied by the narrative. They have access to events impossible for them to attend. Access to any and all events that occur on stage is unavailable for other characters. Principal and supporting characters are bound by their actual bodies, unable to be in two or more places at once. The chorus and audience are multiple, present and absent on- and offstage; they see, hear, and know.

THE MUSICAL THEATER CHORUS

Much has been said about the longing for or rejection of community seen in many musicals, and the songs of the chorus appear intimately tied to the expression of fulfillment or, alternatively, the denial of this ideal community life. In addition, the self-expression that is performed in song mentioned by McMillin and echoed by scholars such as Raymond Knapp ensures that the songs a chorus sings are active and pregnant sites from which to understand the character of a chorus.[26] In this examination of *Allegro* the chorus has been defined by its function, its relationships, and its song. These three aspects have been explored in terms of congruity or incongruity. The chorus performs congruity with itself, other characters, and the audience. Through song the chorus can inform other characters and the audience of important characters and events; it can comment on these same characters and events. In this way it gives the audience insight into what has happened, why it happened, and what is going to be the result. It also sings to reveal the inner lives of other characters. Song, as used by the chorus, opens and closes lines of thought and inquiry. It works to focus the audience on what is important, what is essential. Without "One Foot, Other Foot" the audience watching *Allegro* does not know if the development of Joe from infant to toddler is merely a milestone to note and move forward from, or if it is a significant moment pointing to themes that will be worked out over the course of the musical. Song works to shape the story and the reception of that story.

The many relationships the chorus possesses also have a creative force. In *Allegro* the chorus establishes its relationship with the audience through implicating the audience as fellow actor, tying the two together for the remainder of the musical. The chorus relates to Joe both as an extension of him, speaking his thoughts and feelings before he can even formulate them, and as a benevolent observer who can identify what he is experiencing and sympathize with him. The relationship the chorus develops with itself is the most complex. The chorus is the community, performing presence and absence while expressing intimate and distant knowledge. In "Yatata" the chorus performs community, sings subversion, and resides in the liminal space of knowing and not knowing itself. These various relationships are all constructed through the songs of the chorus. In "Opening," the chorus narrates the event, introduces three main characters, and demonstrates the reaction of the community, showing through their song the importance of Joe and the intense connection the community feels to him. Thus the "Opening" chorus shifts from a description of the baby to an expression of the entire town's joy at his birth, and it is the fluidity with which the chorus is able to mutate between its various subject positions, articulated in separate sections above, that is perhaps its most important feature.

Songs sung by the chorus are powerful. A song can give information, comment to explain a particularly important moment, or reveal intimate information about a character's inner thoughts, desires, or dreams. A song works performatively to form a relationship, complicate one, and even to make actors where there used to be only audience members. When the chorus sings in *Allegro*, it is both inside and outside the world, singing about the world to the audience and participating in the world on stage. Through song the chorus shares in the audience's gaze and draws the audience into the action of the musical. Song enables the chorus to form relationships, impact the audience and other characters, and fulfill the functions assigned to it. Most importantly, the performative power of song creates the existence of the chorus as a discrete character. It is not a collection of individuals, nor a sanitation worker, ignored and underappreciated. Through song, the chorus performs its identity as a singular character, though multiply embodied.[27] Song works to make the character called the chorus visible, audible, and performative.

ACKNOWLEDGMENTS

The research, the initial presentation, and drafting of this chapter were completed while the author worked as a grant writer for the non-profit company Music Theatre of Wichita.

1. "Enter Mr. DiMaggio," *Smash*, NBC (20 February 2012).
2. "Allegro," Internet Broadway Database. Online. Available: http://ibdb.com/production.php?id=1787. November 27, 2012.
3. "Oscar Hammerstein II," preface to Oscar Hammerstein, *Allegro* (New York: Alfred A Knopf, 1948), x.
4. Searching for both *Allegro* and *Oklahoma!* in the licensed performance listings that the Rodgers and Hammerstein Organization maintains reveals the popularity of the latter and the absence of the former in current musical theater repertoire. Online. Available: http://www.rnh.com/now_playing.html. November 27, 2012.
5. *Out of My Dreams: Oscar Hammerstein II*, PBS, March 3, 2012.
6. Aristotle, *Poetics* (Mineola, NY: Dover Publications, 1997), 36.
7. John Potter, "Ensemble Singing," in *The Cambridge Companion to Singing*, ed. John Potter (Cambridge: Cambridge University Press, 2000), 158–64.
8. Jessica Sternfeld, *The Megamusical* (Bloomington: Indiana University Press, 2006).
9. Further study of the idea of a continuum in musical theater groupings should take place, exploring moments of multiple bodies singing one thing, many things and the area in between. The quintet "Tonight" in *West Side Story* is an instance where five characters sing individual lines, but where the possibilities for multiple voices singing one line are often explored. In the vocal score published in 2000, created to serve also as a piano/conductor score, a note states that if the scene is staged with more than the designated five characters the Jets and Sharks should sing with their respective leaders. Leonard Bernstein and Stephen Sondheim, *Vocal Score West Side Story* (Milwaukee, WI: Boosey & Hawkes, 2000).
10. Scott McMillin, *The Musical as Drama* (Princeton, NJ: Princeton University Press, 2006).
11. McMillin, *The Musical as Drama*, 80–81.
12. Lead characters such as Huckleberry Finn in *Big River* or the Balladeer in *Assassins* often serve as narrators or commentators, but groups such as the household servants in *The Secret Garden* also perform the function.
13. Hammerstein, *Allegro*, 3.
14. Ibid., 51.
15. Ibid., 67.
16. Ibid., 145.
17. The support for the song as a direct, private communication rather than a figment of Joe's imagination or byproduct of his own dissatisfaction with his practice in Chicago is shown in the final scene of act 2 when the chorus sings a section of "Come Home." In this scene some chorus members are costumed as Chicago residents and some as residents of Joe's hometown. The chorus's spoken lines in this scene indicate that the voice that Joe recognizes and is eventually persuaded by is the voice connected to the chorus of townspeople. While the townspeople are described as existing in Joe's mind in the libretto, in both of these scenes their embodied presence locates them in the space of Joe's mind and in his immediate surroundings, suggesting their physical presence in the hometown. This repetition highlights the spatial differences the chorus performs, both present and absent, as it communicates the inner desires of the townspeople for Joe's physical presence with them.
18. Hammerstein, *Allegro*, 40–41.
19. Ibid., 6–7.
20. Richard Rodgers and Oscar Hammerstein II, *Allegro*, vocal score (New York: Williamson Music, 1948), 203–8.
21. Hammerstein, *Allegro*, 133–35.
22. For McMillin's discussion of music's ability to reach and reveal subtext, transforming it into song and movement that can be shared and most importantly performed, see *The Musical as Drama*, 76.

23. Rodgers and Hammerstein, *Allegro*, vocal score, 178–90.
24. Ibid., 11.
25. The complication of the appearance of Joe on stage in *Allegro* is significant and will only be touched on in this chapter. Until the actor portraying Joe was seen on stage, Joe had no lines he communicated to other characters, but his inner thoughts were heard. The chorus spoke these inner thoughts, though the blocking clearly showed that Joe's location was most often in the auditorium, seemingly implicating the audience in the performance of Joe's character.

    The implications of treating the audience as a fellow actor in the musical are significant, and are also beyond the scope of this chapter.
26. See Raymond Knapp's *The American Musical and the Performance of Personal Identity* (Princeton, NJ: Princeton University Press, 2006).
27. Knapp states in *The American Musical and the Performance of Personal Identity* that it is not through song that one knows *who* a character is, but *that* a character is (131).

CHAPTER 17

Singing and Dancing Ourselves

The Politics of the Ensemble in

A Chorus Line (1975)

MILLIE TAYLOR

In 2007 I attended a performance of *Fingerprint* (2007) devised by a British music theater company called The Shout.[1] The Shout was a sixteen-voice a cappella choir that created original and provocative new music theater works.[2] What was really exciting about the performance was the way in which the choir members were clearly all individuals who used their own experiences and voices, their diverse cultural backgrounds and vocal techniques, in the creation and performance of a work about conformity. Their website advertizes that

> The choir aims to be a group whose personalities are revealed by the music and who are given freedom to sing solos and to improvise, and yet a group capable of homogeneous effort; it aims to explore the possibilities of sixteen individuals and of a single voice with sixteen components.[3]

Fingerprint was notionally about a new British citizenship test set in a classroom where students were preparing for the test.[4] The work explored the compromise between being a good citizen, and not losing one's own individuality and cultural identity, and to do this it drew on the individuals in the choir to represent themselves, but also to be a singing community. This tension between the choir as a unified singing community and the choir as a group of individuals with diverse voices and contexts sparked my interest because it identifies the performers as both individual *and* group, and through the content of the work they became a microcosm of society. The choir in this piece could be perceived both as a group of diverse individuals representing the functioning of a multicultural society in a postmodern world, and as a coherent singing machine whose corporate operation could be understood to represent the undifferentiated mass in a binary reading of the functioning of a capitalist economy or a Fordist production line.

This idea of performers as simultaneously individuals and community germinated in my mind, and led me to question what we mean by ensemble works and the ensemble, and what the consequences of ensemble performances are for their performers and audiences. The ensemble is understood here, in response to the work of The Shout, as a group of performers who perform their individuality in small group performances, but who are also required to work together for the good of the whole as a creative team and, in this case, as a choir. And developing this argument one step further, since the structures of performance reflect and performatively refashion contemporary society, analyzing the structures, functions, and reception of ensemble performances must tell us something about our society, and therefore something about ourselves.

The hit Broadway show *A Chorus Line* (1975)[5] also explores the compromise between individuality and community, as the performers in the staged audition are required to demonstrate their individuality in order to get a job that requires absolute conformity. Bruce Kirle describes the ways in which *A Chorus Line* stages the paradox of conformity for the "me" generation as a desire for mediocrity; the dancers can only achieve the insider status represented by a job in the chorus line through the mediocrity of anonymity.[6] In this chapter I argue against that reading, positing the view that *A Chorus Line* both in its narrative and in its structure creates a balanced tension through which both individuality and conformity are maintained. *A Chorus Line* is taken as a key example that reveals something about the ensemble musical and its politics. Although the musical is about a chorus line, its story and the way it is performed and received celebrates the individuals, their interactions, and their relationships; it celebrates the ability of performers to represent individuality within and through community. This balanced tension allows that despite the requirement for conformity to styles, techniques, and methods, performers rely on originality and individuality to express character and to achieve unique performances of song and dance.

Building on the idea of performativity that is the theme of this book, we can take a step further and read the work of the performers not only as a performance in a particular time and place, but as a performative enactment of a sense of self and ensemble. And this is particularly significant in *A Chorus Line* because the dancers are performing not only to us, the audience, but also to Zach, and to each other. So the song and dance becomes a self-conscious and explicit performative re-enactment of individual identity, even as these individual voices and bodies also performatively construct a group, ensemble, or community for the audience. This reading of *A Chorus Line* is then reflected on in a further doubling, as a performative reading of the structures and politics of society is revealed that is constructed and reconstructed through the performances of single and group identities.

The structures and politics of society as they are revealed in film musicals have been discussed in Richard Dyer's article "Entertainment and Utopia," which provides a contextual backdrop for contemporary discourses about the politics of structure and the representation of community in musicals. Through reconsidering that article, this chapter identifies in *A Chorus Line* a utopian politics of individuality and difference.[7] The same is probably true of many other ensemble musicals. *Company* (1970) is arguably one of the first ensemble musicals, and its title suggests the musical deals with a company, a community, an ensemble, and it is performed by an ensemble as I use the term here.[8] *Company* also demonstrates its "ensemble-ness" in interesting ways as it negotiates the balance between Bobby, the individual, isolated loner, and the group of bickering, intimate couples, "those good and crazy people [his] married friends!"[9] But perhaps, in exploring Dyer's approach, it is useful to be challenged to read against the grain, and here is a musical that has the word "chorus" in its title, that has been perceived as glorifying conformity, mediocrity, and anonymity, and which requires its company to be a chorus of individuals. So *A Chorus Line* is read against the received wisdom as an ensemble musical in a multicultural society where all bodies and voices are experienced as equally human, individual, and diverse. This creates a framework for reading the ensemble musical as performatively redefining the tension between individual and community, local and global.

THE MUSICAL THEATER ENSEMBLE

In musical theater of the past forty years or so the term "ensemble musical" has developed specific meanings; an ensemble musical is created by a group of performers who enact the narrative in its entirety; the narrative, plot, or concept is the sum of the interactions of the group of characters.[10] There are no supernumeraries or chorus commenting on plot or enlisted simply to add vocal volume or choreographed action in support of the narrative being enacted by "principal" characters. Many of Sondheim's works, including *Into the Woods*,[11] *Assassins*,[12] and *Company*, are ensemble works in which the onstage company is a group of protagonists. Each performer in the ensemble has his or her own role and relationships and often a through line in the narrative, though a performer might also play multiple roles; the performer playing the airline hostess in "Barcelona" (*Company*) might also play other parts (and in an actor-musician production may accompany the performance by playing an instrument or several), but she is always an individual within the ensemble. *Cats* allows each character within the ensemble a moment to communicate individual characteristics to the audience,[13] and the performer retains that persona throughout the whole evening, never becoming an anonymous body even when performing in unison. Given the diverse characters, actions, and relationships, the ensemble as a whole rarely does work in unison; instead each cat maintains physical characteristics that mark the unique and idiosyncratic performance of that cat's identity within the group.

The development of ensemble musicals during the 1970s was not so surprising since, as Stacy Wolf remarks, "these musicals were created during an era when feminism and progressive communal ideals entered mainstream thought."[14] This is in stark contrast to the chorus of the golden age of the Hollywood film musical in which "the musical seeks to bridge the gap [between audience and performer] by putting up 'community' as an ideal concept."[15] This is the difference identified in this chapter between a community of individuals—where the community articulates diverse identities—and an anonymous mass without opportunities to articulate individual identities. The choral mass of voices creates a unified or polyphonic sound and a dynamic experience for audiences that is greater than the sum of its parts, but it limits the textural diversity that individuality can offer. One might think of the anonymous singing and dancing communities of the Rodgers and Hammerstein musicals (including *Allegro* discussed in the previous chapter) or the robotic similarity of the dancing girls in Busby Berkeley films to identify the lack of individuality and excessive conformity that signified this communal ideal. Yet the experience of hearing or watching the group perform is spectacular, even as it represents community through an idealized conformity and anonymity. This division of labor might be argued to reflect a capitalist politics critiqued by Theodor Adorno as mass culture and a product of the culture industry, and it still has a useful place in contemporary musicals, though the choreography is not generally as uniform as in Berkeley's films. Examples include *Billy Elliott* (2005),[16] with its chorus of dancing policemen and miners, or *Wicked* (2003),[17] whose chorus performs as "Monkeys, Students, Denizens of the Emerald City, Palace Guards and Other Citizens of Oz,"[18] all of whom are essentially anonymous.

However, there is the potential for confusion in the term "ensemble" in musical theater studies as a result of the conflation of the ensemble with "ensemble numbers" and the "ensemble effect." Scott McMillin's *The Musical as Drama* contains a chapter devoted to analysis of "the ensemble effect," identifying the "drive toward ensemble performance in the musical dramatic form."[19] In many musicals there is a process whereby a number begins between one or two characters and builds up to a larger group or choral climax, and through this "the musical fulfils its intentions in the teamwork of ensemble performance, no matter how many good solos are heard along the way."[20] This is a feature of operatic finales including, for example the famous act 2 finale of *The Marriage of Figaro* (1786).[21] That finale combines a gradual increase of protagonists onstage, the development of the plot enacted physically and in recitative, and musical sophistication as the characters maintain their own characters and stories in a coherent sung ensemble. Whether the group in question is a group of protagonists or incorporates in the latter stages a larger, anonymous chorus, the effect McMillin explores is the buildup of voices leading to communal singing that works musically as a simultaneous expression (albeit of competing ideas) and sonic climax.

The dynamism of community singing and its performative effect on audiences is such that at times creative teams replace plot development with the sensual affect achievable through communal singing or dancing. Each has its place and its effect. Interaction between character, plot, and individual performance, in concert with harmonic, climactic, and spectacular use of the group, creates a dynamic and diverse experience for audiences. This diversity is an essential feature of musical theater, whose dynamic range is often greater than can be experienced in works without song or dance.

The plot of *A Chorus Line* exists in real time and is the staging of an audition for a new dance show, during which a group of dancers who have won through the first stage of the audition are asked to talk about their lives, which they do in songs and dances as solos, duets or small groups. Tension is created as the dancers attempt to second-guess what the director wants from them so that they can satisfy his desires and get the job. For the audience tension grows as they get to know and empathize with the characters; the knowledge that they can't all be successful and what that means for the individuals becomes increasingly poignant. There is a subplot of a past relationship between the director (Zach) and one of the dancers (Cassie), but the main point of interest is the backstage story of dancers' lives. The appearance of reality is achieved by using characters and stories developed through a verbatim process, and from this material solo songs and dances emerge that expand the audience's understanding of, and identification with, characters.[22] The appearance of reality emerges, also, from the reflexivity of the design and staging; an audition in an empty theater space as seen in figure 31.

Since the music fits the characters, and the characters are individual and diverse, the music is necessarily eclectic. Paul Laird records that the tap number "I Can Do That" has the rhythmic character of 1930s jazz with melodic blues touches, that "At the Ballet" alternates between a rock beat and a waltz with speech rhythms in the rock section, while the montage section built around "Hello Twelve, Hello Thirteen" includes many sections in different styles to fit the characters, including an easy rock ballad for "Nothing" and gospel for the end.[23]

Figure 31 A view from behind the dancers reveals the audition space and the diversity of bodies in the group. Photo courtesy of Sony Picture Classics/Photofest. © Sony Picture Classics.

For McMillin the ensemble is the subject of the musical.[24] Stacy Wolf identifies the montage "Hello Twelve, Hello Thirteen" as the central point of the musical, which focuses on individuals finding their identity as they go through adolescence to adulthood. By contrast the final number "One," structured according to McMillin's "ensemble effect," explores the essential tension in A Chorus Line, that the "labor of self-individuation was for naught."[25] Although the personal reflections created through the collaborative process can lead to the impression that the show is about individualism, for McMillin the achievement that matters is the achievement of absolute conformity in an ensemble performance.[26]

Bruce Kirle reads the musical as tracing the tensions between insider and outsider, between individual autonomy and corporate economy reproduced as the individual hard work and talent of each dancer that can only be rewarded as a result of the loss of identity required to become a cog in the wheel of the ideal chorus line.[27] What is interesting in A Chorus Line, though, is that while the company is straining to conform to requirements, the director is asking them to articulate their individuality, highlighting, for the audience, the tension between individuality and conformity. Kirle explains that the glory for the chorus members lies in their willingness to sacrifice their identity in what he describes as corporate America's celebration of mediocrity. This is a change from the glorification of community in the work of Rodgers and Hammerstein and represents a change in musical theater. Rather than the faceless mass as foil for the virtuoso soloist, which together represented the ideal community structure, Kirle describes the community as conformist; an unindividuated mass, revealing the changed political landscape since the 1940s and 1950s. The ensemble musical blurs the binary distinctions still further and thus challenges the idea of massification and conformity. Kirle argues that the spectacular finale where all the individuals are consumed into the company production number is a horrifying spectacle of anonymity whose shadow overwhelms the audience in the reflections of the mirrors placed so that spectators are forced to identify with the plight of the auditionees.[28] In the end, though, Kirle takes a Foucauldian perspective when he recognizes that A Chorus Line represents a site of struggle, focusing on how dominant forces are coped with, evaded, or resisted.[29] It is this struggle, or rather the tension between the representation of individuality and conformity to external pressures, that will develop in the examples that follow.

In the libretto song listings the central sequence of A Chorus Line is one long section entitled "Hello Twelve, Hello Thirteen, Hello Love" performed by the "Company." But in the body of the text there is fluidity as the focus shifts between individual stories, between speech, song, and dance, and between this and the rest of the work. There are five other numbers listed as company numbers and one, "What I did for Love" as "Diana and Company." Of the others, three are solos (for Mike, Diana, and Val) and three are small group numbers ("And...," "At the Ballet," "Sing!"). What this simple exercise reveals is the small number of solo songs in the work, and yet my memory of the work is of individual voices and experiences being revealed. If one looks further into the script and score, the reason for this discrepancy is revealed; in the company numbers there is very little unison or homophonic singing but individual parts and lines, stories, and speeches in a conversational and fluid exchange.

Figure 32 Priscilla Lopez as Diana sings "Nothing," listened to by the group. Photo courtesy of Photofest. © Photofest.

Structurally the vocal score is different, and the difference between these two artifacts is instructive. In the vocal score the same central sequence is separated into four parts entitled "Montage—Part 1 ('Hello Twelve' Mark, Connie)," followed by "Montage—Part 2 ('Nothing')," "Montage—Part 3 (Don, Judy, 'Mother')" and "Montage—Part 4 (Judy (cont), Greg, Richie)." The basic discrepancy between the listing in the vocal score and libretto reveals something about the construction of this musical and its fluidity. Separate sections of soliloquy in speech, song, dance, and discussion form the central part of the narrative as revealed in the libretto, but musically it is one long montage that is divided into four parts. The whole is almost continuously underscored and the parts are linked by a refrain that includes the title "Hello Twelve, Hello Thirteen, Hello Love." Within the montage there are quite long sections or individual "numbers" that are more clearly identified in the score, including the songs "Nothing," "Mother," and various versions of the refrain "Hello Twelve." The sections don't have defined or applause-inducing beginnings and endings (except at the end of "Nothing"); there is a fluid movement between individual expression and group interaction. This can be seen in the performance of "Nothing" in figure 32, during which the company listens to Diana's story standing immediately behind her. The difference between vocal score and libretto reveals this blurring between solo and group, number and dialogue, scene and song, individual and group.

The musical structures and the verbal structures don't map exactly onto each other since the musical themes and structures form different coherent groups than those perceived in the lyric/dialogue writing. The result is a fluid performance that is not easily articulated in titles and indexes, lyrical and musical forms, song, dance, and dialogue, and one that articulates resistance to a binary structure of group and individual.

Looking in a little more detail at the lyrical content of "Hello Twelve" reveals a chronology of sorts that begins as the group discusses being twelve or thirteen "Too young to take over, too old to ignore,"[30] before discussing early sexual experiences, dance training, and relationships with parents. These disparate stories, which often have no clear beginnings or endings, fade into and out of focus. Then they come together in a central "faster rock" section in which all the characters sing parts of their stories in a polyphonic ensemble. By this time the lyrics reveal that "suddenly I'm seventeen."[31] Richie then leads the final section on college and the start of adult life. This results in an ensemble song during which diverse individual characters' lines are merged into a polyphonic pattern to create an ensemble effect, and performers move fluidly between individual expression and community cohesion.

The narrative of individuals moving between groups, and performing different identities within those groups, is one of the performative features of this work. The characters tell stories and perform identities from stages of growing up. As they recognize shared experiences, a cohesive group identity develops that is performed as the shared experience of being a dancer. During this montage diverse stories feed into a common identification with the shared moment, revealing the performative experience that occurs in life as individuals become parts of groups who share one aspect of life, but perform different identities in other groups. Judith Butler constituted gender identity as a performative act, which has been developed in performance studies to reveal the performance of identity to be citational; becoming sedimented and normalized through repetition. "By stressing performative citationality, Butler allows us to see how [Turner's] theory of ritual may be generalized to understand both transgressive and normative performance."[32] During this montage a series of performative identities emerges to articulate similarity and difference among the characters, conformity and individuality within the group.

During an earlier montage "I Hope I Get It" the performers sang in unison or in groups of anonymous characters, but the action continued in spoken scenes over musical underscore as different characters were introduced by name, responded to comments, or sang short sections. The whole was thematically and musically one continuous number so that the result appeared as a montage of thematically related musical material accompanying speech, solo, small group, and unison singing, and through which a number of characters were introduced. This first number revealed the inner tension of the show as a whole, the negotiation between individual character and conformist song and dance in an ensemble show. At this point the separate identities had not become established so the unison singing and thematic similarity represented an anonymous mass that then became much more clearly differentiated by the time of "Hello Twelve." In the later montage the singers not only speak to Zach as individuals but begin to compare their experiences and develop a group identity that alters the power relationship with Zach.

The identification of "Hello Twelve" as a montage in four parts (in the vocal score) also begins to reveal the thematic nature of each of the sections. The sections are not related simply to individuals or even a precise chronology, but are thematically focused, with overlaying of materials, motifs, and the development of relationships. Montages are a useful device to juxtapose materials and suggest diverse and complex readings of characters and situations, while the musical continuity serves to unify and draw the materials into revealing juxtapositions. The result of a montage can be to compress information that is thematically related and to reveal its similarities and differences within a relatively short space of time. In this case it allows a lot of information to be performed about many of the characters so that the audience can experience them as diverse individuals. At the same time, both narrative and music are performing the group as a continuum with similar experiences to share and a similar musical theme to articulate. This is accomplished through a range of diverse musical styles that signify personalities or moods within the overall unity of the montage. Just as singers move between articulating individual and group sentiments, the structure of the montage has musical continuity and repetition but is comprised of diverse musical genres and voices.

The discrepancies in the listings in the score and libretto articulate these tensions. None of the written texts reveals the entire structure or the developing relationships in this part of the work; rather there is a negotiation between the libretto, the score, and the performance that reveals the potential meanings of the work. This montage draws together stories and responses to particular themes of growing up, adolescence, and early adulthood. It identifies similarities between characters, but does so through the performance of individual experiences, dances, and songs, articulated through diverse musical genres and a repeated recognizable theme that is representative of the group identity.

By contrast, the version of "One" that the company sings to accompany the final performance of the rehearsed routine introduces two separate themes that are then sung in a double chorus. This is a classic device in musical theater and a type of "ensemble effect." It is also the number that has led academics to read this final conformity as revealing something about a capitalist society. In the score this song is identified as the Bows, and so it exists outside the narrative, but clearly in the performance it is the climax of the show, the place where the performers have changed clothes and perform as though in the performance for which they have auditioned (figure 33). There is a question whether this separation strengthens or weakens the interpretation, and produces another tension or paradox for interpretation: that it is only after the narrative is completed that the conformity that is so denigrated is enacted onstage.

Before that, within the show the song is sung and danced partly in unison and accompanied by a number of polyphonic threads: counting; speaking dance steps; individual characters reminding themselves of instructions, and so on. Diane needs to "Fill the phrase," Judy remembers to "Lead with the hip. Follow thru."[33] The song moves into four parts. Then it is sung in unison beneath the final scene between Cassie and Zach. Zach reveals his perspective; Cassie is special, so he wonders how

Figure 33 The company performs "One." Photo courtesy of NYSF/Photofest: © NYSF.

she can really want to be like the chorus line, which is immediately revealed as a line of unison singers and dancers with dissonant music and a change of lighting that supports Zach's viewpoint. Cassie reveals her perspective and the one that the narrative has pursued: that every member of the chorus line is special and individual. Paul's accident is the next scene, after which Zach asks the question—"what do you do when you can't dance anymore?"[34] This question is ultimately followed by the final response to that question, the song "What I did for Love." The show concludes with the audition results before the Bows present the final version of "One."

The montage structure of the work maintains a fluid movement between individual and group that reveals the narrative and the performed nature of character identity. The structure of the work contributes to the way in which the fluidity and the tension are represented; individuality and community are simultaneously maintained.

THE PERFORMATIVITY OF VOICES AND BODIES

A Chorus Line contains a narrative of difference and diversity that is expressed through a vocal and physical language that is equally diverse. Musical genres and dance styles are used to represent the individuality of characters. As a supplementary layer, the performers' individual personalities are revealed in the performative choices they make in the interpretation of those characters, their songs, and dances. Butler reminds us that "identity is discursively constituted, the effect rather than the cause of the sequence of acts which give it the appearance of substance."[35] This suggests that it is through particular vocal and musical utterances that the identity of the singer is fashioned, and also suggests that performers can reconstitute the performance they give. So rather than the identity of performer or character being external to the instances of song and dance in a work, it is through the physical and vocal utterances of song and dance that the identity of both character and performer is fashioned.

The vocal mechanism functions in the same way across cultures, though the voice varies from person to person, as a product of the relationship between resonance, articulation, and breath. Perhaps there may be physical genetic similarities that create similarities of sound resulting from particular physiologies, such as the bone structure or the shape of resonating cavities, but these are overlaid with cultural and linguistic patterns that are so ingrained that they appear "natural." The language of a singer can affect resonance and placement, use of the tongue, and articulation, but culture also informs training and the musical genres to which the singer is attuned, its scales and structures. So when Roland Barthes speaks of the "materiality of the body speaking its mother tongue,"[36] he might be referring either to the physiological or to the cultural, or indeed, to an indecipherable concatenation of the two. The same is true of dancing bodies whose sociocultural context is performed through physiology, technique, and interpretative gesture. Dancers extend their bodies in particular shapes, use gestures derived from cultural background, and within performance express character through movement and stillness. In the ways they express genre patterns, and use them as a framework, they express individuality and cultural context in their bodies. Fred Astaire's dancing is different from Gene Kelly's, which is different again from that of Greg Hines. Each body reflects the physiological and cultural patterns from which it is constructed, but each performs the identity it wants to reveal through those cultural patterns.

Singers, like dancers, can alter the vocal placement, the timbre of the voice, the intonation against modal or tonal pitches, the articulation against rhythm, the use of ornamentation, to become multiple, individual, and hybrid vocalists. They perform identity within a cultural context that is articulated in their voices; they sing through anticipated patterns, stereotypes, and techniques to suggest readings and to create characters, but those patterns also perform the unique choices, journeys, and contexts of the singer. The work of The Shout explores this complexity of utterance at the level of the individual and the group. Mike Henry, a member of the group, said that as an individual choir member you "use the voice in a way that is appropriate to the dramatic intent. You don't necessarily have a definition for it [. . .] you don't really define by genre, but it has a kind of tactile quality to it."[37] I would suggest that this ability to transform and respond in a tactile way to the sounds being created by others is the result of an individual's hybrid musical understanding and performative ability. Henry identified how he could change the timbre of his voice to reflect different musical styles and perform himself as an individual or harmonize with the group. This requires an understanding of placement and tone color alongside tuning and ornamentation in relation to genre.

The narrative of *A Chorus Line* explores this as Cassie is repeatedly reminded of the ways in which she must blend her gestures to merge with the group. Choir members learn to blend their voices by listening carefully to the sound of the whole, ballet dancers in the corps raise their legs and arms to exactly the correct angle by close observation of their peers. The narrative of *A Chorus Line* not only gives the characters opportunities to work in both of those ways—performing their individuality and harmonizing with the group—but it gives the same opportunities to the performers. The physical and vocal utterances, the songs and dances of *A Chorus Line*, discursively reveal the characters and performers as unique individuals and part of the Broadway dance community.

So Cassie's assertion that the members of the line are all special is borne out by the audience's experience of the physical and vocal gestures, the utterances, the performative identities of each individual performer. Moreover, the narrative is reflexive of the performance of identity audiences experience in their own lives; the interaction of group conformity and individuality reminds the audience that their own identities are multiplicitous, and that these performances of group and personal identity are familiar.

A UTOPIAN ENSEMBLE

In "Entertainment and Utopia" Richard Dyer analyzed musical films as entertainment and arrived at a categorization of nonrepresentational signs that was designed to reveal the utopian values of musical film.[38] His categorization challenges a politics that denigrates musical film entertainment as escapist based simply on analysis of narrative, but argues instead that the utopianism musical films espouse can be explored at the level of structure and signification. In particular, he notes the relationship between the complex meanings of signs and their sociocultural situations. He arrives at five categories of entertainment's utopian sensibility that I have paraphrased as follows: energy—the capacity to act vigorously; abundance—the conquest of scarcity or the enjoyment of sensuous material reality; intensity—experiencing of emotion directly, fully, unambiguously; transparency—relationships between characters or between performers and audience; community—togetherness, sense of belonging, network of relationships.[39] His argument is that each of these is performative, as each of these features is revealed in the structures of the work as something desirable, and is then recreated for audiences in the experience of a utopian entertainment. In this chapter I have been focusing on one of these, community, though the others are clearly present in the performance. Energy is apparent in the work and the skill of the dancers. Abundance is present in the excess of voices and bodies constantly interacting and performing, separately and together. Intensity is revealed in the emotional highs and lows the characters reveal about their personal lives, and most fully experienced in Paul's fall, which reveals the dancers' essential vulnerability. Transparency occurs in the growing relationships between the performers, and in the developing understanding between Zach and Cassie.

Community, I have been arguing, is revealed as something rather complex that reflects a contemporary society, and that is formed through simultaneous awareness of individuality and conformity.

Dyer proposes that entertainment creates a tension between speaking to the real experience of the audience and drawing attention to the ideological gap "between what is and what could be."[40] He shows that, while in *Gold Diggers of 1933* the narrative suggests that performing in a show is the solution to the Depression-induced problems of the characters, the nonrepresentational signs in the film both reinforce and contradict this narrative. Thus he demonstrates that musicals, through their mix of narrative, structure, and nonrepresentational signs, provide the potential for contradiction and complexity latent within them.[41] The complexities revealed through such contradictions point to the ideological gaps that musical film "managed" in order to present a utopian entertainment. His analysis therefore reveals something about society, its politics, and its ideologies.

Dyer's categorization was developed from a Marxist politics in the 1980s and applied to musical films of the golden age. It is still a useful touchstone and provocation when analyzing how entertainment functions through the complex juxtapositions of its narratives, its structures, and its affects, but it is perhaps worth revisiting it in relation to the ensemble of protagonists to reconsider the relationships of individuals and groups in contemporary society. It also derives from a rather more passive understanding of the audience experience. That relationship is now perceived in quite different ways. Audience response is regarded as performative in that audiences are active in the construction of meaning in cinema and in theater; however, in theater the audience's affective excitement also feeds back into an energy exchange with the performers. Beginning from Dyer's categorization reveals the ways in which our interpretation of community has shifted, and thus demonstrates the contingent and dynamic nature of reception. At the same time the performativity of the ensemble enacts a different aesthetics and politics than that articulated by Dyer as "community," revealing the diverse ways we are performed in the community songs and dances of our entertainments.

In *A Chorus Line* there is tension in the narrative between individuality and conformity, as success is related to the ability to function as an individual *and* an empathetic community. This is mirrored in the performativity of the characters/performers, and in the construction of the relationships and the musical numbers. This is different from an aesthetics that celebrates the anonymity of a community member in juxtaposition with a principal character. Where Dyer argued for a politics of the film musical that identified community as one of the utopian aspirations of society, a contemporary Western politics might read within community an aesthetics of diversity, a politics of difference. This ensemble musical represents that aesthetics in its plot, its development process, and its nonrepresentational signs, even as the end of the narrative reveals the conformity required of the chorus line. The work thus manages the ideological gap between real equality and the contemporary world. The ensemble allows individuals to shine at times, but at other times they function as part of a group, and in the fluidity of the relationships power and resistance are continually revealed and questioned.

The UK experienced cultural diversity and celebrated multicultural difference in the last thirty years or so, while the United States' melting pot occurred rather earlier and possibly resulted in a greater sense of congruent national identity. This may be reflected to some extent in the ways in which musical theater is theorized and read in our two countries. Interestingly, Raymond Knapp's two volumes on the American musical mirror these concerns. Having written about the ways in which the American musical projected an American national identity through the assimilation or otherwise of its diverse communities in "its much ballyhooed 'melting pot,'"[42] Knapp continued his project by observing the ways in which individual and alternative identities are performed onstage and in the world. As he says, national and personal identities "tend in opposite directions, the former toward a single, relatively stable abstraction, and the latter toward a multiplicity of possibilities expressed and experienced in more concrete terms."[43] He identifies a dramatic shift "as we move from considering a background, group identity, to considering more closely the individuals occupying the foreground."[44] While he identifies these themes in different musicals, I'm conceptualizing the way in which the ensemble musical represents a fluid and resistant dramatic tension between these extremes within itself. This is the tension that I argue occurs in *A Chorus Line*. The individual and group singing and dancing performs this dynamic, and by the end of the work the individuals occupy the foreground of the audience consciousness but are nonetheless able to maintain a position within the background group identity. My experience of the performance was that my eyes were drawn to individuals and mind to the task of identifying them even during the conformity of the bows. This is clearly a much more utopian reading than those of McMillin, Wolf, and even Kirle.

At the same time, 2005, Jen Harvie, in *Staging the UK*, discovered a range of identity formations in the UK that allowed identity to be "multiple, mutually contingent, and mutually embedded—simultaneously holding in tension multiple determinants."[45] It is this sense of the copresence of an individual sung or danced identity and communal singing and dancing that seems to be the epitome of what ensemble musicals perform. I'm relating this multiplicity of identity formation to the dynamic diversity of contemporary Western societies, within which hybrid and diasporic communities create affinities with local and global contexts. There is no stable identity but one that is multiple and diverse, that is experienced locally and within a global context.

The analysis in this chapter tries to draw away from the dialogical extremes of individual and group, and frame identity as something more fluid and performative; to read the musical theater ensemble as the outward expression of the tensions between, for example, a coherent and shared experience of life as a dancer in New York, and multiplicitous personal identities that are performed through songs and dances. This narrative is then perceived to reflect the tensions of identity within and between communities and countries. Such a reading might be considered hopelessly utopian; Harvie points out that critics of this type of approach observe that such diversity and multiplicity is a function of privilege, and that difference can be assimilated and homogenized, repressed instead of supported.[46] However, I am being deliberately utopian and speaking about our privileged Western experience, drawing on Dyer's exploration of the utopian in musical film entertainment and questioning what a contemporary liberal democracy sees as its lack, its gap to be filled. And the question of identity in a shifting global world is a key source of unease from which entertainment must provide escape, solace, reconciliation, and hope.

The implication of this is that those ensemble works that maintain the structural tension between individual and group reflect a contemporary politics of diversity within community. The eclectic styles within the music might be seen as a reflection of such a cosmopolitan diversity drawn together within a communal expression. This is in contrast to the binary understanding of community as the experience of the suppression of individual identity, or as the anonymous mass. It is this tension that was apparent in the critiques of *A Chorus Line* discussed above, in which some commentators suggested that conformity won out over individuality. Given the arguments above, "One" in *A Chorus Line* is perhaps more complex, with the community cohesion celebrated at the end *because* of audience awareness of the diverse individual stories. The spectacle at that moment is performatively experienced as a dynamic and intense excess that also retains the ideological tension between community and individuality not in its own right, but because of what has preceded it during the rest of the show dramatically, structurally and performatively. And that includes the ironic fact that a lyric about individuality, "One," is performed by a unified group. The group performs as one, but a "one" that is constructed of unique individuals who blend their performances into the moment of spectacle. The focus of the mirrors on the audience extends that gaze so that audiences see themselves as individuals *and* part of a larger cohort.

SINGING AND DANCING OURSELVES

It is perhaps instructive that the ensemble musical has replaced the chorus/principals binary in many contemporary musicals, and not only for economic reasons, but because the ensemble gives rise to the opportunity for performative identities to emerge, through which the musical's narrative is deepened and its performances rendered more complex. As a reflection of contemporary life, the tension between community and individual has featured in the content of a wider group of musicals, from *Assassins* to *Avenue Q* (2003). Scott McMillin speaks of musical theater as having coherence rather than integration: "Coherence means things stick together, different things, without losing their difference."[47] The universalizing tendency has gone, as has the binary reading of power relations. In song and dance this new aesthetic of coherence and difference would include the individuality of solos and special tricks, moments of nonconformity alongside moments of togetherness. One can discover such a pattern in blues and jazz, where music results from a group of instrumentalists creating a coherent whole that supports opportunities for individual expression. Rock music also allows individual expression within a coherent harmonic structure and performance framework, and actor-musician shows foreground individual skills and techniques that create the performance of the whole. The musical and physical gestures of song and dance are thus perceived as moments in a larger work that give expression to the performative identities of characters and actors as complex individuals, and just as songs and dances are subsets of the larger work, so too the individual sounds and gestures of the performers are the subsets that become the performance.

Then, to go further into a political reading of the reception of performance, what I have argued is that the structural tension of the ensemble musical as a community of individuals reflects contemporary society. In this way the changing nature of musical theater, as it is perceived in the songs and dances of the ensemble musical, has transformed from solo with chorus to a dialogue between individuals and groups. This signifies a new politics of diversity that can be read by audiences and understood in relation to the social, cultural, and political contexts beyond the theater. The ensemble musical might be argued to embody optimism; the balanced tension between individual and group, local and global, points to the ability of society to maintain and celebrate diversity within community in our cosmopolitan societies. Ensemble musicals might thus propose a utopian future in which individuals within a community are able to perform their own identity and to resist the urge to conformity even while maintaining their presence within community. This is an entertainment and a society in which diverse audiences might perceive themselves to be represented. By empathetically embodying the performance, we, the audience members, are able to perceive our multiple selves and the ways our physical and vocal gestures create our identities. We become aware of our individuality and diversity, of our multiplicity and our communal power, and that we are able to sing and dance ourselves.

NOTES

1. This chapter was largely written before the 2013 production of *A Chorus Line* opened at the London Palladium, but it has informed this final version.
2. The company suspended its activities in 2011, though members of the choir continue to work on projects as individuals and in new small combinations.
3. Online. Available: www.theshout.org/pages/aboutdetail.htm. February 28, 2011.
4. "A Life in the UK" (cultural test) and language test commonly known together as the citizenship test was introduced for people applying for Indefinite Leave to Remain in the UK or British citizenship. The aim was to offer guidance on cultural and social values and practices. It quickly became the source of media commentary and comedy, especially as it was obvious that many nationals would not pass it. It is still a requirement. Online. Available: http://lifeintheuktest.ukba.homeoffice.gov.uk/. October 25, 2012.
5. James Kirkwood, Michael Bennett, and Nicholas Dante are credited on the libretto, published by Applause, 1975. Marvin Hamlisch and Edward Kleban are credited on the vocal score published by Morris and Co., 1975.
6. Bruce Kirle, *Unfinished Show Business* (Carbondale: Southern Illinois University Press, 2005), 51.
7. Richard Dyer, "Entertainment and Utopia," in *Only Entertainment* (London: Routledge, 2002).
8. Stephen Sondheim and George Furth, 1970.
9. Sondheim and Furth *Company*, libretto (New York: Theatre Communications Group, 1996), 14.
10. Apologies to musicians and creative teams, this chapter refers specifically to the ensemble of onstage performers. While I realize there are other larger groups involved in the creative process, for the purposes of this chapter I focus entirely on the onstage world.
11. Sondheim and Lapine, 1987.
12. Sondheim and Weidman, 1991.
13. Lloyd Webber and Elliott, 1981.

14. Stacy Wolf, *Changed for Good* (Oxford: Oxford University Press, 2011), 19–20.
15. Jane Feuer, *The Hollywood Musical* (Basingstoke: Macmillan, 1993), 3.
16. Elton John and Lee Hall, 2005.
17. Steven Schwartz and Winnie Holzman, 2003.
18. As listed in the program and the CD booklet.
19. Scott McMillin, *The Musical as Drama* (Princeton, NJ: Princeton University Press, 2006), 78.
20. Ibid., 79.
21. Wolfgang Amadeus Mozart and Lorenzo Da Ponte, *The Marriage of Figaro*, 1786.
22. The devising process for this musical is documented by some of its participants, though the account is somewhat partisan. See Viagas, Lee and Walsh, *On the Line: The Creation of "A Chorus Line"* (New York: Morrow, 1990). *A Chorus Line* began with taped sessions, but ultimately not all those involved in the taped sessions were in the production, and some performers acted the parts of other performers from the taped sessions. The show ran for fifteen years and there have been many tours of the production with new casts who recreated the words, voices, actions, and physicality of the first cast, but even the first cast were not necessarily the originators of the material they performed. This is a necessity within the commercial sector, where profits are recouped from a production over a long period, and where audiences in many parts of the world want to see a Broadway production. It is possible that the physical and vocal diversity was increased, but the authority and ownership that derived from the taped sessions and workshops was reduced as a result of the process of recreation.
23. Paul Laird, "Choreographers, Directors and the Fully Integrated Musical," in *The Cambridge Companion to the Musical*, ed. William A. Everett and Paul R. Laird (Cambridge: Cambridge University Press, 2008), 233.
24. McMillin, *The Musical as Drama*, 98.
25. Ibid., 125.
26. Ibid., 99.
27. Kirle, *Unfinished Show Business*, 128 and 151.
28. Ibid., 152.
29. Ibid.
30. Kirkwood, *A Chorus Line*, 57.
31. Ibid., 79.
32. Jon McKenzie, "Genre Trouble: (The) Butler Did It" in *The Ends of Performance*, ed. Peggy Phelan and Jill Lane (New York: New York University Press, 1998), 222.
33. Kirkwood., *A Chorus Line*, 112.
34. Ibid., 129.
35. Sarah Salih, *Judith Butler* (New York: Routledge, 2004), 91.
36. Roland Barthes, "The Grain of the Voice," in *Image-Music-Text* (London: Fontana Press, 1977), 182.
37. In an interview by the author.
38. Richard Dyer, "Entertainment and Utopia," in *Only Entertainment*, 19–35 (London: Routledge, 2002).
39. Ibid., 22–23.
40. Ibid., 27.
41. Ibid., 35.
42. Raymond Knapp, *The American Musical and the Representation of National Identity* (Princeton, NJ: Princeton University Press, 2005), 8.
43. Raymond Knapp, *The American Musical and the Performance of Personal Identity* (Princeton, NJ: Princeton University Press, 2006), 1.
44. Ibid., 11.
45. Jen Harvie, *Staging the UK* (Manchester: Manchester University Press, 2005), 7.
46. Ibid., 192.
47. McMillin, *The Musical as Drama*, 209.

EPILOGUE

Performativity as Writing

Friday July 27, 2012. Former Beatle Sir Paul McCartney led 80,000 people singing the familiar refrain from "Hey Jude" in a remembered experience that has passed into cultural memory. The performativity of his gestures, for those present, for those watching at home, and for those who later accessed excerpts on YouTube or read about the experience, was individual and distinctive. Diverse effects continue to resonate with us, to act on us, as the memories expand outward into our shared history, until eventually they dissolve like the ripples in a pond. But they never completely disappear; they have been performed and their performativities continue to affect us, to resonate as experience and memory, and to be rearticulated when reactivated by current circumstances.

And like our shared but different responses to that performance of "Hey Jude," the thing that we have discovered in the course of this book is that our approaches to the performativity of song and dance are diverse. Performativity can result from shared but different parts of a performance, different approaches to its analysis, different understandings of its affects, and they continue to resonate and to be reactivated within and through this writing. We don't want to pin down definitions of performativity that interrupt its dynamic activity, its intensity, or its affect, but in order to exemplify its diversity we have categorized areas of performativity as Dramaturgies, Transitions, Identities, Contexts, Practices, and Community. These categories are only some of those that might be apparent to other theorists in other circumstances. What these have done, though, is to draw together examples of song and dance through their affect rather than through their location; to allow a new story to emerge about the ways in which these gestures of music theater have operated.

Rather than subsets or interruptions to the narrative of music theater, song and dance have become active features, provocations to a teleological perception of music theater. Their performativity, multiplicitous and complex as it has been revealed to be, alerts us to the excess, the overstimulation, the affective overperformance of music theater. The excess of physicality and vocality observed in the preceding chapters offers an opportunity to read the individual gestures of song and dance and the larger framing of music theater in counterpoint, in synchrony, and in chorus. The texture of performativity in music theater, containing as it does the gestures of song and dance, is perceived, therefore, to be dense, interwoven, dialogical, and paradoxical.

Moving away from the idea that music theater is a repertoire of works is a useful exercise. It allows us to engage in an approach to our field that is not restricted by disciplinary ideologies, it allows us to see connections between what may typically appear to be very different art forms, and above all, it allows us to explore and discuss the metaphysical dynamics of performativity that are so fundamental to performance. On the other hand, in doing this we lose the security of the work itself, the score and libretto that act a little bit like a lifeline to a high-wire act. In the text, we have a tangible object of study, authenticated documentation against which we can cross-reference our thoughts, and the specter of authorial authority to validate our claims. Here we have moved away from this security, and like the high-wire act we balance in a daring performative gesture of our own.

Yet paradoxically, we choose to exercise our high-wire act not on the high wire, but as a text: we do not perform our performative gesture in performance, but instead try to translate or stabilize the errant performative dynamics we have been discussing in the fixity of the scholarly text. To explore performance and its performativity in writing is a particular challenge, one that itself becomes a performative act. Two performative acts, then: the first, to cut across the grain, reading gestures that are disembodied, so to speak, a *dance* with the music, not the partner; the second, to filter this back in the language of the scholar, to sing and dance our own gestures, transcribed into the format of an academic book. Is this the "twice-behaved behavior" that to Richard Schechner defines performance?[1]

The trouble with writing about performance has been discussed extensively in recent performance studies literature. Contemporary writings on practice as research explore the value of embodied, tacit "know-how" and emphasize the difficulty of articulating this in the language of the written word.[2] As Lynette Hunter writes, "any *theory* is always on the edge of articulation because it's trying to talk about things that haven't been said before. This makes it difficult to communicate theory within the conventional discourse of conference and publication."[3] Once thought becomes reified into writing, it ceases to think. More than this, though (as twice-behaved behavior), in John Freeman's words, "all research is performative [...] inasmuch at least as it possesses the capacity to change, to make things happen."[4] The writing triggers thoughts that flutter off on their own, which is why Hunter qualifies her comment in evocative (performative) language, writing of "the precipitous edge of not-said concepts and feelings that theory attempts to bring into being through the process of its performance."[5]

Thus in writing about song and dance we metaphorically perform our own song and dance, which is why we suggest that music theater can become a critical methodology for scholarly study. Here the song and dance is undeniably metaphorical, but acutely so in the sense that our thoughts and our practice are themselves disciplinarily guided by the performative competence of our (interdisciplinary) performance practice—we think in the mode of song and dance, as it were, and articulate these thoughts through writing in songlike and dancelike gestures.

This may not be such a facetious comment, especially in an age when different modes of understanding and learning are recognized and targeted in educational systems. Furthermore, two interesting examples of performative writing offer the suggestion that perhaps dance at least (or let us be faithful to our ongoing commitment to the mutual expressive gesture of *song and dance*) can become an expressive gesture that can communicate more effectively than the rigid codes of language.

Perhaps not surprisingly, the first example comes from Jacques Derrida, whose own work consistently problematizes language yet performs (extremely performatively; even theatrically) in the material of that language. In discussing Stephen Mallarmé he calls into conceptual space the idea of the ballerina as a metaphorical embodiment of writing's performativity, and he talks of three ways in which the ballerina's pirouette can help us to understand the performativity of the scholarly text. The first is in the way that writing, "like the dancer's pointed toe, is always just about to pierce with a sign, with a sharp bit of nothing, the page of the book or the virginal intimacy of the vellum."[6] Here Derrida is evoking the sexual act and in particular the breaking of the hymen that is "the consummation of a marriage, the identification of two beings, the confusion between two. *Between* the two, there is no longer difference but identity."[7] Two, as it were, become momentarily one, though not exactly as the Spice Girls would have it.[8] In a chain of metaphors, Derrida evokes both the pirouette and the sexual act as the point at which the thought of a writer and the thought of a reader come into union. The second way Derrida sees the pirouette as emblematic of writing is in the fact that "Dance [...] appears to me to necessitate real space, or the stage."[9] In this he implies that writing too, like the dance, needs to move physically in time and space, flowing from the confines of the page to gain its momentum, its performativity. Finally, Derrida traces the developmental evolution of that performativity away from the union—the immediacy—of the encounter and through the dimensionality of time and space: "in turning incessantly on its point, the hieroglyph, the sign, the cipher moves away from its 'here and now,' as if it were endlessly falling, forever here en route between here and there."[10] Thus Derrida finds in the metaphor of the dance a way of describing the fluidity and flow of performative dynamics; he could just as effectively have used song—what else do Rodgers and Hammerstein do when they sing (in song) that "the hills are alive with the sound of music"?

The second example of performative writing is the brainchild of scientist John Bohannon, whose intriguing "Dance Your PhD" initiative seeks to find ways of articulating complex scientific theories without the hindrance of language. Bohannon explains his idea to an academic audience in a "spellbinding choreographed talk" at TEDx Brussels in November 2011.[11]

> The experiment is not the end of the story because you still have to transmit that knowledge to other people. [...] If you're trying to give someone the big picture of a complex idea to really capture its essence, the fewer words you use, the better. In fact, the ideal may be to use no words at all. I remember thinking, my friend could have explained that entire experiment with a dance.

Bohannon practices what he preaches, because his talk, delivered on a large, open stage space, is illustrated not with a PowerPoint presentation (he teases us that these are, in their inefficiency, a threat to the global economy), but with a supporting cast of dancers from Black Label Movement. As he explains complex molecular processes and chemical reactions, the dancers use their bodies in space to emulate the behavior of the molecules, adding not only a performative dynamic to his talk, but also a visual way of understanding the science. Bohannon's proposal here is clearly a bit of a gimmick. His idea is simply to replace the mediatized imagery of the PowerPoint with the live performance of dance, which in itself is cute but rather impractical on several levels; as he himself blogs, "the majority of PhD dances [in 'Dance your PhD'] are pretty bad (though most are at least amusing in some way)." However, the efficacy of his proposal is not the point of using Bohannon's lecture as an example. What certainly does grip its audience is the performative energy of this presentation, performative in part because of the physical impact of the dance, but just as performative because it presents an academic audience with an unfamiliar performance idiom and an unlikely fusion of science and art.

In presenting his performance in this way, Bohannon exploits his performative competence in an interdisciplinary gesture that merges two discrete and usually unpaired idioms; in fact, this is also what Derrida does, fusing his talent for imaginative creative writing with his ability to intellectualize complex theoretical philosophy. That both of these individuals lean more toward dance as a vehicle for their expression than song perhaps indicates that their way of thinking is more inclined toward an understanding of the physical gestures and patterns of the body in visual space than the vocalic gestures and patterns of the song in audible space.

Although we should not consider the diverse contributors to this collection as thinking uniformly, it is certainly worth considering the fact that we are all conversant with the dynamics of performance and in particular of performances that involve music and dance. Many of us practice as well as theorize in this field, and in habituating our bodies and voices into the sort of corporeal practice that our own music theater practices demand, we also habituate our minds into associative patterns of expression. We perform the hieroglyphs that communicate these diverse and complex spatial dynamics and our responses to them.

This then, is the ending point. Another performativity has been enacted with little comment throughout this volume. That writing, in the end, draws the diverse psychologies and disciplinary trends of this group of scholars into a collection with the rich texture of a vocal ensemble or dancing troupe. Thus the final gesture of this collection of songs and dances is the performativity of its writing, of how the writing makes possible a rethinking of music theater through the performative gestures of its songs and its dances.

NOTES

1. Richard Schechner, *Between Theater and Anthropology* (Philadelphia: University of Pennsylvania Press, 1985), 36.
2. See Robin Nelson, "Modes of Practice-as-Research Knowledge and Their Place in the Academy," in Ludivine Allegue et al., *Practice-as-Research in Performance and Screen* (New York: Palgrave Macmillan, 2009), 112–30.

3. Lynette Hunter, "Theory/Practice as Research: Explorations, Questions and Suggestions," in *Mapping Landscapes for Performance as Research: Scholarly Acts and Creative Cartographies*, ed. Shannon Rose Riley and Lynette Hunter (Basingstoke: Palgrave Macmillan, 2009), 230–31.

4. John Freeman, *Blood, Sweat and Theory: Research through Practice in Performance* (Farringdon: Libri Publishing, 2010), 62.

5. Hunter, "Theory/Practice as Research," 230–1.

6. Jacques Derrida, *Dissemination*, trans. Barbara Johnson (London: Athlone Press, 1981), 240.

7. Ibid., 209.

8. Derrida proceeds to critique the idea that "Two become one": "it does not follow [...] that there is now only one term. [...] The confusion or consummation of this hymen eliminates the spatial heterogeneity of the two poles in the 'supreme spasm,' the moment of dying laughing. By the same token, it eliminates the exteriority or anteriority, the independence, of the imitated, the signified, or the thing," 209–10. By contrast, the Spice Girls, in their 1996 hit, repeat to fade.

9. Derrida, *Dissemination*, 241.

10. Ibid.

11. John Bohannon, "John Bohannon: Dance vs. PowerPoint, a modest proposal," *TED: Ideas Worth Spreading*, online. Available: http://www.ted.com/talks/john_bohannon_dance_vs_powerpoint_a_modest_proposal.html. November 22, 2011.

BIBLIOGRAPHY

Abbate, Carolyn. "Analysis." In *The New Grove Dictionary of Opera*, ed. Stanley Sadie, vol. 1, 116–20. London: Macmillan, 1992.

Abbate, Carolyn. *In Search of Opera*. Princeton, NJ: Princeton University Press, 2001.

Abbate, Carolyn. *Unsung Voices: Opera and Musical Narrative in the Nineteenth Century*. 1991; reprint Princeton, NJ: Princeton University Press, 1996.

Adams, Rachel, and David Savran, eds. *The Masculinity Studies Reader*. Malden, MA: Blackwell, 2002.

Adcock, Craig. "Marcel Duchamp's Gap Music: Operations in the Space between Art and Noise." In *Wireless Imagination: Sound, Radio and the Avant-garde*, ed. Douglas Kahn and Gregory Whitehead, 105–39. Cambridge, MA: MIT Press, 1992.

Adler, Patricia A. Steven J. Kless, and Peter Adler. "Socialization to Gender Roles: Popularity among Elementary School Boys and Girls." *Sociology of Education* 65: 3 (1992): 169–7.

Adorno, Theodor W. "The Curves of the Needle." *October* 55 (1990): 48–55.

Adorno, Theodor W. "The Form of the Phonograph Record." *October* 55 (1990): 56–61.

"All about the Music." *Across the Universe*. Sony C8283549. DVD.

Allain, Paul. "Gardzienice: A Village, a Theatre, and a Cultural Crossroads." *New Theatre Quarterly* 2 (1993): 48–58.

Allain, Paul. *Gardzienice: Polish Theatre in Transition*. Amsterdam: Harwood Academic Publishers, 1997.

Altman, Rick. *The American Film Musical*. Bloomington: Indiana University Press, 1987.

Anderson, Laurie. *Big Science*. 2007, 1982. Warner Bros. Records. Nonesuch 130428-2. Compact disc.

Anderson, Laurie. *Bright Red*. 1994. Warner Bros. Records 9 45534–2. Compact disc.

Anderson, Laurie. *Home of the Brave*. 1986. Warner Bros. Records 9 25400-2. Compact disc.

Anderson, Laurie, dir. *Home of the Brave: A Film by Laurie Anderson*. 1986; Burbank, CA: Warner Reprise Video, 1990. VHS.

Anderson, Laurie. *Stories of the Nerve Bible: A Retrospective 1972–1992*. New York: Harper Perennial, 1994.

Anderson, Laurie. *The Ugly One with the Jewels and Other Stories*. 1995. Warner Bros. Records 9 45847-2. Compact disc.

Anderson, Laurie, and Celant Germano. *Dal Vivo*. Milan: Fondazione Prada, 1999.

Aristotle. *Poetics*. Mineola, NY: Dover Publications, 1997.

Artaud, Antonin. *The Theatre and Its Double*. Trans. Mary Richards. New York: Grove, 1958.

Ashman, Howard, and Alan Menken. *The Little Mermaid*. 1989. Walt Disney Records 60841-2, CD-018, D190113. Compact disc.

Auslander, Philip. "Going with the Flow: Performance Art and Mass Culture." *TDR* 33: 2 (1989): 119–36.

Auslander, Philip. *Liveness: Performance in a Mediatized Culture*. New York: Routledge, 1999.

Austin, J. L. *How to Do Things with Words*. 2nd ed. Oxford: Clarendon Press, 1975.

Bakhtin, Mikhail. *Rabelais and His World*. Trans. Hélène Iswolsky. Bloomington: Indiana University Press, 1984.

Bakhtin, Mikhail. *Toward a Philosophy of the Act*. Trans. Vadim Liapunov, ed. Vadim Liapunov and Michael Holquist. Austin: University of Texas Press, 1993.

Banfield, Stephen. *Sondheim's Broadway Musicals*. Ann Arbor: University of Michigan Press, 1994.

Barba, Eugenio. "The Deep Order Called Turbulence: The Three Faces of Dramaturgy." In *The Performance Studies Reader*, ed. Henry Bial, 252–62. London: Routledge, 2004.

Barba, Eugenio. *Whispering Winds*. Odin Teatret Film & CTLS, Denmark: Holstebro, 1997. DVD.

Barletto, N. "The Role of Martha Graham's Notebooks in Her Creative Process." *Martha Graham: Choreography and Dance* 5: 2 (1999): 53–68.

Barthes, Roland. *Camera Lucida*, Trans. Richard Howard. New York: Hill & Wang, 1981.

Barthes, Roland. *Image, Music, Text*. Trans. Stephen Heath. London: Fontana, 1977.

Barthes, Roland. *The Grain of the Voice: Interviews (1962–1980)*. Trans. Linda Coverdale. New York: Hill and Wang, 1985.

Baudelaire, Charles. *Paris Spleen and La Fanfarlo*. Trans. Raymond N. Mackenzie. Indianapolis: Hackett, 2008.

Beckett, Samuel. *Happy Days*. London: Faber and Faber, 2006.

Beckett, Samuel. *Not I*. In *Complete Dramatic Works*, 373–83. London: Faber and Faber, 1986.

Bell, Marty. *Broadway Stories: A Backstage Journey through Musical Theatre*. New York: Limelight Editions, 1993.

Ben-Zvi, Linda, ed. *Women in Beckett*. Urbana: University of Illinois Press, 1990.

Berkson, Robert. *Musical Theater Choreography*. New York: Backstage Books, 1990.

Berlin, Irving. "A Pretty Girl is Like a Melody." New York: Irving Berlin, Inc., 1919.

Besson, Mireille, Federique Faïta, Isabelle Peretz, Anne-Marie Bonnel, and Jean Requin. "Singing in the Brain: Independence of Lyrics and Tunes." *Psychological Science* 9: 6 (1998): 494–98.

Beynon, John. *Masculinities and Culture*. Buckingham: Open University Press, 2002.

Bigand, Emmanuel, Barbara Tillmann, Bénédicte Poulin, Daniel A. D'Adamo, and François Madurell. "The Effect of Harmonic Context on Phoneme Monitoring in Vocal Music." *Cognition* 81: 1 (2001): B11–B20.

Billington, Michael. "Metamorphoses/Elektra." *The Guardian*, February 2, 2006. Online. Available: http://www.guardian.co.uk/stage/2006/feb/02/theatre?INTCMP=SRCH. March 10, 2011.

Björk. *Selmasongs*. 2000. Elektra 62533-2. Compact disc.

Bleeker, Maaike. "Disorders That Consciousness Can Produce: Bodies Seeing Bodies Onstage." In *Bodycheck: Relocating the Body in Performing Art*, eds Maike Bleeker, Steven De Belder, Kaat Debo, Luk Van den Dries and Kurt Vanhoutte, 131-60. Amsterdam and New York: Rodopi, 2002 .

Block, Geoffrey. *Richard Rodgers*. New Haven: Yale University Press, 2003.

Blood, Anne J., and Robert J. Zatorre. "Intensely Pleasurable Responses to Music Correlate with Activity in Brain Regions Implicated in Reward and Emotion." *Proceedings of the National Academy of Sciences of the United States of America* 98: 20 (2001): 11818–23.

Blood, Anne J., Robert J. Zatorre, Patrick Bermudez, and Alan C. Evans. "Emotional Responses to Pleasant and Unpleasant Music Correlate with Activity in Paralimbic Brain Regions." *Nature Neuroscience* 2: 4 (1999): 382–87.

Bohannon, John. "John Bohannon: Dance vs. PowerPoint, a Modest Proposal." *TED: Ideas Worth Spreading*. November 22, 2011. Online. Available: http://www.ted.com/talks/john_bohannon_dance_vs_powerpoint_a_modest_proposal.html. December 12, 2012.

Bonnel, Anne-Marie, Federique Faïta, Isabelle Peretz, and Mireille Besson. "Divided Attention between Lyrics and Tunes of Operatic Songs: Evidence for Independent Processing." *Perception and Psychophysics* 63: 7 (2001): 1201–13.

Bradbury, Raymond. *Fahrenheit 451*. London: HarperCollins, 2008.

Bradley, Ian, ed. *The Complete Annotated Gilbert and Sullivan*. New York: Oxford University Press, 1996.

Brestoff, Richard. *The Great Acting Teachers*. Lyme, NJ: Smith and Kraus, 1995.

Brook, Peter. *The Empty Space*. London: Penguin, 1968.

Bruner, Jerome. "Life as Narrative." *Social Research* 54: 1 (1987): 11–32.

Buck-Morss, Susan. *The Dialectics of Seeing: Walter Benjamin and the Arcades Project*. Cambridge, MA: MIT Press, 1989.

Burrows, David. *Sound, Speech and Music*. Amherst: University of Massachusetts Press, 1990.

Butler, Judith. *Bodies That Matter: On the Discursive Limits of "Sex"*. New York: Routledge, 1993.

Butler, Judith. "Critically Queer." In *The Routledge Queer Studies Reader*, ed. Donald Hall and Annamarie Jagose, 18–31. London: Routledge, 2012.

Butler, Judith. *Gender Trouble: Feminism and the Subversion of Identity*. New York: Routledge, 1990.

Butler, Judith. "Performative Acts and Gender Constitution: An Essay in Phenomenology and Feminist Theory." In *Performing Feminisms: Feminist Critical Theory and Theatre*, ed. Sue-Ellen Case. Baltimore: John Hopkins University Press, 1990, 270-82.

Cage, John. *Song Books*. New York: C.F. Peters, 1970.

Calvo-Merino, Beatriz, et al. "Action Observation and Acquired Motor Skills: An fMRI Study with Expert Dancers." *Cerebral Cortex* 15 (2005): 1243–49.

Carlson, Marvin. *The Haunted Stage: The Theatre as Memory Machine*. Ann Arbor: University of Michigan Press, 2001.

Carlson, Marvin. *Performance: A Critical Introduction*. London: Routledge, 1996.

Carlson, Marvin. "Theatre and Dialogism." In *Critical Theory and Performance,* ed. Janelle G. Reinelt and Joseph R. Roach, 313–24. Ann Arbor: University of Michigan Press, 1992.

Causey, Mathew. "The Screen Test of the Double: The Uncanny Performer in the Space of Technology." *Theatre Journal* 51: 4 (1999): 383–94.

Cavarero, Adriana. *For More Than One Voice: Toward a Philosophy of Vocal Expression*. Trans. Paul A. Kottman. Stanford, CA: Stanford University Press, 2005.

Chion, Michel. *Audio-Vision: Sound on Screen*. Trans. W. Murch and C. Gorbman. New York: Columbia University Press, 1994.

Chion, Michel. *The Voice in Cinema*. Trans. Claudia Gorbman. New York: Columbia University Press, 1999.

Chow, Rew, and James A. Steintrager. "In Pursuit of the Object of Sound: An Introduction." In *Differences* 22: 2–3 (2011): 1–9.

Cioffi, Kathleen. "New (and Not-So-New) Alternatives." *Contemporary Theatre Review* 15: 1 (2005): 69–83.

Citron, Stephen. *The Musical from the Inside Out*. London: Hodder & Stoughton, 1991.

Cline, Patsy. *Patsy Cline*. 1962. Decca ED 2707. LP.

Clover, Carol. "Dancin' in the Rain." *Critical Inquiry* 21 (1995): 722–47.

Clum, John. *Something for the Boys: Musical Theater and Gay Culture*. New York: St. Martin's Press, 1999.

Cohen, Allen, and Steven. L. Rosenhaus. *Writing Musical Theatre*. New York: Palgrave Macmillan, 2006.

Comotti, Giovanni. *Music in Greek and Roman Culture*. Trans. Rosaria V. Munson. Baltimore: Johns Hopkins University Press, 1991.

Connell, R. W. *Masculinities*. 2nd ed. Cambridge: Polity, 2005.

Connor, Steven. "Chiasmus." *Studies in Musical Theatre* 6: 1 (2012): 9–27.

Connor, Steven. "De Singulatu: The Life and Times of the Sob." Paper presented at the "Breaking Voices" Symposium, London College of Fashion, June 7, 2008. Online. Available: http://www.bbk.ac.uk/english/skc/lectures.htm. October 22, 2008.

Connor, Steven. *Dumbstruck: A Cultural History of Ventriloquism*. New York: Oxford University Press, 2000.

Conquergood, Dwight. "Performance Studies: Interventions and Radical Research." *Drama Review* 46 (2002): 145–56.

Conrad, Peter. *Romantic Opera and Literary Form*. Berkeley: University of California Press, 1977.

Cook, Amy. "Interplay: The Method and Potential of a Cognitive Scientific Approach to Theatre." *Theatre Journal* 59 (2007): 579–94.

Cook, Amy. *Shakespearean Neuroplay: Reinvigorating the Study of Dramatic Texts and Performance through Cognitive Science*. Basingstoke: Palgrave Macmillan, 2010.

Cook, Nicholas. *Analysing Musical Multimedia*. Oxford: Oxford University Press, 1998.

Coppolillo, Henry P. "Maturational Aspects of the Transitional Phenomenon." *International Journal of Psychoanalysis* 48 (1967): 237–46.

Cox, Nell (producer). *Jammin': Jelly Roll Morton on Broadway*. New York: PBS, 1992. Videocassette.

Cross, Ian. "Music as a Social and Cognitive Process." In *Language and Music as Cognitive Systems*, ed. Patrick Rebuschat, Martin Rohrmeier, John A. Hawkins, and Ian Cross, 315–28. Oxford: Oxford University Press, 2011.

Cross, Ian, and Iain Molley. "The Evolution of Music: Theories, Definitions and the Nature of the Evidence." In *Communicative Musicality*, ed. Stephen Malloch and Colwyn Trevarthen, 61–82. Oxford: Oxford University Press, 2009.

Crowder, Robert G., Mary Louise Serafine, and Bruno H. Repp. "Physical Interaction and Association by Contiguity in Memory for the Words and Melodies of Songs." *Memory and Cognition* 18: 5 (1990): 469–76.

Culley, R. C. "An Approach to the Problem of Oral Tradition." *Vetus Testamentum* 13: 2 (1963): 113–25.

Cumming, Naomi. "The Subjectivities of 'Erbarme Dich.'" *Music Analysis* 16: 1 (1997): 5–44.

Czekanowska, Anna. *Polish Folk Music: Slavonic Heritage, Polish Tradition, Contemporary Trends*. Cambridge: Cambridge University Press, 1997.

Czekanowska, Anna. "The Teaching of Ethnomusicology in Poland: Experiences and Prospects." *Acta Musicologica* 58: 1 (1986): 24–35.

Damasio, Antonio. *The Feeling of What Happens: Body, Emotion and the Making of Consciousness*. London: Vintage, 2000.

De Marinis, Marco. "The Performance Text." In *The Performance Studies Reader*, ed. Henry Bial, 232–51. London: Routledge, 2004.

De Vries, Hilary. "The Wolfe at the (Stage) Door." *Los Angeles Times*, March 3, 1991. Online. Available: http://articles.latimes.com/print/1991-03-03/entertainment/ca-103_1_jelly-roll-morton. December 7, 2012.

DeCasper, Anthony J., and Melanie J. Spence. "Prenatal Maternal Speech Influences Newborns' Perception of Speech Sounds." *Infant Behavior and Development* 9: 2 (1986): 133–50.

DeFrantz, Thomas F. "Foreword: Black Bodies Dancing Black Culture—Black Atlantic Transformations." In *EmBODYing Liberation: The Black Body in American Dance*, ed. Dorothea Fischer-Hornung and Alison D. Goeller, 11–16. New Brunswick, NJ: Transaction Publishers, 2001.

Derrida, Jacques. *De la grammatologie*. Paris: Les Éditions de Minuit, 1967.

Derrida, Jacques. *Dissemination*. Trans. Barbara Johnson. London: Athlone Press, 1981.

Derrida, Jacques. "Heidegger's Ear: Philopolemology (Geschlect 4)." In *Reading Heidegger* ed. John Sallis. Trans. John P. Leavey Jr. 163–219. Bloomington: Indiana University Press, 1991.

Derrida, Jacques. *Margins of Philosophy*. Trans. Alan Bass. Chicago: University of Chicago Press, 1982.

Derrida, Jacques. *Of Grammatology*. Trans. Gayatri Chakravorty Spivak. Baltimore: John Hopkins University Press, 1976.

Derrida, Jacques. *Speech and Phenomena*. Trans. David B. Allison. Evanston, IL: Northwestern University Press, 1973.

Dixon, Steve. *Digital Performance: A History of New Media in Theater, Dance, Performance Art and Installation*. Cambridge, MA: MIT Press, 2007.

Dolan, Jill. *Presence and Desire: Essays on Gender, Sexuality and Performance*. Ann Arbor: University of Michigan Press, 1993.

Dolan, Jill. *Utopia in Performance*. Ann Arbor: University of Michigan Press, 2005.

Dolar, Mladen. "The Burrow of Sound." *Differences* 22: 2–3 (2011): 112–39.

Dolar, Mladen. *A Voice and Nothing More*. Cambridge, MA: MIT Press, 2006.

Dowling, Tim. "The Armchair Olympics: It Begins!" *The Guardian*, July 27, 2010.

Drake, Sylvie. "Stage Review: 'Jelly' Struts Its Stuff at Mark Taper." *Los Angeles Times*, March 8, 1991, 1.

duCille, Ann. "The Shirley Temple of My Familiar." *Transition* 73 (1997): 10–32.

Dyer, Richard. "Entertainment and Utopia." In *Only Entertainment*, ed. Richard Dyer, 19–35. London: Routledge, 2002.

Dylan, Bob. *Bringing It All Back Home*. Sleeve notes. CBS 62515, 1965.LP.

Eliot, T. S. *The Complete Poems and Plays of T. S. Eliot*. London: Book Club Associates, 1969.

Elkin, Michael. "'Jelly' on a Roll; Jewish Women Part of Black Musical's Success." *Jewish Exponent* (Philadelphia), August 21, 1992, 9X, 147.

Emmerson, Simon. *Living Electronic Music*. Kent: Ashgate, 2007.

"Enter Mr. DiMaggio." *Smash*, NBC, February 20, 2012.

Erlmann, Veit. *Reason and Resonance: A History of Modern Aurality*. New York: MIT Press, Zone Books, 2010.

Everett, William A., and Paul R. Laird, eds. *The Cambridge Companion to the Musical*. Cambridge: Cambridge University Press, 2002.

Fadiga, Luciano, Laila Craighero, and Alessandro D'Ausilio. "Broca's Area in Language, Action, and Music." *The Neurosciences and Music III—Disorders and Plasticity: Annals of the New York Academy of Science* 1169 (2009): 448–58.

Farmer, Brett. *Spectacular Passions: Cinema, Fantasy, Gay Male Spectatorships*. Durham, NC: Duke University Press, 2000.

Fedorenko, Evelina, Aniruddh D. Patel, Daniel Casasanto, Jonathan Winawer, and Edward Gibson. "Structural Integration in Language and Music: Evidence for a Shared System." *Memory and Cognition* 37: 1 (2009): 1–9.

Feuer, Jane. *The Hollywood Musical*. Bloomington: Indiana University Press, 1982.

Feuer, Jane. *The Hollywood Musical*. 2nd ed. Basingstoke: Macmillan, 1993.

Firmat, Gustavo Pérez. *Literature and Liminality: Festive Readings in the Hispanic Tradition*. Durham, NC: Duke University Press, 1986.

Fischer, Gerhard, and Greiner Bernhard, eds. *The Play within the Play: The Performance of Meta-theater and Self-Reflection*. Amsterdam: Rodopi, 2007.

Fischer-Lichte, Erika. *The Transformative Power of Performance: A New Aesthetics*. Trans. Saskya Iris Jain. New York: Routledge, 2008.

Frank, Jonathan. "Spotlight on Jason Robert Brown." *Talkin' Broadway*, 2000. Online. Available: http://www.talkinbroadway.com/spot/jrb1.html. February 20, 2012.

Frankel, Aaron. *Writing the Broadway Musical*. New York: Da Capo Press, 2000.

Frederickson, John. "Technology and Music Performance in the Age of Mechanical Reproduction." *International Review of the Aesthetics and Sociology of Music* 20: 2 (1989): 193–220.

Freeman, John. *Blood, Sweat and Theory: Research through Practice in Performance*. Farringdon: Libri Publishing, 2010.

Freud, Sigmund. "Beyond the Pleasure Principle." In *The Standard Edition of the Complete Psychological Works of Sigmund Freud*, trans. and ed. James Strachey, vol. 18, 1–64. London: Vintage, Hogarth Press, and the Institute of Psychoanalysis, 1920.

Frith, Simon. *Performing Rites: On the Value of Popular Music*. Cambridge, MA: Harvard University Press, 1996.

Frith, Simon. "Why Do Songs Have Words?" In *Lost in Music: Culture, Style and the Musical Event*, ed. Avron Levine White, 97–98. New York: Routledge, 1987.

Gallese, Vittorio, L. Fadiga, L. Fogassi, and Giacomo Rizzolatti. "Action Recognition in the Premotor Cortex." *Brain Research* 119 (1996): 593–609.

Garafola, Lynn. "The Travesty Dancer in the Nineteenth Century." *Dance Research Journal* 17: 2 and 18: 1 (1985–86): 35–40.

Gates, Henry Louis, Jr. *The Signifying Monkey: A Theory of Afro-American Literary Criticism*. New York: Oxford University Press, 1988.

Gautier, Théophile. *The Romantic Ballet*. London: C. W. Beaumont, 1947.

Gelles, Barrie. "*Glee* and the 'Ghosting' of the Musical Theater Canon." *Popular Entertainment Studies* 2: 2 (2011): 89–111.

Genette, Gérard. *Narrative Discourse Revisited*. Trans. J. E. Lewin. New York: Cornell University Press, 1988.

Gervain, Judit, Francesco Macagno, Silvia Cogoi, Marcela Peña, and Jacques Mehler. "The Neonate Brain Detects Speech Structure." *Proceedings of the National Academy of Sciences of the USA* 105 (September 2008): 14222–7.

Gilbert, W. S., and Arthur Sullivan. *The Mikado*. Directed by John Michael Phillips and Andrew Wickes. London: BBC, 1992. VHS. Online. Available: https://www.youtube.com/watch?v=ZRCbKHegzZk. December 2, 2012.

Gioia, Ted. *The History of Jazz*. New York: Oxford University Press, 1997.

Goebbels, Heiner. "Text als Landschaft: Librettoqualität, auch wenn nicht gesungen wird." In *Komposition als Inszenierung*, ed. Wolfgang Sandner, 64–70. Frankfurt am Main: Verlag der Autoren, 2002.

Gold, Sylviane. "Steven Hoggett is the Anti-dance Choreographer." *Los Angeles Times*, April 10, 2012. Online. Available: http://articles.latimes.com/print/2012/apr/10/entertainment/la-et-steven-hoggett-20120410. June 10, 2103.

Goldberg, Vicki. "High Tech Meets Goo with Blue Man Group." *New York Times*, November 17, 1991.

Gonçalves, Fernando do Nascimento. *Fabulaçoes eletrônicas: Poéticas da comunicaçao e da tecnologia em Laurie Anderson*. Rio de Janeiro: E-papers, 2006.

Gontarski, S. E. *Beckett's Happy Days: A Manuscript Study*. Columbus: Ohio State University Libraries, 1977.

Goodwin, Andrew. *Dancing in the Distraction Factory: Music Television and Popular Culture*. London: Routledge, 1993.

Gottschild, Brenda Dixon. *The Black Dancing Body*. New York: Palgrave Macmillan, 2003.

Grant, Barry Keith. *The Hollywood Film Musical*. Malden, MA: Wiley-Blackwell, 2012.

Green, Stanley, ed. *Ten Great Musicals of the American Theatre*. Radnor, PA: Chilton Book Company, 1973.

Grosbras, M-H, Jola, C, Kuppuswamy, A. and Pollick, F. "Enhanced Cortical Excitability Induced by Watching Dance in Empathetic and Visually Experienced Dance Spectators." Paper prepared for the conference "Kinaesthetic Empathy: Concepts and Contexts," Manchester University, UK, April 22–23, 2010.

Grotowski, Jerzy. *Towards a Poor Theatre*. Ed. Eugenio Barba. London: Methuen, 1969.

Hamlisch, Marvin, and Edward Kleban. *A Chorus Line*. Vocal score. New York: Edwin H. Morris, 1975.

Hamm, Charles. *Irving Berlin: Songs from the Melting Pot: The Formative Years, 1907–1914*. New York: Oxford University Press, 1997.

Hamm, Charles. *Music in the New World*. New York: Norton, 1983.

Hamm, Charles. *Yesterdays: Popular Song in America*. New York: Norton, 1983.

Hammerstein, Oscar. *Allegro*. New York: Alfred A. Knopf, 1948.

Hart, Dorothy. *Thou Swell, Thou Witty: The Life and Lyrics of Lorenz Hart*. New York: Harper & Row, 1976.

Harvey, Jonathan. "The Metaphysics of Live Electronics." *Contemporary Music Review* 18: 3 (1999): 79–82.

Harvie, Jen. *Staging the UK*. Manchester: Manchester University Press, 2005.

Hayles, N. Katherine. *How We Became Posthuman: Virtual Bodies in Cybernetics, Literature, and Informatics.* Chicago: University of Chicago Press, 1999.

Henson, Karen. "Introduction: Divo Worship." *Cambridge Opera Journal* 19: 1 (2007): 1–10.

Hickok, Gregory. "Eight Problems for the Mirror Neuron Theory of Action Understanding in Monkeys and Humans." *Journal of Cognitive Neuroscience* 21: 7 (2008): 1229–43.

Hill, Constance Valis. *Tap Dancing America: A Cultural History.* New York: Oxford University Press, 2010.

Hoban, Phoebe. "Euripides in Bacchanal (it's Also One of His Plays)." *New York Times,* April 13, 2005, E7.

Hodge, Alison, ed. *Actor Training.* New York: Routledge, 2010.

Hodge, Alison. "Gardzienice's Influence in the West." *Contemporary Theatre Review* 15: 1 (2005): 59–68.

Hong, K. Michael. "The Transitional Phenomena: A Theoretical Integration." *Psychoanalytic Study of the Child* 33 (1978): 47–79.

Hood, M. "The Reliability of Oral Tradition." *Journal of the American Musicological Society* 12: 2–3 (1959): 201–9.

Hornby, Richard. "Musicals Revived." *Hudson Review* 45: 3 (1992): 452–58.

Horton, Paul C. "Language, Solace, and Transitional Relatedness." *Psychoanalytic Study of the Child* 39 (1984): 167–94.

Horton, Paul C. *Solace: The Missing Dimension in Psychiatry.* Chicago: University of Chicago Press, 1981.

Hulton, Peter, and Dorinda Hulton, eds. *Gardzienice, Poland.* Exeter: Arts Archives, 1993. DVD.

Hunter, Lynette. "Theory/Practice as Research: Explorations, Questions and Suggestions." In *Mapping Landscapes for Performance as Research: Scholarly Acts and Creative Cartographies,* ed. Shannon Rose Riley and Lynette Hunter, 230–6. Basingstoke: Palgrave Macmillan, 2009.

Hutchins, Ernest. *Cognition in the Wild.* Cambridge, MA: MIT Press, 1995.

Hutera, Donald. "Religion and Ritual." *Glasgow Herald.* May 1, 1989, n.pag.

Jacobson, Alan. "Across the Universe: Julie Taymor Made the Most Spectacular Film of the Year. Too Bad Nobody Noticed." Online. Available: http://www.brightlights-film.com/61/61universe.php. April 10, 2012.

Jakobson, Roman. *The Sound Shape of Language.* The Hague: Mouton de Gruyter, 2002.

Janacek, Gerald. *Zaum: The Transrational Poetry of Russian Futurism.* San Diego: San Diego State University Press, 1996.

John, Elton. *Elton John.* 2004, 1970 by DJM Records. Island Records B0003607-36. Compact disc.

Johnson-Spence, Jennifer, dir. "Episode 185/186: ATW's Working in the Theatre: Production: 'Jelly's Last Jam'." American Theatre Wing, CUNY TV, September 1, 1992. http://www.cuny.tv/audiovideo.

Jola, Corinne. "Merging Dance and Cognitive Neuroscience." In *The Neurocognition of Dance: Mind, Movement and Motor Skills,* ed. Bettina Blasing, Martin Puttke-Voss, and Thomas Schack, 203–34. Hove: Psychology Press, 2010.

Jourdain, Robert. *Music, the Brain and Ecstasy: How Music Captures Our Imagination.* New York: Harper Collins, 2002.

Jowitt, Deborah. "Dancing Masculinity: Defining the Male Image Onstage in Twentieth-Century America and Beyond." *Southwest Review* 95 (2010): 227–42.

Jowitt, Deborah. *Time and the Dancing Image.* Berkeley: University of California Press, 1988.

Kaiero, Ainhoa. "Technological Fiction, Recorded Time and 'Replicants' in the Concerts of Laurie Anderson." *TRANS: Transcultural Music Review* 14 (2010). Online. Available: http://www.sibetrans.com/trans/a10/technological-fiction-recorded-time-and-replicants-in-the-concerts-of-laurie-anderson?lang=en. October 31, 2012.

Kalb, Jonathan. *Beckett in Performance*. New York: Cambridge University Press, 1989.

Kendrick, Lynne, and David Roesner, eds. *Theatre Noise: The Sound of Performance*. Newcastle: Cambridge Scholars Publishing, 2011.

Kentucky Network, The. "George C. Wolfe." Annenberg/CPB, 1996. Online. Available: http://www.learner.org/resources/series55.html. December 12, 2012.

Kern, Jerome, and Oscar Hammerstein II. *Music in the Air*. Original cast recording, radio broadcast. 1952 by AEI. AEI CD024. Compact disc.

Kessler, Kelly. *Destabilizing the Hollywood Musical: Music, Masculinity and Mayhem*. Basingstoke: Palgrave Macmillan, 2010.

Keysers, Christian. "From Mirror Neurons to Kinaesthetic Empathy." Keynote presentation to *"Kinaesthetic Empathy: Concepts and Contexts,"* Manchester University, April 22–23, 2010.

Keysers, Christian, and V. Gazzola. "Social Neuroscience: Mirror Neurons Recorded in Humans." *Current Biology* 20: 8 (2010): 353–54.

Kimmel, Michael. *Manhood in America: A Cultural History*. New York: Free Press, 1996.

Kirkwood, James, Michael Bennett, and Nicholas Dante. *A Chorus Line*. Libretto. New York: Applause, 1975.

Kirle, Bruce. *Unfinished Show Business: Broadway Musicals as Works-in-Process*. Carbondale: Southern Illinois University Press, 2005.

Kislan, Richard. *Hoofing on Broadway: A History of Show Dancing*. New York: Prentice Hall, 1987.

Kisselgoff, Anna. "Baryshnikov and Feld Rejoin Forces." *New York Times*, March 9, 1995, C13.

Kisselgoff, Anna. "Dance View; Dance and Song Are Cheek to Cheek on Broadway." *New York Times*, July 5, 1992, B1.

Knapp, Raymond. *The American Musical and the Performance of Personal Identity*. Princeton, NJ: Princeton University Press, 2006.

Knapp, Raymond. *The American Musical and the Representation of National Identity*. Princeton, NJ: Princeton University Press, 2005.

Raymond Knapp, "Performance, Authenticity, and the Reflexive Idealism of the American Musical." In *The Oxford Handbook of the American Musical*, ed. Raymond Knapp, Mitchell Morris, and Stacy Wolf, 408–22. Oxford: Oxford University Press, 2011.

Knowlson, James. *Damned to Fame: The Life of Samuel Beckett*. London: Bloomsbury, 1996.

Koelsch, Stefan. "Neural Substrates of Processing Syntax and Semantics in Music." *Current Opinion in Neurobiology* 15: 2 (2005): 1–6.

Koelsch, Stefan, Thomas C. Gunter, D. Yves von Cramon, Stefan Zysset, Gabriele Lohmann, and Angela D. Friederici. "Bach Speaks: A Cortical 'Language-Network' Serves the Processing of Music." *NeuroImage* 17: 2 (2002): 956–66.

Koelsch, Stefan, Thomas C. Gunter, Matthias Wittfoth, and Daniela Sammler. "Interaction between Syntax Processing in Language and in Music: An ERP Study." *Journal of Cognitive Neuroscience* 17: 10 (2005): 1565–79.

Koelsch, Stefan, Burkhard Maess, and Angela D. Friederici. "Musical Syntax Is Processed in the Area of Broca: An MEG Study." *NeuroImage* 11: 5 (2000): 56.

Koestenbaum, Wayne. *The Queen's Throat: Opera, Homosexuality, and the Mystery of Desire*. Cambridge, MA: Da Capo Press, 2001.

Kohn, Martin F. "The Celluloid Source: Movies Provide a Well of Inspiration for the Musical Stage." *Detroit Free Press*, March 17, 2002.

Kosinski, Dariusz, ed. *Polish Theatre Perspectives: Theatre "Out of the Spirit of Music"*. 2: 2 (2011).

Sedgwick, Eve Kosofsky. *Performativity and Performance*. New York: Routledge, 1995.

Kramer, Lawrence. *Music as Cultural Practice 1800–1900*. Berkeley: University of California Press, 1990.

Kramer, Lawrence. "The Mysteries of Animation: History, Analysis and Musical Subjectivity." *Music Analysis* 20: 2 (2001): 153–78.

Kramer, Lawrence. "Unsung Voices: Opera and Musical Narrative in the Nineteenth Century by Carolyn Abbate." *Nineteenth-Century Music* 15: 3 (1992): 235–9.

Kristeva, Julia. *Revolution in Poetic Language.* Trans. Margaret Waller. New York: Columbia University Press, 1984.

LaBelle, Brandon. *The Site of Sound # 2: Of Architecture and the Ear.* Ed. Brandon LaBelle and Claudia Martinho. Berlin: Errant Bodies Press, 2011.

Lacan, Jacques. *Écrits: A Selection.* Trans. Bruce Fink. London: Norton, 2004.

Lacan, Jacques. *Family Complexes in the Formation of the Individual.* Trans. Cormac Gallagher. 1938. Unpublished.

Lacan, Jacques. *Playing and Reality.* 1971; reprint, London: Routledge Classics, 2005.

Lacan, Jacques. "Position of the Unconscious." In *Écrits: The First Complete Edition in English,* trans. Bruce Fink, 703–21. 1964; New York: Norton, 2007.

Lacan, Jacques. *Les quatre concepts fondamentaux de la psychanalyse (Sem 11).* Paris: Seuil, 1973.

Lacan, Jacques. *The Seminar of Jacques Lacan. Book VII: The Ethics of Psychoanalysis.* Trans. Dennis Porter, ed. Jacques-Alain Miller. 1959–60; New York: Norton, 1997.

Lacan, Jacques. *The Seminar of Jacques Lacan. Book XI: The Four Fundamental Concepts of Psychoanalysis.* Trans. Alan Sheridan, ed. Jacques-Alain Miller. 1973; New York: Norton, 1998.

Lacan, Jacques. *The Seminar of Jacques Lacan. Book XVII: Psychoanalysis Upside-Down/The Reverse of Psychoanalysis.* Trans. Cormac Gallagher. 1969–70. Unpublished.

Lacan, Jacques. "The Subversion of the Subject and the Dialectic of Desire in the Freudian Unconscious." In *Écrits: The First Complete Edition in English,* trans. Bruce Fink, 671–702. 1960; New York: Norton, 2007.

LaChiusa, Michael John. *Bernarda Alba: Libretto.* New York: Rodgers and Hammerstein Theatricals, 2007.

LaChiusa, Michael John. *Bernarda Alba: Piano-Vocal Score.* New York: Rodgers and Hammerstein Theatricals, 2007.

LaChiusa, Michael John. "Interview by Ira Weitzman." *Lincoln Center Theater,* March 13, 2006. Online. Available: http://www.lct.org/showMain.htm?id=178. December 7, 2012.

LaChiusa, Michael John. "Interview by Thomas Cott." *Lincoln Center Theater.* November 17, 1999. Online. Available: http://www.lct.org/showMain.htm?id=95. December 7, 2012.

Laing, Heather. "Emotion by Numbers: Music, Song and the Musical." In *Musicals: Hollywood and Beyond,* ed. Bill Marshall and Robynn Stilwell, 5–13. Exeter: Intellect Books, 2000.

Laird, Paul. "Choreographers, Directors and the Fully Integrated Musical." In *The Cambridge Companion to the Musical,* ed. William A. Everett and Paul R. Laird, 220–34. Cambridge: Cambridge University Press, 2008.

LaPointe-Crump, Janice. "Of Dainty Gorillas and Macho Sylphs: Dance and Gender." In *The Dance Experience,* ed. Myron Howard Nadel and Marc Raymond Strauss, 2nd ed., 159–72. Hightstown, NJ: Princeton Book Company, 2003.

Lawley, Paul. "Stages of Identity: From Krapp's Last Tape to Play." In *The Cambridge Companion to Beckett,* ed. John Pilling, 88–105. New York: Cambridge University Press, 1994.

Lehman, Engel. *The American Musical Theatre.* Rev. ed. New York: Macmillan, 1975.

Leknes, Siri, and Irene Tracey. "A Common Neurobiology for Pain and Pleasure." *Nature Reviews Neuroscience* 9: 4 (2008): 314–20.

Levitin, Daniel J. *This Is Your Brain on Music: The Science of a Human Obsession.* New York: Plume, 2007.

Levitin, Daniel J. *The World in Six Songs: How the Musical Brain Created Human Nature.* New York: Dutton Adult, 2008.

Levitin, Daniel J., and Vinod Menon. "Musical Structure Is Processed in 'Language' Areas of the Brain: A Possible Role for Brodmann Area 47 in Temporal Coherence." *NeuroImage* 20: 4 (2003): 2142–52.

Levitin, Daniel J., and Anna K. Tirovolas. "Current Advances in the Cognitive Neuroscience of Music." *The Year in Cognitive Neuroscience 2009: Annals of the New York Academy of Sciences* 1156 (2009): 211–31.

Lidji, Pascale, Pierre Jolicœur, Patricia Moreau, Régine Kolinsky, and Isabelle Peretz. "Integrated Pre-attentive Processing of Vowel and Pitch: A Mismatch Negativity Study." *Annals of the New York Academy of Sciences* 1169: 1 (2009): 481–4.

Lloyd Webber, Andrew, and Charles Hart. *The Phantom of the Opera*. 1987 by Polydor. Polydor 831 273-2 Y-2. Compact disc.

Lodge, Mary Jo. "Review of Spring Awakening." *Theatre Journal* 60:3 (2008): 460–62.

Lowerre, Kathryn. "Fallen Woman Redeemed: Eliot, Victorianism, and Opera in Andrew Lloyd Webber's *Cats*." *Journal of Musicological Research* 23: 3 (2004): 289–314.

Loxley, James. *Performativity*. New York: Routledge, 2007.

Lyotard, Jean-François. *The Postmodern Condition: A Report on Knowledge*. Trans. Geoff Bennington and Brian Massumi. Minneapolis: University of Minnesota Press, 1979.

MacInnes, John. *The End of Masculinity*. Buckingham: Open University Press, 1998.

Maess, Burkhard, Stefan Koelsch, Thomas C. Gunter, and Angela D. Friederici. "Musical Syntax Is Processed in Broca's Area: An MEG Study." *Nature Neuroscience* 4: 5 (2001): 540–5.

Magee, Jeffrey. "Irving Berlin's 'Blue Skies': Ethnic Affiliations and Musical Transformations." *Musical Quarterly* 84: 4 (2000): 537–80.

Mampe, Birgit, Angela D. Friederici, Anne Christophe, and Kathleen Wermke. "Newborns' Cry Melody is Shaped by Their Native Language." *Current Biology* 19: 23 (2009): 1994–7.

Margolick, David. *Strange Fruit: The Biography of a Song*. London: HarperCollins, 2001.

Marshall, Rob, dir. *Nine*. Los Angeles: Weinstein Company / Relativity Media, 2009. DVD.

Marshall, Rob, and John DeLuca. "Director's Commentary." *Nine*. Directed by Rob Marshall. Los Angeles: Weinstein Company/Relativity Media, 2009. 114 mins. DVD.

McAfee, Noelle. *Julia Kristeva*. New York: Routledge, 2004.

McCallumo, Conrad. "Why They Call It the Blues." *The Star*, November 13, 2007. Online. Available: http://www.thestar.com/living/article/275759. March 28, 2012.

McConachie, Bruce. *Engaging Audiences: A Cognitive Approach to Spectating at the Theatre*. New York: Palgrave MacMillan, 2008.

McKenzie, Jon. "Genre Trouble: (The) Butler Did It." In *The Ends of Performance*, ed. Peggy Phelan and Jill Lane, 217–35. New York: New York University Press, 1998.

McKenzie, Jon. *Perform or Else: From Discipline to Performance*. New York: Routledge, 2001.

McLean, Anna Helena. Interview by Konstantinos Thomaidis. London. December 7, 2008.

McMillin, Scott. *The Musical as Drama*. Princeton, NJ: Princeton University Press, 2006.

McMullen, Anna. *Theatre on Trial: Samuel Beckett's Later Drama*. New York: Routledge, 1993.

Menon, Vinod, and Daniel J. Levitin. "The Rewards of Music Listening: Response and Physiological Connectivity of the Mesolimbic System." *NeuroImage* 28: 1 (2005): 175–84.

Merleau-Ponty, Maurice. *Phénoménologie de la perception*. Paris: Gallimard, 1976.

Metz, Christian. *Le signifiant imaginaire: Psychanalyse et cinema*. Paris: Christian Bourgois Éditeur, 2002.

Miller, D. A. *Place for Us: Essays on the Broadway Musical*. Cambridge, MA: Harvard University Press, 1998.

Monks, Aoife. " 'The Souvenir from Foreign Parts': Foreign Femininity in Deborah Warner's *Medea*." *Australasian Drama Studies* 43 (2003): 32–46.

Monro, David Binning. *The Modes of Ancient Greek Music*. Oxford: Elibron Classics, 2005.

Moon, Christine, Robin Panneton Cooper, and William P. Fifer. "Two-Day-Olds Prefer Their Native Language." *Infant Behavior and Development* 16: 4 (1993): 495–500.

Moore, Tracey, and Allison Bergman. *Acting the Song: Performance Skills for the Musical Theatre.* New York: Allworth Press, 2008.

Morris, Rebecca. "Hope Clarke (Choreographer) (People)." *American Theatre* 11: 10 (1994): 53–4.

Most, Andrea. *Making Americans: Jews and the Broadway Musical.* Cambridge, MA: Harvard University Press, 2004.

Murray, David. "Capriccio (ii)." In *The New Grove Dictionary of Opera—Grove Music Online—Oxford Music Online,* ed. Stanley Sadie. Online. Available: http://www.oxfordmusiconline.com/subscriber/article/grove/music/O900991. March 28, 2012.

Nattiez, Jean-Jacques. *Music and Discourse: Toward a Semiology of Music.* Princeton, NJ: Princeton University Press, 1990.

Nazzi, Thierry, and Franck Ramus. "Perception and Acquisition of Linguistic Rhythm by Infants." *Speech Communication* 41: 1 (2003): 233–43.

Nelson, Robin. "Modes of Practice-as-Research Knowledge and Their Place in the Academy." In *Practice-as-Research in Performance and Screen,* ed. Ludivine Allegue et al., 112–30. New York: Palgrave Macmillan, 2009.

Nettl, Bruno. *Folk and Traditional Music of the Western Continents.* 3rd ed. Englewood Cliffs, NJ: Prentice Hall, 1990.

Nixon, Will. "Profile: Playwright George C. Wolfe." *American Visions* 6: 2 (1991): 50–52.

Niziolek, Grzegorz. "Gardzienice: 'Elektra.'" *Le Théâtre en Pologne–The Theatre in Poland* 1: 2 (2004): 41–44.

Nye, Sean. "From Punk to the Musical: South Park, Music, and the Cartoon Format." In *Music in Television: Channels of Listening,* ed. James Deaville, 143–64. London: Routledge, 2011.

O'Malley, Sheila. Online. Available: http://www.sheilaomalley.com/?p=9942. April 10, 2012.

Out of My Dreams: Oscar Hammerstein II. PBS. March 3, 2012.

Overy, Katie, and Istvan Molnar-Szakacs. "Being Together in Time: Musical Experience and the Mirror Neuron System." *Music Perception* 26: 5 (2009): 489–504.

Parker, Andrew, and Eve Kosofsky Sedgwick. "Sexual Politics, Performativity and Performance." In *The Routledge Reader in Politics and Performance,* ed. Lizbeth Goodman and Jane de Gay, 172–77. London: Routledge, 2000.

Patel, Aniruddh D. *Music, Language and the Brain.* New York: Oxford University Press, 2008.

Perani, Daniela, Maria Cristina Saccuman, Paola Scifo, Danilo Spada, Guido Andreolli, Rosanna Rovelli, Cristina Baldoli, and Stefan Koelsch. "Music in the First Days of Life." *Nature Precedings,* July 2008. Online. Available: http://precedings.nature.com/documents/2114/version/1. March 28, 2012.

Peyser, Joan. *The Memory of All That: The Life of George Gershwin.* New York: Billboard Books, 1998.

Phelan, Peggy. *Unmarked: The Politics of Performance.* London: Routledge, 1993.

Phelan, Peggy, and Jill Lane, eds. *The Ends of Performance.* New York: New York University Press, 1998.

Pöhlmann, Egert, and Martin L. West. *Documents of Ancient Greek Music: The Extant Melodies and Fragments Edited and Transcribed with Commentary.* Oxford: Oxford University Press, 2001.

Poizat, Michel. *The Angel's Cry: Beyond the Pleasure Principle in Opera.* Trans. Arthur Denner. 1986; Ithaca, NY: Cornell University Press, 1992.

Potter, John. "Ensemble Singing." In *The Cambridge Companion to Singing,* ed. John Potter, 158–64. Cambridge: Cambridge University Press, 2000.

Poulin-Charronnat, Bénédicte, Emmanuel Bigand, François Madurell, and Ronald Peereman. "Musical Structure Modulates Semantic Priming in Vocal Music." *Cognition* 94: 3 (2005): 67–78.

Pountney, Rosemary. "*Happy Days* at the National Theatre." (1976). Online. Available: http://www.english.fsu.edu/jobs/num01/Num1Pountney2.htm. December 20, 2008.

Pountney, Rosemary. "On Acting Mouth in *Not I*." *Journal of Beckett Studies* 1 (1983): 81–5.

Prather, Pamela. Interview by Konstantinos Thomaidis. Gardzienice, Poland. September 12, 2009.

Prescott, Nick. "Across the Universe." Online. Available: https://dspace.flinders.edu.au/jspui/bitstream/2328/7496/3/Prescott_Across_the_Universe.pdf. April 10, 2012.

Prosser, Jay. "Judith Butler: Queer Feminism, Transgender, and the Transubstantiation of Sex." In *The Routledge Queer Studies Reader*, ed. Donald Hall and Annamarie Jagose, 32–59. London: Routledge, 2012.

Ramsey, Burt. *The Male Dancer: Bodies, Spectacle, Sexualities*. New York: Routledge, 1995.

Randolph, Laura B. "*Jelly's Last Jam* and the Pain and Passion of Gregory Hines." *Ebony* 47: 11 (1992): 116–9.

Ratajczakowa, Dobrochna. "In Transition: 1989–2004." Trans and ed. Paul Allain and Grzegorz Ziolkowski. *Contemporary Theatre Review* 15:1 (2005): 17–27.

Rice, Tim, and Andrew Lloyd Webber. *Jesus Christ Superstar*. 1972. Fanfare SIT 60006. LP.

Richards, Thomas. *At Work with Grotowski on Physical Actions*. New York: Routledge, 1995.

Richmond, Keith. *The Musicals of Andrew Lloyd Webber*. London: Virgin Publishing, 1995.

Riefenstahl, Leni. *Triumph of the Will*. [Short version] Online. Available: http://www.youtube.com/watch?v=v6WMXd8ZqmM&feature=related. December 5, 2012.

Rizzolatti, Giacomo, and Corrado Sinigaglia. *Mirrors in the Brain: How We Share our Actions and Emotions*. New York: Oxford University Press, 2008.

Robertson, Paul. "Music, Mind and Brain." Paper presented at the King's College London, Music Colloquium series, London, December 5, 2007.

Rodgers, Richard, and Oscar Hammerstein II. *Allegro*. Vocal score. New York: Williamson Music, 1948.

Rodman, Ron. "'Coperettas,' 'Detecterns,' and Space Operas: Music and Genre Hybridization in American Television." In *Music in Television: Channels of Listening*, ed. James Deaville, 35–56. London: Routledge, 2011.

Rodosthenous, George. "*Billy Elliot The Musical*: Visual Representations of Working-Class Masculinity and the All-Singing, All-Dancing Bo[d]y." *Studies in Musical Theatre* 1: 3 (2007): 275–92.

Rolnick, Katie. "Gregory Hines: America's Ambassador of Tap." *Dance Teacher* (2010). Online. Available: http://www.dance-teacher.com/content/gregory-hines. December 7, 2012.

Rose, Jodi. "Why Bridges? Why Sound?" In *The Site of Sound # 2: Of Architecture and the Ear*, ed. Brandon LaBelle and Claudia Martinho, 187–195. Berlin: Errant Bodies Press, 2011.

Rosenthal, Harold, and John Warrack. *The Concise Oxford Dictionary of Opera*. Oxford: Oxford University Press, 1987.

Ross, Barry. "Challenges Facing Theories of Music and Language Co-evolution." *Journal of the Musical Arts in Africa* 6 (2009): 61–76.

Rowell, Charles H. "'I Just Want to Keep Telling Stories': An Interview with George C. Wolfe." *Callaloo* 16: 3 (1993): 602–23.

Rychly, Maciej. "Untitled Note." In *Metamorfozy, Music of Ancient Greece*, 9–19. CD booklet.

Sacks, Oliver. *Musicophilia: Tales of Music and the Brain*. New York: Picador, 2007.

Salecl, Renata, and Slavoj Žižek. *Gaze and Voice as Love Objects*. Durham, NC: Duke University Press, 1996.

Salih, Sarah. *Judith Butler*. New York: Routledge, 2004.

Salimpoor, Valorie N., Mitchel Benovoy, Kevin Larcher, Alain Dagher, and Robert J. Zatorre. "Anatomically Distinct Dopamine Release during Anticipation and

Experience of Peak Emotion to Music." *Nature Neuroscience* 14: 2 (2011): 257–62.

Sammler, Daniela, Amee Baird, Romain Valabrègue, Sylvain Clément, Sophie Dupont, Pascal Belin, and Séverine Samson. "The Relationship of Lyrics and Tunes in the Processing of Unfamiliar Songs: A Functional Magnetic Resonance Adaptation Study." *Journal of Neuroscience* 30: 10 (2010): 3572–78.

Sandla, Robert. "Meet the Hunnies and a Honey." *Dance Magazine* 56: 11 (1992): 76–77.

Savran, David. *A Queer Sort of Materialism: Recontextualizing American Theater*. Ann Arbor: University of Michigan Press, 2003.

Schafer, R. Murray. *The Soundscape: Our Sonic Environment and the Tuning of the World*. Rochester: Destiny Books, 1994.

Schafer, R. Murray. *When Words Sing*. Toronto: Berandol Music, 1970.

Schechner, Richard. *Between Theater and Anthropology*. Philadelphia: University of Pennsylvania Press, 1985.

Schechner, Richard. *Performance Theory*. 1988; reprint, New York: Routledge, 2003.

Schechner, Richard. "What Is Performance Studies Anyway?" In *The Ends of Performance*, ed. Peggy Phelan and Jill Lane, 357–62. New York: New York University Press, 1998.

Scherzinger, Martin. "When the Music of Psychoanalysis Becomes the Psychoanalysis of Music." Review essay on *Listening Subjects: Music, Psychoanalysis, Culture* by David Schwartz. *Current Musicology* 66 (1999): 95–114.

Schön, Daniele, Reyna Leigh Gordon, and Mireille Besson. "Musical and Linguistic Processing in Song Perception." *Annals of the New York Academy of Sciences* 1060 (2005): 71–81.

Schuller, Gunter. *Early Jazz: Its Roots and Musical Development*. New York: Oxford University Press, 1986.

Schwarz, David. *Listening Subjects: Music Psychoanalysis, Culture*. Durham, NC: Duke University Press, 1997.

Schwegler, Robert A. "Oral Tradition and Print: Domestic Performance in Renaissance England." *Journal of American Folklore* 93: 370 (1980): 435–41.

Sebesta, Judith. "From Celluloid to Stage: The 'Movical,' *The Producers*, and the Postmodern." *Theatre Annual* 56 (2003): 97–112.

Sebesta, Judith. "Introduction." In *Women in American Musical Theatre: Essays on Composers, Lyricists, Librettists, Arrangers, Choreographers, Designers, Directors, Producers and Performance Artists*, ed. Bud Coleman and Judith Sebesta, 1–8. New York: McFarland Press, 2008.

Sebesta, Judith. " 'Real Men' Watch Musicals: *The Full Monty* and Post 9/11 Masculinity." *Studies in American Culture* 31: 1 (2009): 1–12.

Serafine, Mary Louise, Robert G. Crowder, and Bruno H. Repp. "Integration of Melody and Text in Memory for Songs." *Cognition* 16: 3 (1984): 285–303.

Serafine, Mary Louise, Janet Davidson, Robert G. Crowder, and Bruno H. Repp. "On the Nature of Melody-Text Integration in Memory for Songs." *Journal of Memory and Language* 25: 2 (1986): 123–35.

Serrano, Juan, and Jose Elgorriaga. *Flamenco, Body and Soul: An Aficionado's Introduction*. Fresno: California State University, 1990.

Serres, Michel. *Genesis*. Trans. Geneviève James and James Nielson. Ann Arbor: University of Michigan Press, 1995.

Shaw, Fiona. "Buried in Beckett." *The Guardian*, January 23, 2007. Online. Available: http://www.guardian.co.uk/theguardian/2007/jan/23/features11.g21?INTCMP=SRCH. December 20, 2008.

Shaw, Marc Edward, and Elwood Watson. *Performing American Masculinities: The 21st-Century Man in Popular Culture*. Bloomington: Indiana University Press, 2011.

Small, Christopher. *Musicking: The Meanings of Performing and Listening*. Hanover, NH: University Press of New England, 1998.

Smart, Mary Ann. *Mimomania: Music and Gesture in Nineteenth-Century Opera.* Berkeley: University of California Press, 2004.

Smith, Susan. *The Musical: Race, Gender and Performance.* London: Wallflower, 2005.

Sommer, Sally. "Tap Dance and How It Got That Way." *Dance Magazine* 62: 9 (1988): 56–60.

Sondheim, Stephen, and George Furth. *Company.* Libretto. New York: Theatre Communications Group, 1996.

Sondheim, Stephen. *Finishing the Hat: Collected Lyrics (1954–1981).* London: Virgin Books, 2010.

Staniewski, Wlodzimierz. "Baltimore Interview with Richard Schechner." *Drama Review* 113: 1 (1987): 137–63.

Staniewski, Wlodzimierz. *"Gardzienice" Practising the Humanities.* Gardzienice: Dialog and Institut Teatralny, 2005. CD-ROM.

Staniewski, Wlodzimierz. "*Iphigenia at A*...: Oxford Lecture." Paper presented at Magdalen College, Oxford, October 26, 2009.

Staniewski, Wlodzimierz, and Alison Hodge. *Hidden Territories: The Theatre of Gardzienice.* New York: Routledge, 2004.

Staniewski, Wlodzimierz, Alison Hodge, and Peter Hulton, eds. *Hidden Territories: The Theatre of Gardzienice.* Arts Archives. New York: Routledge, 2004. CD-ROM.

Stearns, David Patrick. "Hines Taps His Deeper Talents; 'Jelly' Role Earns Him a Tony Nod." *USA Today*, May 29, 1992, 1D.

Stearns, David Patrick. "*Jelly's Last Jam* on a Rocky Tour Road." *USA Today*, November 21, 1994, 6D.

Stearns, Peter. *Be a Man! Males in Modern Society.* 2nd ed. New York: Holmes, 1990.

Stefanics, Gábor, Gábor P. Háden, István Sziller, László Balázs, Anna Beke, and István Winkler. "Newborn Infants Process Pitch Intervals." *Clinical Neurophysiology* 120: 2 (2009): 304–8.

Steinbeis, Nikolaus, and Stefan Koelsch. "Comparing the Processing of Music and Language Meaning Using EEG and fMRI Provides Evidence for Similar and Distinct Neural Representations." *PloS ONE* 3: 5 (2008): 1–7. Online. Available: http://www.plosone.org/article/info%3Adoi%2F10.1371%2Fjournal.pone.0002226. March 28, 2012.

Sternfeld, Jessica. *The Megamusical.* Bloomington: Indiana University Press, 2006.

Steyn, Mark. *Broadway Babies Say Goodnight: Musicals Then & Now.* London: Routledge, 1999.

Stokes, Adrian. *Tonight the Ballet.* London: Faber & Faber, 1942.

Stucker, Richard. *Bernarda Alba.* Original Off-Broadway Cast. April 5, 2006. Theatre on Film and Tape Archive, New York Public Library for the Performing Arts: Lincoln Center, directed by Graciela Daniele. Videocassette [Beta], 89 mins.

Sullivan, Nikki. *A Critical Introduction to Queer Theory.* New York: New York University Press, 2003.

Sun, William H., and Faye C. Fei. "The Colored Theatre in Los Angeles." *TDR* 36: 2 (1992): 173–81.

Swain, Joseph P. *The Broadway Musical: A Critical and Musical Survey.* 2nd ed. Lanham, MA: Scarecrow Press, 2002.

Taplin, Oliver. *Greek Tragedy in Action.* London: Methuen, 1978.

Taplin, Oliver. *Pots & Plays: Interactions Between Tragedy and Greek Vase-Painting of the Fourth Century B.C.* Los Angeles: Getty Publications, 2007.

Tawa, Nicholas. *The Way to Tin Pan Alley: American Popular Song, 1866–1910.* New York: Schirmer Books, 1990.

Taylor, Millie. "Experiencing Live Musical Theater Performance: *La Cage Aux Folles* and *Priscilla, Queen of the Desert.*" *Popular Entertainment Studies* 1: 1 (2010): 44–58.

Taylor, Millie. "'If I Sing': Voice, Singing and Song." *Studies in Musical Theatre* 6: 1 (2012): 3–7.

Taylor, Millie. *Musical Theatre, Realism and Entertainment.* Surrey: Ashgate, 2012.

Taymor, Julie, dir. *Across the Universe.* Sony C8283549. DVD.

Thelan, Lawrence. *The Show Makers: Great Directors of the American Musical Theatre.* New York: Routledge, 2002.

Themelis, Konstantinos. *Enestos Diarkeias: Synantisi me ton Jerzy Grotowski* [*Present Continuous: A Meeting with Jerzy Grotowski*]. Athens: Indiktos, 2001.

Toop, David. *Haunted Weather: Music, Silence and Memory.* Chatham: Mackays, 2005.

Totton, Robin. *Songs of the Outcasts: An Introduction to Flamenco.* Portland, OR: Amadeus Press, 2003.

Trainor, Laurel J. "The Neural Roots of Music." *Nature* 453: 7195 (2008): 598–99.

Trainor, Laurel J., and Christine A. Zacharias. "Infants Prefer Higher-Pitched Singing." *Infant Behavior & Development* 21: 4 (1998): 799–805.

Traister, Bruce. "Academic Viagra: The Rise of American Masculinity Studies." *American Quarterly* 52: 2 (2000): 274–304.

Travers, Peter. "Across the Universe" Review. Online. Available: http://www.rollingstone. com/movies/reviews/across-the-universe-20071018. April 10, 2012.

Trehub, Sandra E. "The Developmental Origins of Musicality." *Nature Neuroscience* 6: 7 (2003): 669–73.

Trehub, Sandra E., Erin E. Hannon, and Adena Schachner. "Perspectives on Music and Affect in the Early Years." In *Handbook of Music and Emotion: Theory, Research, Applications*, ed. Patrick N. Juslin and John A. Sloboda, 645–68. Oxford: Oxford University Press, 2010.

Tucker, Linda G. *Lockstep and Dance: Images of Black Men in Popular Culture.* Jackson: University Press of Mississippi, 2007.

Turner, Cathy, and Synne K. Behrndt. *Dramaturgy and Performance.* London: Palgrave, 2008.

Turner, Victor. *The Anthropology of Performance.* New York: Performing Arts Journal Publications, 1988.

Turner, Victor. "Are There Universals of Performance in Myth, Ritual, and Drama?" In *By Means of Performance*, ed. Richard Schechner and Willa Appel, 8–18. New York: Cambridge University Press, 1990.

Turner, Victor. *Drama, Fields and Metaphors: Symbolic Action in Human Society.* Ithaca, NY: Cornell University Press, 1974.

Turner, Victor. *From Ritual to Theatre: The Human Seriousness of Play.* New York: PAJ Publications, 1982.

Tusa, John. "Interview with Deborah Warner." 2001. Online. Available: http://www.bbc. co.uk/radio3/johntusainterview/warner_transcript.shtml. March 24, 2008.

Van Aken, Kellee Rene. "Race and Gender in the Broadway Chorus." Ph.D. diss., University of Pittsburgh, 2006.

Van Gennep, Arnold. *The Rites of Passage.* Chicago: Univeristy of Chicago Press, 1960.

Van Leeuwen, Theo. *Speech, Music, Sound.* London: Macmillan, 1999.

Verstraete, Pieter. "The Frequency of Imagination: Auditory Distress and Aurality in Contemporary Music Theatre." PhD diss., University of Amsterdam, 2009.

Vertov, Dziga, dir. *Man with a Movie Camera.* Cinematography by M. Kaufman. USSR (1929). Online. Available: http://archive.org/details/Chelovekskinoapparatom-ManWithAMovieCamera. September 4, 2012.

Viagas, Robert, Baayork Lee, and Thommie Walsh. *On the Line: The Creation of "A Chorus Line."* New York: William Morrow and Company, 1990.

Walsh, Michael. *Andrew Lloyd Webber: His Life and Works.* New York: Harry N. Abrams, 1997.

Warren, Jason D. "How Does the Brain Process Music?" *Clinical Medicine—Medicine, Music and the Mind* 8: 1 (2008): 32–36.

Weiss, Allen W. *Transformation of Lyrical Nostalgia.* Middletown, CT: Wesleyan University Press, 2002.

Weiss, Allen W. *Varieties of Audio Mimesis: Musical Evocations of Landscape.* Berlin: Errant Bodies Press, 2011.

West, Russell, and Frank Lay, eds. *Subverting Masculinity: Hegemonic and Alternative Versions of Masculinity in Contemporary Culture*. Amsterdam: Rodopi, 2000.

Whitelaw, Billie. *Billie Whitelaw ... Who He?* London: Hodder and Stoughton, 1995.

Wilder, Alec. *American Popular Song: The Great Innovators*. New York: Oxford University Press, 1972.

Wilk, Max. *They're Playing Our Song: Conversations with America's Classic Songwriters*. New York: Da Capo Press, 1997.

Willis, Cheryl. "Tap Dance: Manifestations of the African Aesthetic." In *African Dance: An Artistic, Historical, and Philosophical Inquiry*, ed. Kariamu Welsh Asante, 145–59. Trenton: Africa World Press, 1996.

Winkler, Todd. *Composing Interactive Music: Techniques and Ideas Using Max*. Cambridge, MA: MIT Press, 1998.

Winnicott, Donald W. *Playing and Reality*. London: Routledge Classics, 2005.

Winnicott, Donald W. "Transitional Objects and Transitional Phenomena: A Study of the First Not-Me Possession." *International Journal of Psychoanalysis* 34 (1953): 89–97.

Wolf, Stacy. *Changed for Good: A Feminist History of the Broadway Musical*. New York: Oxford University Press, 2011.

Wolf, Stacy. *A Problem Like Maria: Gender and Sexuality in the American Musical*. Ann Arbor: University of Michigan Press, 2002.

Wolfe, George. C. "Defining Identity: Four Voices." *New York Times*, May 24, 1992, E11.

Wolfe, George C., Susan Birkenhead, Jelly Roll Morton, and Luther Henderson. *Jelly's Last Jam*. New York: Theatre Communications Group, 1993.

Wollman, Elizabeth, and Jessica Sternfeld. "Musical Theatre and the Almighty Dollar: What a Tangled Web they Weave." *Studies in Musical Theatre* 5: 1 (2011): 3–12.

Wood, Graham. "Why Do They Start to Sing and Dance All of a Sudden? Examining the Film Musical." In *The Cambridge Companion to the Musical*, ed. William A. Everett and Paul Laird, 2nd ed., 305–24. Cambridge: Cambridge University Press, 2008.

Wright, Jill Gold. *Creating America on Stage: How Jewish Composers and Lyricists Pioneered American Musical Theater*. Saarbrucken: VDM Verlag, 2009.

Youngren, William H. "Unfairly Convicted: A Current Broadway Show Has It Wrong about Jelly Roll Morton." *Atlantic* 272: 1 (1993): 98–103.

Zarifi, Yana. "Staniewski's Secret Alphabet of Gestures: Dance, Body and Metaphysics." In *The Ancient Dancer in the Modern World*, ed. Fiona Macintosh, 389–410. Oxford: Oxford University Press, 2010.

Žižek, Slavoj, and Mladen Dolar. *Opera's Second Death*. London: Routledge, 2002.

INDEX

Printed in Great Britain
by Amazon